THE COMMERCIAL THEATER INSTITUTE

GUIDE TO

PRODUCING

PLAYS AND MUSICALS

THE COMMERCIAL THEATER INSTITUTE
GUIDE TO
PRODUCING
PLAYS AND MUSICALS

EDITED BY FREDERIC B. VOGEL AND BEN HODGES

THEATRE & CINEMA BOOKS

The Commercial Theater Institute Guide to Producing Plays and Musicals
edited by Frederic B. Vogel and Ben Hodges
Copyright © 2006 by Ben Hodges and the estate of Frederic B. Vogel

BOOK DESIGN BY PEARL CHANG

Library of Congress Cataloging-in-Publication Data

   The Commercial Theater Institute guide to producing plays and musicals / edited by Frederic B. Vogel and Ben Hodges ; forewords by Gerald Schoenfeld and Jed Bernstein.
         p.   cm.
   Includes bibliographical references and index.
   ISBN-13: 978-1-55783-652-6 (pbk. original)
   ISBN-10: 1-55783-652-3 (pbk. original)
      1. Theatre—Production and direction. 2. Musicals—Production and direction. 3. Theatrical producers and directors—United States--Interviews. I. Vogel, Frederic B. II. Hodges, Ben. III. Commercial Theater Institute.

   PN2053.C618 2006
   792.02'32—dc22
                              2006023523

Applause Theatre & Cinema Books
19 West 21st Street, Suite 201
New York, NY 10010
Phone: (212) 575-9265
Fax: (212) 575-9270
Email: info@applausepub.com
Internet: www.applausepub.com

Applause books are available through your local bookstore, or you may order at www.applausepub.com or call Music Dispatch at 800-637-2852

Sales & Distribution

North America:
   Hal Leonard Corp.
   7777 West Bluemound Road
   P. O. Box 13819
   Milwaukee, WI 53213
   Phone: (414) 774-3630
   Fax: (414) 774-3259
   Email: halinfo@halleonard.com

Europe:
   Roundhouse Publishing Ltd.
   Millstone, Limers Lane
   Northam, North Devon EX 39 2RG
   Phone: (0) 1237-474-474
   Fax: (0) 1237-474-774
   Email: roundhouse.group@ukgateway.net
   Internet: www.halleonard.com

I think only people in the theatre know what a producer is.
The public does not know.
It knows a writer writes, and an actor acts,
and a director tells them what to do.
A producer raises money.
Well, he does, and in some cases that's all he does.
But the workers in the theatre know that this is not the real thing.
A producer is a rare, paradoxical genius–
hard-headed, soft-hearted, cautious, reckless,
a hopeful innocent in fair weather,
a stern pilot in stormy weather,
a mathematician who prefers to ignore the laws of mathematics
and trust intuition,
an idealist, a realist, a practical dreamer,
a sophisticated gambler, a stage-struck child.
That's a producer.

—OSCAR HAMMERSTEIN II

For Fred

CONTENTS

Gerald Schoenfeld

Gerald Schoenfeld is chairman of the board of The Shubert Organization, a theatrical organization engaged in the ownership and operation of legitimate theatres in the cities of New York, Philadelphia, Washington, D.C., and Boston.

The Shubert Organization has been an essential factor in the rejuvenation of the theatre industry which has been accompanied by the emergence of The Shubert Organization as an active and vital force in the production of such distinguished theatrical attractions as *Indiscretions, Dirty Blonde, Passion, An Inspector Calls, The Grapes of Wrath, The Heidi Chronicles, Amadeus, The Life and Adventures of Nicholas Nickleby, Cats, Jerome Robbins' Broadway, The Most Happy Fella, Children of a Lesser God, Dancin', Whoopi Goldberg, Pygmalion, Ain't Misbehavin', The Gin Game, A Streetcar Named Desire, Lettice & Lovage, Dreamgirls, Chess, Sunday in the Park with George, Les Liaisons Dangereuses, Little Shop of Horrors, Skylight, Closer, The Blue Room, Amy's View, Dance of Death,* and *Amour.*

Mr. Schoenfeld has committed himself and his organization to a vigorous participation in community and civic affairs in a continuing effort to renew the theatre district and the surrounding area of Times Square. He has been an organizer and a catalyst in the effort to effect the changes required to reverse the trend of deterioration of the midtown area. A leader in uniting theatre with business, residential, and labor communities, he is dedicated to the restoration of New York City as the premier city in the Empire State.

Mr. Schoenfeld is chairman of The League of American Theatres and Producers, Inc. He is a member of the board of NYC & Company and is chairman of the Mayor's Midtown Citizens Committee.

Mr. Schoenfeld received his BS from the University of Illinois, his LL.B from New York University School of Law, and also attended Massachusetts Institute of Technology and Columbia University.

Mr. Schoenfeld was formerly a member of the faculty of Yale Drama School and is presently a member of the faculty of Columbia University School of the Arts. In 1999, he received an honorary degree of Doctor of Humane Letters from the City University of New York (CUNY) and in 2001 he received a Doctor of Humane Letters from Emerson College.

Foreword

GERALD SCHOENFELD
Chairman, The Shubert Organization

Several years ago, Fred Vogel came to see me about his project, The Foundation for the Extension and Development of the American Professional Theatre (FEDAPT). I welcomed Fred's idea because it was the first time that anyone had created a program that related exclusively to the Broadway theatre, or as it is commonly referred to, commercial theatre. Until then, courses in theatre at colleges and universities were devoted almost exclusively to not-for-profit theatre.

Later, FEDAPT evolved into the current Commercial Theater Institute (CTI). When Fred asked me for assistance in finding a venue for CTI's classes, I agreed that The Shubert Organization would furnish the Lyceum Theatre for an annual weekend seminar. That first seminar took place in 1985 and has continued ever since. Fred also developed a ten-week CTI course dealing with all aspects of the commercial theatre and taught by working theatre professionals. I was pleased that he invited me to lecture about the Broadway booking contract. My participation became an annual event for many years.

Fred Vogel was an innovator and a dedicated advocate of the role of the Broadway theatre. He understood the need for it to flourish in the hands of educated and competent professionals. He was my friend and a Broadway leading man in a very important role in the American theatre community.

The seasoned contributors included within this publication share Fred's belief that the best way to learn is by doing, that the development of theatre is a collaborative effort, and that we all have a duty and responsibility to do what we can to ensure its proliferation. The knowledge and wisdom that is to be gained from the collective experience of these men and women will hopefully inspire you to follow your passion in the same way that they have all done so ardently.

Jed Bernstein

When he stepped down from his position at the League of American Theatres and Producers, in 2006, Jed Bernstein completed a nearly eleven-year run as the head of Broadway's national trade association.

Under Jed's leadership, the League embarked on a series of new programs that furthered the organization's mission of fostering increased awareness of and interest in Broadway theatre. These programs include Kids' Night on Broadway, a national audience development initiative; the transformation of Broadway on Broadway into a televised event; the annual summertime Broadway Under the Stars concert; Act II, a collaboration with Theatre Communications Group that brings together commercial producers and not-for-profit theatres; and an industry-wide corporate sponsorship program for Broadway that has resulted in cash and measurable in-kind support of over $135 million in seven years. He also produced several notable one-time events including Broadway's participation in the 1998 NBA All-Star Game half-time show, and Broadway Meets Country, in conjunction with the 2005 Country Music Awards.

Jed was instrumental in leading Broadway's recovery after 9/11. Among other efforts, he produced and directed New York Loves America, a fourteen-city concert tour starring Sandy Duncan.

In addition to his League responsibilities, Jed has lectured at the Commercial Theater Institute, NYU, and Yale University's Schools of Management and Drama. He currently holds board appointments with Broadway Cares/Equity Fights AIDS, The Actors' Fund, the Times Square Alliance, and NYC & Company.

Jed looks forward to continuing his work with his entertainment industry colleagues as an independent producer of Broadway shows, television, and special events.

Foreword

JED BERNSTEIN

President, The League of American Theatres and Producers

On Thursday, September 13, 2001, nearly 100 producers, theatre owners, general managers, and union leaders gathered at the offices of the League of American Theatres and Producers to talk about our future, considering the horrors of the preceding forty-eight hours.

Fifteen minutes into the meeting, my assistant handed me a note to tell me that all of the members on the shift on 9/11 of Engine 54, which takes care of Broadway theatres, had been confirmed dead. For most people in the room, this news brought the enormity of the tragedy crashingly close to home.

Soon after, grief was replaced by fear. What was to become of our city? And on a practical as well as personal level, what was going to happen to Broadway? The prospect of terrorism making people afraid to gather together in public places such as theatres was a very real one. Furthermore, with over one-half of Broadway made up of domestic and international visitors, tourism in our city might be affected for months, if not years. In fact, given the relatively small capitalization of a Broadway show, after forty-eight hours or more of darkened theatres, would the twenty or so shows that were playing on September 10 even be able to reopen?

In the weeks and months that followed, Broadway not only survived, but prospered. By June of 2005, by almost every measurement, Broadway was exceeding its 2001 levels by a clear margin.

Why did this happen? Some of it was luck. Some of it was the tremendous spotlight that our city leaders focused on us. The resiliency of our audiences, the quality of our productions, the ability that entertainment has always shown to uplift people in times of crisis, the millions of tourists and visitors; they were all important elements as well. But a critical part of the credit for Broadway's comeback was its producers—their good old-fashioned, measured risk-taking, combined with vision and inspiration.

At its best, the art of producing can be noble, life affirming, emotionally fulfilling, and, yes, profitable. At its worst, it can break your heart and bank account in ways you never dreamed possible.

For decades, theatre professionals believed that producers were born, not made. You couldn't teach the unteachable. Being a great producer was all about instinct and natural ability.

But then, along came Fred Vogel. He believed that commercial theatre producing was susceptible to smart management principles, as in any other discipline. And for nearly twenty-five years, he built CTI into a program that has now served over 7,500 participants.

This text captures the thinking of some of the best and brightest teachers from CTI over the years. It represents a terrific cross section of Broadway's leaders and covers the complete gamut of topics from labor relations to show marketing, and back again.

You won't find a substitute for taking a CTI course, or, heaven forefend, the knowledge you gain from actually producing a show. But the reader will find this an invaluable resource on the whys and wherefores of producing for the commercial theatre.

Broadway didn't die on September 11, 2001. In fact, it has only gained in strength. A strong industry (be it in Fort Worth or on 42nd Street), needs strong managers. It needs new enthusiasms, if it is to thrive into the next millennium. This book will help you, to help theatre, get there.

Ben Hodges

PHOTO BY KRISTIN HOEBERMANN

As an actor, director, and/or producer, Ben Hodges has appeared in New York with The Barrow Group Theater Company, Origin Theater Company, Daedalus Theater Company, Monday Morning Productions, the Strawberry One-Act Festival, Coyote Girls Productions, Jet Productions, New York Actors' Alliance, and Outcast Productions. Additionally, he has appeared in numerous productions presented by theatre companies that he founded, including the Tuesday Group and Visionary Works. Based on Hodges' Showcase production of award-winning playwright Wendy MacLeod's *Things Being What They Are*, a full production was staged at Seattle Repertory in 2003. On film, he can be seen in *Macbeth: The Comedy*.

In 2001, he became director of development and then served as executive director of Fat Chance Productions Inc., and the Ground Floor Theatre, a New York-based nonprofit theatre and film production company. *Prey for Rock and Roll* was developed by Fat Chance from their stage production into a critically acclaimed feature film starring *The Sopranos'* Emmy winner Drea de Matteo, Gina Gershon, and Lori Petty. Additionally, Fat Chance produced the American premiere of award-winning Irish playwright Enda Walsh's *Misterman* Off-Broadway, as well as conducted numerous readings, workshops, and productions in their Ground Floor Theatre, their mission statement being to present new works by new artists.

In 2003, frustrated with the increasingly daunting economic prospects involved in producing theatre on a small scale in New York, Ben organized NOOBA, the New Off-Off-Broadway Association, an advocacy group dedicated to representing the concerns of expressly Off-Off-Broadway producers in the public forum and in negotiations with other local professional arts organizations.

He also serves on the New York Innovative Theatre Awards Committee, selecting outstanding individuals for recognition Off-Off-Broadway, and as vice-president of Summer Stage New York, a professional summer theatre program in Fayetteville, New York.

Ben served as an editorial assistant for many years on the 2001 Special Tony Honor Award–winning *Theatre World*, becoming the associate editor to John Willis in 1998, and co-editor earlier this year. Also an assistant for many years to Mr. Willis for the prestigious Theatre World Awards given for Broadway and Off-Broadway debut performances, Ben was elected to the Theatre World Awards Board in 2002 and currently serves as executive producer for the annual ceremony. In 2003, he was presented with a Special Theatre World Award in recognition of his ongoing stewardship of the event. He has also served as executive producer for the 2005 LAMBDA Literary Foundation "Lammy" Awards, given for excellence in LGBT publishing.

Forbidden Acts, the first collected anthology of gay and lesbian plays from the span of the twentieth century, edited and with an introduction by Hodges, was published by Applause Theatre and Cinema Books in 2003 and became a finalist for the 2004 LAMBDA Literary Award for Drama. He also is a contributing editor to *.dot* magazine.

In 2005, Ben founded and currently serves as executive director of The Learning Theatre, a 501(c)(3) nonprofit organization incorporating theatre into the development and lives of autistic and learning disabled children.

He holds a BFA in Theatre Acting and Directing from Otterbein College, and lives in New York City.

Preface: The Buck Starts Here

BEN HODGES
Executive Director, The Learning Theatre

At the completion of the Commercial Theater Institute (CTI) fourteen-week seminar in April 2004, I approached Fred Vogel with the idea for this book with three goals. I wanted liberal arts graduates to know that they have creative and exciting career options other than being the next Tom Cruise or Julia Roberts. I wanted to share with all theatre people everywhere the invaluable information in the seminar, from experts in all disciplines, for anyone who wants to work professionally in the theatre. The final goal was to spread the development of theatre on every level, particularly new work, which is usually the most difficult to find (read: fund).

Just out of college in 1992 and having landed Off-Off-Broadway, I was rapidly confronted with the reality of living and working in New York, where an uninviting artistic landscape still pervaded the city following the real estate boom in the 1980s. Theatre rental for rehearsal and performance was difficult if not prohibitive. Other economic challenges such as the costs of advertising (before e-mail blasts) forced me to juggle many roles in order to get anything to the stage as I eventually segued from acting into directing and producing. I aspired to Broadway but I had to start somewhere and unfortunately found painfully few resources or organizations to help me make it there (or anywhere).

But upon my participation in the Commercial Theater Institute's three-day seminar in 2003, I realized that I was not alone in the trenches. There were more warriors fighting the battle of rising theatre rental and insurance costs and other issues than I imagined. During a question and answer period, I bit the bullet and raised the specter of the Actors' Equity Basic Showcase Code, the greatest plight I believe facing developmental theatre producing in New York. The cathartic response of exasperated sighs, cheers, and applause by the hundreds of assembled producers was explosive. I was besieged by sympathizers immediately following the seminar, one in tears at how much she had charged on her credit card to put on a show, helpless to recoup due to the Code's restrictions. I instantly became a de facto figurehead for a Code reformation movement. Fred Vogel took notice at my determination to persuade Equity to initiate changes to the Code and teamed up with me to do something about it—unfortunately so far, to little effect. But somewhere along the path of panels, discussions, and meetings with Actors' Equity administrators, Fred also enlisted me to participate in the more extensive 2004 CTI fourteen-week seminar, the basis of this book.

Now three years after I undertook the deconstruction of the Actors' Equity Showcase Code and my activism to amend it, I have tried every approach to work through the Code—the only production option open to most Off-Off-Broadway producers, who actually outnumber the total of Broadway and Off-Broadway producers combined. But the Code carries with it restrictions on producers who choose to utilize Equity actors, such as limited amounts of rehearsal and performances, as well as ticket price caps that do not keep pace with inflation, among many others. My resulting analysis has concluded that by greater artistic and financial restrictions being placed on producers on the developmental level than any other, the Code effectively makes it more difficult to recoup a twenty thousand dollar investment in an Off-Off-Broadway production than it is to return a $14 million investment in a Broadway musical. It boggles many an artistic mind that Code producers, many of whom are showcasing their own work as actors, directors, and writers (i.e., those who are taking the greatest chances in New York and can least afford to by bringing new work to the stage), are doing so encumbered by the most stringent Equity restrictions in the country. Conventional wisdom would dictate that in the most competitive and economically challenging market in the country that Equity agreements and contracts like the Code be *more* conducive to the development of new work rather than *less* so. Those agreements already in place in Los Angeles or Chicago, for instance, routinely provide even twenty-something producers and actors with the ability to make a living and achieve greater visibility from having the opportunity to run their shows for longer lengths of time and charge a more reasonable ticket price. At the very least these agreements should be examined by Equity for possible ratification in New York.

Ultimately, however, my conclusion is that the Code, devised decades ago and responding to the concerns of another era, is in truth no longer applicable to the scale of developmental productions now being produced in New York. A new and mutually acceptable contract should be negotiated by Equity and producers on *every* level. We feed each other, after all.

Neither Code reformation nor a new agreement will happen, however, despite numerous ongoing newspaper articles and other essays on the topic, until:

1. Off-Off-Broadway producers via those organizations that purport to represent them engage in an active dialogue with Equity in an organized way about the seriousness of this issue. It affects not only the ability to produce work, but actors' opportunities for work as well, including potentially valuable subsidiary rights. Those rights cannot be actualized if plays with the potential for transfers to larger venues never make it to the stage in the first place.

   When I pleaded for action on the Code at its top levels, a representative from A.R.T./N.Y. (Alliance of Resident Theaters of New York) responded that the organization does not make a distinction between Off-Broadway and Off-Off-Broadway; it considers Off-Off-Broadway to be a part of Off-Broadway and as such falls under its jurisdiction. Through its web site, A.R.T./N.Y. also claims a membership of "close to 400 not-for-profit and related organizations," including many that function on the Off-Off-Broadway level. It then remains a mystery why A.R.T./N.Y. is largely silent and/or complacent when the issue of the Code periodically bubbles to the

The Ben Hodges co-production of the 2002 Off-Broadway American premiere of Enda
Walsh's *Misterman*. Pictured is George Heslin as Thomas Magill.
Photo courtesy of Origin Theatre Company.

surface, released by A.R.T./N.Y.'s own members, the press, or otherwise.
Are not the concerns of hundreds of producers, directors, and actors who
consider this the most serious issue to threaten developmental theatre in
decades enough to prompt a dialogue between A.R.T./N.Y. and Equity?
A.R.T./N.Y. is, of course, a beneficial, productive, and crucial member of our
collective artistic and professional community (as is Equity, of course), but
focusing on rising space and insurance costs, while valid concerns, without
addressing the terminally ill Code is a little like throwing coal in the engines
of the Titanic even after it's hit the iceberg. It still sinks, no matter how
earnestly you shovel.

Real estate and insurance costs will always be subject to the rules of a
free market economy, and the Greek chorus lamenting those reasons for the
demise of artists and theatre companies in New York City is easily joined.
It also makes for great and easy press. But it requires far more courage for
producers or actors, or their appointed representatives to face their own
failure to the cause, when silent for fear of controversy, retribution, or bad

press. The time has come for the most visible and well-financed arts service organizations to aid their dues-paying members, or explain why they are not doing so, especially on the most important issue facing them in New York developmental theatre history.

2. Equity actors (many of whom are themselves producers—especially Off-Off-Broadway), realize the detriment of this Code to their current and future creative efforts as well as employment prospects, and lobby their own leaders to do something about it.

I have been unable in over three years of analysis to find anything ultimately beneficial in the Code to either producers or actors—in fact, all aspects are starkly antithetical to the goals of all members of a production, *especially* actors. Truncated rehearsal/performance schedules prevent crucial word of mouth, press, and media exposure for actors, limiting possibilities for transfer that would trigger valuable subsidiary and corollary rights. They restrict box office for producers thereby inhibiting the potential for compensation for actors, designers, and stage managers. (Although not required to, many producers—including myself—routinely pay all members of a production and on a most favored nations basis, more than standard requisite reimbursement of travel costs. Given greater freedom of production, we would happily do so in a greater way.)

But Equity also does not consider the Code an employment opportunity (the Code allowing that actors may leave a production up until opening or thereafter, even during the run of a production, though producers may have been invested up to twenty thousand dollars), locking in a Catch-22 that allows neither the producer nor the actor guaranteed to walk away with anything other than a stage credit. None of these or many other arguments, thus far, have resonated, however, with the leaders of Equity, even though "14.4% of all members are employed in live theatre in any given week or that their median earnings are less than seven thousand dollars a year." (Equity's own numbers).* Considering these figures, are there truly that many other options open to many Equity actors better than the kind of opportunities in many high quality productions that the public has come to expect from today's Off-Off-Broadway? It would seem that the prospect of producers on such a large scale stepping in to actually create employment

* Pace, Guy. "2004-05 Theatrical Season Report: Earnings, Employment, Membership, and Finance," Nov. 10, 2005. http://www.actorsequity.org/docs/about/2005_Annual_Report.pdf (July 2, 2006).

opportunities would be welcomed, not thwarted. Are threats of utilizing non-union actors the only idea that results in motivation to discussion on both sides—a threat that serves no one?

I am an optimist, and so I continue to propose a solution to this issue that someone in a position of power in Equity as well as the corresponding parties in A.R.T./N.Y. and other prominent producing membership organizations will step forward and champion. From either a vastly revised Code to ideally, a new and contractual arrangement in-between the Code and the Mini-Contract that would provide for: (1) larger budgets, (2) greater production values, (3) increased ticket prices, (4) a longer schedule of rehearsal and performances, (5) compensation for actors with accompanying subsidiary and corollary rights for productions that transfer, and (6) increased visibility and opportunities for all by more opportunities for public, press, and media attention—it's time for us to work together and realize that a rising tide lifts all boats.

But my ideas for improvements to the Code were in no way extraordinarily unique projects for Fred Vogel. He spent twenty-five years as director of the Commercial Theater Institute, seventeen years as head of FEDAPT, and at least that long as a producer and/or investor of over fifty Broadway and Off-Broadway productions. During that time he nurtured many of those who appear in these pages, as well as countless thousands of others, arming them with the knowledge and nuance of all aspects of this business, all the while reveling in the continued education he received in return. Fred would teach what could be learned, although he would be the first to say that most everything could never be. He was a nonpareil diplomat—a Shubert Alley Superman who was able to leap obstacles separating Actors' Equity Association and The League of American Theatres and Producers in a single bound. He was beholden to none, and therefore, to all. That alone secures Fred's place in the pantheon of true theatre originals.

Whether it be his newly diagnosed illness, my constant badgering, or both, Fred eventually acquiesced in the idea for this book in the summer of 2004, and like Woody Allen cherry picking actors for his films, dutifully descended upon those included here with yours truly, his *assistant director*, in tow, he explained that they had been *chosen* for inclusion in this publication, and instructed them what their part would be, and on occasion, even what he wanted them to say (the prescriptions eventually loosened a bit).

One of the only publications approaching the purview of the work before you is Stephen Langley's thirty-year old *Producers on Producing*. Now somewhat a novelty (as were then many producers), it runs the gamut from larger than life impresarios such as Alexander H. Cohen holding court on *showbiz* to *far out rapping* by progenitors of the newly rediscovered street theatre.

But the intervening years since the publication of *Producers on Producing* have seen the nonprofit/commercial theatre relationship, as well as the industry of commercial theatre producing in totality evolve, and although complicated (or simplified) by monoliths such as Disney and Clear Channel, do so beyond any few men or women's occasion to dominate it. The glass curtain of theatrical producing has now been parted, if not completely drawn, for anyone who can follow cash flow as closely as a chorus boy. Ultimately, theatre's postmodern innovators, many of whom included here, are the product of a more collaborative, laissez-faire network, all in it together to be sure prior to 9/11, but now even more so.

The New York Times reported in its June 12, 2006 issue (the morning after the 60th annual Tony Awards), that the 2005–2006 Broadway season set records in attendance (12 million), and grosses ($862 million),* and so while the demise of Broadway and the theatre can be argued (conventional wisdom dictating—if not the *official* figures—that 80 percent of Broadway shows initially lose money). And although sometimes those odds can be increased by touring and subsidiary considerations but by no means guaranteed to do so), to undertake commercial theatre producing in this day and age is to fly—as a child on a magic carpet ride—in the face of every cynical crosswind blowing through Times Square. What follows is the collective and unprecedented story of twenty-eight such adventurers, as disparate and accomplished as those in any field, who have sat down with legal pads and laptops to tell their stories of commercial theatre producing.

There is more in these pages about producing Broadway and by a more accomplished and diverse group of professionals than has ever been assembled in print. But if you manage to make it to producing on Broadway, much of your work will be undertaken by the combination of a general manager and theatrical attorney. So as much as this is for the Broadway producer, it is even more so for the Off-Broadway, Off-Off-Broadway, regional, community, institutional, and college theatre producer or investor (or student thereof), who must, out of necessity, assume the role of or hire any or all of those players included here throughout the course of their professional life.

---

* Campbell Robertson, "At the 60th Tony Awards, It's 'History' and a Haircut," "Broadway Bestows Honors on the Directors of 'The History Boys' and 'Sweeney Todd,'" *The New York Times*, Sec. B, page 1, June 12, 2006.

Fred Vogel resisted, however, the thought of this being thought of in that way as a *How to...* book, as ultimately he thought that the only way to learn how to produce was by doing it. It was his greatest hope, as well as mine, then, that those of you who read this publication will ultimately have the same contagious and infuriatingly glorious experiences producing as those who appear within its pages.

In 2006, when movies are turned into musicals are turned into movies are turned into..., it is dangerous in this business to herald anything as truly original. (More than one new play or musical has been skipped for a good—or any—*Sex and the City* rerun.) Buried under the hype of the hit-making machine, however, lives the theatre producer and the producer's allies, clinging to the ingenuous belief that by sharing a story they can impact a life; maybe even change the world just a little bit, leaving it in some measure better than how they found it. I got into this business for a lot of the self-serving reasons that kids do. I have remained in it for the very grown-up reason that storytelling has the power to change the world. And sometimes, *sometimes*, be it on the page or on the stage, you find an original story to tell, and sometimes, just *sometimes*, you find you have a hit in your hands.

Note on Text:

For the benefit of the reader, industry terms otherwise used within the publication that have definitions that may not be easily recognizable to the reader and are ultimately defined in the glossary are italicized upon their first occurrence with respect to each contributor's chapter.

Acknowledgments

All of the below have contributed generously to this publication, but a few have gone above and beyond the call of duty: Ric Wanetik, David Hagans, and Yvonne Ghareeb, and their associates Steven Gelston, Kim Jackson, and Mollie Levin at Ricochet, Ric, David, and Yvonne becoming Fred's eyes and ears at the end of his life, thereby allowing him to accomplish much work on this publication; Michael Che, Brad Hampton, Wilson Valentin, Scott Denny, Fred Cantor, and Robert Zimmerman, all of whom gave me professional editorial advice and assistance, as well as crucial personal support; Susan Cosson and Lesa Reed, who transcribed (and impeccably) the audiotapes of the seminar and interviews herein; Sue Cosson, who couriered the audiotapes to and from their respective destinations; Kay Radtke, Pearl Chang, Brian Black, and Britt Augenfeld at Applause Theatre and Cinema Books, and especially to Michael Messina, publisher of Applause Theatre and Cinema Books, whose compassion and support during this process was unwavering; Renée Isely Tobin and Bob, Kate, Eric, Laura, Anna, Foster, and Lucky Tobin, who provided intermittent and restorative stints for me at their Connecticut home during pivotal times over the past three years; my fellow alumni of the 2004 CTI fourteen-week seminar; and Bob Ost of Theater Resources Unlimited, who awarded me a scholarship in 2004 to attend the CTI fourteen-week seminar, providing me the invaluable opportunity that I have now hopefully helped to share a measure of with you.

Not *Also Rans*: Epitacio Arganza; Seth Barrish, Lee Brock, Eric Paeper, and The Barrow Group Theater Company/The Barrow Group School; Todd Blass; Nicole Boyd; Helen Guditis and the Broadway Theater Museum; Fred Caruso; Jason Cicci, Monday Morning Productions, and Summer Stage New York; Christopher Cohen; Richard Cohen and George Wilson; Greg Raby and Daryl Roth Productions; Cori Silberman and David Binder Productions; Robert Dean Davis; Carol and Nick Dawson; Carmen Diaz; Diane Dixon; Pamela Lloyd, James Love, and Dodger Theatricals; Rebecca Frank and The Dramatists Guild; Amanda Dubois; Craig Dudley; Marshall Vickness, DeWayne Snype, and Eliran Murphy Group; Amy Luce and Epstein, Levinsohn, Bodine, Hurwitz & Weinstein; Emily Feldman; Stanley Morton Ackert III and Gersen, Blakeman, and Ackert; Valerie Black-Mallon, Kristine Urnikis, and the Goodman Theatre; the late Charles J. Grant Jr. and Zan Van Antwerp; Laura and Tommy Hanson;

Esther Harriot; Richard M. Henderson Jr. and Jennifer Henderson; Richard M. Henderson Sr. and Patricia Lynn Henderson; Ron Nicynski and Harriet Leve Productions; Al and Sherry Hodges; David Howe, Delia Washington, and Hudson Scenic Studio; Leonard Jacobs; Billy Zavelson and The Karpel Group; Gretchen, Aaron, Eli, and Max Kerr; Jane, Lynn, and Kris Kircher; Brigitte Lacombe and Janet Johnson; Patty Casterlin, Seth Popper, Roxanne Rodriguez, Christina Warner, Zenovia Varelis, and The League of American Theatres and Producers; Tim Deak, Kim Spanjol, and The Learning Theatre; David Lowry; Ronni Mandell; Joey Levy and Mark Platt Productions; Cecelia McCarton and the staff of the McCarton Center/The McCarton School; Joseph Melillo; Barry Monush and *Screen World*; Virginia Moraweck; Wren Longno and The New Group; Jason Bowcutt, Shay Gines, Nick Micozzi, and the staff and respective voting committees of the New York Innovative Theatre Awards; Petie Dodrill, Craig Johnson, Rob Johnson, Dennis Romer, Katie Robbins, Dr. John Stefano, Dean Jo Ann VanSant, Ed Vaughan, the late Dr. Charles O. Dodrill and the staff of Otterbein College/Otterbein College Department of Theatre and Dance, Kathie Packer; Hugo Uys and the staff of Paris Commune and Shag; John Philip, David Plank; Shea Martin and PMK; Angie and Drew Powell; Ryan Hill, Robert Jones, and The Producing Office; Richard Rainville; Carolyn, David, and Glenna Rapp; Ron Reeves; Robert Rems; Don Suma and Richard Kornberg Public Relations; Justin Zell and Roger Gindi Theatrical Management; Jeutan Dobbs, Sydney Davalos, and Roundabout Theatre Company; Kate Rushing; Bill Schaap; Madeline Austin and The Shubert Organization; Andy Apostolides, Matt Britt, Joaquin Esteva, Susan Grushkin, Brandon Mikolaski, Shelly Morzov, and Serino Coyne; Emmanuel Serrano; William Jack Sibley, Hannah Richman Slosberg and Jason Slosberg; Danielle Tandet and SpotCo; Susan Stoller; Sam Holtzapple and Susan Quint Gallin Productions; Allison Graham, Henry Grossman, Lucy Nathanson, Michael Riordan, John Sala, Mark Snyder, Laura Viade, Michael Viade, Rachel Werbel, and the staff of *Theatre World* and the John Willis *Theatre World/Screen World* Archive; Jamie deRoy, Patricia Elliott, Peter Filichia, Leigh Giroux, Doug Holmes, Tom Lynch, Kati Meister, Matthew Murray, and the board of The Theatre World Awards, Inc.; Harry Haun, Howard Kissel, Frank Scheck, Michael Sommers, Doug Watt, Linda Winer, and the voting committee of The Theatre World Awards, Inc.; Yufen Kung and Tony Origlio Public Relations; Keith Blau, Chris Urstlin, and Universal Studios; Adam Blanshay, Emily Erstling, Liz Frankel, and Waxman Williams Entertainment; Jack Williams, Barbara Dewey, and the staff of the University of Tennessee at

Knoxville; Milena Urbaez and West 37th ARTS Group; Sarah and Bill Willis; Shane and Bill Wolters. I once read that Maureen Dowd's heroes were famous people's personal assistants. The names of many of those such heroes are listed above, peppered among those of many good friends and devoted family members. I emphatically second Ms. Dowd's sentiment, and thank all of them, also now considered friends, especially for not calling me off as I continually called their bosses.

Frederic B. Vogel

PHOTO BY MARTHA SWOPE

Frederic B. Vogel created the Commercial Theater Institute in 1982, the first workshop ever conducted to train producers for commercial Broadway, Off-Broadway, and road productions. These workshops have included seminar leaders including producers, general managers, theatre owners, press agents, literary agents, theatrical attorneys, and others in the commercial theatre. Over fifty participants in these programs have gone on to produce with distinction On and Off-Broadway.

Having invested in over fifty Broadway and Off-Broadway productions, Mr. Vogel co-produced the Tony Award-nominated *Marlene*, and co-produced *Shakespeare's R&J* Off-Broadway, R.T. Robinson's *The Cover of Life* in fall, 1994, at the American Place Theatre, and co-produced the Off-Broadway musical *Lust* in June 1995. For seventeen years, Mr. Vogel headed FEDAPT (The Foundation for the Extension and Development of the American Professional Theatre), which offered development and technical assistance to over 500 theatres, dance organizations, performing arts centers, and other arts projects throughout the United States.

Prior to this, Mr. Vogel was the assisting director for the Performing Arts Division at the 1962 Seattle World's Fair, which presented more than 125 international theatrical and concert attractions. He supervised the International Special Events Program and served as the director of the Film Program, which premiered films from all over the world. Mr. Vogel subsequently was appointed special events director for the New York State Commission on the World's Fair for the New York Pavilion at the World's Fair, a position he held from 1963–65. As general manager for Lumadrama (a son e lumiere) at Independence Hall in Philadelphia, PA, Mr. Vogel coordinated this tourist and educational program with the U.S. Department of the Interior and was responsible for its operation.

Beginning his theatrical career as an actor at the age of nine, Mr. Vogel appeared in Broadway, Off-Broadway, the summer stock circuit, television, and film before switching his creative priorities to the *front office*. He has held administrative positions in summer theatre, music events, Off-Broadway, and created and supervised Broadway Theatre Leagues (Columbia Artists Management) throughout the U.S. For several years Mr. Vogel served as an independent arts management consultant for a variety of organizations. Additionally, he has been a stage manager, box office treasurer, subscription and group sales manager, publicity director, general manager, and producer. He has lectured at leading universities and arts management programs throughout the United States, and has served as an arts consultant for the Ford Foundation in Indonesia.

In 2003, he produced and distributed the independent film, *A Tale of Two Pizzas*.

Introduction

FREDERIC B. VOGEL
Director, Commercial Theater Institute

You have just read a play that a friend of yours has written or, more likely, was written by a friend of a friend. You really love it and you think it's a surefire hit. It might even be a political, social, or philosophical subject you are passionate about. You need, you must, you *have* to produce it.

It is the collective goal of the contributors of this book to provide as much clear-cut information as possible on producing for the *commercial* theatre, as well as to identify the tools necessary to undertake and succeed on that journey. We will see that success has many definitions—more than the number of people who undertake producing—from Seattle to Shubert Alley. However, your chance of obtaining any measure or success, such as it is, will be exponentially increased by following the prescriptions and prohibitions set forth here. It is also crucial to understand the world in which commercial theatre producing takes place, as well as to examine the producing process itself, and to that end we will attempt to provide an objectivity of the world in which we work, how the world influences the decisions we make, and how within this world decisions are sometimes made for us. *Webster's New Collegiate Dictionary* defines "process" as "a series of actions

---

* Henry Bosley Woolf, *Webster's New Collegiate Dictionary* (Springfield, MA: G. & C. Merriam Company, 1975), 917.

or operations conducing to an end."* The process of producing is complex, with every single step related to the whole. Every step and aspect of any process is interrelated and interdependent, so then, the execution of the process of theatrical producing must happen in the context of the full sensibility of the work being created and of the world in which it is being created.

This book will also help you determine if you actually wish to produce in the commercial theatre, or if you should instead go into a safer and more secure profession. Some of these include brain surgery, quantum physics, and air traffic control. A practitioner of any of these endeavors would have a better guarantee of money, peace of mind, and most certainly a more routine way of life than that of theatrical producing. If, however, you frequently crave putting your security, ego, and sense of self-worth on the line, then you may want to further explore producing a play or musical in the commercial theatre.

I had the great opportunity and good fortune to be hired as associate director of the Performing Arts Division of the Seattle World's Fair, the theme of which was "Century 21." From 1961–62, Seattle was the center of my universe. I handled several major world-class attractions such as the Royal Dramatic Theatre of Sweden and the Banraku Doll Theatre of Japan (its first appearance in the Western World). We had an excellent team of professionals from the New York theatre world working together with the Hurok Organization, which was the major concert management company at the time. On our team was a man who has subsequently remained my close friend, Robert Brannigan, whose chief responsibility was to see that the backstage needs of each performing group were met. I was the youngest member of the performing arts staff and, though eager and assertive, inexperienced. In a meeting one day I asked Robert a question to which he replied, "As compared to what?" I stopped talking and had an epiphany that would guide me throughout my entire professional life—my question could not be answered, nor could any other, without a clear *context* in which to compare it.

The process of producing demands that your work as an individual be understood within the context of the others with whom you work. More importantly, to be produced, your project must be understood by your entire team within the context of everything that has come before, as well as that which is currently around you. So, then, as the director of the Commercial Theater Institute for over twenty-three years, I assert that context is the governing principle by which the careful construction of the tapestry of a play or musical is crafted, one thread at a time. The craftspeople presented here, in whose calloused hands you will rest for the next several hundred pages, will collectively attempt to contextualize producing, to demystify that which is occasionally considered mystical and sometimes given to misunderstanding (and even suspicion), and hopefully and ultimately help you to discover that which I have said is so difficult to discover—the *there* there.

THE DEVELOPMENTAL PROCESS OF PRODUCING PLAYS AND MUSICALS

The major issue to be addressed by any producer is how to structure the *developmental* process of a work. As a producer embarking on a first project, what is the best way to evaluate the viability of a play or musical? I have worked in the professional theatre since my late teens and I am fairly certain that I know how to read a play. I do not feel as confident about how to read a musical because it requires some ability to read and understand music sufficiently enough to visualize and hear it on stage.

However one may feel about a play after reading it, nothing gives you the insight into the work like hearing and seeing a reading by professional actors. I urge anyone interested in looking for material to produce to attend as many *readings* of new work as possible, and to go to Off-Off-Broadway theatres, or frequent local or *regional* theatres producing new works. If you come across a new work that interests you, ask the theatre about the *disposition rights* to the work. Who controls it? Is it under *option* to anyone? If so, who? If not, you need to find out how to reach the playwright in order to determine if the author has representation. Obtaining an option involves a process of negotiation. I learned early in my career that the best executive—and a producer is that and much more—is aware of their weaknesses and, importantly, is aware of those components of the business about which they are ignorant. For example, I would never option a property without having an experienced *theatrical attorney* handle the negotiation. Although you may have a great friendship or personal relationship with the author, each side being represented by an attorney will help sustain that relationship as well as a more harmonious partnership into the future.

SELF-PRODUCING

Over the years of my conducting the Commercial Theater Institute, a number of writers of plays and musicals have attended the seminars in hopes of learning how to produce their own works. In my judgment, a series of root canals may prove less painful. The basic laws of physics do not allow for you to be in two places at once, and in any case, playwriting and producing are two very different and separate full-time positions, each in need of the undivided attention of those who respectively undertake them. (However, authors, like new parents, do not give birth to ugly offspring, so if you are a playwright, I will offer the following suggestions about self-producing):

After *Oklahoma!, Carousel,* and *South Pacific* had all opened, Oscar Hammerstein was asked how he had managed to create so many masterpieces in the American theatre. He replied, "Three things: collaboration, collaboration, collaboration." Because each element of the producing process is a priority, you need to define the steps that will lead you to your desired goals. Finding collaborators may depend on where you live. I also recommend that authors find and collaborate with a professional director. If you live in or near a major city with an active professional theatre community, finding a director should not be too difficult. Contacting professional theatres for recommendations may also be productive. In your search, remember that you are looking for a director who has experience with new works. A friend of mine once told me that there are two kinds of plays—*new* and *used.* So a director whose resume includes working with new material will be a logical collaborator.

I always have better trust in my evaluation of works after having heard them read by professional actors. Even a *cold* (unrehearsed) *reading* will enlighten an author as to what degree the work sounds like what they intended. In any community where there are professional theatres—either commercial or *nonprofit*—a pool of actors will be available. Just listening to a piece being read will be beneficial, even in your own living room. In addition, hearing the actors' comments can help determine the next steps in development. Is the work ready to be mounted on any level of production, or is the consensus that rewrites should be made before a production? Directors are often the best to offer questions and options for a playwright to consider as the work evolves.

The greatest challenge for writers is to be able to maintain a producer's dispassionate objectivity about their own work. I was once contacted by the creator of a work that he described as a musical with a cast of six or seven principal actors (the roles for two of which already had stars attached); a chorus of forty that would appear in two short scenes; and a budget, he predicted, which was one-third that of anything I could imagine, given what he was describing. As I listened, I realized he had no idea that the *weekly nut* (running costs) of the production he was envisioning would be astronomical. But he loved his work and was sure he could produce it himself. (For only one example of the problems with his scenario, a chorus member is paid as much for performing in two scenes as they would if they performed in *all* scenes.) I would never suggest to a writer that anything be cut if the cast size is key to the artistic vision, but there must be a balance between what is necessary to fulfill the vision as well as the practical and financial realities of producing. In life, there may be many battles, but in the arts, the one that you will take up arms to fight the most will be that of art versus commerce. Self-producing dictates that you will be fighting that battle with, and within, yourself.

SOME FURTHER THOUGHTS ABOUT DEVELOPMENT

Whether it is the writer/producer or any other producer who has optioned a work, the developmental process is an ongoing one. How many readings? How much rewriting? How much time will be allotted? These factors will be determined throughout the process, given that all the key people involved have agreed on the same destination as well as on all the steps to get there.

Prior to any reading or staging, the ground rules for conducting it must be set. What is to be accomplished at the reading? Is the reading for the author to determine if there is any interest from additional or potential producers? Or is it to test the working relationship of the author and the director? Is it solely for the writer to hear it read aloud to see what works and what doesn't? Unless there are well-articulated goals, no realistic determination can be made of what was accomplished or what it is to be accomplished immediately thereafter. You may find, however, just how easy it is to get caught up in an enthusiastic audience reaction from family and friends. They are no doubt heartfelt responses, so it is advisable to add as many impartial and theatrically sophisticated attendees as possible to assure you an ultimately objective array of feedback.

A writer once told me an interesting and apocryphal story of Thoreau's response when told that Alexander Graham Bell had sent the first voice message over a wire. "What did he say?" Thoreau asked. I share the same curiosity when asked to evaluate a play, musical, or film. What is the story about? Who is telling it? Who are they telling it to? Why are they telling it? I want authors to be absolutely clear in telling me what *they* want to tell me. The developmental process, then, will likely require the creators to go through a series of clarifying steps, including as many readings and developmental productions as possible, to reach a level that satisfies the entire team.

INVESTING AND RAISING CAPITAL

Somehow I think the fear of asking anyone to invest with you can be turned upside down, and possibly be seen as your choosing to exclude a theatre lover from participating in an amazing adventure.

There are a myriad of reasons an individual may have for investing in a commercial production. I think for the first time producer, they will find that people willing to consider investing will do so because of the relationship to the person who solicits them, rather than for an affinity for the project itself. I have, on occasion, invested in shows in the past solely because of my belief and interest in the individual producer. Investors may be intrigued by investing in a play or musical that espouses a political point of view or a social theme commiserate with their own views, or often a particular playwright, actor, or director will motivate an investor to participate in a show. There are in point of fact as many reasons for someone to invest their disposable income in a show as there are investors wanting to invest. Likewise, there are as many reasons *not* to invest as there are tears shed on a closing night.

In order to approach any investor, you will need the appropriate papers prepared by your attorney and a budget prepared by your *general manager*. Even while you are in the process of obtaining rights to your work, you should have an idea of the general manager you want to work with. If not before, I suggest that at least by the time the *option agreement* is being negotiated with the playwright that you undertake your search for a general manager. In this way, you have an idea of your desired general manager's schedule and can be certain that it is someone who can devote the time to work satisfactorily with you. And, perhaps most importantly, you will have an idea of the level of *capitalization* needed to bring your project to a selected *venue*, which will arm you with important information in advance of approaching potential investors.

The fees for both your attorney and your general manager should be discussed in your respective first meetings with them. Both should want to read the script and, if it is a musical, hear the score (should a recording be available). If the work is being performed in a reading or a staged at a venue available to your other prospective team members, you should notify them. If they can see the piece it will help them determine the project's needs, and since you will be negotiating their fees, each will be in a position to judge the time and degree of the workload required of them and can give you a more realistic estimate for their services.

It is wise to discuss with the author possible *attachments* to the contract of a director, actor(s), choreographer, and so on, before any option is signed. If the author has made some commitment to a director or anyone else for a commercial production, then that must be taken into the option considerations. You may choose not to employ someone the author has already committed to, and instead choose to *buy them out* of the deal altogether. This potential action and related cost should be explored with both your attorney and the general manager; it is ultimately an artistic as well as financial decision.

The Frederic B. Vogel co-production of the 1999 Tony-nominated production of *Marlene*; book by Pam Gems; additional lyrics by Haven Gillespie; co-produced by Ric Wanetik. Pictured is Siân Phillips as Marlene Dietrich.
Photo by Mike Martin, X Martin/Jet Set/Dennis Taranto,
courtesy of the John Willis Theatre World/ Screen World Archive.

Right away we reach the chicken or the egg stage of the producing process when we consider raising money as a producer. Do you have any indication of your ability to raise any capital for financing this project? Do you have monies in hand or do you have potential sources needed to hire an attorney to negotiate an option and funds to pay for the option? The attorney's fee is negotiable. So is the option payment. The details for this important process are best left to your attorney.

Raising capital, then, is an important reality you must face in order to produce work you are passionate about and want to see on stage. Most people who have attended CTI programs in the past initially want to be shown *The Way*—a magic formula for raising money. I usually offer the following suggestions:

1. Get a legal pad and make a list of everyone you've known since childhood—family members, schoolmates, *all* of them. Then add anyone who did business with your family like your doctors and real estate people who bought and sold property with your family. Then list (to the best of your knowledge) the financial status of each person in regard to your estimate of their disposable income. Consider: could they have an amount from $2,500–$100,000? Might they be willing to take a gamble on your production? (If you don't know for sure, make a guess.)

2. After you have a decent number on your list of names, contact them. Ask, "If I were to produce a theatrical work, would you consider joining me?" You are not asking them to *invest*; you are asking, *"If,"* as in "If I were to be involved on a project as a producer, would you at least be responsive enough to hear an entire proposition?"

3. Take your time going through this process. You want to find out, at least, if you have the beginning of a pool of investors. This pool is about your greatest asset as a producer.

4. You should seriously consider being an *associate producer* on a Broadway or Off-Broadway production. An associate producer is someone who, in exchange for bringing investors on board a production, will receive at least three benefits:

    • Billing (usually under the title)

    • A negotiated percentage of the producer's share of the profits

    • What may be the most important: a possible access to attend meetings where discussions regarding casting and other key components give you a "place at the table."

There is a publication that you will find invaluable called the *Theatrical Index*, a weekly newsletter that lists information on all productions On and Off-Broadway (both commercial and nonprofit productions). It chronicles shows currently running as well as works in rehearsal, in preparation for rehearsal, and those under option for production in the foreseeable future. If you would like to get experience as an associate producer, the *Theatrical Index* tells you what works have been optioned and who is producing them. You will have the information you need to contact a producer's office to request a meeting and to express your interest in raising money for the production. It is important that you have taken the preliminary steps of creating a list of your potential investors before you contact the producer's office. This allows you to have a sense of your ability to deliver investors in the amount the producer(s) may require. For example, if it is a musical with a $10 million budget, you may not be able to participate as an associate producer your first time out. If you think you can raise, say, fifty- to one hundred thousand dollars, this amount will be very attractive to producers of Off-Broadway productions where budgets often range from $400–600 thousand (which will no doubt will have increased by the time of this printing).

Before approaching any potential investor, it is important that you meet with the production's attorney to discuss any and all legal issues required of your approach to potential investors. No matter where a potential investor resides, there are state rules and regulations that pertain to their solicitation—these are referred to as *Blue Sky Laws*. Also, there must be a clear understanding by anyone soliciting investments of all the details of investing before moving forward, as there are very specific legal requirements as to what can be mentioned and how the investment process is described.

Let me add here that I have never enjoyed raising money. I wrote grants for seventeen years as the head of FEDAPT (The Foundation for the Extension and Development of the American Professional Theatre), a nonprofit in need of subsidizing (as well as an acronym). When I began as a commercial producer, I remained in the money raising business through two Broadway productions and five Off-Broadway productions, and in doing so always recalled the writing on a sign in the coffee shop window I frequented when I first arrived in New York: "As you amble through life, whatever be your goal, keep your eye upon the doughnut and not upon the hole." My doughnuts have always been the works I had to see produced on the stage, while the money needed from investors was the means. It's sort of like the tanks of gas we need to drive to Nirvana.

BUILDING A TEAM

If you are seriously considering producing commercially, I suggest that you first identify an experienced general manager as well as a theatrical attorney whom you would like to include in your endeavor. The importance of a general manager cannot be stressed enough. They will guide you through the jungles and minefields of union negotiations, *theatrical licensing*, and "ride herd" over every penny spent throughout the life or your project. This means obtaining the option, development of the work, raising of capital, and overseeing the rehearsals and run of the show.

An attorney who has represented a commercial producer or has had some track record in the commercial theatre is your best bet. I caution you to make certain you use an attorney with a theatre practice, and a lawyer in New York with a theatrical practice who deals with all of the issues of commercial theatre will simply be more informed than any other. I advise you to interview a few attorneys to make certain there is a meeting of the minds. More than likely, the attorney will want to read the play, get to know you, and assess your ability to raise the capital necessary to produce the work. Most of the people I have met through the Commercial Theater Institute have a lawyer in their family or in their close circle of friends, and even though they may be a lawyer proficient in real estate or tax law, I urge every producer to seek out an attorney with experience in the New York commercial theatre. I offer as a caution that film and television businesses are very different from the commercial theatre, and I encourage you to speak to an attorney who is proficient in the latter.

ADVERTISING, MARKETING, AND PUBLICITY

Once upon a time, the selling of tickets for a Broadway show was mostly dependent on names of star performers, playwrights, or composers and lyricists. Today the marketing of a Broadway, Off-Broadway, or even Off-Off-Broadway production is a far more complex process requiring more money, time, and most importantly, the combined skill, talent, and commitment of a team of experienced marketing and promotionally minded people.

Decades ago, your production team would have included only a *press agent* and an *advertising* agency. There were seven daily New York newspapers and the reviews pretty much determined the fate of your production. Today the process has changed significantly. Your team will still include a press agent and an advertising agency, but will also likely include a *marketing* director or team, forming a trio of efforts to *put butts in seats*, as they say. The goal is to make your production less dependent on reviews. We have fewer and fewer newspapers, and a growing power of other media, and the day when a show's fate rests in the hands of one or several reviewer, is quite possibly now behind us.

1. **THE ADVERTISING AGENCY** There are currently three major advertising agencies in New York that specialize in serving theatrical productions. It is crucial to consider these agencies for any production in which you are involved. The nature of advertising for New York theatre requires a flexibility that any of the three can handle. In addition, these agencies have expanded to include marketing services such as direct mail, promotional opportunities, and other options. You and your general manager should approach each of these agencies once they have read the work, or seen a reading or a showcase. Actually you should make every effort to get everyone you are considering for your team to attend. In my experience, capable professionals are more likely to join a project because of its quality and their enthusiasm for a project may make their remuneration somewhat more flexible.

2. **THE PRESS AGENT** Your press agent is a crucial member of your marketing team. As the title implies, they are responsible for providing information about the production to all media, as well as placing any items, stories, and photos therein. These items are considered as part of the news, and an addition to paid advertising. The press agent will be a member of the ATPAM union (Association of Theatrical Press Agents and Managers). Your general manager, also, will most likely belong to ATPAM and fully understand union contracts.

3. **MARKETING AND PROMOTIONS** The third member of your team is a marketing and promotions person, or firm. This additional team component has become necessary in recent years to address the continuing complexity of marketing theatre. As theatre people, we tend to assume that the general public is as interested in going to the theatre as we are, and we read ads and articles about the latest plays and musicals in development and previews. The ticket buying public is much more likely to buy because of great word of mouth than what they may read. Of course, the more theatregoers and the general public alike hear about a show and the more familiar the title becomes, the more we are aware of its presence. In addition, a marketing and promotions person is responsible to arrange whatever cross promotions will give a show greater name recognition.

SUI GENERIS

During the first year of the Commercial Theater Institute, one of the speakers used the phrase, *sui generis*. Since I had won the Latin Prize in the seventh grade at St. Leonard's Academy, I was thrilled I knew what it meant. *Sui generis* means "unique unto itself," (my translation). Although similar to something else, the differences are sufficient to be both peculiar and rare, hence, unique. Each and every production of a play or musical is *sui generis*. For example, there is no such thing as a standard budget for a four-character, one-set play. Since all decisions are based on the evaluations and judgments of facts, costs, and other tangible elements in an artistic and financial context, the mixture of different ingredients will lead to different conclusions.

⤙

As a result of my spending all these years listening to virtually every theatre professional involved in the process of producing, I feel that I have an invaluable amount of information, insight, and understanding to share with anyone who believes they have the passion to produce, or even with anyone who is curious to learn about the nature of commercial producing. So when I was approached by writer/producer Ben Hodges (who was himself an alumnus of CTI) with the idea for this book, I thought the time may be right. It was a cautious "Yes," as I felt it impossible to write a "*How to...*" book, but ultimately realized that the wealth of CTI information should indeed be collected and shared.

I also think it is of value to the reader for me to explain how and why CTI was created, and what it was designed to accomplish. As the head of the nonprofit organization FEDAPT from 1970–1987, I led a group of management consultants committed to working with nonprofit theatres in developing viable board and management structures that could support their respective artistic missions. This meant that our team of consultants was drawn from highly experienced managing directors, development directors, business managers, and marketing directors throughout America and would be individually assigned to work with an existing nonprofit *resident* theatre or other theatre in its genesis. We were all committed to the goal that the only excuse for the failure of a theatre closing should be an artistic one, not the failure to maximize its earned and contributed income, its fiscal accountability, its board support of its clearly stated mission statement, or its overall management and staff structure.

Almost from the beginning of this burgeoning of professional resident theatres across the country, there were reports of the artistic excellence of the work in many of the theatres. In fact, even some early productions created in nonprofit venues were being seen both On and Off-Broadway. The production that was for me the seminal influence leading to the birth of CTI occurred on Broadway in October 1968, with the opening of *The Great White Hope*, a play which had been developed and staged as the third production of the 1967–68 season at the Arena Stage in Washington, D.C. Under the leadership of its artistic director, Zelda Fichandler, Arena Stage clearly demonstrated that the artistic level of these nonprofit theatres was on par with the New York theatre district. Upon its *transfer* to New York, *The Great White Hope* garnered Tony Awards for Best Play, Best Actor in a Play (James Earl Jones), and Best Actress in a Supporting Role (Jane Alexander), in addition to the 1969 Pulitzer Prize for Drama for playwright Howard Sackler. The fifteenth-month run of the play constituted a commercial as well as an artistic success. However, as this was at the very beginning of the collaborative relationship between *for-profit* and nonprofit theatres, the Arena Stage did not have a contract with the playwright that specified any kind of billing (e.g., "originally produced at Arena Stage"), nor any financial participation in the future of the production created at their venue, contract components which are now included in virtually every agreement today between writers of new works and nonprofit theatres. There was nothing dishonest or untoward about this production being produced in New York by a commercial producer, but it was clear to me at the time that both sectors—the nonprofits as well as the for-profits—needed to develop clear and effective relationships, and engage in a dialogue about the purposes of each.

During those early years, I realized that my heroes in the growing and exciting world of nonprofit theatres were members in top management who made the creation of the art of the theatre a viable, fiscally functional, and accountable reality. Without those people and their excellent producing skills, no audiences in the cities all over America would have realized the great enjoyment and fulfillment that comes from sitting in a theatre and watching so many talented artists and craftsmen ply their trades to astonish and delight. It was this collected insight, understanding, and wisdom that best allowed me to see my name above the title as a producer.

I began my theatre career as an actor and worked On and Off-Broadway as well as in television and film. During that time I was like so many theatre artists who I meet today. They usually believe they exist on the *artistic side* and producers exist on the *business side*. In truth, it is not possible to make a financial decision in the producing process that does not have an artistic impact, or vice versa. The battle of art and commerce in the commercial theatre is less a battle and more of a struggle about the best means for the management structure to serve and support the art itself. If it weren't for our great producers who have not only the taste but also the management skills that they do, none of us would have ever seen (*insert your favorite show here*), which, of course, changed your life in all the ways you recall it did.

My thanks to Hal Prince for producing *Follies* as well as his other musical treasures, as well as to Robert Whitehead for *Member of the Wedding*, two productions of *Medea*, and countless other memorable shows, to David Merrick for *Hello, Dolly!* and *42nd St.*, and to Kermit Bloomgarden, Stuart Ostrow, The Dodgers, and The Shubert Organization, The Nederlanders, Jujamcyn…I cannot mention them all, but you get the point—*we're all in it together.*

As you read what follows here, I hope and believe you will develop an understanding of what it means to be a producer, shared with you by those included here who most certainly do. And even if you decide not to embark on the journey of producing, it is my hope, then, that you will have an enhanced appreciation and understanding of the producing process, which will at least enhance your pleasure of going to the professional theatre—which you must always, *always,* continue to do.

The Developmental Process of Producing Plays and Musicals

The artistic material that feeds you, will feed others,
and ultimately, seed the artistic future of our art form.
—HAL PRINCE

David Binder

David Binder has spent the last decade bringing new artists and audiences to the theatre. He produced the first Broadway revival of Lorraine Hansberry's classic *A Raisin in the Sun*, starring Sean Combs, Audra McDonald, Phylicia Rashad, and Sanaa Lathan. The production, directed by Kenny Leon, won two Tony Awards and was widely recognized for bringing in the most diverse audience Broadway had seen in decades. David is the original producer of John Cameron Mitchell and Stephen Trask's rowdy, loud, and ultimately sweet rock 'n' roll musical *Hedwig and the Angry Inch*. Off-Broadway, at *De La Guarda*, a group of flying Argentines literally lifted a young international crowd off its feet for more than six years. David has brought the show everywhere from London to Las Vegas, and Tokyo to Tel Aviv. With Lisa Kron's *2.5 Minute Ride* (New York and San Francisco), and Kenny Lonergan's *Lobby Hero* (with The Donmar in the West End), David has showed his support for new writing that is polemical, political, and hilarious. David recently produced *The Public Sings: A 50th Anniversary Celebration* for the Public Theatre with Meryl Streep, Natalie Portman, Ben Stiller, and Mike Nichols, among many others. He is currently represented in the West End with The Donmar production of *Guys and Dolls*.

WET AND HAPPY,
OR HOW TO HOLD ON TO YOUR INSPIRATION

DAVID BINDER
David Binder Productions

The following is drawn from a speech made at *Untitled: An Anti-Conference For Brand and Design Provocateurs,* an event hosted by Coca-Cola in San Francisco, California, on November 8, 2005.

In the theatre, the producer often starts with nothing.

You often don't have a director. Or actors. Or a theatre. Or money. There's no audience. Sometimes you don't even have a script. All you have is an idea, and that idea for the producer is the entire reality.

Putting on a show—be it in a tiny fringe *venue* or under the blaring lights of Broadway—is a famously daunting task. I always marvel at how anyone is able to get *anything* on. So how—over the course of years mounting a show—in the face of incredible odds, do you hold onto your inspiration? What pushes you through?

↓

I'm having dinner with my friend John Cameron Mitchell. It's 1993. At the time, John was a successful Broadway actor and I was a young producer, whose credits included a number of one night special events.

John is restless to write something of his own. He's going on about a character around which he wants to create a show. The character, he tells me, is named Hansel, and he's living a sorry life in communist East Berlin.

I nod my head, listening carefully.

"To get out," John explains, "he gets a sex change operation so he can escape with an American GI to the West. But the operation ends up being botched and Hansel, now Hedwig, ends up living in the American South, alone, penniless, a woman. All he's left with is an angry inch."

"O.K.," (I say tentatively, not quite sure what John is talking about). He goes on: "Hedwig ends up raising a kid who becomes a rock star. The rock star runs out on Hedwig too, and the whole thing revolves around the search for identity and Plato's *Symposium* and oh—one other thing… it's a musical."

About that time, on a plane, John meets Stephen Trask, an enormously talented singer/songwriter with a band called Cheater. He loves the idea of Hedwig and the two begin to collaborate, with Stephen writing the songs and John the book. As the two continue to *develop* it further, Hedwig's story grows more complex. I don't fully understand it. Still, I am completely inspired by John's vision and the way in which he wants to bring rock 'n' roll into the theatre. I decide I want to produce the show.

The next thing you know I'm downtown at a club called Squeezebox. It's 2:00 a.m. On stage, John (as Hedwig), and Cheater are voraciously reworking a cover of David Bowie's "Boys Keep Swinging." Nearby, I'm holding wigs and someone has spilled beer on me. But I'm sorta wet and sorta happy because we're off and running.

Over the next few years, we would put together more and more of what would become *Hedwig and the Angry Inch*. What starts as an elaborate character sketch gradually becomes a full-blown piece, with Stephen's original songs replacing the covers. The small size of the show (John, plus one other actor and four musicians) makes it possible to put it up for a night or two at a time, and we do so in a variety of venues (Fez and the Public Theatre among them). The show develops a following of East Village gay boys and downtown hipsters and fashionistas (people who *never* go to the theatre), and that for me is really exciting.

In February 1997, we mount the first full-scale production at the Westbeth Theatre Center. The tiny budget is just twenty-nine thousand dollars, painstakingly raised from eight investors. No one wants to invest in a show they can't understand and I can't wholly explain. It doesn't help that between all of us we have almost no relevant track record. Everything is borrowed or begged for. We now have a director, Peter Askin, and a design team and a company manager, but it's still a mom-and-pop operation being run out of my fifth floor walk-up Village apartment. (We have to run to the corner copy shop to receive faxes.)

But the show is fantastic—unlike most anything I've seen. The production garners attention and buzz and succeeds in launching *Hedwig* out into the world, where it will subsequently become an Off-Broadway hit and an internationally acclaimed film.

✦

I hear from a friend that there's this show from South America where there's no seats and the audience moves around the space, as if at a nightclub. Most of the action, I'm told, takes place in the air, high above, on bungee cords. I figure I have to check it out.

So I get on a plane and go see it at a theatre festival in Montreal, Canada. I head to this performance space in a funky neighborhood, where I'm ushered into a big dark room with the rest of the audience.

I always think that a show should be bigger than the theatre that it's in. Like a rockin' party, a successful show should be bursting at the seams.

The creators of this piece, *De La Guarda,* also seem to understand this idea. As the evening begins, the actors literally bust through the paper ceiling down into the audience. Accompanying the action is a pumping tribal soundtrack unlike anything you ever hear in the theatre. There's drums and chanting and it sounds like the Roxy at 4:00 a.m. on a Saturday night.

Next, it begins to rain—no, *storm*—BIG TIME. And while I'm standing there in the middle of all if it, getting soaked, and the winds coming at me, someone plunges down from the ceiling and hoists me up to the rafters twenty or thirty feet above the crowd. While I'm happily soaring up high in the arms of a hot, wet Argentine, I decide I'm bringing this show to New York, one way or the other.

As my partners and I get going in doing just that, it's clear everyone thinks we're nuts because this show is hugely expensive to mount. Plus, the *weekly operating expenses* are astronomical. Clearly, it's a show for young people and conventional wisdom says that young people don't go to the theatre. They don't spend forty-five dollars on something they can't even describe.

I reason with a friend that the kids spend way more than forty-five dollars on a new pair of shoes, so why wouldn't they spend that much on a theatre ticket? My friend argues that shoes, for the most part, have been meeting expectations for hundreds of years; the theatre mostly hasn't.

We need to find a big open space with incredibly high ceilings in Manhattan— no easy task. I spend six months looking at old nightclubs, warehouses, and disused city buildings. I have a huge stroke of luck when I find out that the producer Daryl Roth has just bought an old bank on Union Square that she's about to convert into a theatre. My partners and I tell her to hold off—the raw space is perfect as is. With the theatre and the *capitalization* in hand, we open in the summer of 1998, about a year after my trip to Montreal.

But no one comes. June. July. August. The show is hemorrhaging tens of thousands of dollars a week. For the most part, the critics are dismissive. Much of our staff, completely at a loss as to what to do, quits or we have to let them go.

Still, the small audiences are loving it and word of mouth is growing.

I'm passionate about *De La Guarda* and it is a great pleasure to attend every night. I find it thrilling to experience again and again. That excitement gets me up in the morning and gives me the energy to go to the office and fight for the show.

To spread the word, we give out literally thousands of free tickets each month. We target people in fashion, publishing, and entertainment. We invite literally the entire staff of *GQ* one week, and then all the people at MTV the next. These audiences (who never go to the theatre) love *De La Guarda,* and they start to make it a quintessential word of mouth phenomenon.

Fall comes. September. October. We're still losing tons of money. But our word of mouth campaign is working and some of the biggest stars in the world make it to the show. Leonardo DiCaprio, Cameron Diaz, and Harrison Ford, among others, come to *De La Guarda,* and the reports of the stars' "flying" hits the papers. The celebrity coverage hugely raises the shows profile and we actively pursue more. Madonna, Janet Jackson, Britney and Justin all make their way to 15th Street. At Thanksgiving, we are truly grateful, because the show is solidly making money every week.

The show would go on to become a huge hit with a young international crowd, playing at the Daryl Roth Theatre for seven years. It would be produced around the world—everywhere from London to Tokyo, Las Vegas to Tel Aviv.

➤

In the summer of 1999 I saw a production of Lorraine Hansberry's *A Raisin in the Sun* at the Williamstown Theatre Festival. The production, for me, has a lot of flaws—but the play sings out. Hansberry jumps out from 1959 and grabs me and it is thrilling. *Raisin* plays as if it were written this morning. For me, it has a great story, one that has a lot to say about the way we live in America now.

I meet with the Hansberry estate and I get the *rights* to do the play on Broadway. But no one has any idea why I want to do this play. White people tell me that it's a Black play and that Black audiences won't come to Broadway. Black people tell me that it's dated.

I pursue Denzel Washington to star. When I hear he's in New York I drop him a note at his hotel. He immediately calls and says he'll do it.

Over the course of a year I talk to him numerous times, but my *general manager* isn't getting anywhere with his representation. I hear from others around town that he's telling everyone he's indeed doing it. Then I hear from still others that he's not—that he's changed his mind. I eventually move on.

But the pool of African-American stars is small to begin with, so there's a limited number of places to turn. Some actors think the play is simply not relevant. Others are clearly afraid of stepping into the shoes of Sidney Poitier, Ruby Dee, Claudia McNeil, and the rest. Still, others are guided by their managers and agents, who prescribe to the Broadway dictum that Black plays don't work here. It's pretty discouraging.

There are yet more meetings and phone calls and letters. Finally, I have a *casting* scenario that actually looks possible. In October 2002, the *New York Post* scoops me. Under the headline:

RAISIN' HOPES: B'WAY GRAPEVINE ABUZZ ON REVIVAL

Michael Riedel writes, "FINALLY, a revival to get excited about: Lorraine Hansberry's *A Raisin in the Sun,* starring Laurence Fishburne and Angela Bassett." But Fishburne pulls out. And then Bassett leaves the project.

As months, then years go by, the Hansberry estate grows incredibly frustrated. It's a battle for my team and me to keep going. I have spent tens of thousands of dollars and literally thousands of hours pushing the project and I'm nowhere. I've extended my *option* three times. It becomes clear that my general manager has lost faith in me as well as in the production ever happening, and she quits. Everything is a struggle.

Somewhat resigned and defeated, in summer 2003, after four years of slogging through, I escape to Fire Island. And there I meet this guy, Carl Rumbaugh. I tell him my whole tale and he says, "You have to meet my business partner because she's Black and she knows everyone in Black entertainment." So I go off to meet this woman, Susan Batson.

Susan and I hit it off immediately. It turns out she is the acting coach to the stars. Ten minutes into the meeting she asks me if I have ever thought of Sean Combs for the role. I say "No. Never." "Well," she says, "would you be open to him?" And I say, "Yes," because at this point, why not? She says, "OK, let's call him." And right there, she picks up her cell and calls him and he answers. "Ma," as Sean calls her, "Did I do something wrong, Ma?" She explains she's sitting there with a young man who is going to produce *A Raisin in the Sun* on Broadway and would he be interested in the part of Walter Lee?

So he comes in to audition for the casting director and me and he's pretty damn good. We bring in the director Kenny Leon, and the Hansberry estate for his callback and he impresses everyone.

Everything then happens incredibly fast. I put the rest of the cast together. Audra McDonald, Phylicia Rashad, and Sanaa Lathan will co-star. The mash up of the four stars is incredibly exciting. Each comes from a different background and will bring their fan base, providing us with a potentially enormous and diverse audience. For a moment, it feels like things are finally coming together.

But there's yet another huge obstacle—there's a Broadway *booking* jam. No one wants to give me a theatre. I think I'm losing my mind. It's just two weeks before we go into rehearsal when the tenant at the Royale, the jewel house of The Shubert Organization, announces they are closing, leaving the theatre vacant.

I also need $2.6 million yesterday. But no one wants to invest. I'm a first time Broadway producer, with a first time Broadway director and a first time Broadway star. People wonder how Sean will be on time eight shows a week, that is, if he bothers to make it at all. I hear jokes about an industry pool where people are betting how far we will get before we shut down. People think it's going to be one of those legendary disasters.

I put up over $420 thousand on credit cards and credit lines from the bank. I borrow from friends. When those loans are due, I return the money and borrow from others. I keep moving forward, because that's all I can do. Being a producer is often like being a magician. You have to create the illusion for everyone that it's all moving forward all the time.

In the middle of all of it, we put the show on sale, but the tickets are not moving. We change courses, taking much of our money out of *The New York Times* and instead put it on the subways and the radio. We do street *marketing* in front of clubs and concert events.

And somehow, unfathomably, we make it to the first preview. It is immediately clear that there is something exciting going on both on stage and out in the house. The show looks great. Over the course of previews, the performances evolve and it's exciting to watch. As for the audience, it is primarily African-American. By the end of the run it will be 80 percent Black and represent many generations. You have hip-hop kids from downtown and families from Harlem and sexy couples on dates, all sitting next to one another.

Opening night is incredible. Everyone's there: Beyoncé and Jay-Z, Ossie Davis and Ruby Dee. Spike Lee and Ed Bradley and Iman. Oprah. It rains mercilessly, but our spirits, well…! As I make my way in the rain to the opening night party, I am very wet and very happy. In the following days, you can't pick up a paper or turn on the TV without hearing about *Raisin*.

The show becomes the second highest grossing play in the history of Broadway. We win Tony Awards. Hundreds of people wait on the street during the last week of the run for up to two days for cancellations. The line stretches east on 45th Street, across Shubert Alley, and onto 44th Street. The show takes on a life of its own. The success is crazy. I'm more exhausted and more exhilarated than I have ever been in my life.

✦

Looking back now at the years developing and producing *Hedwig and the Angry Inch,* mounting *De La Guarda*, and putting together *Raisin in the Sun*, it's interesting to think about inspiration; to think about what got me through it.

First and foremost was an incredibly rich, complicated set of ideas at the center of each project: a rock 'n' roll musical that truly rocks and engages the personal, social, and geopolitical tensions between "East and West, man and woman, slavery and freedom"*; a performance piece that dismisses all the traditional physical constructs of theatre; a play from 1959, widely considered dated, that actually had a lot to say about dreams and identity, family, and race.

None of the ideas driving these projects, or the paths these projects would take were simple, clear, or easy. I realize now that they held me in fact *because* they were so challenging. I know now that if I can wholly and clearly understand an idea from the outset and readily see its path, then it's probably not worth pursuing. Because if a project is that simple, chances are, in the end, it won't sustain the audience or me.

Of course, the artists whom I worked with on each project pushed me from day to day with their passion, their vision, and their views of the world.

And finally, and most importantly, it's the audiences who proved the biggest inspiration. Theatre is ultimately about community and that is something that we have less and less of today. I know what I want my community to look like. It's *not* the audience that we traditionally associate with Broadway. I want my community to look like New York City.

The theatre exists in its own entirely ephemeral world. Unlike television and the movies, live theatre is about the interaction between audience and performer. Nothing exists for very long, and at the end of the night, it's up to each person to keep their own record (and they often differ quite a lot, depending on who you ask). In a way, the thing that pushes me through more than anything else is something that is truly impossible to identify. Like the experience of theatre, there is no way to capture or define what makes

* John Cameron Mitchell, *Hedwig and the Angry Inch,* (Woodstock: The Overlook Press), 15. From the musical *Hedwig and the Angry Inch*, by John Cameron Mitchell and Stephen Trask, text Copyright 1998 by John Cameron Mitchell, music and lyrics copyright 1999 by Stephen Trask.

inspiration—it must simply be experienced. But at the end of the night, after everything and when the lights come down, all I know is that it was worth it.

The David Binder co-production of the 2004 Tony Award-winning revival of *A Raisin in the Sun*, by Lorraine Hansberry. Pictured are Sanaa Lathan, Alexander Mitchell, Phylicia Rashad, Sean Combs, and Audra McDonald.

Photo by Joan Marcus, courtesy of the John Willis Theatre World/Screen World Archive.

Amy Danis and Mark Johannes

MARS Theatricals has produced the following productions on Broadway: *Swing!* (six Tony Award nominations); *Little Shop of Horrors* (Tony and Outer Critics Circle nominations); National Tours: *Swing! Little Shop of Horrors*; Off-Broadway: *Tabletop* (Drama Desk Award for Best Ensemble), *World of Mirth* (Drama Desk nomination), *My Old Lady* (Lortel Award, Drama Desk nomination), *Cookin'*, *BUG* (four Lortel Awards, including Best Play) and two OBIE Awards (Best Ensemble, Best Design Team).

AN INDEPENDENT VIEW–FROM MARS

AMY DANIS AND MARK JOHANNES
Partners, MARS Theatricals

AMY DANIS

I didn't set out to be a producer. I was happy to sing, dance, or act in a show—
any show. A worker bee, that was me—no responsibility beyond learning lines
and blocking. Then my true personality won out. When asked why I became a
producer, I reply, "Because I'm bossy." If there is one thing I have, it's an opinion,
and I figured if I was unhappy with the plays and musicals that were being
produced, I should get down in the trenches and see what I could do about it.
It sounds like this decision was made over coffee one Sunday afternoon, but it
actually was a long time coming.

My husband and I were both actors. I had been a dancer/choreographer as
well, and we were both becoming disillusioned with theatre in general. When
we realized we should get involved in producing, the first hurdle was discovering
exactly how one does that. We knew that each of us had twenty years of theatrical
experience, but none in the *business* of theatre, and there was much to learn. To
test the waters, we took the Commercial Theater Institute weekend seminar on
producing. After the first day I knew I was hooked, and I was naïve enough to
think I was going to be a producer. Not wasting any time, I handed out computer-
generated business cards to a few producers who had spoken to us that weekend.
I announced my intention to *associate produce* on *any* project, in order to learn
the ropes, and that is how it started. This was going to be my fourth career and I
knew I had a lot of catching up to do. I hadn't worked in a producing office, and
I was over forty and in a hurry. And I don't think you can learn to be a producer
unless you are actually producing.

The term associate producer can mean a few different things. In our case it
meant we raised money for someone else's project, using their name and track
record to do so. We associate produced on the Broadway musical *Swing!* with
a large group of producers. We sat in on most meetings and soaked up what we
could. Associate producers can also be large *investors* who enjoy being involved
in the project, but are not necessarily interested in eventually running their own

project. These producers are invaluable since there are few producers who can take on the large risk alone. Our reason for associate producing was clear: we needed the education that cannot be acquired any other way. Once at the table, every meeting became graduate school, and every comment, strategy, and decision was filed away for the time we would produce our own projects. We were fortunate to be able to express an opinion or two, and we were never made to feel our presence was merely being tolerated. We learned lessons that cannot be found in a book or a seminar. Likewise, we found that one is taught by those you hire, so we are ever humbled, which is as it should be. Every *advertising* agency, *marketing* consultant, *press agent*, and *general manager* had knowledge to impart.

As *independent producers*, we may partner with larger producing groups on Broadway shows, but that will never be the only way we produce. It takes too much money and too many investors, or both. And investors are hard to find, harder to keep, and impossible to impress. Only if you deliver a hit will you have any stature in their eyes. And why should you? After all, you are more likely to lose money than return it at a profit. We have acquired investors in many ways, even making cold calls from a list of people who had indicated to us they wished to invest. Many of them had clearly stretched the truth, as I soon found out, but a few were for real. Some of our investors are friends and some are family (the hardest money to take). If you are fortunate to have someone calling you asking for a piece of your show (and it does happen), take that person to dinner, ASAP! I have been told by a few aspiring producers, that they are waiting to produce until they have "collected" an investor base. In my humble experience, this is the *great stall*. You must have a project to entice an investor. No one is going to promise you money based on your good looks or your stated goal to produce great art. You can only produce if you are willing to raise money or write a check, if need be. So here's what I know after a mere six years: I know that you never know. I know there used to be a formula for putting up a show: find the property, get the rights, raise the money, hire the team, rent a theatre, and wait for the reviews. However, that is only one way a show gets produced. At any given moment, you may be asked to reinvent the wheel in order to get to opening night.

When we began, our intention was to produce new plays in New York. We like dark and edgy material, but producing the edgier playwrights had become very risky and was not the norm commercially. This is as much a reflection of the changing times and the changing audience as it is of anything. A commercial Off-Broadway play that can sustain a run is a rare thing. Which brings us to *BUG*, by Tracy Letts. Letts wrote *Killer Joe* a few years ago, and that show was considered a downtown success, because it got good reviews *and* it *recouped*. We loved it. When we were introduced to the script of *BUG*, we jumped on it, knowing it was our kind of project. But should we do it? We had produced three other commercial Off-Broadway plays, for $500–950 thousand apiece, and all of them had failed to find an audience or pay back investors. So how would we produce *BUG*? Our choice was to do it "down and dirty" for very little money, so that if/when we failed, it would be only a small failure. How's that for optimism? We had one partner, and the three of us split up the job of general manager to save money. We had never done any of the day-to-day general managing that goes on, and it was the best course in producing I will ever survive. I learned more lessons from this experience than I can recount. Our partner also had relationships with agents and with Actors' Equity that helped immensely when it came time to negotiate contracts. We watched and learned, calling in a lot of favors along the way. On Feb. 29, 2004, the stars aligned, *The New York Times* first-string critic gave us a *money review*, and we started selling tickets. (It should be noted that *BUG* closed Jan. 31, 2005. It recouped and went into profit soon thereafter, with the sale of the publishing and film rights).

Some have asked why a married couple would decide to work together in this emotional and volatile business, fraught with stress and turmoil. It never

The MARS Theatricals production of the
2004 OBIE Award-winning *BUG*, by Tracy Letts. Pictured are
Michael Shannon as Peter Evans and Shannon Cochran as Agnes White.
Photo by Gabe Evans, courtesy of the John Willis Theatre World/Screen World Archive.

occurred to me to do otherwise. I knew that producing was going to be difficult, if not impossible, and I wanted a buddy along for the ride. Besides, it was just another journey and we were already traveling together anyway. I think our varied but similar theatrical backgrounds enhance the partnership. Do we always agree? Certainly not—in fact, I think our differing views keep us honest and grounded.

One assumes the moral here is: where there's a will, there's a way, but it should not be stated so simply. There would be no story to tell, had it not been for the on-the-job training we received from other producers who happened to need our investors and money for their projects. We benefited from their years of experience, and the favors we called in for *BUG* were earned from our respective apprenticeships on their productions. In the end, this is a very small business. The actor we hire today may end up at our producing table as an associate in the future, and each new venture will assuredly teach us something else. At least, one can hope so.

MARK JOHANNES

After twenty-odd years of living as performers in New York, my wife Amy Danis and I reached the point where we felt that there was a dearth of intriguing, imaginative, and provocative plays being presented here and decided to look into producing to see if we could do something about it. At the time, we even had a prospective project in tow. What we didn't have was a clue as to how to go about producing it. After a weekend spent at one of the Commercial Theater Institute's three-day seminars, though still relatively clueless, we at least had some inspiration, incentive, and a direction in which to travel. We felt the first step for us was to sign on as associate producers on someone else's project, raise some money for it, and follow the process with experienced producers at the helm. We made our interest known to a couple of professionals who had spoken on panels during the CTI weekend and eventually found ourselves raising some money as associate producers on the Broadway musical *Swing!*

We were fortunate indeed to have fallen in with the Frankel/Routh/Viertel/ Baruch group (the lead producers on *Swing!*), who mentored us by generously sharing their knowledge and acumen and answering and re-answering our many questions. We were thirsty for information and we asked, listened, and learned from producers, general managers, company managers—anyone who could explain a strategy, break down a budget, and just generally share their prior experience. As we have gone on to work with this partnership on a total of five productions since that time, it seems a great example of how one experience or opportunity can lead to others.

Eventually it did lead to our original goal to produce on our own. For us that meant Off-Broadway plays and we have now done several. The most recent and best example of what we picked up along the way is undoubtedly *BUG*, by Tracy Letts, a play that ran for eleven months at the Barrow Street Theatre in Greenwich Village. We spent a year with one other producer creating and recreating budgets to come up with a viable (i.e., inexpensive) plan to lose as little money as possible, while putting up a show that we felt had a right to some life in New York, even if that life was measured in weeks as opposed to months or years. Our lack of confidence in expecting an Off-Broadway (or Broadway) play to have much of a run was the product of our past experiences with material of this nature. While we were excited to see these plays realized, we also had come to the conclusion that there might not be a large enough audience to support them for long, however wonderful they were.

BUG survived eleven months Off-Broadway for two reasons: (1) the number of rave reviews and the amount of other press it received upon opening and beyond, and (2) we kept its costs much lower than is usually possible by choosing to wear many of the hats that we would normally have hired others to wear (which is just as important). We did not intend to wear them for that long and, though it somewhat monopolized our producing schedule at the time, it seriously sharpened our skills in many areas. These were some of the same skills that we got our first glimpse of five years ago as associate producers of *Swing!* and without that experience we never could have even attempted to fly solo on this one.

Is this ultimately the way we will choose to produce in the future? That's hard to say. I prefer the hands-on approach but I'm also more aware now of the necessity of being able to rely on others as well. I've certainly learned that nothing in this business turns out quite the way you imagine or plan it, and that may be the most important lesson I've learned from my six plus years of producing theatre. That you must make the best plans you can, endlessly going over and over them, refining them, finessing them, and then be malleable enough to roll with the punches, prepared to paddle your production down an entirely different stream than you had figured (usually in the eleventh hour or later).

We've learned much from many. The commercial theatre producing world is much smaller than most people realize and though allies are obviously much more helpful than adversaries, I can't think of anyone I've met in this business who—by virtue of their experience, acumen, or example—hasn't had something to teach me.

MARS Theatricals will continue to produce theatre one way or another for as long as we believe there is a place for our voice to be heard. Perhaps the key to that lies in that balance between how prepared, yet still adaptable, we can continue to be.

Michael David

From 1980–present, Michael David has served as president of Dodger Theatricals. From 1970–1980 he was the executive director of New York's Chelsea Theatre Center. He has produced 300 plays and musicals in New York, and garnered 134 Tony Award nominations and forty-six Tony Awards.

Broadway productions include: The 2006 Best Musical Tony Award – winning *Jersey Boys*, *Urinetown*, *42nd Street*, *Titanic*, *Dracula*, *The Music Man*, *Wrong Mountain*, *Footloose*, *The King and I*, *High Society*, *1776*, *The Who's Tommy*, *A Funny Thing Happened on the Way to the Forum*, *Mandy Patinkin in Concert*, *Once Upon A Mattress*, *How to Succeed in Business Without Really Trying*, Ralph Fiennes' *Hamlet*, *Guys and Dolls*, *The Secret Garden*, *Jelly's Last Jam*, *Into the Woods* (1987 & 2002), *Big River*, *Prelude to A Kiss*, *Gospel at Colonus*, *Pump Boys and Dinettes*, *Candide*, *Yentl*, and *Happy End*.

Off-Broadway productions include: American premieres of *Drumstick*, Leroi Jones' *Slaveship*, David Storey's *The Contractor*, Edward Bond's *Saved*, Allen Ginsberg's *Kaddish*, Barrie Keefe's *Gimme Shelter*, Jean Genet's *The Screens*, Stanislaw Witkiewicz' *Crazy Locomotive*, Heathecote Williams' *AC/DC*, and Jack Heifner's *Vanities*.

COLLABORATIONS BETWEEN NOT-FOR-PROFIT AND COMMERCIAL THEATRES

A Transcription of a Seminar at the Commercial Theater Institute

MICHAEL DAVID
President, Dodger Theatricals

In years past, the idea that there may be any sort of hand-in-hand between the *bad* people (*commercial* producers) and the *good* people (*nonprofit* artistic directors); the *low-minded* and the *high-minded*; was unacceptable. But inexorably, as those relationships began to develop, it first resulted in a number of compromised nonprofits losing grants. Studio Arena in Buffalo, New York, for instance, was one of the first to combine with a commercial producer, on *The Lady from Dubuque* by Edward Albee. To one it was a *tryout*; to the other, a way to gain needed funds, increase *subscriptions*, and please their constituents. It may be assumed that both thought it a worthy play. The New York State Council made its disappointment with that relationship tangibly clear in the next grant cycle.

That was then. Now these relationships abound. Serving various needs shared and separate; one trying not to adulterate the other. Obviously there are plentiful contracts between nonprofits and the commercial. The fact is, what we (my office, the Dodgers) have done after some twenty of these collaborations, has been to evolve some sort of paradigm for that relationship. If there is nothing else I say of value here, there will at least be a list of issues to be negotiated, as well as a series of comparables, that may help inform those issues. Trust that the not-for-profits actively share this same kind of information among them. But that hasn't been happening among commercial producers; we don't share much in an organized way with one another. So, if nothing else, there will be some twenty deals that you'll know and be able to reference. But I am getting ahead of myself.

There seem to me to be three kinds of producers on Broadway:

1. Producer-as-shopper. You find someone else's successful child and adopt it. Producers are constantly circling over both sides of the Atlantic these days, looking to find the next hit somewhere else that they might bring here to the

Great White Way. (That seems more like presenting to me, but considering how dangerous and unwelcoming *here* is, it makes a lot of sense that you would want to vet something before you bring it in.)

2. Producer-as-investor. You find a child someone else is raising and you support it, and you buy into it. It is a way to learn, have a stake, rooting interest, cocktail party one-liner, and more and more these days a way to have control; as serious, sizable investors acquire a proverbial seat at the table. (It has always seemed to me that democracy and producing are counterproductive, or I suppose, a necessary evil. But that is a discussion for another time.)

3. Producer-as-originator. You cause an idea to happen; you make the baby. And that is—and I don't have to tell you—the most dangerous of these three producing styles. But it is also the most gratifying, the most fun, as well as the most risky.

Tonight we talk primarily about origination, and if you want to originate and if shows are—forgive the metaphor—sort of children, I would contend that Broadway is an extraordinarily dangerous, unwelcoming, expensive, and unsupportive place to raise any child. It's also a place where just being good isn't enough to succeed; where work needs to be artful *and* accessible; where accessible is often not good; where good (or bad) has to pay for itself and pay it's own way. So in terms of parenting, it is placing an amazing load—an amazing burden—on your child to support itself in this unbelievably unhealthy and expensive neighborhood. Was the best thing for *Angels in America* to bring it to Broadway, where it would have to make or *break even* at over $200 thousand per week, on its own, without subsidy? Or would it have been better to have performed Off-Broadway, at say, the Lucille Lortel, where it could break even at under seventy thousand dollars per week and might have run much longer? The argument would be that on Broadway it is in our faces; that it was too important a message not to have been there, and one needed to take a risk to do so. But on Broadway, success is necessarily the mutual accomplishment of art and commerce. Given then the expense, the danger, the risk, the lack of privacy, and the lack of generosity, it's important to learn how to hold and nurture and promulgate the baby before you get there. So, and forgive me—this is hopefully the last baby analogy—but, all babies are different, and yes, no show is the same. They have different *developmental* needs and require distinct strategies.

If we could, the Dodgers would originate everything we do. But some time ago we did consider relative risks, energy, and capital required, and life lost in the process, and determined it would be good business to incorporate some work that had already found success, was familiar, and had titles and stories and melodies that you recognized. So over time we interpolated classics in with the new stuff. And, as you'll see as we go through the list, we've actually included in this developmental model the occasional classic with the new work.

If all shows are unique, and each requires a unique development, then we have utilized a number of means to get smart about the respective baby before it leaves the proverbial nest. Some of these methods that follow are relatively standard, others less so.

Actors' Equity Association provides two paradigms we've used, or "riffed" on: (1) the longer term Workshop, and (2) the Twenty-Hour Reading. Workshops tend to be six to eight weeks in length, with complete casts, little scenery, few musicians, and no paid performances. The Workshop process brings with it to Equity members a consequent sharing in future gross and *subsidiary rights*, and a commitment to a payment of four weeks contractual salary to actors not used if and when the project reaches Broadway. We have used the Workshop format successfully on its own directly preceding a full Broadway production (*Titanic* was too big and complicated to produce twice). With Equity's cooperation we have also messed with this format (e.g., Martha Clarke's wonderfully whacked concept for a new *Hans Christian Anderson*: Everyone flies!) Before its developmental production at San Francisco's ACT, Equity allowed us to do a six-week workshop divided into three, two-week segments. We were able to work in a theatre on wires with the writer and director to generate through trial and error the theatrical vocabulary desired to tell Martha's version of these stories with two weeks on and two weeks off, two weeks on and two weeks off, and so on.

We have also utilized the Actors' Equity 20-Hour Reading with partial casts, on-book, with no scenery or paid performances. Whereas originally intended to prepare for a *reading* of a complete work, we have found them most helpful in a more intensified exploration of a section of a work (How do we end? or begin? Does this act work?) And we have done a series of these short "get togethers" targeting sections of the same show. Between each one the creatives take what they've learned and design the informed itinerary of the next get together. Equity has recently put fairly stringent rules in place governing these Readings, which are (from my point of view) regrettable and harmful to this healthy, economical, and productive development process for new work.

We have also taken the Broadway production rehearsal process and riffed on it as well. With the first Broadway production of *Into the Woods* in 1987, we broke up the conventional rehearsal schedule of seven or eight weeks into two four-week parts. We needed to explore the ending of the show and tested three versions by interrupting the rehearsal period. The cast was hired on full production salaries for Broadway, but the contract with each actor defined the rehearsal period as a twelve-week process: four weeks on, four weeks off, and four weeks on. The actors received a small financial recognition of this accommodation in return. After the first four weeks, we ran each ending, picked one, and took a four-week break. The authors rewrote, and we resumed rehearsal even as the Broadway marquee was going up. Pressure? Yes. But hardly the kind encountered when you are in previews and everyone is publicly taking you apart.

But more than any other, we have utilized the full production of a show within a seminal/commercial relationship; a custodial relationship to explore text, personnel, chemistry, the audience, early critical reactions, staging, costumes, scenery, and even a title. For example, we had a show title we weren't sure of: *Shout up a Morning,* which was a musical by Cannonball Adderley about John Henry we produced at the La Jolla Playhouse. We asked the box office there to keep track of every version of the title buyers used when they called in to order tickets. There were fifty or so different monikers they came up with, and ultimately *Shout Up a Morning* became *Big Man.* (In the end, the title change was not enough.) We have done some twenty of these and with only two exceptions, all have been intended to provide a pause (or stop) when the engagement ended, in order to take the necessary time to apply what was learned. There are so many things to learn about the child, on stage and off. So, we will talk about the seminal/commercial collaboration; a relationship created not to get a Broadway show on cheaply, but to learn how best (or whether) to get it on Broadway at all. Wisdom first, tangible assets—maybe never. Now to the chart.

As we refer to the chart (see *Productions and Contract Terms* on pg.66-69) let's use the original Broadway production of Stephen Sondheim and James Lapine's *Into The Woods* as a start. It was their first collaboration and Lapine would direct. *Into The Woods* was originally read at Playwrights Horizons. After the reading, it was determined to produce the show on Broadway, and rights were acquired by the producing team. It was also determined by everyone that the show had much work to do. Within a short time, the Old Globe Theatre in San Diego expressed a desire to do a production during their 1986–87 season, and as cumbersome and potentially fractious as such a relationship might be, on paper it seemed to suit everyone. We both shared enthusiasm for the project. We had the rights and a core team. They had the theatre, an audience, and an available slot. (And it was about as far away from New York as we could possibly be. We especially liked

PRODUCTION AND CONTRACT TERMS

	INTO THE WOODS Old Globe	SHOUT UP A MORNING LaJolla Playhouse	BIG RIVER ART/Harvard	BIG RIVER LaJolla Playhouse
Term of License	Limited	Limited	Limited	Limited
Control	Non-profit	Non-profit	Non-profit	Non-profit
Liability	Non-profit	Non-profit	Non-profit	Non-profit
Artistic Team	Mutual	Mutual	Mutual	Mutual
Enhancement	200K + 25K contingency	165K	0	65K
B.O. income to	Non-profit	Non-profit	Non-profit	Non-profit
Press Determination	Yes (local crix & press) No (nat'l crix & press)	Yes (local crix & press) No (nat'l crix & press)	Yes (local crix & press) No (nat'l crix & press)	Yes (local crix & press) No (nat'l crix & press)
Tickets	30 total comps with additional paid tickets on request	30 total comps with additional paid tickets on request	30 total comps with additional paid tickets on request	30 total comps with additional paid tickets on request
Billing @ Non-profit (Dodgers)	Invisible	Invisible	Invisible	Invisible
Billing B'way (Non-profit)	Bottom of title page	Bottom of title page	Bottom of title page	Bottom of title page
Continuing Obligations	No first refusals/side letters instead	No first refusals/side letters instead	Some first refusals	No first refusals/side letters instead
Asset Ownership	Available up to value of enhancement	Available up to value of enhancement	Available at cost	Available up to value of enhancement
Future % Gross	1/2 3/4 @ recoup	3/4 1 @ recoup	1.5	0
Future % Net	2 (mother company only)	2	3.75	1 less 65K advance

MERRY WIVES OF WINDSOR Alley Theatre	PRELUDE TO A KISS Circle Rep NYC	SECRET GARDEN Virginia Stage	JELLY'S LAST JAM Center Theatre Group @ Mark Taper Forum	THE WHO'S TOMMY LaJolla Playhouse
Right to one tour	Limited	Limited	Limited	Limited
Non-profit	Non-profit	Non-profit	Non-profit	Non-profit
Non-profit	Non-profit	Non-profit	Non-profit	Non-profit
Mutual	Non-profit	Mutual	Mutual	Mutual
0	50K	400K	350K	500K
Non-profit	Non-profit	Non-profit	Non-profit	Non-profit
Yes (local crix & press) No (nat'l crix & press)	Unlimited	Yes (local crix & press) No (nat'l crix & press)	Yes (local crix & press) No (nat'l crix & press)	Yes (local crix & press) No (nat'l crix & press)
30 total comps with additional paid tickets on request	As needed	30 total comps with additional paid tickets on request	30 total comps with additional paid tickets on request	52 total comps with additional paid tickets on request
Invisible	Invisible	Invisible	Invisible	Invisible
Bottom of title page	Above title	Bottom of title page	Bottom of title page	Bottom of title page
No first refusals/side letters instead	Yes	No first refusals/side letters instead	No first refusals/side letters instead	No first refusals/side letters instead
Available at cost	Available up to value of enhancement	Available up to value of enhancement	Available up to value of enhancement	Available up to value of enhancement
1/2 1 @recoup within 3 years of last performance	3/4 1 @ recoup 1 1/2 @ 125% recoup	1/2 3/4 @ recoup	1/2 3/4 @ recoup	1/2 3/4 @ recoup
0	5	2	2	2

[continues on next page] ⟶

[↪ continued from page 57] **PRODUCTION AND CONTRACT**

	HOW TO SUCCEED.. LaJolla Playhouse	HAMLET Almeida Co-production	HIGH SOCIETY American Conservatory Theater	WRONG MOUNTAIN American Conservatory Theater Co-production
Term of License	Limited	Limited	Limited	Limited
Control	Non-profit	Non-profit	Non-profit	Non-profit
Liability	Non-profit	Non-profit (Weekly running Dodgers)	Non-profit	Non-profit
Artistic Team	Mutual	Mutual	Mutual	Mutual
Enhancement	900K	400K	675K	195K
B.O. income to	Non-profit	Co-production	Non-profit	Non-profit
Press Determination	Yes (local crix & press) No (nat'l crix & press)	Non-profit (London) Dodgers (Bway)	Yes (local crix & press) No (nat'l crix & press)	Yes (local crix & press) No (nat'l crix & press)
Tickets	52 total comps with additional paid tickets on request	As needed	52 total comps with additional paid tickets on request	52 total comps with additional paid tickets on request
Billing @ Non-profit (Dodgers)	Invisible	Invisible	Invisible	Invisible
Billing B'way (Non-profit)	Bottom of title page	Above the title	Bottom of title page	Above the title
Continuing Obligations	No first refusals/side letters instead	Yes- Prior to NYC All consummated before NYC	No first refusals/side letters instead	No first refusals/side letters instead
Asset Ownership	Available up to value of enhancement	Co-production	Available up to value of enhancement	Available up to value of enhancement
Future % Gross	3/4	1/2 Almeida 1/2 Dodgers	1/2	1
Future % Net	3	15% off the top to creatives/ cast then 50/50 split	3	5

TERMS

HANS CHRISTIAN ANDERSON American Conservatory Theater	BARBRA'S WEDDING Philadelphia Theatre Company	DRACULA LaJolla Playhouse	JERSEY BOYS LaJolla Playhouse
Limited	Limited	Limited	Limited
Non-profit	Non-profit	Non-profit	Non-profit
Non-profit	Non-profit	Non-profit	Non-profit
Mutual	Mutual	Mutual	Mutual
1 Million	30K	1.4 Million	900K
Non-profit	Non-profit	Non-profit	Non-profit
Yes (local crix & press) No (nat'l crix & press)	Yes (local crix & press) No (nat'l crix & press)	Yes (local crix & press) No (nat'l crix & press)	Yes (local crix & press) No (nat'l crix & press)
52 total comps with additional paid tickets on request	As needed	52 total comps with additional paid tickets on request	52 total comps with additional paid tickets on request
Invisible	Invisible	Invisible	Invisible
Bottom of title page	Bottom of title page	Bottom of title page	Bottom of title page
No first refusals/side letters instead	No first refusals/side letters instead	No first refusals/side letters instead	No first refusals/side letters instead
Available up to value of enhancement	Available up to value of enhancement	Available up to value of enhancement	Available up to value of enhancement
1/2	1/2	3/4 1 @ 125 recoup	1 1.25 @ recoup
2	2	3	3

that.) The question then became how to create a relationship that serves the piece, our respective needs, and doesn't emasculate either party in the process. Both agreed that much could be gained from such collaboration. And what turned out to be the critical element in such a relationship was the realization that at some time, *your* rights become *their* production. Yikes!

We created a contract which memorialized the relationship and in it we tried to anticipate the kind of behavior presently required of all parties, as well as the consequences for us all afterward, if this worked. Because no matter how collegial the relationship, each party has its own distinct needs and aspirations. Sometimes they align; often they don't. Their future is now; yours, a hoped-for later.

RIGHTS

This chart presumes you have the *first class production* rights to the show already. In all of the following situations, but one (*Prelude to A Kiss*), we had the rights. We then sought out (or were sought out by) an enthusiastic partner, if you will, to put up the show together. It is the fact of having those rights that enables one to create the most equitable of these relationships. So to take this first step, the nonprofit then needs to acquire the rights to *your* show for *their* production. There are two ways this has happened: One, the nonprofit negotiates with the author's representative directly and we consent to that discreet use; or two, it *licenses* those rights from us.

The rights to the Old Globe for *Into the Woods* came from us. In our agreement with the authors for the first class rights, the authors provided us the right to do one developmental production. So we created a limited license directly with the Old Globe that provided terms for authors that were commensurate with the Globe's history and means. That said, I would recommend the nonprofit make an arrangement directly with the authors to get yourself out of the middle of that.

TERM

The term for the use of these rights was for a limited period of time (their subscription period) only, with extensions at our discretion.

PRESS

A provocative area. Who comes—and when—and who doesn't. Our needs do not align. Naturally, the host theatre is eager to celebrate their current accomplishment; while you more than likely want time to make it better and save any *publicity* for later. (If this is, for you, a laboratory until you have perfected the show you want as

The Michael David/Dodger Theatricals co-production of the 1993 Tony Award-winning *The Who's Tommy*; book by Pete Townshend and Des McAnuff; music & lyrics by Pete Townshend. Pictured are Donnie Kehr, Michael Cerveris, and Christian Hoff.
Photo by Joan Marcus, courtesy of the John Willis Theatre World/Screen World Archive.

much privacy as possible.) And so, at the Old Globe we determined that inviting their local critics, including *The Los Angeles Times*, was fine but we drew the line at *The New York Times'* Frank Rich. And in the end, some came anyway (they say they didn't invite them), but we always try to limit national exposure in these circumstances. In our various relationships since, the practice has been that local critics are invited; the national critics are not. The same goes for local press coverage and TV exposure. For example, when *The Who's Tommy* was first presented at the La Jolla Playhouse, even in its early form there, it was a hit. *The Tonight Show* wanted someone for an appearance. That was good for La Jolla and their box office; not good for us. You only do *The Tonight Show* once. We would want (and need) it later. We had to say "No." You're there at the beginning of a journey, and for them it is the theoretical end. Tricky business, this.

ARTISTIC TEAM

With *Into the Woods* there was already a core team. It came with the authors (a few even before the Broadway producers), not to mention its new collaborators, The Old Globe. So when sitting down with The Old Globe to make the contract, the names of the creative team for their production were agreed upon and included. In this case Lapine, who co-wrote, would direct. Sondheim had musical colleagues, and so Paul Gemignani would musical direct and Jonathan Tunick would orchestrate. It went like that. The Old Globe would attempt to hire them under their standard terms, but decisions were made in the beginning as to who they were.

CONTROL

And so it went. Once the details of the production, its team, timing, and budget (with *enhancement*) were determined, we let it go. All the day-to-day control from then on would go to The Old Globe. This was liberating in some ways and frustrating in others, but in all but a few cases, that has been the model, and imperfect as it sometimes is, I can't think of one of these relationships over the years that has not been the better for it. Once the rules are determined, your activity takes place around theirs, not in the middle of it. So, once codified, the control of the future there is theirs.

LIABILITY

Liability therefore, is theirs as well. The balance of any liability, the mess someone makes, the new prop someone wants, etc., is their problem. If they go over budget, if they need radio mics, whatever it is, theoretically in this contract after you've given them the money (we'll talk about enhancement later), the risk in producing there is theirs (sort of). Because the result of their production affects yours, you are hooked no matter what the contract says. And among other things, that does mean that every time something new is needed someone looks at you as the wallet.

ENHANCEMENT

How much will their production cost? How much of that don't they have? More specifically, your enhancement equals the cost of the production; plus the cost of the entire run; less how much they anticipate earning at the box office; less what they have in their budget. And this moment of determining what they can afford and what you add has become a sort of ritualistic dance. I can promise you now that whatever the show, the only available slot in their subscription is the slot budgeted to have a one-person show with no scenery. So, the dance begins. They budget the production using their in-house templates, and then you and your team struggle with them and theirs to come up with the number of additional dollars needed. And yes, you'll be finding that their budget includes the production costs, running costs, and frequently everything but the kitchen sink. The struggle is to come up with a reasonable budget while preserving this new relationship. Note this process is a dangerous one where a Pyrrhic victory can easily occur. You win the budget battle and lose the bigger war with an under-funded show and bad feelings in its wake. In the case of *Into The Woods* at The Old Globe, the process was fair and reasonable. We enhanced their budget by $200 thousand, putting aside an additional twenty-five thousand dollars contingency (just in case). Of course that was eventually contributed too. The total enhancement at The Old Globe: $225 thousand. Today that number would be one million dollars. And fifteen years later that number is one million dollars, for *Tommy, Dracula*, and the recent *Jersey Boys*.

ASSET OWNERSHIP

When all is done, and you are moving on to the next step, you can take with you everything from the closed production at no charge, up to the value of your enhancement—everything not nailed down when you got there. Most often those things are orchestrations, copies, and the like.

INCOME

One hundred percent of the income goes to them; they get it all. And you'll find with rare exception, that is always the case. They would say that in return that you take away what you've learned, with most of future profit and gross intact. Note that The Old Globe included *Into The Woods* in their subscription, and it was Sold Out before anything happened on the stage.

TICKETS

For you, your team, a potential new team member, and of course, the eventual investor, seeing and learning from this seminal production is the prime reason for doing it. For us, this is the best way to introduce something you are excited about to people who might be putting money into it. You introduce it to them when you don't need any money—yet. So tickets are very important. It seems easy enough, however, because these theatres are almost always subscription based and tickets are a very tight commodity. We have created a ticket expectation that seems to work: thirty to forty comps early on (including opening night). Thereafter, thirty or forty a week in any location, that *we* pay for. You *must* have the capability to expose this production to others. The mechanism and amounts need to be determined before you start.

BILLING

Whether it was twenty years ago, when there was much anxiety *attached* to what our nonprofit theatres were doing and who they were doing it with, or now, when such commercial/nonprofit relationships are commonplace, we didn't and don't want our names anywhere—*anywhere*. We don't want to be thanked either (not in print). *Into the Woods* is produced by The Old Globe Theatre. Period. And while we do not want to be *billed* anywhere there; on Broadway, the host theatre would be billed anytime the producers are, in a line (or two) across the bottom of the title page (e.g., "Originally produced at The Old Globe Theatre, San Diego, California." Or nowadays, "World Premiere at…" (Fine with me.)

CONTINUING OBLIGATIONS

Now this is *really* tricky. This production, for you, is in the laboratory. And when you go into the *lab* you want the best people possible. But because more often than not those people you want live somewhere else and expect higher compensation in order to join up, they will want first refusal on the next step. But if the chemistry doesn't work in this lab, you want to be able to make a change. That's why you are paying one million dollars to figure out how it works. For example, we got ourselves into some trouble early on with *Big River* at Harvard when we did give first refusal to a leading actor and, needing to eventually make a change, that actor was paid for a year for not performing the role that we were sure (when he was hired) that no one else could play. So, presuming wisdom is gained during this process, the application of that wisdom must be combined with at least the capability to change the elements that informed it. So, we have no first refusals with personnel that work on these early production collaborations. No actor, director, designer, orchestra, etc. What we *do* do, is create short separation agreements with certain people. Instead of saying we agree to hire you if we move forward to another production, we commit that if we don't, we will pay an additional amount for your taking the early ride. The separation amount is determined by who it is and how confident you are that you're not going to change that chemistry. So on *Into the Woods*, you can give Jonathan Tunick and Paul Gemignani the promise of a lot of money if you don't hire them because you're sure that you will (Note: Actors' Equity does provide a version of this within their contract for the actors in a nonprofit production). This methodology has been relatively successful. The point is that it is critical to include the ability for you to make changes after this first step.

FUTURE SHARING

What if it works? What if it ends up on Broadway? The sharing of future income with your early collaborator makes perfect sense. The amount depends on the nature or state of the work at that particular point of the collaboration. If early, more; if later, less. In the case of *Big River* at the La Jolla Playhouse, we had already collaborated previously on *Big River* at Harvard with ART. So that when the next production was mounted at the La Jolla Playhouse nine months later (after a free look-see in Cambridge), the speculation and corresponding risk was less, but the reward the same. (The accompanying chart will reflect that Harvard received a larger share, La Jolla very small.

GROSS

In the case of *Into the Woods* at The Old Globe, they were doing the first production, before anyone else, they received a royalty of one-half point of the gross, going to three-quarters of a pint of any the future commercial production in our control. (Their royalty share was governed by that of the producer. If there was a pool and the producer was in it, then The Old Globe had to be in that pool. If the producer deferred or waived, then so did The Old Globe.)

PROFITS

The Old Globe also received 2 percent of the profits of the Broadway production (the so-called *mother company* only).

Parenthetically, I believe the production of Stephen Sondheim and James Lapine's *Into the Woods* in 1987 at The Old Globe and had some affect on nonprofit theatres all over the country. Although The Old Globe was well established, the people in San Diego were proud of it and loved it, and it was an overall wonderful operation—suddenly the most important composer in musical theatre was coming and working there. And their production shaped the work that was to eventually go to Broadway, to acclaim, and a long run as well as a *tour* and yes, even (shared) profitability. *Into The Woods* at The Old Globe (and in its own way *Big River* at the La Jolla Playhouse two years before), demonstrated how a partnership comprised of so many disparate elements—and egos—can be mutually and respectfully beneficial. And I think tangentially, the fact of this project, at that theatre, at this time, gave legitimacy to such collaborations in the eyes of the not-for-profit theatres and their funders.

Okay so that's one show.

As we proceed with the rest, I think, in almost every case on this chart, what we expected to take away going in, had nothing to do with the tangible. Risking redundancy, there was nothing about these relationships that was motivated by *getting the scenery built cheaper there and then moving it.* It was predicated by exactly the opposite: the expectation was rooted in the assumption that what we decide we want before, we are likely to want to do differently after; what we know now, we'll know so much better then. And we will build in enough time after to put it to use. And the fact of that depressurizes the whole situation. Aspiring to wisdom rather than inexpensive assets liberates the two parties.

Finally, although these collaborations cause you to increase your eventual Broadway *capitalization* in the amount of the enhancement, and you also risk finding out all too vividly that your beloved child is not near as beloved as you thought, there is nary a person I've met who has done their show once who doesn't salivate at the prospect of doing it again—knowing what they know now. It probably applies to life as well. That said, like life (and the theatre), even with all of the nurturing, sometimes it works and sometimes it doesn't.

A fast couple of things: (1) Remember that more often than not, in the theatre time is at least as valuable as money. Use both wisely. Be prepared. (2) Never forget that show titles are actually names of families—artificially conceived but most singular of families, carefully hand-picked groups of wandering, disparate, and independent souls all assembled for a few moments to land a big idea. So for God's sake, do all you can to not be left trusting the success of the work—your child, that family—to the critics.

A CODA

It seems to me that the distinction between the not-for-profit and the *for-profit*—the seminal theatre and the commercial theatre—is getting fuzzier and fuzzier and, regrettably for me, fuzzier and fuzzier in exactly the wrong texture. My hope for the development of theatre in our country does not rest in commercial producing on Broadway. Those aspirations tend to rest with people whose names I don't know in theatres I don't inhabit. Not that we couldn't do it, or don't do it occasionally, but simply that the challenges that stand before commercial theatre producers, the impediments that exist before putting up anything—in this case something that also has to support itself—seems to stand directly in the path of artfulness, not to mention sustenance. But that's for another time.

Susan Quint Gallin

Susan Quint Gallin is currently a producer of Monty Python's *Spamalot* and of the long-running *STOMP*. She produced *Woman Before a Glass,* Lanie Robertson's one-woman play based on the life of Peggy Guggenheim, starring Mercedes Ruehl; *The Retreat From Moscow* (2004 Tony nominee for Best Play); the 2002 Broadway Revival of *Man of La Mancha*, starring Brian Stokes Mitchell; *The Shape of Things* by Neil LaBute; Jon Robin Baitz's adaptation of Ibsen's *Hedda Gabler*; *Fully Committed* by Becky Mode (2000 Outer Critics' Circle Award); *Cowgirls* by Mary Murfitt and Betsy Howie; *Angels in America* by Tony Kushner (five Tony Awards and the Pulitzer Prize for Drama); *From the Mississippi Delta* by Dr. Endesha Mae Holland; Bock and Harnick's *The Rothchilds* (revival); *Other People's Money*, by Jerry Sterner (1988 Outer Critics' Circle Award; New York and national tour); *Burn This* by Lanford Wilson; and the London production of David Mamet's *The Cryptogram*. She is the first recipient of the Robert Whitehead Award for Outstanding Producing.

OTHER PEOPLE'S MONEY

SUSAN QUINT GALLIN (A CONVERSATION WITH)
Susan Gallin Productions

BEN HODGES: Do you want to tell us how you got started?

SUSAN QUINT GALLIN: I'm sure that 99 percent of the people working in theatre were members of their high school drama club! Recently I was talking to a friend who is a theatre critic, and she said that when she was in high school, she told her English teacher that she wanted to be a theatre producer and her English teacher said, "Impossible!" and ultimately she became a critic. In high school I wrote and essay about wanting to do theatre criticism and my English teacher said, "Impossible!" and I became a producer. We both had a love for the theatre, but the limitation of our teachers' vision certainly influenced the paths we took. I was working on a daily television show and also *developing* properties on my own, mostly for children's television. I worked for *Entertainment Tonight* when it went on the air (which I never put in my credits because people in theatre do not want to see a television background), and this led me indirectly into the theatre. I was developing *Today I Am a Fountain Pen* for television with Israel Horovitz. Israel's play *North Shore Fish* opened at the WPA to very positive reviews. There were a number of producers who were interested in moving it to a *commercial* Broadway production, including the Weisslers. He asked me if I wanted to produce it with them. He then introduced me to the Weisslers. I remember feeling overwhelmed by the realization that to produce you didn't have to be born into the theatre; that you didn't have to be the son or daughter of an established producer. As long as you had the ability to raise money, you could begin to work in the theatre, and if your taste and instincts were good, you could continue. A magical kingdom had been opened to me, and I knew I had found work that was deeply satisfying. I decided not to go ahead with Israel's play (we couldn't cast it the way we wanted—that is, couldn't get the star we wanted—the phenomena of needing a star is not as new as people seem to think). I started to look for a producer who I could learn from, and a play that intrigued me. I looked around a bit and met Jim Freydberg. Jim was producing Lanford Wilson's *Burn This* with John Malkovich. I read the play, was fascinated by it, and thought Jim would be a good teacher. He was, and it was a great experience. I'm proud when I say that that production of *Burn This* was my first experience in the theatre. When the play was revived by the Signature Theatre Company a few years ago, it made me realize I've been in this business a long time!

HODGES: And the original production was in what year?

GALLIN: 1988.

HODGES: So, from working with Jim Freydberg and *Burn This* you moved on to...?

GALLIN: After that experience I was told about the Commercial Theater Institute. It is extraordinarily valuable for anyone interested in producing. People working in all aspects of theatre speak on panels sharing their experience. Every profession should have such a concise "*How to...*" It also provides the participants with a way to hear and meet people in the business and decide if there might be someone they might be interested in working with. Fred Vogel was the heart and soul of CTI and it is hard to imagine it without him. But there are wonderful people who will take his position this year—not his *place*, but his position.

Fred invited me to a *reading* and afterwards we went out for coffee with Jeff Ash, who was at that time the head of the theatre department at Grey Advertising. I had been reading scripts. I don't know how I was able to get the word out, but I was reading everything that anybody sent me. They were coming from agents and writers and doormen and waiters. I learned that Jeff had the rights to *Other People's Money* and this was to be his foray into producing. We became partners, and it began an incredible learning experience. To have a first play be so successful was pretty exciting. But I'm getting ahead of myself. We were looking for a director—I can remember this so vividly—a couple of directors passed on it, very discouraging! Jerry Sterner was an unknown writer and it was about a subject that a lot of people in the creative community weren't particularly interested in: corporate takeovers. And many people felt that the moment for the play had passed. It had been given to Mark Lamos at Hartford Stage. There was a call on my answering machine from Mark saying: "It's a great play—let's do it." Ultimately, it turned out that Mark wasn't available to direct, but he wanted it to be part of the season at Hartford Stage. That was the real beginning of my career.

HODGES: So, you've produced with *nonprofits* as well as commercially. What are the differences, in your mind?

GALLIN: The relationship with a not-for-profit at that time was very different from the way it is currently. We granted the rights to Hartford Stage and they had creative control. We had already agreed that Gloria Muzio would direct before we proceeded. It was a Hartford Stage production—it was their mandate as a theatre developing new plays to have complete creative control. It was comfortable going ahead in this manner because we had had many discussions and all seemed to envision the play in the same way. But I emphasize it was definitely their production. The enhancement was a small amount of money—forty thousand dollars. We did participate, because we got to know each other and they were comfortable with us, but there was never any doubt about the fact that they had the final decision. I have had experiences since then, one being developing a musical with Seattle Rep. Also a supportive relationship, but very different. Basically, they gave us the tools to work with, the space, the actors and the support staff, and we were on our own—all the artistic decisions were ours. Sharon Ott was the artistic director at the time and was very supportive but didn't influence artistic decisions.

The economics of theatre have become such that commercial theatres need help from not-for-profits. Equally, not-for-profits need help from commercial producers. It has caused not-for-profits to allow commercial producers to have more artistic control in their theatres. If a play or musical that is developed in a not-for-profit theatre *transfers* to a commercial production, the originating theatre receives a weekly royalty and piece of the profit. It can be a very meaningful amount of income to a theatre. I absolutely understand and that works very well for me, but I also think it is sad that the economy of the theatre has caused this, that the not-for-profits have to have much more of an eye toward the future life of a play and can't be as experimental and daring as they once were. It causes some theatres to work with established writers as opposed to taking a risk with a new voice.

HODGES: If I am a playwright, how do I get you to see my play?

GALLIN: When I started in the business, all you had to do is hand it to me and I read it. Because I think that taste is so specific, nobody else can read for me. If I have a talent, it's recognizing good writing. For me to be interested in spending at least the next year of my life involved in the work, it needs to have resonance to me personally. In other words, the play has to deal with something that is of importance to me. Nobody else can know that. Now I read plays that come from writers and agents who I work with who have an idea of what my taste is. Let me back up a bit—I'm a commercial producer. I raise money. I'm in business. I don't have the luxury of producing a play just because I like it. I have investors and if they are not making money, then I am not in business any more. So I feel as though I have to find a play that for me has resonance. That is, about something that matters to me, but at the same time is commercial, has an audience. I am always looking for a well-written play that will provoke an audience. If the audience is talking about the play at intermission it is the best thing that could possibly happen. For me, a play should make people think about things in a way that they hadn't before.

HODGES: Do you go to readings of plays and/or workshops, and are you more inclined to go to something that is staged than a reading?

GALLIN: I do go to readings occasionally—I would actually rather read a play. The business has changed there also. Agents used to give producers plays and the producers tried to set it up in a not-for-profit theatre. But now the agent wants to have a production in a not-for-profit theatre, and have producers come and see it. So the dynamic between the agent, writer, and producer is different. In some ways the agent is doing the producer's work. Sometimes it is advantageous, but ideally I would like to be involved before any of the creative team has been chosen. I do go to readings, especially if an agent is persistent! There are some plays that I have read that I know, honestly, I haven't been able to quite grasp. I need to see a reading.

HODGES: But, it does happen that you'll actually read a play *cold*, without having seen a reading, and decide that it's something you would like to produce?

GALLIN: Most of what I've done fits that category. *The Retreat from Moscow*, for instance. I read it and I was just bowled over by it. At that time Mike Nichols had the rights to it and, sadly, it wasn't available. I thought the writing was beautiful. The author, Bill Nicholson, dealt with relationships in a way that hadn't been done before—it was a serious play about marriage. The same thing was true of *The Shape of Things*. I read it and was fascinated by it. I thought it was very provocative and there was an audience for it, possibly a much younger audience. It was being done by the Almeida Theatre in London. I got in touch with Jonathan Kent, the artistic director at the time, and we worked out an agreement for me to produce it commercially after the Almeida run. In that case it was their production. It opened to great reviews in London and I had the rights to move it, which I did.

Right now I'm working on a musical based on the movie *Desperately Seeking Susan*, with the music of Blondie. It was brought to me by Peter Michael Marino. He had written a treatment for the musical. It had tremendous appeal to me and I thought it had a big heart. I *optioned* the rights to the movie from Darcie Denkert and Dean Stolber at MGM, Deborah Harry got very excited about the idea, and Ron Kastner became my partner. And the process begins!

HODGES: So, it's a combination of personal resonance and what you feel is commercial viability?

The Susan Quint Gallin co-production of the 2004 Tony nominated production of *The Retreat From Moscow*, by William Nicholson.
Pictured are Eileen Atkins as Alice and John Lithgow as Edward.
Photo by Joan Marcus, courtesy of the John Willis Theatre World/Screen World Archive.

GALLIN: Yes. There's a little overlap where a play that is commercial is also well written. There are often well-written plays that I like that I don't think have a big enough audience. As a commercial producer, whether I'm right or wrong, I have to believe there is an audience that will want to see this play.

HODGES: You brought *The Shape of Things* to New York, so maybe you can just take us through the process of how that happens?

GALLIN: Maybe it would be good to compare *The Shape of Things* with *The Retreat from Moscow*. I read *The Shape of Things* and found it provocative and interesting as only Neil LaBute can be. The Almeida Theatre was doing a production. I got in touch with them, and agreed to *enhance* their production for a very fair amount of money. I got the rights to bring it to New York, and to co-produce it commercially in London. In that case they cast it; it was their production. It opened to great reviews and was a big hit in London. Everybody in New York wanted to be my partner! I had met Stuart Thompson and was interested in his *general managing* it, and I hoped he would want to produce it with me. He had read it and really liked it, went to see the production, decided to produce and general manage. It was a lesson. The production transferred exactly as it was in London with Paul Rudd, Fred Weller, Rachel Weisz, and Gretchen Mol. Everybody in New York wanted to be involved. I kept making calls saying, "Do you mind investing less so that I can bring some new investors in?" It opened in New York and didn't get good reviews. It ran six months and was made into a movie and I am proud of the production, but it wasn't a commercial success. There is no sure thing.

The Retreat from Moscow had been optioned by Mike Nichols when I read it. There was an actor *attached* to it, but when that actor dropped out, Mike Nichols wasn't interested in going forward. Stuart Thompson had read the play also and was very interested in it. We optioned it. It did have a production that wasn't well received at a theatre festival outside of London. We felt that the play was a finished piece and didn't need a production outside of New York. Dan Sullivan read it and agreed with us, and signed on as the director. We then started the *casting* process. It has over the years become increasingly more important to have stars. It was also a play that needed actors with serious acting "chops." It was not a play that could be done by someone who had never been on a stage before. The first person who came on board was Eileen Atkins. Then we spent months thinking about who to cast as her husband. We were thinking only of English actors. One day Daniel Swee, who was casting, called and said, "I know he is not English, but he has played English—what about John Lithgow?" It seemed like such a perfect choice I knew that John would want to do it. He read it, loved it, and said yes. We were thinking about Ben Chaplin to play the son, and got a call from Mark Epstein, Ben Chaplin's manager, saying, "You know I read *The Retreat from Moscow*—would you consider Ben Chaplin?" and I said "Oh, yes, we will consider him." [*Laughs*]. It was the best kind of producing experience for me, because it was taking material that I really loved, beautiful writing, putting the pieces together, and putting it on stage. I'm not a writer. I can't write something that will express what I want to say, but I can produce it and that is what this play was. It was a play about something I wanted to deal with in the theatre. The audience reaction was incredible. I was getting calls from people who were moved and affected by it when they saw it in previews. And you can tell a difference. You can hear a difference in the theatre when people are really excited. The *press agent* said, "You know you have a hit." Hmmm….It opened to unfavorable reviews. Again, we ran six months, which was the length of the actors' contracts, and I couldn't be prouder, and I would not have done anything any differently. But, unfortunately it wasn't a commercial success. A producer was quoted as saying that you can't do straight plays in New York commercially, and I thought to myself, "That not true—he just had some bad experiences." I am tending to agree now. Possibly there are one or two plays a year that are successful, but you absolutely have to have *The New York Times* behind you. It's been proven with musicals that if there is an audience that's supporting a musical it doesn't need a great review to survive and flourish. But, there is such a small audience for serious straight plays that if you lose a part of that audience because you haven't gotten a great review in *The New York Times*, you probably can't survive. That's unfortunate.

HODGES: Because you are one of the only people who is contributing to this book who can really talk about the process of taking something from the stage into film production, can you talk a little bit about that?

GALLIN: You normally have a negotiated percentage of what the author receives from the outset. But, it is very unusual for the theatre producer to get the film rights. Sometimes you try to get a *right of first negotiation*, which is more of a possibility. When I produced *Other People's Money*, the film rights had already been sold, but we would participate. Because the play was very successful, the sale price was increased—a miracle. *Other People's Money* was *capitalized* at $400 thousand and the film rights were about $200 thousand. We received a percentage of that, around one hundred thousand dollars to the *Other People's Money Limited Partnership,* which is meaningful. In general, I'm not interested in film, but I do think, "If I produced a play, and I am so intimately involved in its development, it would be interesting to produce the film." At the least, you share in the author's *subsidiary rights.*

HODGES: Also, you said something that I want to go back to: you had everyone coming at you to invest in *The Shape of Things.* So you have had enough successes that I think you can talk about this—when investors are disappointed, how do you maneuver that territory, tilling the soil for future productions while keeping your investor base happy?

GALLIN: My investors are very happy. I asked one of my investors—who has been with me from the very beginning (and has invested the amount which I've asked for in each show—not the same percentage of every show). I asked him to check with his accountant to see where he is in the big picture and his profit is much better than the stock market on a great year. But, there are certainly investors who have invested in the one or two plays that haven't made money, and I've had one investor who invested in *STOMP* and nothing else—major windfall! I would recommend that an investor look at theatre investments as a mutual fund. It's best if they decide that they are backing a person they have faith in—and are going to invest in everything that they produce—then I think there is a good chance that they will come out ahead, or at least, a better chance.

HODGES: Does your investor pool change?

GALLIN: Yes, it changes. I have people who have been investing with me from the very beginning. But each show brings new people. Last year I produced a play *Woman Before a Glass* about Peggy Guggenheim. There were people involved in the art world to whom this appealed. Occasionally someone comes into my life and asks if they may have the privilege of investing in theatre—I like that question!But I have also turned down investors if I have sense that they don't understand the nature of a theatre investment.

HODGES: What is the first thing you say to someone if they say they want to put their money in one of your shows?

GALLIN: I say that you have to think about it as writing a check and ripping it up and throwing it away. [*Laughs.*] On the other hand, I also tell potential investors that I have made a lot of money for people. It is much more difficult for me to find material that meets all my criteria for production than investors. Often my enthusiasm for a play causes people to invest when I'm not actually approaching them as an investor.

HODGES: So whether it's *Other People's Money*, *The Shape of Things*, or *Retreat from Moscow*, you've gotten the rights and you've brought it to New York. With respect to budget and the size of the production, how much do you personally strategize *marketing* and publicity, with respect to each show? Or do you hire your *advertising* and marketing company and turn it over to them completely?

GALLIN: We do it together. I know the press agent knows better than I do about press, and the advertising agency knows better about advertising, but I am certainly opinionated. When we sat at our first advertising meeting at SpotCo for *The Retreat From Moscow*, we agreed that we had a play with revered actors and a title that was misleading. We knew that the ads needed to have photographs of the actors and language that was enticing—that it explained that it was a play about the dissolution of a marriage, not a history lesson about the Napoleonic Wars. The agency took this information and presented us with a campaign that we thought was classy, enticing, and presented our three actors. It did all of that and was very simple and classy.

HODGES: How has working on a musical been different for you than working on a play?

GALLIN: Well, I keep saying I'm really a play person, but when Peter brought me the treatment for *Desperately Seeking Susan*, I loved the idea and was just seduced by it.

HODGES: It was only an idea?

GALLIN: It was a treatment based on a movie with existing music. I got really excited about the combination of the two elements. The book is written, a new song has been written, and we are in the process of deciding who will direct. Musicals are more difficult creatively because you have many elements that have to come together. There isn't one creative voice but usually three—book, music, and lyrics—that need to come together as one. I think even though I haven't been *about* musicals, it's the next step. It's bigger, in that there are also many more elements to the production. Each play that I have produced has been exciting to me—there are always new lessons to learn! But I know what it's like to open a play. A new musical is a big learning curve. I've produced musicals before but not as one of the lead producers.

HODGES: Finally, what would you like to say about this business to someone who is twenty-five years old, that you wished you had known when you were that age?

GALLIN: When I started in the business as part of the producing team on *Burn This*, there was no formal way of working with an established producer. I just spent time at Jim's office and kept calling him and asking him questions. Now it is formalized, there is a meeting at the advertising agency every week, and all the people who have a producer credit are at that meeting. They don't have decision-making ability, but they come to the meeting and they can voice their opinion. The advertising, press, marketing, and management all give their reports. If taking the Commercial Theater Institute is college, joining in on the production of an established producer is graduate school. What I see some people doing is staying in graduate school and not taking the leap to find material and produce on their own. There is nothing like it! There are so many young producers working in the theatre. Maybe this has to do with the arts management programs that certainly didn't exist when I was in college.

When I was taking the Commercial Theater Institute seminar, Gail Berman and Susan Rose talked about producing *Joseph and the Amazing Technicolor Dreamcoat*. What I loved about hearing them talk about that experience was that they were really honest and said that looking back, they didn't know what they were doing. But they were feisty and smart and they kept at it, made mistakes, and corrected them. They had a very successful production, and went on to wonderful careers. I was listening to them and I thought that if you are really passionate about theatre, then you can figure it out. You can produce. If you love theatre, put all your energy into it. There is nothing more exciting—and so worthwhile!

Kevin McCollum

Kevin McCollum has won Tony Awards for Best Musical for *RENT,* currently on Broadway, touring the country, and a major motion picture, as well as for *Avenue Q,* currently on Broadway and which played at the Wynn Resort in Las Vegas. In 1995, Mr. McCollum co-founded The Producing Office with Jeffrey Seller. The Producing Office is represented on Broadway by *RENT,* the winner of the 1996 Pulitzer Prize for Drama. More recently he produced the debut stage production of *Irving Berlin's White Christmas* at the Curran Theatre in San Francisco. In 2002, Mr. McCollum produced Baz Luhrmann's Broadway production of Puccini's *La Boheme,* which won two Tony Awards. Mr. McCollum is a graduate of the University of Cincinnati College Conservatory of Music, and has a master's degree from the Peter Stark Program at the University of Southern California.

BUSINESS AS UNUSUAL

KEVIN McCOLLUM
Partner, The Producing Office

I have never believed that a producer's job is to raise money. That is like saying an actor's job is simply to read lines. The marginalization of a producer's role in theatre today as just a money person is very destructive to the ecosystem that is musical theatre. I feel a producer's job is to help create an environment and provide the tools and philosophy that enable a new work to grow into its fullest potential. There are practical and creative realities that every good producer must navigate, but I can assure you that raising money is the last, and in many ways the easiest, one of them.

The far more difficult aspect of being a producer is approaching the act of producing as a big *"What if?"* *What if* this story is placed with this librettist or if these melodies are put with these lyrics? Or, *What if* this director worked with this librettist, or that lyricist to continue to shape a work that is still not finding its footing? All of these disciplines require artists with their own unique voice as well. I think about all of these things when deciding what to produce and how to produce it.

I have never produced in the same way twice. I don't believe there is a formula to follow in producing a show *commercially* in today's market. It is too expensive and too dynamic, with too small of a global audience, to do it the way you did it before. How many sequels have you seen in musical theatre that even got produced, let alone work? *Funny Lady* comes to mind as the only one I know—and that was a film. Such is my case. I produce this way because I believe people go to the theatre because they are thirsty for a song, melody, and story that transcends watching something get blown up. We see so much of that in today's society and it appears to me that it's nothing out of the ordinary anymore; it's not surprising. However, a melody and lyric that touch your emotional center is more powerful than you can ever anticipate, even if you have heard it before. When we go to the theatre we want the hair on the back of our neck to stand and our eyes to well with tears because of the shear brilliance of that surprise.

So how do you start? First, you must understand that all theatre is research and *development*. It is not manufacturing. The movie business employs a manufacturing model because it's less costly on a per capita basis. Once a movie is made, it lives on and has a shelf life that doesn't demand another human being to sustain it after it is captured by the camera. However, theatre must be invented at every performance—every matinee and evening, one day at a time. It is never the same twice. Every performance has its own unique fingerprint and economic equation. The longer a show runs, the more it costs, and your audiences begin to diminish, which is antithetical to a successful manufacturing business. Unfortunately, the labor and real estate economics involved in the theatre industry are structured like manufacturing, which is why it is so difficult to produce today. But, that is for another book. If you approach producing as a research and development model, your goal is to enter the marketplace with the least amount of cost and test the market to see if anyone likes what you've created.

In the theatre, the most important part of the business—and the most expensive part—is pulling in a paying audience. A full-page color ad in the Sunday edition *of The New York Times*, at the time of this writing, is $105 thousand. For most of the shows running on Broadway today, pulling in an audience is much more expensive per week than the costs of the director, writers, and actors *combined*! The challenge is how to place your musical in an environment where a paying audience will not only come to your show, but also give you necessary information and feedback about how good or bad your show is.

However, before you begin your producing, you should have a philosophy as to *why* you are producing something; that is your first goal. Producing just so you can be a producer does not count as a philosophy...unless you are wildly wealthy and have a jaded view of yourself...and a low self-esteem. Your second goal is to find a place for your musical to be seen. The *venue* should constitute an economic equation, providing enough money for the creative team in order to hire the necessary talent to tell your story. This equation should also aid in accessibility, by means of attracting an audience that can start spreading the word about the play. This is why many of my shows have been produced Off-Broadway or *out-of-town* before coming to Broadway.

RENT and *Avenue Q* were both the result of starting small by *enhancing* an Off-Broadway theatre company's production in order to see how the audiences would react to something my producing partners and I already thought was pretty fantastic. It's a collaborative effort, really. Internally, you collaborate with your colleagues. Externally, and perhaps most importantly, you collaborate with your audience by making yourself available to new ideas through community, interests, and input.

With *RENT*, Jonathan Larson, the author of the entire musical, knew that he wanted to have a workshop at the New York Theatre Workshop. He had initiated a reading that I saw in 1994. The show was in great need of structure, but the music completely propelled me immediately into bliss. I had never heard such a brilliant mix of music theatre lyricism with a rock 'n' roll score. Jonathan's voice was unique, but work was needed. Jeffrey Seller and I, along with Allan S. Gordon, agreed to give to the New York Theatre Workshop the money they would need to fully produce a workshop production. They needed the money because, to do it right, we would have to hire the director, musical director, actors, rehearse for five weeks, and perform for seven weeks. They could only foot half the bill and we agreed to pay the rest. Consequently, we acquired the commercial rights from Jonathan so that if it captured the audience's imagination and became a hit, we could produce it commercially. (To clarify hit, I mean a financially successful venture where the entire *capitalization* is *recouped* and profit earned.)

You know the rest of the story, but what this illustrates is that we knew a lot going into it. We knew we were producing it because of Jonathan's unique talent, and we knew New York Theatre Workshop was the perfect venue with the perfect

The Company of the 10th anniversary production of the 1996 Tony Award-winning *RENT*; a Kevin McCollum co-production; book, music, and lyrics by Jonathan Larson.
Photo by Joan Marcus, courtesy of the John Willis Theatre World/Screen World Archive.

creative staff—Jim Nicola, director Michael Greif, and musical director Tim Weill—all deserve so much of the credit in bringing our show to the audience that would usher Jonathan's brilliant musical into the world.

We enhanced *Avenue Q* differently because we already held the commercial rights when we approached The Vineyard Theatre and The New Group about our wonderfully eccentric group of talented puppet characters who were dealing with *real* life. We felt the audiences that *subscribe* to both The New Group and The Vineyard Theatre were the kind of audiences that would be up for an adventure of life lessons given by puppets who speak the truth about the human condition. This groovy audience was very important to us because we really needed to figure out how audiences would relate to seeing actual puppeteers manipulate the puppets and still be able to fall in love with the furry characters. We had no idea if it would work and we needed people to start talking about it. If we had not enhanced the Vineyard/New Group production of our show, we would have had to spend millions on *advertising*. Instead, we found a theatre to work with at a fraction of the cost to show the adventurous theatregoer our show, and let them tell their friends. It also enabled our wonderful creative team—director Jason Moore, and authors Jeff Marx, Robert Lopez, and Jeff Whitty—to work with the talented Doug Abel and Scott Elliott. It is part of human nature to tell your friends what you liked about something you saw and why. Our job was to bring together the best audience possible for our show and let them tell us what to do with it. It is my guess that in the ever-shrinking world that we live in, the most rewarding and profitable experience will be a renaissance of consciousness built entirely upon collaboration in every sense of the word.

Avenue Q and *RENT* both moved to Broadway, not because we needed to produce a Broadway show, but because we decided to produce something we loved with an affordable model. We listened to the audiences that came to those initial productions, we collaborated, and realized that we had no choice but to move them to Broadway...

Harriet Newman Leve

Ms. Leve is presently a producer of the award-winning New York and national tour productions of *STOMP*, created and directed by Luke Cresswell and Steve McNicholas, and the critically acclaimed, large format motion picture entitled *Pulse: a STOMP Odyssey*. Currently she also is producing the Broadway production of Martin McDonagh's *The Lieutenant of Inishmore*, the Off-Broadway production of Sherry Glaser's *Family Secrets*, directed by Bob Balaban, and the national tour of the Broadway production of Eve Ensler's *The Good Body*.

Recent productions include the Off-Broadway production of the international hit musical *Shockheaded Peter*, the Broadway production of Eve Ensler's *The Good Body* directed by Peter Askin; the South African production of *Jocasta Rising*, written and directed by Carol Michèle Kaplan; August Wilson's *Ma Rainey's Black Bottom*, directed by Marion McClinton and starring Whoopi Goldberg and Charles Dutton; Eve Ensler's *Necessary Targets*, directed by Michael Wilson and starring Shirley Knight and Diane Venora; the Tony-nominated Broadway production of Arthur Miller's *The Crucible*, directed by Richard Eyre and starring Liam Neeson and Laura Linney; and the Broadway production of *Hedda Gabler*, directed by Nicholas Martin and starring Kate Burton.

Other notable New York productions include the Tony-nominated Broadway production of *The Diary of Anne Frank*, directed by James Lapine and starring Natalie Portman and Linda Lavin; *Twilight: Los Angeles, 1992*, written and performed by Anna Deavere Smith and directed by George C. Wolfe; the Olivier Award–winning production of *Kat and the Kings*, book, lyrics, and direction by David Kramer and music and arrangements by Taliep Petersen; Alan Ayckbourn's *Communicating Doors*, directed by Christopher Ashley and starring Mary-Louise Parker, Patricia Hodges, and David McCallum; and Alan Zweibel's *Bunny Bunny*:

Gilda Radner—A Sort of Romantic Comedy, directed by Christopher Ashley and starring Bruno Kirby and Paula Cale.

Her Los Angeles productions include Larry Kramer's *The Normal Heart*, directed by Arvin Brown and starring Richard Dreyfuss, Kathy Bates, and Bruce Davison; Wendy Wasserstein's *Isn't it Romantic*, directed by Gerald Gutierrez and starring Christine Estabrook and Joan Copeland; Sam Shepard's *The Curse of the Starving Class*, starring Carrie Snodgress and Andrew Robinson; the original production of Sherry Glaser's *Family Secrets*; Dinah Manoff's *Telegram from Heaven* starring Renée Taylor; Mark Rothman's *Excess Baggage* starring Larry Miller; and Claire Chafee's *Why We Have a Body*.

Ms. Leve was also director of development for Tony Bill Film Productions and taught film workshops at the American Film Institute in Los Angeles.

She is a partner in the new theatre complex 37 ARTS, which has three Off-Broadway theatres, in addition to studio and rehearsal space for Mikhail Baryshnikov's company, and she is a member of the League of American Theatres and Producers. Ms. Leve was on the Board of Directors of New York Stage and Film for four years.

YOU NEVER FORGET YOUR FIRST TIME

HARRIET NEWMAN LEVE
President, Leve Productions

As they say, you never forget your first time. Mine was at the Canon Theatre in Beverly Hills, California, on a warm October evening—my very first opening night as a theatre producer, and I was thrilled, nervous, excited, and terrified. Together with three partners, I was producing the West Coast premiere of Wendy Wasserstein's *Isn't it Romantic*, which had been a hit in New York City. As the audience began to arrive, I wondered whether we were crazy to bring this very New York play to Los Angeles. We had no big *name* stars in the production, just an amazing cast of wonderful actors. What made us think that people would come? (Especially people in Los Angeles, for whom theatre is mostly an afterthought in an industry town that is ruled by the film and television business.) What would the critics think?

I sat in the audience that night, and as the lights went down, it was hard to stay still in my seat. I looked at the faces of the people sitting there, looking expectantly at the stage. I thought about how much I would have loved to have my parents there, but unfortunately, my mother had recently had a heart attack, and so she and my father were in Miami Beach, Florida, awaiting news of reviews. Christine Estabrook, playing Janie, made her entrance, and the magic began. "You did it!" I remember thinking to myself, "You actually did it. You made your dream come true."

The journey to that opening night probably began when I was growing up in Miami Beach, although that's the long story. The short story is that I had been living in Los Angeles for many years, having moved there to get into the entertainment business. I was working for Tony Bill, the film producer, director, and actor, and I had a number of film and television projects of my own in development at the studios. One of my colleagues, Van Spaulding, who also worked at Tony's company, told me he had seen this great play called *Isn't it Romantic*, which was running at the Lucille Lortel Theatre in New York, produced by Playwrights Horizons. I had gotten to know Susan Dietz, who ran L.A. Stage Company and was an experienced theatre producer, who told me that if I was ever interested in producing theatre, I should bring her a play I liked. I flew to New York to see it and just loved the piece. I met with André Bishop (who was artistic director of Playwrights at the time and is now the artistic director of Lincoln Center Theatre), and told him that I'd like to take the play to L.A., and that I would be working with Susan and L.A. Stage Company. André was very supportive, and spoke to Wendy, who gave it her blessing. To this day I feel indebted to André and Wendy for enabling me to launch my producing career.

Once we had secured the rights, I embarked on my first adventure in learning the art and business of producing. We approached Ellen Krass to join the team, which, by then, included Susan, Van, and myself. Ellen was an experienced TV producer, but also had never produced theatre. Susan was our mentor and our guide. We had an equal partnership among the four of us. The total budget for the production was $200 thousand, and we each had to raise fifty thousand dollars. I was apprehensive about it. Where do you begin? How do you ask people to give money to a business venture that was very risky? And who do you go to? I began by making a list of every person I knew all over the country; people I had grown up with, gone to college with, met in the different cities I had lived in before L.A., and I began calling the people I thought might be interested. My plan was to be completely honest with everyone; to tell them that there were no guarantees of success in the theatre business and that they could lose their entire investment.

I think that something about my honesty and my forthrightness gave people the sense that they could trust me and that I wasn't pulling anything over on them. A lot of people said no, and often it was those I most expected would say yes. But miraculously, I was able to raise exactly what I needed: I found ten people willing to put in five thousand dollars each, and often it was the people I *least* expected would say yes. I have used the same approach every time I've had to raise money for a show, whether it has been a few hundred thousand dollars or $2.3 million, the most I have raised personally for a production so far.

What was great about that first producing experience was that we were not only financiers, but also closely involved in the creative process. Gerry Gutierrez, who had directed *Isn't It Romantic* in New York and received a Drama Desk Award for its direction, was hired to direct our production as well. It was at the first set of auditions that I met Wendy Wasserstein in person, and over the *casting* period and during rehearsals I had a chance to get to know her. Wendy didn't drive, so we put her up in a hotel within walking distance to the theatre, but I would often pick her up to drive her to different places in L.A. that she needed to go, and sometimes we'd have lunch or dinner together. She was such a joy to work with, and her sense of humor was unstoppable, no matter what was happening. She and Gerry were also very close friends, but they both involved us in the pre-production process, which was a great learning experience. It is a huge loss to our theatre community, and deeply sad, that Wendy has passed away, and of course, Gerry died a few years ago as well, completely unexpectedly. I think of them both with enormous fondness, as they are so closely associated with my first steps as an emerging producer.

In addition to raising money and giving opinions on casting, there were numerous other decisions to be made by the producing team about budgets, *advertising, marketing, key art*, rehearsals, previews, the opening night party, and *publicity*. Each of us as producers had one vote, and ironically, the three inexperienced producers often agreed, which meant we sometimes outvoted Susan. She took it well, but once the play had opened and was running, she decided to step down as a producer, but continued *general managing* the production.

So, come opening night, I sat there wondering if the three of us, who had voted with such certainty, had any clue about what we were doing. Would we end up with egg on our faces? We had taken a play that was a success in New York, and was directed by an award-winning director. If it flopped in L.A., there was really only one place to lay the blame—on us. When the last line of the play was spoken, the audience, which had laughed loudly and appreciatively throughout the evening, rose to its feet and applauded. The critics also loved it. We were a hit! The play ran for nine months in L.A., a town where most shows run six to twelve weeks. Because some in our original cast had other commitments, we had to recast a few of the roles to be able to keep it going. My first foray into theatrical producing was a success, and I was hooked. I loved the fact that the whole process—from getting the rights to seeing the play up on its feet—was live and changing. I felt that, as a producer, I was involved in nurturing a living, breathing thing every day. Most of all, I loved the sense of belonging to a community of people who share a commitment to theatre.

There was another aspect to the immense satisfaction I derived from this experience. As I said, I had moved to L.A. many years before with the dream of becoming a film producer, and was fortunate to land my first job in the business with Tony Bill's company. Working for Tony was a formative experience. I met agents, managers, directors, producers, studio executives, and other development people. I learned the business side of the entertainment industry, the importance of forging strong professional relationships, and being the sort of person people like and trust. I also learned to recognize material that speaks to me.

After working with Tony for a number of years, I ventured out on my own as an independent film and TV producer. I had some strong projects and was successful in getting a few of them into development at the major studios. The problem, though, was getting them greenlit—that is, getting to the point where a film would actually go into production. I always felt that I did well where I had control and input (working with the writer and other creative people, *pitching* the projects, persuading executives), but at the point where my control ended—the point at which the studio execs decided whether to invest money in a project—the deal would fall apart. It was frustrating. In contrast, in producing *Isn't It Romantic* I had control over financial and business decisions from the start of the project to its ultimate realization. I realized that in the theatre world, whether a production actually saw the light of day was up to me as the producer. With the success of *Isn't it Romantic,* I bid goodbye to the film business for a number of years and crossed over into theatre producing full-time.

I produced six plays in Los Angeles, including Larry Kramer's *The Normal Heart*, starring Richard Dreyfuss, Kathy Bates, and Bruce Davison; Sam Shepard's *Curse of the Starving Class*, starring Carrie Snodgress and Bradley Whitford (now on television in *The West Wing*); and Sherry Glaser's *Family Secrets*. With the success of these productions, people kept asking me whether I had plans to move to New York. I knew that if I was going to be serious about being a theatre producer, I needed to work there. I was actually born in New York City, but my family moved to Miami Beach when I was a child. I'd always fantasized about moving back, but I hated cold weather and after living in L.A. for fourteen years following a divorce and a move from San Francisco, I didn't feel that I wanted to start my life all over again, yet again. Of course, as with most things in this life, you should never say never. As luck and business would have it, Lee Sankowich, a friend and colleague who had produced and directed the San Francisco production of *One Flew Over the Cuckoo's Nest*, was going to New York to produce and direct *Edith Stein* at the Jewish Repertory Theatre. He asked me to accompany him to help with the producing side of things, so that he could focus on directing. He just needed me to be there for the month of November. I decided the weather couldn't be that bad in November, so I said yes.

And then I said yes to two more offers when I arrived here: the first was the opportunity to join the producing team of *STOMP*, because three of the producers who had originally planned to bring the show to the United States had dropped out. They needed a replacement, and the money to fill the shortfall, very quickly. I was given a copy of a short promotional video showing some excerpts of their work. I loved it! The work struck me as completely innovative and unusual. I called Richard Frankel, who was the general manager and executive producer of the show, and said I was on board. I set about raising my share of the money, which I had to gather in three weeks. While that was happening, I got a phone call from one of the producers of *Twilight: Los Angeles, 1992 (Twilight)*. The one-woman show with Anna Deveare Smith was running at The Public Theatre and selling out every night. Ben Mordecai, the lead producer of the show, among

The Harriet Newman Leve co-production of the 1994
OBIE Award-winning *STOMP*; created and directed by Luke Cresswell and Steve McNicholas. Pictured are performers Theseus Gerard and Theona Wilkes.
Photo by Stuart Morris, courtesy of the John Willis Theatre World/Screen World Archive.

others, wanted to move it to Broadway and was looking for producers to come on board. Once again, time was very short. I went to see the show at The Public and thought it was stunning. I was mesmerized by Anna's performance, watching her transform herself into forty-four different characters, and I knew I had to be a part of it. I told Ben I was on board, and I started to raise money for that show as well. At that point I knew my fate was sealed. I had to move to New York because the following year I would have two openings to go to: *STOMP*, that was opening Off-Broadway, and *Twilight*, which would be my first play to open on Broadway.

Upon arriving in New York, I immediately got caught up in the many meetings, discussions, and decisions that go into producing a play in this city. *STOMP* opened at the end of February 1994, and *Twilight* opened at the end of April the same year. By that time, I had already begun to feel integrated into the New York producing world, because of the people I was getting to know through the production meetings for both shows. I would end up co-producing or collaborating on more occasions with quite a few of the people I had met in those first weeks, which was like jumping into the deep end of a swimming pool to learn to swim—all I needed to do was remember to breathe. I worked with some of the best in the business on those two first productions, and in particular, learned the nuts and bolts of getting a new show off the ground and keeping it going from Richard Frankel and his general management partners. The attention they gave to *STOMP*, and all the aspects of marketing and promoting a show, made a strong impression on me. Today, *STOMP* continues to run in the same Off-Broadway theatre, the Orpheum, where it opened twelve years ago, and ticket sales are still going strong. In addition, the show *tours* the country and has developed a huge following of fans in the U.S. and in the rest of the world. During my association with the show, I have grown close to Luke Cresswell and Steve McNicholas, the two creators of *STOMP*. My connection with them led me, together with Jim Stern (another theatre producer I have worked with a few times), Steve and Don Kempf, and Walden Media, to work with Luke and Steve on developing an idea for a large format film that would explore rhythm and drumming around the world. The result is *Pulse: A STOMP Odyssey,* a film that was released in 2002, has won numerous awards, and continues to play in IMAX theatres across the country and around the world.

My entry into the New York theatre world was a combination of my being in the right place at the right time, and being ready and willing to throw myself into the work at hand without hesitation. Since then, I have steadily built my production company in New York, and have produced a total of sixteen shows, of which eight have been on Broadway.* I have formed a vibrant producing team under the Leve Productions banner, which includes Laura Wagner, who has been involved in my company since 1999, and has risen from assistant to *associate producer* to producer-director of her own projects, and Ron Nicynski, who joined our company in 2004 as a management associate and is now also a producer with his own projects. They each contribute invaluable talent, insight, and perspective to the company's work, and I depend on them for their creative instincts as well as their expertise as organizers and managers.

When I tell non-theatre people that I am a producer, they normally ask what a producer does. I'm not surprised by the question, as before I got into this career, I would have been hard-pressed to explain the job. In the early stages of getting a play off the ground, the main pressures are to secure the rights for the work, hire the director and cast, and hire the production and design team. It sounds straightforward, but it entails juggling a lot of schedules around theatre availability, and at the same time finding the right mix of talents, styles, tastes, and personalities that each member of the creative and business teams are bringing to the table. Of course, the director is key when it comes to choosing the designers and the casting, often because they have excellent relationships with actors, and know when they are looking to do theatre, and what kind of role they may be looking for. Through all of this, too, the general manager, the production team, and the director are making sure that the playwright is happy with the choices that are being made. I also meet with the advertising and marketing team to work out what the key artwork will be for the play's poster, print ads, and playbill.

While managing this initial phase of assembling the troops, I am also responsible for raising funds. To do that, I need offering documents and other legal paperwork, as raising funds for theatre is governed by both federal and state securities laws. I have used the same entertainment lawyer on all productions where I am the lead producer—Nancy Rose—and she is both an exceptional lawyer and a very good friend. Armed with the paperwork, I start making calls. I am usually looking for two types of investors: those who are interested in putting money into a show and getting the perks that go with it such as the opening night party and a sense of being on the inside track of shows that may turn out to be huge successes; and other producers and individuals who take on the job of raising a portion of the money themselves in exchange for greater involvement.

----

* Broadway shows: *Twilight: Los Angeles, 1992*; *Diary of Anne Frank*; *Kat and the Kings*; *Hedda Gabler*; *The Crucible*; *Ma Rainey's Black Bottom*; *The Good Body*; *The Lieutenant of Inishmore*. Off-Broadway shows: *Edith Stein*; *STOMP*; *Why We Have a Body*; *Bunny, Bunny*; *Communicating Doors*; *Necessary Targets*; *Shockheaded Peter*; *Family Secrets*. Overseas: *Jocasta Rising* (South Africa).

Those who contribute a substantial share may end up with prominent credits and an opportunity to attend most of the business meetings relating to the production. Often people come forward who want to be associate producers—typically an entry-level producing credit—which gives them a chance to break into the business. They don't vote on production and business decisions, but they attend meetings and express their opinions.

Once we move into the theatre, I see as many previews as I can. I think it's essential that the creative team know that I am behind them and supporting them as they make choices about how to improve the play. I give notes on the text, the design, the performances, and other elements, and solicit comments from my two producing associates, Laura and Ron, who each have specific tastes and very good ears and eyes for what works theatrically, as well as friends and colleagues in the theatre whose judgment I trust. I pass these on to the director only, as they are the person best placed to determine what notes are most appropriate to share with the playwright, the performers, and how they fit into the director's overall vision of the play. As we work toward opening night, the tension and suspense mount by the minute. The critics start attending, and at some point the show is *locked*—that is, no other changes are made to the direction, text, or design elements of the show. Of course, there are often technical problems to be ironed out, and the usual day-to-day challenges that arise when a company of creative people is collaborating on a new enterprise. There are also still numerous decisions to be made, from deciding who will be invited to opening night, to choosing the opening night gift for everyone who has been involved in the production, and deciding on seating locations in the theatre. I always try to ensure that my investors are well taken care of, because without their participation and enthusiasm, I know the show would not have happened.

The night itself arrives, and no matter how often I do this, I never get used to it. I feel the same nervous excitement I felt at my very first opening in L.A. I always think, "Maybe I'm crazy to think audiences will want to see this," and "What will the critics think?" It's impossible to predict. I've had shows that critics hated and audiences loved and flocked to; shows that critics admired but audiences were not moved to go see; shows where everything came together and they were both critical and audience successes; and shows where neither happened. And the job of a producer does not end on opening night. Once the reviews are out, we have to figure out how to keep people coming, build the audience, and maintain the show's profile. Advertising, marketing, and publicity become key.

So, why do I do it? Well, it's not for the money. And I don't think that anyone who does it just for the money would last very long in this business. Theatre producing is very risky. There is no reliable formula for a success. But I firmly believe that if you persevere, know your taste and trust it, and commit yourself to doing the best possible production of plays that touch your soul, at some point all the elements come together in the magical way that creates a hit. I was fortunate to experience that early on with *STOMP*, and some of the other plays I've produced have generated similar excitement.

I love Alan Ayckbourn's work, and I was able to get the rights from him, personally, to produce *Communicating Doors*. Mary-Louise Parker performed the lead role and she was brilliant, and the cast was altogether superb. We presented the play Off-Broadway, and it got great reviews and was a huge hit with audiences. We Sold Out a number of shows during previews, and had a sizeable advance for a small theatre. We ran to huge houses for three months—the length of time that Mary-Louise was available to do the show—and then she had to leave to shoot a film. We recast, and the replacement actress was wonderful in the role, but Mary-Louise had been a big draw and we lost momentum with her departure.

So, really, why do I do it? It has to be for the love of it. Even if a show *fails* in the sense that it doesn't run for as long as I'd hoped, or it gets mediocre reviews, or doesn't draw audiences, I have the satisfaction of knowing I put my energies into something meaningful to me. A number of productions I have produced have been nominated for awards, including *Twilight*, my very first Broadway production, which was nominated for a Tony Award for Best Play. It didn't win, but as corny as it sounds, just being there felt like a huge win to me. Since then both *The Diary of Anne Frank* and *The Crucible* were nominated for Tony Awards as revival productions. The range of material I have been drawn to is quite wide: from smart, innovative comedies such as those by Ayckbourn to plays with extremely important social and political messages such as the work of Eve Ensler. I have produced two of her works: *Necessary Targets*, about women in Bosnia dealing with the aftermath of war, and her current one-woman show, *The Good Body*, which opened on Broadway and has subsequently toured nationally. Eve is someone with a great ability to inspire and to change people's ways of thinking and operating. She is truly a force to be reckoned with, and I feel fortunate to have her as a close friend, and honored to have helped her take her voice to people all around the country.

So, I guess I do it because, as much as I put into it, I get even more out of it. I believe that theatre people understand that in order to get, you have to give. Great theatre in America doesn't just happen overnight and show up on Broadway. It is usually nurtured through the many not-for-profit theatres around the country. I have had the privilege of working with a number of theatres and enhancing their productions of new plays that I think should be given a longer or bigger productions on the commercial stage. I was on the board of New York Stage and Film for four years, and I participate in the Commercial Theater Institute programs, mentoring new commercial producers. Very recently, I have expanded my role in the business by becoming a co-owner of a new theatre complex, 37 Arts, which opened in 2005. My partners in this exciting venture are Alan Schuster, Kevin McCollum, Jeffrey Seller, and Dan Markley. The complex, built entirely from the ground up and beautifully designed by architect John Averitt, also houses the Baryshnikov Arts Center, which serves as a creative laboratory, meeting place, and performing space for a vibrant community of experimental artists from dance, music, theatre, film, design, and visual arts.

I have learned a lot from many different people so far, and I know there is even more for me to discover about this business. I think I can sum up the most important lessons I've learned as follows: Be dedicated. Be generous. Be inclusive. Don't get greedy. More specifically, share your knowledge with others. Be caring and considerate. Work collaboratively. Think *Big*. Help your colleagues and peers in this business and they'll (most likely) help you. Don't be stubborn or negative. Don't rush into things sometimes; gut feelings are the way to go, but other times you have to stop, sit back, and rethink. Return all your calls. Don't be afraid to be a feminist. I have worked with some wonderful women producers, including Jennifer Manocherian, Amy Nederlander, Willa Shalit, and Linda Brumbach. All of us believe that we can and should make a difference in the work we choose to do. And of course, what more inspiration to be a feminist would you need than to work with Eve Ensler. Be discriminating in the work you choose to produce. There is a lot of material out there clamoring to be shown, and a lot of people want you to pick theirs. That can be a pretty heady experience, but if you aren't careful, you can spread yourself too thin as a producer. I like to be very involved and have a grasp of what is going on day to day with my shows. If I had too much on my plate, that would be impossible. So I choose carefully, and I rarely have any regrets. And finally, be willing to experiment, take risks, and open your mind to new ideas.

Because I love the sense of discovery, I have traveled to some distant and exotic places, in search of new work, or to help produce or develop work. I went with Eve to Croatia when she was creating *The Good Body*, and have been to see the *STOMP*-ers perform at the Acropolis in Athens. I also caught up with them in Paris, and while filming *Pulse: a STOMP Odyssey.* I went with them to Salvador in Brazil to experience the amazing Carnivale. I have also developed strong relationships with the theatre community in South Africa, where my partner of ten years, Carol Kaplan, is from, and I brought the South African musical, *Kat and the Kings,* to Broadway. I go there frequently to see new theatre and I have also produced in South Africa.

Theatre producing has turned out to be the perfect fit for me. I love the challenge that a new production presents. I am not daunted by the task of raising money, as I care passionately about the projects I choose. To be able to combine my love for theatre with my business skills, and earn a living doing it, is a great gift that I get to enjoy every day.

Daryl Roth

Daryl Roth is privileged to have produced five Pulitzer Prize-winning plays: *Proof* by David Auburn (2001 Tony Award Best Play, New York, National Tour); *Wit* by Margaret Edson (New York, London, and national tour); *How I Learned to Drive* by Paula Vogel; *Three Tall Women* by Edward Albee (New York, London, and national tour); and *Anna in the Tropics* by Nilo Cruz.

Recent productions include: Sandra Bernhard's *Everything Bad and Beautiful,* Kenny Finkle's *Indoor/Outdoor,* Bob Morris' *Assisted Loving,* and Brian Copeland's *Not a Genuine Black Man.*

Broadway productions include: Edward Albee's *Who's Afraid of Virginia Woolf?* (2005 Tony Nomination for Best Revival of a Play); Tony Kushner and Jeanine Tesori's *Caroline, or Change* (2004 Tony Nomination for Best Musical); Edward Albee's *The Goat, or Who Is Sylvia?* (2002 Tony Award for Best Play); Charles Busch's *The Tale of the Allergist's Wife* (2001 Tony Award Nomination for Best Play, and national tour); Oscar Wilde's *Salome, the Reading* starring Al Pacino; *Medea* starring Fiona Shaw; *Bea Arthur on Broadway*; Anna Deveare Smith's *Twilight: Los Angeles, 1992* (1992 Tony Award Nomination for Best Play); and *Nick & Nora* by Arthur Laurents, Charles Strouse & Richard Maltby, Jr.

Off-Broadway credits include: Paul Grellong's *Manuscript*; Will Eno's *Thom Pain (based on nothing)*; Stephen Guirgis' *Our Lady of 121st Street* directed by Philip Seymour Hoffman; Mathew Lombardo's *Tea at Five* starring Kate Mulgrew; Alan Bennett's *Talking Heads* starring Lynn Redgrave; George C. Wolfe's *Harlem Song* at the Apollo Theatre; *The Play About the Baby* by Edward Albee; *The Bomb-itty of Errors*; *Snakebit* by David Marshall Grant; *Defying Gravity* by Jane Anderson; *Camping with Henry and Tom* by Mark St. Germain; *Old Wicked Songs* (Pulitzer Prize Finalist, New York and London) by Jon Marans; *The Baby Dance* by Jane

Anderson; *Closer Than Ever* by Richard Maltby Jr. and David Shire; and *De La Guarda*, which ran for seven years as the inaugural production at the Daryl Roth Theatre, a landmark building on Union Square in New York, New York.

Film credits include the Charles Busch film *A Very Serious Person*, Emmy-nominated HBO feature *Dinner with Friends,* based on Donald Margulies' Pulitzer Prize-winning play, directed by Norman Jewison. Other film productions include a documentary, *The Lady in Question*, based on the career of Charles Busch, and a feature film based on the John Searles' novel, *Boy Still Missing*.

Ms. Roth serves on the board of directors of Lincoln Center Theatre, the Sundance Institute, New York State Council on the Arts, and the Albert Einstein College of Medicine.

Ms. Roth was recently profiled in *The New Yorker* and included in *Crain's* "100 Most Influential Women in Business." Awards and honors include: The National Foundation for Jewish Culture's Patron of the Arts Award, The Jewish Theological Seminary's Louis Marshall Award, The Albert Einstein College of Medicine Spirit of Achievement Award, The National Corporate Theatre Fund's Chairman Award, and The Tisch School of the Arts Award for Artistic Leadership.

Dedicated to nurturing and supporting theatre artists, The Daryl Roth Creative Spirit Award is given annually to an artist who has demonstrated exceptional talent and promise in his or her field. Recent recipients include: directors: Michael Wilson, Michael Mayer, Mark Brokaw, Steven Williford; playwrights: Sinan Ünel, Sybille Pearson, Edwin Sanchez, Kia Corthron, Karen Hartman; designer G.W. Mercier; actor Debra Monk; and The New Dramatists.

FOR THE LOVE OF THEATRE

DARYL ROTH (A CONVERSATION WITH)
Producer, Daryl Roth Productions

BEN HODGES: Let's talk a little about your background—how you got into this business, or, more specifically, *why* you did.

DARYL ROTH: I think they're actually interrelated, because the why I got involved is because I always loved theatre and as a child (which is the beginning of it all), I was lucky enough to live not so far from New York in New Jersey, and I was lucky enough to have parents who were very excited by the cultural arts. They would take my sister—who is a few years younger than myself—to the theatre and to puppet shows, everything age appropriate, so as I grew up I had the good fortune of having been exposed to theatre, and when I was old enough as a teenager I was able to come by myself on the bus to New York and I would go to a matinee and just think I had the best time in the world, which I did! So my background in theatre starts a lot as a person just loving it and being mesmerized by and just totally swept into the magic of it all, like many young people are. The why of it for me doesn't have a simple answer—it's just something that I felt very drawn to and compelled to want to try and do. It came for me later in life, as you know. I had raised my family and had a career. I always felt a little longing to do something in theatre and yet I was qualified to do nothing in theatre. I wasn't trained as an actor; I wasn't able to do anything in the technical field; I did have an art and design background, but not clearly in set design. I knew nothing in these specific areas of theatre. I did not know how to general manage. I am actually not so good with numbers to this day [*Laughs.*], but I did know how to put things together and I did—I think—do a pretty terrific job raising my family. I think my skills in putting things together and being able to nurture a group of people gave me some bit of confidence that maybe I could figure out how to do this mysterious thing called producing. It is eighteen years ago that we are speaking about, and I don't know that I knew about Fred Vogel and CTI then. I didn't know how to go about this, so my first step was getting involved in not-for-profit theatres just to sort of let people know that I was here to learn, listen, and I wanted to get to know how things were done.

My initial experience was sitting on the board of City Center, which at the time was organizing what eventually became *Encores!* (It was a committee of people trying to figure out how to resuscitate old musicals.) I met people and I was invited to *readings*, and I started getting a little bit of an open door—a little bit of an invitation into a world that I didn't know about but was dying to know more about. My first production was *Closer Than Ever*, which came about as a result of my being invited to Eighty Eights (which no longer exists), and listening to these trunk songs that David Shire and Richard Maltby Jr. had written. They entrusted me with the idea that I brought to them, which was to try to make something out of the evening of songs because all these songs were talking to me; they were sort of age appropriate; they were relationship appropriate; they were all about making changes in your life and trying to see opportunities. And I think I was influenced (as sappy as it sounds), by *The Celestine Prophesy*, which I always remember—in essence—the residue of that book for me being, "Walk by everything with your eyes open because you never know what you are walking by and may miss. Keep yourself open to it all." It just seemed to me that this opportunity was one that I couldn't let pass by and, I don't know, I felt somehow empowered (God knows why because I wasn't particularly confident), to say, "Could I do something with this?" And lo and behold they said, "Yes, try." That was the beginning for me. We figured out how to get to Williamstown. We workshopped it through the summer, somehow we got it to the Cherry Lane Theatre, and somehow it ran for nine months and somehow it was recorded by RCA. It just gave me my first opportunity. It was not a huge success by any stretch of the imagination, but it made me realize that O.K., I think I can do this… I think I can do this—which is all anybody needs to feel. They just need to think that they can do it because you never say to yourself I can't do it. Once you say you can't do it, and then this is *so* the wrong business to be in. Every time you do a new project and, let's say it doesn't work well, then you say, "Oh, my God, I can't do this." But, you say that for five minutes or a few months and you say, "O.K., what am I going to do next?" If you really want to do this, you need resilience!

HODGES: Moving from *Closer Than Ever*, what were some of the other productions you began to work on—in the *nonprofit* world or otherwise?

ROTH: Nonprofit was another side of my life that existed—and very strongly, because I believe that it is very important to be involved philanthropically, whether it is in theatre, if that is your interest, or medical research, if that is your interest. So, part of me is always involved. The nonprofit, as it relates to theatre then, for me, was figuring out ways to work with not-for-profit theatre in helping them establish new writers, which I saw was my interest really. I figured I needed to find a niche because there were a lot of people producing that had more experience and really knew what they were doing. I was kind of like the Nike commercial, you know? Just Do It. So I thought O.K., what am I interested in? I am interested in new writers who other producers may not be interested in. I'm interested in ideas that might be too challenging for other people to tackle. I'm interested in family drama. I'm interested in gender issues. My son is gay—I have always been very hungry to learn more and understand, so that was on my list. I was interested in things that have issues of identity at the core: Whatever community someone is in, I was curious to explore why you often feel different when on the outside. That can be gender, religion, race—whatever; those are things that were in my own bag of curiosity. So I decided with all of those interests, I would then seek out ways to find work that addressed that big pot full of interesting issues for me. I decided that if I went to the not-for-profit theatre (some of the smaller ones who would actually welcome my help), that it would be a very good way to get to know who the writers were that people were interested in. It would be a way for me to offer not only economic encouragement, but encouragement. I could actually say, "O.K., let's work on this together, and I will be able to take it to the next step, a commercial production, which is not what your mandate is." So that was on my mind. Some of these things are sort of circles that came together unexpectedly, like *Old Wicked Songs*, which you mentioned at the CTI seminar.

I had read this play and was interested in trying to produce it and got a call from a young man, Seth Barrish, who was head of The Barrow Group. Seth said that he was very interested in this play, too, and actually wanted to direct it, and asked was there a way we might work together. I thought that sounded like a great idea. That is exactly what I thought was a safe way to birth this play. And so we joined forces on *Old Wicked Songs*, and it became a very good model actually, not only for my way of producing, but for other people, too, who always felt (surprisingly to me) that the not-for-profit people were *here* and the commercial people were *over there*. It was almost like a competition of sorts, and a feeling that people shouldn't join together and make things work. This kind of collaboration wasn't done seventeen or eighteen years ago at all. People would give donations and that would be the end of the relationship. So that was a very good thing that I think I can actually feel proud about starting, and making a model that worked for everybody. I have done that to this day. I have *enhanced* projects for not-for-profit theatre companies and some have worked and have gone on to have commercial productions and some have not worked past the not-for-profit stage. But I still feel happy that I helped make something happen that wouldn't have happened otherwise.

HODGES: How does *developing* a work with a nonprofit differ from the developing a work for a commercial production, especially at the beginning of the process?

ROTH: The major difference has to do with the guarantee that we will get at a not-for-profit theatre. They have a subscriber base. They will schedule it in for three, four, five weeks (whatever their particular run of show is), and you will definitely see the production come to fruition. If you develop something on your own and it's strictly commercial, you may or may not decide to actually go through with the production. You can work on developing it. You can have readings, you can have workshops, and then when it comes to raising what is now, let's say, anywhere between $500 thousand and one million dollars in today's Off-Broadway market, you may decide not to do the production. But, you will have developed it. That's one difference. The second difference is that the monies are less. So if you enhance a play at a not-for-profit theatre and you give $50–$200 thousand (which is a big chunk of the not-for-profit budget) versus it being a drop in the bucket for a commercial production. You have the economic difference. A third and important difference is that you have a safety net. Once the play is produced in a not-for-profit theatre the safety net—good reviews or bad reviews—is that it gets done, people get to see it, and it will have an afterlife, hopefully. The bad thing about doing it commercially is that if it doesn't work, there is very little afterlife available, and you will have blown the entire budget. The writer has no safety net within which to fall. Commercially, it will cost a lot of money to put it up. If it doesn't work and it is over, it's a harder fall—there is just no cushion. So there are some differences. Now that is not to say that I wouldn't take a playwright and do a commercial play outright. I have and I will continue to, but sometimes its better to try it in a not-for-profit, make sure it works, and then carry it on to the commercial production. If it doesn't work, O.K., so you lost the enhancement money, but a play was born and maybe it will have a life in the regional theatre. Maybe it will just encourage a playwright to write again! That is truly enough.

HODGES: You're clearly talented at knowing good writing. But how do you gauge whether or not a play or musical is going to be marketable? How much is that a consideration before you move into production, be it with a nonprofit or on your own commercially?

ROTH: It is really a hard question to answer because it has to do with whether or not a play just catches the wind, so to speak, and whether it catches the wind has to do with a series of things. Is it well reviewed? Do audiences respond? Does it come at a time when people are open to whatever the subject or the material is? Sometimes you are ahead of your game or ahead of the times—I've had that happen to me, I think, where it just wasn't the right time for a particular play. So, it's a hard question to answer. I would say, though, that the marketing of a play is most successful when it is being marketed on the wings of good reviews. If a play starts in a not-for-profit theatre and gets good reviews and then you decide to take it on to a commercial production, you then have something to market. You have reviews and you've got five, six, or seven weeks of audiences walking out of the theatre and spreading good word-of-mouth. If you do a show initially as a commercial production, you are starting at day one and if the reviews are good, you are in heaven. If they are not, it's a truly difficult challenge. I think that there is no way to gauge how people are going to respond to any given play (and I have said this ad nauseam to people who've asked), that you have to love the project you have chosen to do because the challenges are just so great. If you love what you are doing and you totally believe in what it is, then you will fight as hard as you can to get the editorial stories, to get the marketing people to go out there and sell that product—you will do everything you know how to help make it work because you want it so much, and you believe in it so much. It is especially hard when the critical response is at best mixed. So if you don't believe in it 225 percent, don't do it.

HODGES: And that leads me into what I was going to ask you about next, which was *Nick & Nora*. Because I was on an internship in the Stuart Howard *casting* office and on the roller coaster that was *Nick & Nora*—

ROTH: Many years ago. Many years ago. [*Laughs.*]

HODGES: [*Laughs.*] As that was at the beginning of your career, somewhat—

ROTH: It was right at the beginning of my career.

HODGES: How did that affect you? I am wondering if and how you questioned yourself about what you were doing. What was that process like? How you decide to close a show—let's talk a little bit about that.

ROTH: *Nick & Nora* for me was a good and bad experience, I would say. First of all I was very junior on that producing team. I was an associate producer. It was the first musical that I had stepped up to the plate to get involved with, and my connection was actually through Richard Maltby, Jr. who was, as I mentioned, the co-writer of *Closer Than Ever*. He was working with Charles Strouse and Arthur Laurents on *Nick & Nora* and they were looking for more producers. They invited me into meet some of the main producers which I did and it was Liz McCann, Jimmy Nederlander, and Terry Allen Kramer. I was excited by the idea because I actually loved *The Thin Man*, on which it was based. I love the mysteries and love the style of the time—the genre was great.

HODGES: And we had just had *City of Angels*, so...

ROTH: There was sort of ...

HODGES: ...an excitement about that time.

ROTH: And it was, in fact, a beautifully written piece of material. However, as we all know, it didn't work. But, why it didn't work gave me the best lessons in producing that I could have had. I mean, especially early on in my career, where I was able to sit around the table and witness what didn't work, how things could be handled differently. I wasn't in a position of authority, so I hadn't really the opportunity to have a voice, but that was O.K.—I was on my learning curve. What I would say I learned most effectively was that the creative team really has to have a shared vision, and if they don't, it is very hard to steer this huge animal known as a musical forward. So that was something interesting to observe. Nobody was right or wrong. It was just they weren't quite all on the same page. I think the other thing that was difficult was that everything was being done in front of the public eye and out-of-town. Anytime anything happened, it was written about; it was talked about. There was no privacy to let people just work it out. I saw that as a big issue and not healthy for theatre. I know how important it was for people to be openly collaborative. I, for one, think of myself as a very collaborative person. I like to be able to dialogue with people, and I like to be able to have everybody say what they have to say, and then come to a consensus. That seems to me to be the healthiest way to produce, whether it is a huge musical or a small Off-Broadway play. Failure is something that is so much a part of theatre that you can't really be afraid of it. You can't be in theatre and not experience it. You just know that it is part of it. It is not good and it is not easy. It is hurtful and disappointing and you feel so responsible (or at least I do). You feel so responsible for the people that are working for you on the project, that it is just awful. And I had it again sixteen years later with *Mambo Kings*. I had every great expectation for this musical to be just wonderful. When we were out-of-town, it wasn't working the way it needed to to bring it into Broadway and we had to end it out-of-town. It was much more painful to me than with *Nick & Nora* because it was my production and I was working with my son, Jordan, which made it even more painful that we didn't have a success to share, but rather had to deal with everything that wasn't on track. So the failure thing never gets easier, but it is so much a part of this business that if anybody learns anything—I am going back to the question of what I learned—what you learn is that you're going to fail (just as you're going to succeed). Know that and try to deal with it in the healthiest way you can. Don't push it aside like it doesn't mean anything and say, "Oh well, you know, things didn't work out and la dee da." Really dissect it and understand what went wrong, and try to dialogue with yourself about what you should have seen earlier, or what you could have done differently. Examine it and then lick your wounds. It was a long time after *Mambo Kings* before I even felt like do anything at all. But, then you say, "O.K., look, this is a career, this isn't a project by project thing here—you have to look at the big picture, the grand sweep." I would say this to anybody who might read this book and wants to be a producer: Don't look at your work project by project by project. It is very important to say that what you end up giving is a body of work. What you end up being responsible for is the overall view of what you thought important enough to put out there and to produce. You can't go by every success because that would be foolhardy, too, and you can't go by every failure because that would be foolhardy too. So you just have to say, "O.K., the big picture is I have done all of this. Some have really made a difference in the world and some have been utter failures, and let's just look at the big picture."

HODGES: When we talked in the fourteen-week seminar, I asked you about how involved you get with writers in their work. I think the largest surprise for me of becoming a producer was how involved I was with the writer or the creative teams, especially when working on a developmental level—sometimes for a year or two in developing a script. And because you talk about working with smaller nonprofit theatres, is it productive? How do you decide how much to be involved or not to be involved? How much do you feel now a script needs to be completed before you become involved in production?

ROTH: It is a good question. There are a few answers: I think that it depends on the writer. When you talk about someone like Edward Albee for example, there is very little development that a producer will have with a playwright like Edward. Edward is iconic. Edward is one of the most brilliant minds with whom theatre has ever been gifted. So, while you as a producer will not have much to do with the script with Edward, you will have a lot to do with offering

The Daryl Roth co-production of the 2002 Pulitzer Prize
and Tony Award-winning *The Goat, or Who Is Sylvia?* by Edward Albee.
Pictured are Bill Irwin as Martin and Sally Field as Stevie.
Photo by Carol Rosegg, courtesy of the John Willis Theatre World/Screen World Archive.

thoughts on casting and thoughts on what's in previews—little nips, little tucks. So he would be at one end of the spectrum.

On the other end of the spectrum might be a new writer who is anxious for your input. You need a sounding board who wants to be collaborative with a producer because they can benefit from what you might have to offer. Some writers don't like to discuss their work until they feel it is quite finished. And then a producer can either *option* it as is, knowing that there might be some changes as you get into rehearsals, or, know that the playwright has finished this play and you may take it or you may not. It primarily has to do with playwrights. Many playwrights that I have worked with who write the play and have gone through so many drafts and so many efforts until they have come up with what they feel is their finished play. Then you get into rehearsal and they see it in the hands of the actors and they themselves see things need to be adjusted, or changed, or trimmed, or expanded upon, or some character might need more development, or another character could be completely eliminated. So it is a question that doesn't have a simple answer.

I personally am very happy to option a play after I have read it feeling that it is near completion; I actually don't want to be in the development of writing a play with a playwright—for me that doesn't work as well. I can comment, I think, intuitively and wisely, but I am not a dramaturge, and I am not a playwright. I can only react to what I feel is ringing untrue, and could be more sincere or feel more honest in the voice of whatever character. I can respond instinctively to plot lines. I can respond to something once it exists. As a producer, I want to take something that I like and help make it better—help make it come alive. I think a producer's job is as a facilitator. I don't think a producer should assume to wear the hat of a writer (or a director for that matter). I think a facilitator is somebody who pulls the best people together, gives their best advice, and then has the wherewithal to step back and say, "You do your job and then I am going to be able to see what you have done and comment on what you've done."

I will say it differs a little bit on screenplays, because I'm in the process of having a book that I have optioned adapted for film. I have been more involved with the writer because we know we are both talking about a book that exists and a story that I like in this book that I want to see come to fruition on the screen. Many things from the book need to be pulled out and heightened, and others have to recede or not be present at all. So there is that kind of dialogue that is different than with a playwright who is writing his or her own play.

HODGES: How do you find your scripts? I don't ever advise anyone to send a script cold to a producer in New York, as I think that there are a lot more productive ways for them to develop and produce it initially wherever they are. But if someone reading this feels they have a great play, what are the best steps for them to take to get it produced?

ROTH: In the earlier years I did accept unsolicited scripts. I read a lot of them and quite honestly I felt happy to be reading scripts that were coming to me from all ways, because I was learning a lot about reading plays. I was learning about being discerning. And I also felt a responsibility to respond to the writer—to say what I thought, which I hope was helpful. I did it for years. People thought I was crazy, but I was constantly writing constructive criticism to writers who I didn't even know, but they bothered to send me their play and it was most important to them and I thought the least I could do was respond. Now just because of time and because I am pretty clear now on the kind of play I want to do, I don't accept unsolicited scripts. People now know (these many years later), the sort of thing that I might be interested in. I accept scripts from playwrights who I have worked with before. I accept scripts from other producers I may co-produce with. I accept scripts from friends because they often have a nephew, a niece, a cousin, a sister, or a brother, and I know how hard it is for writers to get anybody to read your work, so I just say sure and sometimes you get a good script! You never know. Mostly though, it is agents' submissions, playwrights that I know, playwrights who are friends of playwrights that I know, and also through the not-for-profit theatres. Another big source for me is New Dramatists, because I have been a big supporter over the years and I read a lot of their members' scripts. Also I'm on the board of Sundance and I read plays that are submitted to the Theatre Lab. More often than not I would rather read a play than a book. I enjoy the form. I really enjoy reading plays. I sort of get into this mode of dialogue and it is like I have this little play going on in my head and I actually like reading that way. I was away this weekend and I took three scripts to read. None of them were plays that I plan to produce, but it is a way to get acquainted with new writers. You never know if a writer will catch your fancy, and that may not be the play they sent you, but you think, "O.K., well, send me something else." I think for a new producer getting unsolicited scripts is not so terrible as long as you can hone your own taste and learn what interests you. I think it is beneficial. It was for me in the beginning.

HODGES: Amy Danis says a producer is a banker, a cheerleader, and a fireman.

ROTH: A banker, a cheerleader, and fireman. O.K., I would add a paramedic. [*Laughs.*]

HODGES: [*Laughs.*] One of the reasons I wanted to interview you was because based on my experience with you, I know you to be a diplomat and you make things happen. You bring people together, facilitate—just as you've talked about. Looking back, what are the resources that you found within yourself that enabled you to get you through some of those times that might help other people reading this to use the same tools, if they find themselves in similar situations?

ROTH: There are a couple of ways I would answer that. I think, some of the things I keep in mind (that might be helpful for someone else to keep in mind) are that when it is all said and done your reputation is all you are going to have, and all you are going to be left with. And so if you give your word to someone, let's just say you give your word to a playwright that you are going to do their play. Don't say yes if you mean maybe. Say yes, and then do it, even if it is a small production, and even if it's a reading. Whatever it is that you say your going to do, do. So the first thing I would say to someone is be good to your word. Be honest with people. Don't talk about all the things you are going to do for somebody if you know you are really not able to pull it off. Don't say you are going to produce a play when you know you may not be able to find the money to put it together. Situations obviously always happen where something may get in the way or something being improbable and challenged to the point of defeat. But primarily, be good to your word because your reputation is everything. When you deal with people—deal fairly. It is a terrible business. There is not a lot of financial gain for anybody including producers (unless you have a huge hit). This is a labor of love for anybody in the business. So put yourself in the mix of an equal partner in the project. Be one of the people on the team trying to make it happen. In other words, as a producer don't set yourself above and beyond in some tutorial place. Everybody has to roll up their sleeves and everybody has to do whatever it takes to make something happen. It is a democracy even though most people don't think it is. I know it sounds ridiculous, but because I have a theatre I do a lot of things that other people don't have to do, but I'll take tickets, I'll sweep, I don't care. People look at me and think, "Is she out of her mind?" It is not the *what* that I'm doing—it's the fact that I want to. And everybody who's a producer has to realize that you have to do everything, because everything is really your job. If you have to stick the mailing labels on the postcards to get them out, well, that's your job. That is what you have to do!

I would say that you must keep your mind on the big picture. We sort of talked about this with failure, but you have to keep your mind on the big picture, and realize that you are part of a larger world. The theatre world that we think is so little is—on some aspect—a very rarified world, but it is really a bigger world. What you do has reverberations in the world. You do a really good play; it will take on a life of its own in whatever way it goes out into the ether. And so people should be very cognitive of the fact that anything they do as a producer can have big waves. I think as a producer, one has to think about what their responsibility is, and the material you put out there. For me, I've always tried to put out things that could make a difference for people— that could make them think about the world a little differently. Or, change somebody's opinion about somebody or some group of people. Be politically aware. (I don't mean waving flags.) Being *politic* is what I really want to say. It might be important in the long run. I mean when we did *Wit*, I have to tell you, it made a difference in the world on a large, large scale. I think there are opportunities for young producers (or old producers, as I am one of those), to think about what you are doing seriously, and take to heart what you think is important to you. What you do is a reflection of who you are!

Keep in mind that success is very different for different people. Success in theatre cannot be qualified only by money. It is one of the few professions where success does not equal money; success is balanced by what we have given the world. It is just a different commodity. It is a different rule of commerce, I think. Clearly it is great to be economically rewarded for your work and God knows as a producer you want to try to pay back your investors and you want everybody to be happy. But that can't be the only motivator in this business in my view. I think you should talk to other people about commercial theatre because that has never been my strong suit and it has never really been my motivator. And sometimes, luckily, things I have done have been commercially successful like *Wit* or *Proof,* or *The Tale of the Allergist's Wife,* which was very commercial. But it's not the reason I do something. It is sort of the icing on the cake if it happens, and I hope it does. I guess the final thing I would say is don't give up—have tenacity. Go to the end of the line before you say, "O.K., this isn't going to work." I am in the process right now of having to close a little show that we produced because it just didn't find its audience. We gave it the best shot; we gave it a good production, and people aren't coming. So, be tenacious until you can do no more. I think that is a good lesson for anybody to hear in any business.

I think the other thing about success is to know (and this is a lesson I am still trying to learn), that the success or failure you have in theatre or in any business, is not a reflection on your person. I mean it is for a lot of people (because theatre is such a personal thing). But, it doesn't mean you are a bad person if you fail. There are so many factors that come into play as you said when we first sat down. There are so many things that you actually have no control over. For a person who is sort of controlling—which most producers have as part of their personality—I think that it goes with the territory and that is a good thing. But when you are a person who would like to be in control and yet you have to deal with so many things that are out of your control, it's a very tenuous situation, and it's tricky. I think one has to deal with that in a mature way (and I'm not saying that I always do). In fact, I have gone to pieces many times (people know this). I have often said whenever you close a show it is like a post-partum depression. You feel so depressed and so despondent because of all the things that you feel maybe you should have/could have/would have done, and you make yourself crazy. But it's not personal.

HODGES: What do you say to investors? What do investors need to know?

ROTH: When they don't get their money back? [*Laughs.*]

HODGES: [*Laughs.*] I didn't think it was a complicated answer. I just wanted to ask the question. [*Laughs.*]

ROTH: It is a good question to ask because what I say to people before I take the investment is "Please, please understand clearly this is a risky business. Do this play because you really think it is important to do and have a chance and like it, or you want to support what I'm doing, or it speaks to you. Do it for the right reasons and we will all hope to get your money back for you, but we may not. Please do it because you believe in this play (or the playwright); or what the subject is; or if you just want to have some fun and you want to do something good for the cultural arts of this world. I like to say to people to consider it a donation in a way that you might donate to a theatre company in your town. Consider it a philanthropic gift to the arts. It has the opportunity to repay, but it may not. You would never get angry if you gave money to a museum—wouldn't expect to get it back—you would feel good that you gave money to a music organization or a dance company. You would feel good about the giving—the philanthropy of it. I say to investors to think about this in that way, because you are making something wonderful happen and you are giving something a chance to have a life. So it is easier to say it up front than it is at the end of the day. I don't promise anything. I can't. On the other hand, I have had plays that continue to pay profits. We get checks for *Three Tall Women* from 1994 because it is done all over the place. Or *Proof*—I just got a check that I am so happy to send back to investors—so happy. I mean nothing makes me feel better than being able to send back profits. It is just a funny business and it doesn't happen often enough, especially in the world of plays, which is where my life is centered. In the musical world—you can speak to any producer of a musical, a big successful musical and you're talking a whole different story and you have a whole different discussion. To be clear, the discussion we're having is really based on challenging dramatic plays, because that is what I have chosen to do. If you spoke to Margo Lion and she told you about *Hairspray*, or talk to Bob Boyette and Bill Haber about *Spamalot*, or the Dodgers about *Jersey Boys*. I mean those are great stories. That is a different chapter. It is a different world.

HODGES: You own a theatre, so you're one of the people uniquely positioned to be able to talk about what producers need to know about working with theatre owners.

ROTH: Owning the theatre for me is an advantage because I can choose work. Now I have three spaces. I have a 299-seat theatre and I have a little cabaret downstairs which is seventy seats. But by owning a theatre and having space,

I can choose to do things that I might not necessarily choose to produce if I didn't know that I had a home in which to produce them. So for me it gives me the opportunity to look at some smaller plays that are appropriate for the space. The 299-seat theatre worked so well for *Thom Paine*, and I can make it economic for myself because if there are weeks when things are not going well, I can just not charge rent. I learned very beautifully about owning a theatre with my experience early on in producing *Baby Dance* at the Lucille Lortel Theatre. Lucille was a great mentor of mine and she was actually called the Queen of Off-Broadway because I think she really did the most for Off-Broadway in her day. When I was producing *Baby Dance* there, all the producers loved this play and Lucille loved this play. She taught me the early lesson that if you believe in the play and if the critics don't like you and you get terrible reviews, you must still give it a go. The way to do that best is to have the theatre owner by your side, who also believes in the play and hasn't taken it in just as a booking because it is rent coming in, but has chosen that play because they too believe in the power of it. So they become your ally. I have tried to do that as a theatre owner when people come to me. I don't take things that I don't like very much because I want to be able to help them make it work. Now that doesn't mean that a play coming into my theatre is going to be successful because I like it. It doesn't mean that at all. But if a play comes into my theatre I will help them keep it there if they have bad times. So, I think a producer needs to enlist the theatre owner as their ally—as their partner in a way. Now on a larger scale, the Broadway producers and theatre owners often invest in the plays that come into their theatres. It is then a different scenario—usually they'll invest to ensure them getting the hot play into their theatres or because they really love it and want to for whatever their reasons are, but by having a vested interest in what comes into your theatre, it is better for the producer. If you have a choice of theatres, go with the theatre that loves the play. Because ultimately it is going to be challenging—in any given scenario there's going to be a challenge, and you are going to need that theatre owner on your side or at least being supportive of your efforts to be tenacious in keeping it going. As a theatre owner I don't want something in my theatre that I don't like, because I need to be supportive of it. Even though it is not my production, I am affiliated with it in a way so that it is a bit of my reputation, too.

HODGES: Well, there again, responsibility.

ROTH: It comes back to responsibility and it comes back to reputation. Because I will say when I had *De La Guarda* (which is what opened up my theatre space),

I loved it so much! I just thought it was innovative and exciting and really out there, and I loved the excitement plus energy that it brought into what was just a space. I was very supportive and became one of the producers of it, because I wanted to be an ally of the project. I think that it is important for producers to approach the theatre owners as they would approach an investor (whether or not they get an investment from that person doesn't matter), but they have to be able to share their enthusiasm. They have to be able to let the theatre owner understand why they are so passionate about this work, and the theatre owner must catch that fever.

HODGES: You are also uniquely positioned to talk about moving a theatrical property into film. Susan Gallin says she almost never gets any film rights to the plays that she produces.

ROTH: It's true for all of us. That is the way the agents write the contracts. [*Laughs.*] It's not such good news.

HODGES: [*Laughs.*] So are there rules or considerations for people to keep in mind when they are optioning a property or if they have interest in it from a film company?

ROTH: I think the rules are loosening a little bit, and I think that the agents of the writers now understand that there are certain producers who do have the wherewithal and the connections to carry the play onto its next step. And then conversely, there are theatre producers who are also film producers (like Scott Rudin), who do both so well, who is clearly positioned to take anything into film. The best way for a new producer to have that opportunity available is to work with very new writers whose agents will be thrilled and delighted to think that someone might be interested. Legally, as we speak today (and I do think it is changing a little bit), what you will get most often is the right to negotiate. You won't get the rights but you will get the right to negotiate or meet an offer. It is upsetting. I will say that you can help be a conduit of material, which is a good thing for a theatre producer to be able to do. I was that on Donald Margulies' play, which I did not produce in theatre. But, I loved it and thought it cinematic enough, and was able to get it to HBO who did make the movie *Dinner with Friends*. You can be—as a theatre producer—a conduit of material and then become a part of the project. But it is not the norm to get the movie rights as a theatre producer, unless you are aligned with a movie company and you go in with the clout of that partnership from the beginning. It seems to me that the producer who is putting up the risk money to get the play done should have the opportunity to do that. So I am not quite sure how that will resolve itself and I know it is a case-by-case situation. But, I ask for it all the time, and I think we are making inroads a bit. If I wanted to say, "O.K., fine then, I won't produce this play unless I get the film rights," in certain situations that kind of heavy handedness might work, but only for a new playwright who is just beginning. It doesn't seem like it is fair but I guess there are two sides to the story.

HODGES: You are known for looking to expand the audiences which theatre attracts, in other words minorities and different ethnic groups. Shara Mendelson talks about the audiences being there, that it's a myth that they aren't.

ROTH: I do look out for opportunities to be able to really expand the audiences that theatre attracts, so when we are talking about plays like *Anna in the Tropics* or *Our Lady of 121st Street* with the Latin audience, it was my hope to try to put work out there that would engage an audience that isn't necessarily invited into theatres regularly. You have to pursue them. The audiences are there but they have to be invited into work that they are interested in seeing. You should talk to David Binder about *A Raisin in the Sun*, because the truth of the matter is that if you give people what they are interested in and what they can relate to, what means something in their life, then they will come sit in the audience. It is a simple equation. Part of what I like to do is find those works and I like new voices. There are a lot of new wonderful Latin voices, Nilo Cruz being only one of them. So developing audiences and reaching out into the world of minority playwrights is really good and exciting. I mean it is the same thing that we said when we first sat down—it is just going through things you think are important to you and maybe it will be important to other people. So if it is finding the next great gay playwright, you know, then if people say it's old news, big deal—if it means something to you then you go for it. If it means something for you to find women's voices—for me that was the beginning of a very interesting relationship with Jane Anderson, Paula Vogel, and Maggie Edson and so many other writers, because I was very interested in including their voices. I was really interested in seeing strong female characters on stage. And, I don't mean characters like *Medea* (which I happen to have produced), but strong women facing challenges in their life—that is what was very interesting to me. It still is, but it was much more interesting to me when I was searching for the plays I wanted to produce. Those women playwrights for me just totally encapsulated writing about women who didn't start off strong, but who did the journey—took the trip—and ended up very strong, enlightened, and/or very enabled. That to me was fascinating…fascinating. I still actually find that when I read plays I look for strong female characters because now I look out for actors that I love. I am always reading and looking for what is the next Mary-Louise Parker part; or Judith Light; or Kathy Chalfant; or Debra Monk. I read that way now. I guess it is about whatever you want to try and to focus on as a producer—not exclusive of anything else, but maybe that is where you will find your footing if you try to lean on what it is that really fits you, or you want to speak to others about.

HODGES: Thanks, Daryl.

ROTH: Thank you.

Roche Edward Schulfer

PHOTO BY MATT CASHORE

Roche Edward Schulfer is celebrating his twenty-fifth season in his current position as executive director of the Goodman Theatre. During that time, he has supervised over 300 productions and over one hundred world or American premieres. Mr. Schulfer inaugurated the Goodman's annual production of *A Christmas Carol*, which has become a Chicago holiday tradition for the past twenty-seven seasons. During his tenure with the Goodman, the theatre has received numerous local and national awards for excellence, including Tony Awards for *Death of a Salesman, Long Day's Journey Into Night*, and the Tony Award for Outstanding Regional Theatre. In 2003, *TIME* named the Goodman Theatre the Best Regional Theatre in the U.S. Mr. Schulfer is a founder and current chairman of the League of Chicago Theatres, and has served on grant panels for the National Endowment for the Arts, the Illinois Arts Council, and the Department of Cultural Affairs. Mr. Schulfer has been recognized for his work by the City of Chicago, the *Chicago Tribune, Chicago* magazine, *Crain's Chicago Business*, the Illinois Arts Alliance, the Arts and Business Council, the League of Chicago Theatres, the American Arts Alliance, Lawyers for the Creative Arts, Columbia College, and the Chicago Jaycees. He currently teaches at the De Paul Theatre School. Mr. Schulfer is a graduate of the University of Notre Dame and was the chairman of its Cultural Arts Commission.

COMMERCIAL PRODUCER-RESIDENT THEATRE COLLABORATIONS

ROCHE SCHULFER
Executive Director, Goodman Theatre

What is the history of partnerships between *not-for-profit* theatres and *commercial* theatres? Have they been successful? How do these partnerships work? And should they be encouraged? In this chapter I will provide perspectives on these questions based on my experience of negotiating over twenty-five collaborations with commercial producers as executive director of the Goodman Theatre.

Throughout this chapter I will use the term *resident* rather than *regional* to refer to not-for-profit theatres that operate outside and within the New York metropolitan area. To me, the term *regional* theatre dates back to the early days of the not-for-profit theatre movement when these theatres were defined by their relationship to the perceived national theatre center—New York City. Today, *resident* theatre more accurately describes a not-for-profit theatre with an ongoing history in a community and a strong connection to local artists, audiences, and supporters.

There are two principal forms of partnerships between commercial producers and resident theatres. The first is based on creating a new production that originates at the resident theatre and then moves to a commercial *venue*. In this case, the partnership between the commercial producer and resident theatre is established at the beginning of the production process. Commercial producers also partner with resident theatres on the *transfer* of resident theatre productions. Here, the original production is created by the resident theatre without the involvement of a commercial producer. The success of the production leads to the partnership and the transfer to the commercial theatre. In this chapter I will mainly focus on the former, partnerships that are formed to create new productions, since these pose the greatest challenges to both parties.

THE HISTORY OF COMMERCIAL PRODUCER-RESIDENT THEATRE COLLABORATIONS

Until the latter half of the twentieth century, New York City was the unquestioned center of the American theatre. New plays, revivals, and musicals originated in New York, On or Off-Broadway, and then went on the *road* to the rest of the country, and the world. *Regional* theatre consisted largely of academic, community, dinner, and experimental theatres. Beyond road productions, large-scale professional theatre was virtually nonexistent outside of New York.

In the 1960s things began to change. Thanks to visionary artists, extraordinary producers, community leaders, W. McNeill Lowry and the Ford Foundation, the National Endowment for the Arts, the Internal Revenue Service, and Danny "Subscribe Now" Newman,* resident theatres were established in cities across America. From a handful of companies in the '60s, the movement has grown to well over 500 theatres that annually produce hundreds of plays, employ thousands of professionals, and serve an audience in the millions according to information compiled by Theatre Communications Group.

The growth of the resident theatre movement quickly caught the attention of commercial producers. Since many of these companies were founded by former New York based theatre professionals, collaborations with commercial producers were soon being explored. The 1969 transfer of the Arena Stage production of *The Great White Hope* to Broadway is considered by many to mark the beginning of commercial–resident theatre relationships. Just a few years later The Public Theatre/New York Shakespeare Festival production of *A Chorus Line* moved to Broadway and made theatrical history—along with millions of dollars for The Public Theatre.

In the 1970s, commercial-resident theatre collaborations rapidly expanded as producers shopped new productions to resident theatres and looked for possible transfers. For commercial producers, these collaborations meant reduced risk and the potential for increased profits. For resident theatres, working with commercial producers provided high profile productions and revenue from royalties or *enhancement* money (the initial financing provided by a commercial producer to augment the budget of the resident theatre).

---

* Danny Newman was a theatre publicist who was hired in the 1960s by The Ford Foundation to work with nonprofit resident theatres on developing subscription campaigns as the basis for their annual attendance. His book, *Subscribe Now*, which is still in print, was the bible for a generation of arts marketers, literally drafting many of "the rules" for marketing the arts in the nonprofit world.

Over twenty-five years, partnerships between commercial producers and resident theatres led to a seismic shift in the American theatre. By the mid-1990s, the majority of Broadway productions had their origins in the not-for-profit theatre. The traditional pattern was reversed—now productions came from resident theatres to Broadway and then went out on the road. Broadway was largely transformed into a showcase for work that had originated elsewhere. Furthermore, not-for-profit theatres fostered the emergence of a new generation of playwrights whose careers did not depend on Broadway productions.

HAVE COMMERCIAL PRODUCER-RESIDENT THEATRE PARTNERSHIPS BEEN SUCCESSFUL?

The vast majority of partnerships between resident theatres and commercial producers have been successful—at least offstage! But this has not been a marriage made in heaven. The economic risk for commercial producers has significantly increased since any *out-of-town tryout* is expensive. Due to the risks surrounding commercial productions, resident theatres have not generated the additional revenue they anticipated. Some partnerships have ended with bitter disputes about artistic control and financial promises with both commercial producers and resident theatres feeling exploited.

HOW SHOULD PARTNERSHIPS BETWEEN COMMERCIAL PRODUCERS AND RESIDENT THEATRES WORK?

In my experience, commercial-resident theatre partnerships fail when the parties allow their emotions to override their business sense. A successful partnership can be achieved if commercial producers and resident theatres keep the following facts in mind:

It is a partnership.

Like any partnership, a commercial-resident theatre partnership can only succeed if each partner understands and sympathizes with the goals of the other. The ultimate goal of the commercial producer is to produce a successful production that will return a profit to the investors. The resident theatre's ultimate goal is to produce a season of plays that serve artists and audiences while maintaining the long-term financial health of the organization. If commercial and resident theatre producers do not accept and respect these goals, there is likely to be tension surrounding every decision connected to the production.

The play is the thing.

While commercial and resident theatre producers may have different ultimate goals, they have an essential common goal: creating a production of the highest quality. Without a great production, no one's goals will be achieved. Despite the stereotypes, the fact is that all great producers are motivated by a passion for the theatre. There are commercial producers with an unrivalled love of the art and resident theatre producers who are obsessed with ticket sales. But all producers have the responsibility of providing circumstances in which artists can do their best work. If commercial producers and resident theatres work toward the goal of creating an outstanding production, they will make good decisions and reach appropriate compromises.

Who's in charge?

In a partnership between a commercial producer and resident theatre on a new production, the resident theatre has the final artistic and budget control of the initial production. The commercial producer should not attempt to exert artistic control or force budget adjustments on the resident theatre, despite the commercial producer's interest in the production. This is because the resident theatre producer is ultimately responsible for producing an entire season as well as maintaining the financial stability of the institution. The resident theatre cannot divert a disproportionate amount of its budget to support one production. But the resident theatre must also be sensitive to the goals of the commercial producer. There is no easy solution to the issue of who's in charge. There will be intense discussions about all aspects of the production from *casting* to *advertising*. Partnerships with commercial producers will put an enormous strain on a resident theatre under the best of circumstances. At the same time, commercial producers are going to feel frustrated because they lack final control over the initial production at the resident theatre.

Let's make a deal.

When commercial producers and resident theatres collaborate, a fair business deal is essential. Over the years, these deal points have evolved:

1. The resident theatre participates in the gross box office receipts and *net profits* of all productions under the auspices of the commercial producer.
2. The resident theatre participates in income generated by the production from the sale of *subsidiary rights* (such as film and television productions), either from the playwright or the producer.

3. The resident theatre may receive enhancement money from the commercial producer for the initial production.

4. The commercial producer may negotiate the purchase of the sets, props, costumes, and sound tapes from the resident theatre.

5. The commercial producer will provide the resident theatre with appropriate credit for all subsequent productions. This may include title page credit and/ or above the title *billing*, bios of the theatre and lists of key staff and trustees in the program, and credit in advertising materials.

The artistic control of the subsequent production (or transfer) reverts to the commercial producer. Having said this, if a good partnership has been established, the resident theatre will be included in future decisions by the commercial producer. Furthermore, the resident theatre should have ongoing artistic input based on the theatre's relationship with the artists involved in the production, especially the writer and director. This will certainly be true if the director of the production is the artistic director of the resident theatre.

A problem that almost always occurs in commercial producer-resident theatre partnerships is reaching an agreement on the production budget, especially when enhancement money is being negotiated. This is due to the fact that commercial producers and resident theatres budget from completely different points of view. The resident theatre's budget is based on an entire season—not just an individual production. The direct expenses for each production are limited to the salary and materials required for that play. The production budget does not include the overhead of the company, which includes *general management, subscription* costs, facilities, and ongoing personnel. Commercial producers create a budget based on one production and effectively establish a company to produce it. All expenses are included in the production budget from artists to advertising to management. In addition, resident theatres project ticket sales from an annual perspective, assuming that some productions will sell better than others but that total sales will reach the goal for the season. Resident theatres do not look at the profit from a single production. Commercial producers, of course, are concerned with nothing but profits—starting with the first week of production. These very different points of view make budget and enhancement money negotiations complicated. Ultimately, enhancement money is one of the deal points that commercial producers and resident theatres must negotiate.

It is essential that commercial producers and resident theatres become aware of industry standards before attempting to enter into a partnership. Obtaining perspectives from other producers and good legal counsel is essential. It is also critical that both parties become well versed in the potential impact of existing labor agreements, particularly with Actors' Equity Association, the United Scenic Artists, the Society of Stage Directors and Choreographers, and the Dramatists' Guild. Both parties must know the precedents that exist in agreements between commercial producers and resident theatres. Theatre Communications Group, the League of American Theatre Producers, and the League of Resident Theatres are all sources for information and perspective.

It is my opinion that the generally accepted range of financial participation by resident theatres in commercial partnerships does not adequately recognize the contribution that the resident theatre makes to the production. The direct and indirect investment of the resident theatre should be included in the capitalization for the commercial production. The resident theatre's financial participation should be proportionate to its investment. The current range of financial participation by resident theatres in net profits and *gross weekly box office receipts* is not based on this formula, but rather on an arbitrary range of percentage participation that has evolved over the years. Commercial producers argue that any increase in the financial participation of resident theatres would make it impossible to attract investors, given the risks of commercial productions. At the same time, the inadequate level of financial participation will make commercial partnerships less and less attractive to resident theatres.

Show me the money.

A resident theatre should not incur additional production expenses in connection with a commercial partnership unless the resident theatre has received the money from the commercial producer. It sounds easy but the vast majority of commercial–resident theatre partnerships that fail do so because the resident theatre spends money that it does not have. Resident theatres must meet the dates on the subscription schedule. They cannot move them back while negotiations continue with the commercial producer. So in order to meet production schedules, some resident theatres will increase their budgets based on a verbal promise from the commercial producer. But, if the production is not well received, the enhancement money may disappear and the resident theatre will be left with a deficit. It is essential that resident theatre producers remember the first rule of negotiations: who has the leverage? If the resident theatre is not prepared to abandon a planned production, then it must make the best deal possible in the shortest period of time and focus on supervising the process. If you do not have leverage, do not waste your time in extended negotiations. Remember that half of nothing is nothing but a small percentage of a lot of money is a lot of money.

What do you believe?

The growth of commercial–resident theatre partnerships has increased the number of high-profile productions available to not-for-profit theatres. Often these productions involve distinguished artists and potential financial benefits. But a resident theatre cannot enter into a partnership with a commercial producer unless the proposed production clearly serves the artistic mission of the resident theatre first. At the Goodman, the overwhelming majority of our collaborations with commercial producers have been on transfers of successful Goodman productions. Our most well-known commercial collaboration, Arthur Miller's *Death of a Salesman*, directed by Robert Falls, began as a Goodman Theatre production. When we chose to produce *Salesman,* we were informed that a Broadway production would be impossible under any circumstances. We said that was fine, we just wanted to produce the play for our audiences in Chicago. The production was planned as part of the ongoing collaboration between artistic director Robert Falls and actor Brian Dennehy. It also reflected our mission of producing the work of the American master playwrights. No commercial producer was involved. Today, most people assume that our production was the out-of-town tryout for the fiftieth anniversary production of *Salesman*. All producers can do is present work they believe in—after all, if producers knew what productions would succeed with audiences, Broadway would be a very happy place!

WHAT IS THE FUTURE FOR PARTNERSHIPS BETWEEN COMMERCIAL PRODUCERS AND RESIDENT THEATRES?

Collaborations between commercial producers and resident theatres have had a major impact on the vitality of the American theatre over the past thirty years. These partnerships have led to the production of important new plays, exciting revivals, and dynamic musicals, while reducing expenses and expanding revenue for commercial producers and resident theatres. These collaborations have also increased employment opportunities and wages for many theatre artists. Partnerships have been established as an important business strategy for resident theatres and commercial producers. In fact, while cultural organizations in other disciplines are being urged to collaborate with commercial interests to expand revenue, American theatre producers have been engaged in this practice for decades!

What does the future hold? For a variety of reasons I think that we will see fewer partnerships that involve commercial producers and resident theatres that are located outside of New York City. For example:

In recent years, most commercial productions of non-musicals on Broadway were built around TV or movie stars whose name recognition would likely sell out the production in a limited run. It is rare now that a commercial production of a drama or comedy is predicated on an open-ended run. The 1999 Goodman Theatre production of *Death of a Salesman* with Brian Dennehy ran for nine months on Broadway with the original cast, subsequently *toured*, and then was produced in London for six months. Now, the prospect of a production proceeding on this path seems unlikely if not unthinkable. The limited run star system for non-musicals on Broadway eliminates the commercial producer's economic incentive for launching a production in partnership with a resident theatre outside of New York. Furthermore, stars are not inclined to make the time and travel commitment necessary for a resident theatre and Broadway run.

At the same time, the majority of commercial productions of musicals on Broadway are now very large productions that are planned to run for years, without stars, and with high tourist appeal. Only a handful of resident theatres outside of New York have the resources to provide a commercial producer with the economic incentive that would lead to a partnership on a new musical production. It has now become increasingly appealing for commercial producers to develop musicals in an "old-fashioned" out-of-town tryout where the commercial producer controls the budget, *marketing*, schedule, and ticket price. Chicago is one city that has seen a marked increase in commercial tryouts of new musicals, including *The Producers* and *Movin' Out*.

Three of the largest not-for-profit theatres in New York City (Lincoln Center Theatre Company, Manhattan Theatre Club, and Roundabout Theatre) have become Broadway producers through their relationships with the theatrical unions, the League of American Theatre Producers, and the Tony Committee. Since these theatres operate multiple stages and have the capacity to produce new work, revivals, and musicals, they add enormous artistic vitality to the Broadway season. They also provide a ready-made opportunity for commercial producers to collaborate on the development of new productions and/or transfers. When you add the diverse repertory of the other major not-for-profits in New York (such as The Public Theatre and Playwrights Horizons) it becomes evident that commercial producers can find resident theatre producing partners right in their own backyard. Given the logistics and economics of transfers and collaborations within New York City, commercial producers no longer have an urgent need to look beyond the Hudson for partnerships with resident theatres.

More than ever, commercial producers in New York are looking to London as a source for new productions. The status and/or star-power that come with productions from the West End, National Theatre, and Royal Shakespeare Company have always been appealing to American producers (and audiences). Now commercial producers have expanded their search to include many more London theatres and are formalizing relationships with them to promote the export of more productions to New York.

While these factors, among others, may reduce the number of partnerships between commercial producers and resident theatres across the country, there could be long-term benefits to the American theatre:

Thanks to the growth of the resident theatre movement over the past fifty years, professional theatre has become a part of the fabric of life in communities large and small across the country. But the concentration of producers and arts media in New York obscures this fact and instead makes it appear that the leading indicator of the health of the American theatre is the Broadway season. This minimizes awareness of the artistic, social, and economic impact of resident theatres outside of New York, as documented by Theatre Communications Group for decades. But as Broadway productions rely more and more on the diversion-seeking tourist audience (over 60 percent according to the League of American Theatre Producers), it makes the commercial production of most plays even more risky—if that is possible! For example, as of this writing there are no formal plans in place for the production of the final works by August Wilson or Arthur Miller in New York. If the production of new works by artists of this stature has become an endangered species on Broadway, it may focus more attention on the many outstanding new plays and revivals that are produced by resident theatres across the country each year.

New types of partnerships may develop between resident theatres and commercial producers. One example would be to expand on the producing model that the late Ben Mordecai developed to produce the work of August Wilson. His strategy involved a co-production of each play, presented at several resident theatres over the course of one or two years, and ending with a commercial production in New York. This provided an extraordinary amount of development time for the artists. In addition, an arrangement was usually made with a not-for-profit New York theatre to make the production available to their subscribers, generating word of mouth and advance interest in the play. Another example is the process by which the musical *The Light in the Piazza* by Adam Guettel and Craig Lucas reached New York. In this case, a collaboration evolved

The 2004 Goodman Theatre production of *The Light in the Piazza*;
book by Craig Lucas; music and lyrics by Adam Guettel; which subsequently won the
2005 Best Musical Tony Award upon its transfer to Broadway. Pictured are Wayne
Wilcox as Fabrizio Naccarelli and Celia Keenan-Bolger as Clara Johnson.
Photo by Liz Lauren.

among three not-for-profit theatres, leading to the creation of a beautiful new work. The Intiman Theatre in Seattle provided the initial impetus and production. The Goodman Theatre joined Intiman as co-producer, which increased the resources for the initial production. Next, *Piazza* was given a second full production at the Goodman with resources for the authors to completely revisit their approach to the material—from design through casting. Although the production was a success in Chicago, there was no interest in a commercial Broadway production—the musical had no stars and was too modest in size and scope; in other words, too *artistic* for Broadway. The development of *The Light in the Piazza* had been closely monitored by Lincoln Center Theatre Company and they were very interested! Ultimately, Lincoln Center Theatre agreed to provide a fully *capitalized* new Broadway production in the Vivian Beaumont Theatre, giving the creators the opportunity to continue to evolve and refine the work. The success of this strategy is apparent since *The Light in the Piazza* won six Tony Awards and has enjoyed more than a year-long run as of this writing.

The critical issue facing the American theatre is that both commercial producers and resident theatres exist in an entrepreneurial industry that is very undercapitalized. No not-for-profit theatre or commercial producer has the resources to consistently enable theatre artists to work to the best of their ability—and make a living. All producers know that the best work on stage occurs when artists have the time and resources to develop that work—through commissions, rehearsals, workshops, previews, and so forth. Collaborations between and among resident theatres and commercial producers can increase the available capital for productions and ultimately the quality on stage. Hopefully, resident theatres and commercial producers will continue to work as partners and explore new forms of collaboration in the future.

Resident theatre and commercial producers should find more ways to work together as advocates for the American theatre as an industry—an industry that provides works of art and entertainment to millions of people; an industry that is comprised primarily of small, undercapitalized businesses; and most importantly, an industry that has an enormous impact on the social fabric of our country. Only then will we create an environment in which resident theatres and commercial producers can enable our theatre artists to reach their full potential.

Elizabeth Williams

Elizabeth Williams has produced On Broadway and around the world since 1989 and received the Tony Award for Best Musical for her production of *Crazy for You* (1992), and Best Revival for *The Real Thing* (1999) and for *One Flew Over the Cuckoo's Nest* (2000). Together, as partners in Waxman Williams Entertainment, Anita Waxman and Elizabeth Williams have garnered seventy-one Tony nominations and sixteen Tony Awards, more than any female producing team in history.

Ms. Williams' and Ms. Waxman's recent Broadway productions include *Bombay Dreams*, *Gypsy*, *Flower Drum Song*, *Topdog/Underdog*, and *Noises Off*, as well as London West End productions of *By the Bog of Cats*, *Ragtime*, *Hitchcock Blonde*, and transfers of the Donmar Warehouse productions of *The Real Thing*, *Boston Marriage*, and *Lobby Hero*. Ms. Williams and Ms. Waxman served as executive producers of an unscripted reality series entitled *The Scholar*, which aired on ABC-TV in spring, 2005, working with partners Jaye Pace, Shannon Meairs, Martin/Stein Productions (Steve Martin and Joan Stein), and Carsey Werner. Through her company Four Corners Productions, Ms. Williams' productions include *Crazy for You*, *Into the Woods*, *The Secret Garden*, and *Moon Over Buffalo*.

From 1984–1989, Ms. Williams served as vice president of Mutual Benefit Productions, a wholly owned subsidiary of Mutual Benefit Financial Service Company, and, subsequently, Fifth Avenue Productions. Mutual Benefit Productions and Fifth Avenue Productions created art and theatre investment funds and served as the American financiers for Cameron Mackintosh by syndicating theatrical partnerships and helping to finance the West End, Broadway, and Australian and U.S. national touring companies of *Les Misérables*, *Phantom of the Opera*, and *Miss Saigon*.

Ms. Williams has served on the board of directors of the 52nd Street Project and is a past chair of the board of directors of the New York Theatre Workshop.

FROM THE WEST END TO BROADWAY

ELIZABETH WILLIAMS
Producer, Waxman Williams Entertainment

In 1982, I was approached to serve on the board of Art Investment Funds, involving working with galleries in London and New York City and created by Mutual Benefit Financial Service company—a wholly owned subsidiary of Mutual Benefit Life Insurance Company. Little did I know the career shift that lay ahead of me as a result of my association with Mutual Benefit, then one of the ten oldest insurance companies in the United States. I was an academic at the time, teaching the Art Humanities Survey at Columbia College while finishing my dissertation in Ancient Near Eastern Archaeology. While serving on the board of the Art Fund, I advised them to buy modern art (rather than ancient), due to the legal and ethical issues that are so much in the news today. As a result, I was also quickly drafted to review plays and musicals submitted to a newly formed unit of the company for funding theatre.

Mutual Benefit's research of the theatre scene had led them to believe that producing theatre in London was far less expensive (and therefore less risky), than originating work on Broadway. Critical reviews of productions in the West End appear in more than twenty British newspapers and tabloids, in contrast to New York's comparably few three primary newspapers, and are published there over several days, unlike the tradition in New York of reviews appearing directly following opening. Thus the power of the critics over the ticket buying public in England is strongly diminished. These facts, combined with the highly literate English audience, the cultural milieu of which encouraged theatregoing from a young age, constituted a fertile environment for new theatrical ventures. For this reason, Henry E. Kates and Karen Crane, then the president and vice president, respectively, of Mutual Benefit, met with British producers, among them Cameron Mackintosh. Cameron gave them the French script and score for Robert Hossein's hit musical *Les Misérables*, which had played to Sold Out houses at the Palais des Sports in Paris. Cameron had taken the project to Trevor Nunn and the Royal Shakespeare Company, as well as to John Caird, who had signed on to adapt it for English audiences. By this time I was teaching at the University of California at Berkeley and Karen shipped me the tapes of the original show, along with a request for a translation in my schoolgirl French.

The Elizabeth Williams co-production of the 1987 Tony Award-winning
Les Misérables; book by Claude-Michel Schönberg and Alain Boublil;
based on the novel by Victor Hugo; music by Claude-Michel Schönberg; lyrics by
Herbert Kretzmer. Pictured is The Company.
Photo by Michael Le Poer Trench, courtesy of the John Willis Theatre World/Screen World Archive.

Although I admired Victor Hugo's book, to which the lyrics in the sing-through show rang quite true, it was the idea of Trevor Nunn and John Caird working with the RSC to adapt it that excited me, as my husband and I had gifted each other the previous Christmas with the unprecedented one hundred dolllar tickets to the RSC's *Nicholas Nickelby,* and had been incredibly impressed. That production remains our single most memorable evening (actually day, as it was eight hours) in the theatre, and we reckoned that creating a musical version of the epic based on the Hugo work could be potentially and equally as amazing.

As *Les Misérables* fit the company's financial strategy to open shows in London in order to lessen the financial risk (with the added benefit of being creatively exciting), it became the first theatrical project funded by Mutual Benefit. Cameron had found no other partners, the Shuberts and many others having turned it down. Mutual Benefit was assigned one-third of the capitalization, Cameron raised one-third, and the RSC contributed one-third to total £900 thousand, which was then at virtual parity with the dollar—amazing to consider today. For this £300 thousand contribution, Mutual Benefit asked not for a royalty share, producer profit points, or producer *billing*, but rather only for an "honorable mention" (as we coined it), hidden in the final credits. The company earned its profits through the fees and commissions added on top of the £300 thousand in the *limited partnership* formed to raise the money, all of which were allowed due to the company's status as a Securities and Exchange Commission registered broker dealer. After *recoupment* of the investors' capital, Mutual Benefit participated in investor profits in a 75/25 percent split (75 percent to the limited partners, 25 percent to the *general partners*). The registered agents of the company did not have an easy time in 1985 of selling the ten-thousand-dollar shares in a Royal Shakespeare Company/Cameron Mackintosh production of Hugo's *Les Misérables*, as you might imagine. We all pitched in to find investors, flying around the country to meet with groups gathered by the company, and eventually turned to our own friends and family, who by then understood our passion for the project.

By this time, I was working for Mutual Benefit and had become a registered representative of the company. I was chosen by the company to greet our investors in London (now including many of my old friends and family), at the opening of *Les Misérables* at the RSC's Barbican Theatre on October 8, 1985. The show ran over three and a half hours that evening, but left me, our investors, and the entire (we believed) audience in exhilarated tears. Contrary to Mutual Benefit's research and theory, the majority of the reviews *did* appear the day following the opening, and despite their number, were universally bad. The poor reception by the press led Cameron, in a meeting held in his offices the next day, to ask me if our investors wanted their money returned. Dumbfounded by his question, I assured him that we were all swept away by the scope of the production and incredibly moved by the story as well as the music. And no, I could not imagine that anyone wanted their money returned. Also while we talked, he received a call from Andrew Lloyd Webber saying that with the terrible notices it was highly unlikely that *Les Misérables* would be able to *transfer* to his Palace Theatre.

All of this background is to illustrate that Mutual Benefit's theory concerning London shows was borne out by this extraordinary musical sailing through its six-week run at the Barbican, becoming the mega hit that we all now know it to be, and running in the West End to this day. Mutual Benefit, for the risk it took, was involved in the Broadway production, the national *tours*, the Canadian, and the Australian productions. Furthermore, Cameron Mackintosh offered us all his subsequent shows, from *Café Puccini* (on which we passed, and after its short run, Cameron said "no more cherry picking," thus we were given the choice of investing in all or none of his shows—we chose the former), to *Phantom of the Opera, Miss Saigon,* and *Follies.* These shows, dubbed by the press as the "British Invasion," established a virtual one-way street of transfers from London to New York.

Rare were the successful shows going in the opposite direction in the late 1980s and 1990s. Although I was fortunate enough to have one hit transfer from Broadway to the West End (1992's Tony Award for Best Musical, the 1993 Olivier Award-winning *Crazy for You*), successful transfers remain far fewer than those from the West End to Broadway.

The rationale for mounting productions in London remains true to this day. Although the domination of long-running British musicals has waned with the closing of *Miss Saigon* and *Les Misérables,* of the ten or more plays produced on Broadway each year, a minimum of two or three transfer from Britain. The majority of these plays or musicals originated in England's subsidized theatres: The National Theatre, and, since the late '90s, The Donmar Warehouse. My partner Anita Waxman and I became involved with The Donmar Warehouse in 1998 when Martin McCallum, Cameron Mackintosh's executive producer, approached us. At that time Martin was president of The Donmar's board. We had produced The Donmar's *Electra* on Broadway, which had transferred from the McCarter Theatre to the Ethel Barrymore Theatre on Broadway in November 1998, and we had also helped finance the transfer of the Sam Mendes hit *Cabaret* from The Roundabout Theatre to Studio 54. With The Donmar hot as a firecracker when Martin approached us, we entered into a *first-look deal* with the theatre at £300 thousand a year for the right to transfer their productions to the West End, and then to Broadway. With our production of *The Real Thing* on Broadway in the spring of 2000, we took home the Tony Award for Best Revival, winning The Donmar its first Tony Award as well.

To help illustrate how the risk remains less when bringing a play from London, I'll discuss *The Real Thing*. David Leveaux directed the revival of Tom Stoppard's *The Real Thing* at The Donmar Warehouse in the summer of 1999. Starring Stephen Dillane and Jennifer Ehle, it received rave reviews. With Sam Mendes and Caro Newling as co-producers and strategists, we determined to transfer the production to the West End's Albery beginning in January 2000. This plan would allow us to transfer the show in spring 2000, to New York if new reviews and ticket sales merited it. The production cost £240 thousand, which could be *recouped* at 80 percent capacity in ten of the twelve weeks. For the West End transfer, the reviews were again raves. Among the reviewers was *The New York Times* critic Ben Brantley, who mentioned the revival positively. We recouped and made a 20 percent profit in the twelve-week run. Meanwhile, we had budgeted the New York production at $2.1 million, (over four times the cost of the British production). We announced a sixteen-week run, strategizing that we would extend for eight weeks. We put together an aggressive *advertising* and *marketing* campaign promoting the hit British show and its stars. We also consciously *branded* it "A Donmar Warehouse Production" in all artwork, print, and on the marquis of the theatre. The show opened to raves (including one from Brantley of *The New York Times*), and went on to win three Tonys, including Best Revival of a Play, as well as those for Best Actor and Best Actress for its stars, Stephen and Jennifer. We recouped and returned a 20 percent profit.

Although I have not done a survey of the profitability of British transfers (it would be an interesting masters thesis for some graduate student), I would wager that far more than three out of ten productions—our generally quoted Broadway ratio—are successful. Certainly my experience bears this out.

Finally, however, I will discuss British shows that we have transferred to New York without having had any involvement in the West End production, which is more unusual for us. We joined ATG, Sonia Friedman, and others in 2001 to bring the revival of Michael Frayn's *Noises Off* to Broadway. Although we considered canceling the production, which was in rehearsals on September 11, 2001, we determined to stay the course. The show proved to be a tonic—almost a catharsis—for audiences, and critics embraced it. Recoupment took six months and we ran almost a year with a 20 percent profit.

In 2004, I saw *Bombay Dreams* in the West End and called Andre Ptaszinski of the Really Useful Group (RUG) to express our interest in a revised *Bombay Dreams* for New York. We wrote RUG and Andrew Lloyd Webber, suggesting certain changes, and worked with Andrew and RUG to bring American collaborators on board to work with their British counterparts. Prime among these new creatives was Thomas Meehan, who worked with the originator Meera Syal to streamline and adapt the story for audiences less familiar with India and *Bollywood* (India's indigenous film industry).

The £4.5 million English production cost $14 million on Broadway. Although we made money in previews, playing to 80 percent capacity houses and *wrapping* around one hundred thousand dollars per day, our reviews were largely bad, with the rare positive one, and our wraps fell precipitously. In *The Wall*

Street Journal, we were number seven on the Zagat list* during previews, but after those reviews we dropped from sight. I had seen this happen with other shows originated on Broadway, particularly *The Secret Garden*. We mounted an aggressive television and printed advertising and marketing campaign emphasizing the sheer entertainment value of the show. Our audience demographics were exciting in that they reflected a broader diversity (30 percent varied race and ethnicity, with as much as 20 percent of that figure South Asian, many of them first time Broadway theatregoers), and 70 percent Caucasian. The ages were 20–60 years old rather than the more typical 30–55. And the income level was $125 thousand, rather than the expected seventy-five thousand dollars. The demographics also showed that we virtually bypassed the New York audience (probably due to the reviews), but captured many U.S. and foreign tourists. The question most frequently posed about the show in features and reviews (including that in *The New York Times*), was whether the show would survive in New York, considering the fewer number of South Asians in the United States than in Britain. We hovered near our *break even* of $475–500 thousand, reasonable for a show our size. In late fall 2004, the producers made a difficult decision to close the show in January 2005, rather than hazard the traditional downturn of the winter months and run through the reserve we had accumulated. We have returned around 20 percent of the investors' capital and expect to return more due to a tour, which was mounted by Theatre of the Stars in spring 2006.

With the strength of the British pound, and the euro, as compared to the dollar, and the unstable times, there may be a turning of the tide in terms of shows transferring successfully from the West End to Broadway. With the successful transfer of *The Producers* to the West End and the impending West End opening of the English-themed *Spamalot* (can *Wicked* and *Jersey Boys* be far behind?), perhaps the Brits will be speaking of an "American Invasion" (at least in terms of musicals), in the coming years! As Fred Vogel would have said, and I now say, "Stay tuned…"

This chapter, suggested by Fred Vogel and his colleague, Ben Hodges, is dedicated to Mr. Vogel and his collaborative spirit, love of the theatre, and many contributions to it. The theatre in New York has lost a giant and I have lost a friend.

---

* Zagat Survey is the world's leading provider of consumer survey-based dining, travel and leisure information, with more than 250,000 voters participating worldwide.

William Craver

William Craver became a part of Paradigm, A Literary and Talent Agency, as a result of its acquisition of Writers & Artists Agency, where he was previously a partner and president of the New York office. He began his career with the distinguished Broadway producer Saint Subber. While in his employ he worked on the original Broadway productions of *Barefoot in the Park*, *The Odd Couple*, and *Plaza Suite*, as well as Mike Nichols' all-star revival of *The Little Foxes*. As general manager or company manager he has worked on more than fifty Broadway and Off-Broadway plays. He ran the business operation of the premiere productions of the *House of Blue Leaves*, *El Grande de Coca-Cola*, and the record-breaking revival of *One Flew Over the Cuckoo's Nest*. He produced two Off-Broadway plays and has been associate producer of a CBS-TV miniseries, a feature film released by Columbia Pictures, as well as co-producer of a Movie of the Week for CBS.

As a literary agent at Writers & Artists Agency, three of his clients—David Auburn for *Proof*, Jonathan Larson for *RENT*, and Robert Schenkkan for *The Kentucky Cycle*—have been awarded the Pulitzer Prize for Drama. *RENT* also won Tony Awards for Best Musical, Book, Music, and Lyrics, respectively, as well as the Drama Critics Circle Award. *Proof* also won the Tony Award, the Drama Critics Circle Award, and the Outer Critics Circle Award for Best Play. Greg Kotis and Mark Hollmann won the Tony Award for Best Score of a Musical, and Kotis for Best Book of a Musical for *Urinetown*. His client, Jerry Zaks, has won four Tony Awards for directing the Broadway revivals *of The House of Blue Leaves* and *Guys and Dolls,* and the original Broadway productions of *Six Degrees of Separation* and *Lend Me a Tenor*. David Henry Hwang won the Tony Award for Best Play for *M. Butterfly*. He is on the boards of The American Theatre Wing, Dramatists Play Service, and The Jonathan Larson Foundation.

YOU CAN TAKE THE AGENT OUT OF THE THEATRE...

WILLIAM CRAVER

Head of New York Theatre Literature Department at Paradigm

People most often ask, "How did you become an agent?" The very simple answer is "Someone asked me." From the first job I had in professional theatre, more jobs came up and I never had to look for employment. How can one be so lucky?

Flashback to mid-July 1979: I was feeling something nagging at the back of my mind. I could not quite figure out what it was. I was sitting in a very nice office on the Warner Brothers Studio lot in Burbank, California. For two years I had been working exclusively in film and television. Luckily I began rather high up as an associate producer for a six-hour miniseries for CBS-TV, followed by the same credit for a Columbia Studios feature film, and eventually became co-producer for a CBS movie of the week. A two-hour movie for television, called a *backdoor pilot*, was made with the idea that if it were successful you could segue right into a television series. The backdoor pilot filled a slot for the network as a movie but it also gave them a look at the potential for a series, usually with the same cast appearing in the movie as would appear as regulars on the series. Warner Brothers had given our company a *housekeeping deal*, which meant they provided us office space and use of the various resources that any big Hollywood studio could provide. In return, we would give them a first refusal to finance and/or distribute any of the feature films we were developing. All of the television shows and feature films we had worked on used real locations, never a studio sound stage. We shot in a prison in Easton, Pennsylvania, the stilt fishing houses in Miami Bay, Stuyvesant Oval (a quaint, short street in New York City with a very period feel to it), an empty mansion on Fifth Avenue, in homes of real people on Shelter Island, and in the very chic River House apartments, to use several examples of the reality to which we were committed. Of course, a production designer was necessary to find the proper location and to make whatever changes were needed to suit the script requirements.

As I sat there that July and not knowing the cause of my brooding, it suddenly occurred to me that a year earlier we were preparing the feature film for Columbia. It was shot in all of the real locations in New York City, including Macy's department store in Herald Square, their warehouse in New Jersey, and finally, on the East River at 58th Street. That scene was shot on a freezing cold night (as only New York can be in February), with a very strong wind blowing off of the East River. We finally had to *wrap*, the term for shutting down for the day, when the camera literally froze, along with all of the humans who were there working.

Finally I figured out what was causing my mood—the movie we were preparing that warm July day in Los Angeles was going to shoot in New York from November through February, which was the same schedule as the previous year. The first shot was to be on the Roosevelt Island Tramway spanning the East River from Manhattan to the Island. Thinking of Manhattan and the locations there made me begin to focus on what my goals for the future were. I did not like the upcoming movie all that much and did not like some of the personnel to be engaged for the film. Luckily, it was not too early in the process that my leaving the production would cause any damage or delays. Within two days I announced that I would not continue in the job or on the movie and would be returning to New York as quickly as possible. I left five days later.

My basic reason for leaving a very well-paying permanent job that also just happened to include working on movies and television and having quite a lot of access to the advantages of the movie industry was simple—the theatre. I had worked in the theatre for many years, it was my first love and I wanted to go back to it. Our movie office in New York was the head office for the company and I spent a great deal of time there, frequently commuting to Los Angeles as needed. Therefore, I still had my apartment in the city and usually took a residential hotel for the time spent out west. It was just a matter of returning to what I had called home for a long time. Easy. Right for me.

I had not worked in the theatre for over two years and really had nothing to come back to or any idea what I might want to do next. There were jobs I was sure I could get or ideas for work that I could easily wrap my mind and energy around. But for ten months I chose not to do anything or even think very much about what to do. Since I had worked so consistently, I was enjoying reading novels, going to movies and the theatre, having dinner with friends, and just living randomly.

There was a woman I had known for a number of years who had decided to become a literary agent and worked out of her living room trying to get playwrights and fiction and non-fiction writers as clients. She developed some interesting clients who began to be successful. The agent lived in my neighborhood and we would occasionally bump into each other or arrange to have dinner together. As playwrights gain some degree of visibility in the theatre, they attract the attention of Hollywood. She had some clients who were being wooed to write a television pilot or a feature film, and she actually had no experience whatsoever in what kind of deals were to be made or what pitfalls were to be avoided. So, she began to call me to find out what to do about those offers she was getting, and I began to coach her on what to look out for and how to deal with specific offers. She began trying to get me to make the calls to work out the deal suggesting that I would present myself as a colleague of hers. By *not* agreeing to do that, my coaching had to become more strenuous and specific, and as a result, she began suggesting that I join her business.

The 2001 Pulitzer Prize and Tony Award-winning
production of David Auburn's *Proof*, represented by William Craver of Paradigm.
Pictured are Mary-Louise Parker as Catherine and Larry Bryggman as Robert.
Photo by Joan Marcus, courtesy of the John Willis Theatre World/Screen World Archive.

I had worked primarily on the non-creative side of theatre as a *general* and company *manager* for Broadway and Off-Broadway shows. These are the positions that do the budgets for productions and to a large degree negotiate the creative contracts for the playwrights, directors, designers, and actors to be involved in a show. My job in film and television was very similar but on a much larger scale than that of the production and financial positions I had previously held in theatre. I had never really considered the idea of becoming an agent, so I kept refusing, but my agent friend kept cajoling. I came to realize that it was a really good idea for me and a logical progression. All of my experience in the theatre and the limited two years in the movie and television business gave me enormous knowledge of what the buyer of talent needed and wanted when making a deal; it was what I had done for years. Therefore, I felt more qualified to represent the talent in knowing what to ask for and what it was possible to achieve for them. Also, I believe I knew the majority of the people in the theatre, so I did not have to explain who I was to anyone I wanted to talk to. It was the perfect fit and there was no learning process to go through. She cajoled and finally, a full ten months after my return to New York, I agreed.

After working six years in that company I got a call asking me to move to Writers and Artists Agency and become not only an agent, but to run the New York Office. To make a long story short, I became an owner of the company and experienced the pleasure of our company being acquired twelve years later by Paradigm, a much larger bi-coastal literary and talent agency, which brings me to today.

Certainly people seeking agents for their work would want to know what some of the expectations are on the part of the client, as well as for the client. A client can reasonably expect that their work will be circulated to those theatres or producers who are looking for new material. The client–agent relationship should obviously be a collaborative one. I am always interested in hearing ideas for where a work might be placed or of previous relationships that the client might have developed in the past. However, the client should not expect that the agent is a mailing service and should be prepared to send material out to anyone who is suggested. In the same way that *casting* directors and directors refer to the type of actor they are looking for, I try to match the play to a particular theatre in relation to the type of plays they have presented in the past.

Several things I mentioned earlier I want to emphasize as very strong points that I believe can be helpful to creating success for those who want to enter the professional world of theatre, film, and television:

> Exercise caution as to how you present yourself and your work. When reading, be as careful as possible about spelling, punctuation, and formatting. (Using "their" instead of "there" or "your" in place of "you're" is especially eye stopping when reading a manuscript.) No matter how engrossed I am in the script, I am literally stopped for a split second when

poor grammar and punctuation jumps out at me. It never hurts to ask questions. If you are unsure of formatting, especially, do not hesitate to ask what is appropriate. When writing a query letter seeking an agent, all of the above suggestions are most important. Remember, it is the first impression (and possibly the last opportunity), to attract the agent's attention.

An agent is not an editor. One of the pleasures of my job is discussing a new work with the writer. Usually, I am the first person to read the material, but it would be presumptuous to discuss it in other than general terms. When a writer has a particular voice or style that is unique to them, I am already familiar with their style or process and it should be understood. If there is a problem with craft or plot line or character development, it is stimulating to bring up my opinions. Making the deal is exciting and fun but hearing the author's process and intent is the most rewarding.

Relationships are often crucial. I mentioned that since I got my first professional job I have never had to look for another. So much of this continued employment has been the result of recommendations by friends or former employers, or else someone merely mentioning that they have asked someone to call me. Treasure and maintain the contacts and friends you make in the industry, as it can pay off in the most unexpected ways.

Working with creative people can be a real pleasure. My career as an agent has paid off more than I could have ever imagined. The joys come from the success of the clients who have won three Pulitzer Prizes, two Tony Awards for Best Musical, two Tony Awards for Best Play, and five Tony Awards for Best Director, not to mention the Drama Critics Circle Awards, Outer Critics Circle Awards, and OBIE Awards. It doesn't get much better than that. But even without the awards, the success is *very* satisfying.

Jack Tantleff

Jack Tantleff began his career working in Broadway and Off-Broadway management and production. In 1979, at the age of 21 he was the associate producer of the Off-Broadway production of *Lone Star & Pvt. Wars* by James McLure at the Century Theatre. He was the company manager of such notable productions as David Mamet's *American Buffalo* starring Al Pacino; A.R. Gurney's *The Dining Room*; and the original New York production of *Jerry's Girls*.

In 1986, he opened The Tantleff Office in a corner of his apartment. His eclectic clientele included playwrights, writers for film and television, directors, choreographers, and designers. Four years later he became the first tenant in the Tribeca Film Center. In 1991, his client Marsha Norman won a Tony Award for her book of *The Secret Garden*, and the following year he represented the Tony Award-winning Best Play *Dancing at Lughnasa* by Brian Friel. Following these successes, in 1993 The Tantleff Office expanded to represent actors and actresses as well.

He was instrumental in bringing the critically acclaimed musical *Side Show* to Broadway, representing most of the creative team, including composer Henry Krieger, book writer and lyricist Bill Russell, director and choreographer Robert Longbottom, costume designer Gregg Barnes, orchestrator Harold Wheeler, and music director David Chase. He also represented a number of company members, including Norm Lewis and its Tony-nominated star Emily Skinner. More recently, he played a significant part in the development of the Broadway musicals *The Full Monty*, *Hairspray*, and *Dirty Rotten Scoundrels*.

His client Ivan Menchell, whose *The Cemetery Club* was the first play Mr. Tantleff represented On Broadway, was supervising producer on the hit TV series

The Nanny and subsequently a producer and writer on the FOX television series *Time of Your Life,* starring Jennifer Love Hewitt.

Other notable clients include playwrights Jeffrey Hatcher, Arthur Kopit, Mark O'Donnell, and Aaron Sorkin, designer David Rockwell, composer/lyricist David Yazbek, and directors David Esbjornson, Des McAnuff, and Francesca Zambello.

For three years, beginning in April 2000, Mr. Tantleff was head of the Literary Division in the New York and Los Angeles offices of Abrams Artists Agency. In June 2003, he joined William Morris Agency as a senior vice president and co-head of Theatre. In 2005, William Morris Theatre clients received twenty-one separate Tony nominations. Mr. Tantleff is a graduate of Sarah Lawrence College, where he studied with Wilford Leach.

THE VIEW FROM HERE

JACK TANTLEFF (A CONVERSATION WITH)
Senior Vice President and Co-Head of Theatre, William Morris Agency

FREDERIC B. VOGEL: As a producer, experienced or otherwise, what does an agent expect of me?

JACK TANTLEFF: I expect a producer to have a real understanding of and passion for the project at hand. Theatre, at least relative to other businesses, has an inexpensive price of admission. With just ten or fifteen million dollars, a producer can mount a major Broadway musical. So an agent must be wary of a producer whose only calling card is money or how to raise money. Much more important is dedication to the property and a real understanding of the business, together which, hopefully, will result in the best possible production, presented and promoted, again hopefully, in the best possible way.

VOGEL: Do you go to a producer, or does a producer come to you?

TANTLEFF: Both. Producers often acquire *underlying rights* and then ask agents to help them assemble the creative team. However, what I like to do is bring together as many creative elements as possible before going to producers. This way the vision is the artists' and you end up, hopefully, with a producer who wants to support that vision, rather than the tail wagging the dog. Of course I realize I say "hopefully" a lot.

VOGEL: You mentioned "underlying rights." Would you explain what you mean?

TANTLEFF: An underlying right is the thing on which a play or musical is based. Broadway musicals, traditionally, often were based on plays or novels. These days it's movies. It always has been unusual to find a completely original Broadway musical, by which I mean a musical not based on something else.

VOGEL: You have spoken at CTI about considering producing earlier in your career. What made you think at that time that you may want to produce?

TANTLEFF: I tend to want to be in charge. Without knowing anything else about the business, I knew, or I thought I knew, that the producer was the equivalent of the president of the company. And this is funny because, I suppose, were I able to, I would have been one of those producers I try to avoid, the ones who simply buy themselves in. I didn't know enough to say: "I want to be a company manager" which, by the way, is a job I later had. Or, in fact, an agent. But I thought I knew what a producer did, and I was presumptuous enough to think I could be one.

VOGEL: Well you certainly worked with very capable people, which has always impressed me. I think it's safe to say that the way you really learn in this business is from everyone else. What process do you go through to find, see, or become aware of new work? And could you explain the differences in doing so from when you were at your own agency, The Tantleff Office, and where you are now, at William Morris? How has the difference in size between those two organizations affected how you work?

TANTLEFF: How I look for material has changed. When I started out, I had to look for writers I could attract pretty much on my enthusiasm and a promise that I would work very hard for them, whatever *that* meant. I also read all kinds of unsolicited material. I asked for recommendations, for favors, anything to meet potential clients. I had to make a name for myself. Today, being at William Morris and having twenty-odd years of experience, people know who I am. But the irony is that now, having more successful clients with greater needs, I spend much more time on fewer people. That's why a big part of my job is to encourage and support the young agents. As Peter Franklin, my partner at William Morris says, they have the jobs we want...

VOGEL: In preparation for Broadway and Off-Broadway plays and musicals, do you deal with the *nonprofit* theatre as well as with potential *commercial* producers? In other words, if your client has a play or musical that you feel is ready, is there a difference in your consideration between the two types of *venues*?

TANTLEFF: The nonprofit is more likely because, just by their very definition, those are the theatres that are more likely to *develop* new material. On the other hand, many commercial producers are hesitant to produce something untested. And, by the way, with good reason. It's dangerous out there! Let's look at the 2004–05 season, which I think is the first time since 1968 when all four best musical nominees were bona fide hits so many months later (don't hold me to 1968, but I believe that's the year). My first point is that it's fantastic but very unusual. However, my bigger point is about the nonprofits: *Spamalot* is the exception; it came to New York without first having a nonprofit production, although it did try out in Chicago. However, *Dirty Rotten Scoundrels, Light in the Piazza*, and *Spelling Bee* all originated at nonprofit theatres. And look at this year: *Jersey Boys* at La Jolla Playhouse, *The Wedding Singer* at the Fifth Avenue Theatre in Seattle, and *The Times They Are A-Changin'* (which is planned for Broadway in Fall 2006) at the Old Globe. It's almost inarguable that *regional* theatres have replaced the commercial *out-of-town tryout*.

VOGEL: Who generally makes the deal with the nonprofit theatre if you are representing the writer? With *Side Show* for example, are you the one who first contacted the regional theatre, or was that the responsibility of a commercial producer?

TANTLEFF: Either, or both. However, *Side Show* is the exception that proves the rule. Although it's a true story, somewhat fictionalized but certainly about real people, it isn't based on any underlying film, novel, or play. Not only that, *Side Show* opened directly on Broadway. But getting back to your question: who would make the deal with the regional theatre? From my point of view, it doesn't matter, provided that my clients are paid appropriately (by whomever), and that if there is commercial interest, then any ongoing obligation to the regional theatre is assumed by the commercial producers. It's the end result that matters, not who prepares the paperwork.

VOGEL: By the way, what is the difference between an agent and a manager? Say you're Kander and Ebb or a team of artists. Who generally represents them? Is there a protocol to follow in dealing with that situation?

TANTLEFF: The difference between an agent and a manager is more distinct than many people imagine. Technically, managers cannot submit clients for jobs and they do not negotiate deals. But whatever the division of labor, of paramount importance (obviously) is that the manager and the agent work together on behalf of their mutual client.

VOGEL: At the Commercial Theater Institute, at least once a week (and sometimes two or three times a week), I'll get a phone call from someone who says they have "produced" a musical, either at some kind of a local facility or community theatre. They say it's a new work, something they or a friend of theirs has written, and that there has been positive audience response. (The audience could have been fifty people selling out only two nights of a six-week run, but they think it's *ready*.) They call and want to know what I could do or what should be done next. What advice do you have for someone in that situation? I don't know what kind of an answer you or anyone could give them, so I wanted to ask you—what process should they go through to maybe answer it on their own?

TANTLEFF: That's a tough one, because chances are the musical in question is not good enough. It's like unsolicited scripts: they're never any good. I know that sounds cynical, but it's a fair representation of *my* experience. Which is that nothing great ever comes unsolicited. A favorite book of mine is *Adventures in the Screen Trade* by William Goldman. It's about the movie business, but its lessons also are applicable to the theatre (by the way, his book *The Season*, which

The 1998 Tony nominated production of *Side Show*; book and lyrics by Bill Russell; music by Henry Krieger; which Jack Tantleff of William Morris Agency was instrumental in bringing to Broadway, representing most of the creative team including the composer, bookwriter, lyricist, and director/choreographer Robert Longbottom. Pictured are Emily Skinner as Daisy Hilton and Alice Ripley as Violet Hilton.

Photo by Joan Marcus, courtesy of the John Willis Theatre World/Screen World Archive.

is about the 1968 Broadway season, is invaluable as well). Early on, Goldman urges the reader to promote themselves and their work to someone—anyone—who might know someone—anyone—who might be able to get their work read or seen by the right person. He writes about the caller who declares he needs to speak to Frederic Vogel. Or, he needs to speak to Jack Tantleff—whomever has their name on the door. (I'm being funny, Fred. He didn't actually mention our names! [*Laughs.*]) But his point, and mine, is this: start with anybody. Get somebody to read or see the work. Because great material finds its way to the top. The same holds true for your community theatre. I believe—and this may be naïve on my part, but I don't think so—that anybody, and especially now with the Internet, can spread the word. They have to get out there, they have to call in favors, they have to pound the pavement. The really great shows get seen. But that other thing, the idea that a little community production is magically whisked off to Broadway, that's *Waiting for Guffman.* It's very charming, but it doesn't really happen.

VOGEL: So in a sense you are saying that networking is not only the best way, but also the most productive way to move anywhere in this business?

TANTLEFF: I think so. In my case, I grew—or advanced—with my clients. In other words, my community of contacts was, for the most part, no more prominent than my most prominent client. Over time, as my clients became more successful, that community broadened. So it's not just networking, but networking appropriately: based on your own success and contacts, the success and contacts of your colleagues, and most important, which people and organizations might realistically be interested in your project.

VOGEL: Is there any marked difference between your talent and skills when you represent a play as opposed to a musical?

TANTLEFF: No. In either case I look for people who are passionate about the material.

VOGEL: You mentioned that you do travel. Would you just explain where you go and why you go there?

TANTLEFF: Los Angeles, because William Morris has offices there, and it's very important to keep in touch with my colleagues in television and motion pictures, both inside the company and out. I go to the London office three or four times a year to cover productions and because London is as great a theatre city as New York. And other cities, although less predictably, to cover productions. For example, in a few months I will find myself in Cincinnati for

John Doyle's production of *Company*, and then in the same week I go to San Diego to cover *The Times They Are A-Changin'*.

BEN HODGES: If I am an Off-Off-Broadway producer you've never heard of and I'm interested in doing either a *staged reading* or full production of an existing property written by one of your clients, on what criteria initially do you base your permission to use that property? I'm of course particularly interested in getting this information to people who may be making these calls for the first time (if I'm right in assuming that you get more calls from people you don't know than from people you do).

TANTLEFF: First, it's important to remember that the property is the writer's, not mine, and therefore the *decision* is the writer's as well. Second, every call gets returned, although not necessarily by me, but again—why do you care who returns your call? Interest in a William Morris property is never a bad thing. And then we do our due diligence: What is the purpose of the reading? Who is the director? Do you have a cast in mind? Are there future plans? Perhaps a conversation with the playwright. But no matter what, it's always a welcomed call.

VOGEL: I say I am a great producer because I've also cleaned the ladies room. I think that what I appreciate about you most is that you've also worked in all echelons of management and have gained some comprehension of the producing process by having done so. Is there anything you feel you would like to add to discussion about the agent—producer relationship and why you feel your background has enabled you to do a better job of representing your clients?

TANTLEFF: I always took the best jobs for which I was qualified (or for which I could pretend to be qualified!) and I needed every single one of them to learn what I know now. My background in management is important because it enables me to have intelligent conversations with managers and producers. I can structure better deals because I am well aware of the financial realities. Since there always is more than one way to skin a cat, this understanding allows me to be more creative in my deal making. Just as important, when a client wants to know why there isn't more money, I actually can tell them. In theatre, pockets are never that deep; every deal on a given production represents a slice of the same pie, and unfortunately the pie is never big enough to make everyone completely happy. So at the end of the day, it's how you slice the pie, and this is where my background in management is so helpful. If I can understand and address the producer's concerns, it's much more likely that he or she will be willing to address mine. Know thine enemy! (Which is a joke, but not really.)

HODGES: I have often found myself, when producing a show Off or Off-Off-Broadway, of acting as a de facto agent for writers who don't otherwise have representation. I want as many different people as possible from within the industry to see the show because if I can get attention for them and for my production, well then a rising tide lifts all boats. How do I best get your attention? I think if we were sitting at the CTI fourteen-week seminar, someone might ask you if it's the postcards, e-mails, *marketing* campaign, or *advertising* that does it best?

TANTLEFF: I participate in these seminars, and I always say the same things: know my name, and spelling counts. Don't tell me your musical is the next *Les Miz*. Don't try to lure me with a cheap price tag, how your show can be produced on a budget. Know something about *me*. I have always advised writers to learn who are a prospective agent's most important clients. It's the best way into that agent's personal tastes, and personal taste is what it's all about. What do I look for in an inquiry? Brevity, surprise, good spelling, "I admire your clients because…and I see myself complimenting your list." But to be completely honest, nobody ever can predict what will catch their eye. However, I will say this: all letters get read. And this: don't send e-mails. E-mail inquiries are an intrusion, and they're *impersonal*. Remember, it's easier to delete an e-mail than to toss away a good personal letter. There's an elegance to letter writing. Or, to put it another way, if you can't write a good letter, what does that tell me about your play?

VOGEL AND HODGES: Thank you, Jack.

Neil A. Mazzella

Neil Mazzella is the president and co-founder of Hudson Scenic Studio, founded in 1980.

As an industry leader, Hudson Scenic Studio has provided custom fabrication, scenic decoration, and theatrical automation for over 200 Broadway and touring theatrical productions. Hudson's major Broadway credits include *Monty Python's Spamalot, Doubt, The Producers, Mamma Mia!, La Boheme, The Lion King, Beauty and the Beast, Chicago, 42nd Street, The Music Man, Movin' Out, Oklahoma! Bring in 'Da Noise, Bring In 'Da Funk, Victor/Victoria, Art, Les Misérables, Miss Saigon*, and *Phantom of the Opera*. Other clients include Disney Entertainment, Blue from American Express, ABC, CBS, NBC, FOX, Canon, Pfizer, Intel, and NYC Ballet.

Mr. Mazzella has served as technical supervisor for over thirty Broadway productions, including *Glengarry Glen Ross* (2005), *The Boy From Oz* (2003), *Long Day's Journey Into Night* (2003), *Private Lives* (2002), *Proof* (2000), and Gore Vidal's *The Best Man* (2000).

He has served on the faculties of Yale School of Drama and Columbia University, and holds a Bachelor of Arts from the State University of New York, and a Master of Fine Arts in Technical Production from Yale School of Drama. He is the chairman of the the Leadership Council of the Yale School of Drama, and a member of the Friars Club of New York.

THE CENTER OF TENSION– THE PHYSICAL PRODUCTION

NEIL A. MAZZELLA
President, Hudson Scenic Studio

In his book *Everything Was Possible: The Birth of the Musical Follies,* Ted Chapin describes the domain in which I work, as "A natural focus for tension between the desires of the designer, the needs of the director, and the producer's budgetary concerns."* How this tension, conflict, or shifting priority plays itself out will dictate how 25 percent of a Broadway production's budget will be spent.

As the owner of Hudson Scenic Studio, I have lived in the center of this rivalry for over twenty-five years. In addition to having built over 150 shows, I have served as the technical supervisor for thirty of them. The balancing act of the technical needs of the production is an ever-growing snowball going downhill. When asked what drove the choices he made as a set designer, Oliver Smith replied, "The needs of the show." He went on to relate that he begins every design with nothing on stage. First, he discovers that the actor will be smoking so he provides an ashtray, followed by a table to put the ashtray on. Next, the show will need a chair to go with the table. Naturally the furniture needs to exist somewhere, so he adds the walls, doors, curtains, carpets, china, pictures on the wall, and so forth. At the end of Oliver's answer you realize that he has designed a beautiful setting just to accommodate someone smoking on stage. Every show starts in a different place with different needs and not all of them are completely in black and white when the process begins. Just think how over budget Oliver's theoretical show would have been if the budget had been formulated without providing for smoking on stage. The ideal budget would be created if the *general manager* had a script permitting him to count the number of scenes, the number of people in the cast, a guarantee as to what theatre he will be in, whether *enhancement* money will be coming from *out-of-town presenters* (permitting an out-of-town *tryout*), the number of stage hands working the show, how many musicians he needs, as well as a host of other unknowns that will directly affect his budget. However, most

---

* Ted Chapin, *Everything Was Possible*, (New York: Knopf, 2003), 61.

managers don't have this information when they are asked to budget a show, so they budget it as if it was a one-set, two-character play, even though the odds of it being so are impossible. The reason being is that most managers believe that only one-set, two-character plays have a chance of *recouping*. We know this is not true because no one would be producing $8–12 million musicals if it were, but philosophically that is where most budgets begin (along with a great deal of faith in the unknown).

As a culture we have always been prone to great leaps of faith. Producing a Broadway show requires it. When President Kennedy said we would put a man on the Moon by the end of the 1960s, what do you think his statement was based on? I am sure no one had yet made up a budget for a lunar landing, and if they had, what would that have been based on? No, we are prone to raising great deals of money and hoping for the best. That is certainly the way we operate when we do a new Broadway show, and tying all the technical elements together certainly requires that.

When we talk about the technical part of the production, we are referring to buying scenery, props, and costumes, along with renting scenic automation, lights, and sound equipment. Once everything is built, bought, or rented, it is all shipped to a theatre, installed, and prepped for rehearsal. The cost for acquiring these elements plus the cost of the labor to install and operate all of them is part of that financial snowball I refer to, which is at the center of the tension we live in.

The first day of rehearsal for *Angels in America: Perestroika* provides a perfect example of how all the various needs of the show tug at each other. Before the cast was called, I—as technical supervisor—attended a production meeting called by the producers. They emphasized how important adhering to the schedule was, as we were about to embark on the second part of Tony Kushner's masterpiece. They told us that we could not afford to cancel performances for *Perestroika*, as we had when we were trying to mount *Part I: Millennium Approaches*. At the end of the speech, the producers looked at the director and asked for assurance that this mandate could be met. Our director then looked at our set designer and asked if we could make it, who in turn looked at me and said that that would be up to me, since setting up the repertory system we were going to use would be my responsibility. I sat there stunned. I considered everyone in the room my friend, and the trust they had shown in me over the years had produced unswerving loyalty on my part, but I had just been offered up for sacrifice by one group of friends (the director and designer), to another. As all eyes focused on me for the reassurance I had always given, when prompted for an answer I asked if we weren't missing someone. They all looked confused, and so I asked, "Where is Tony? And for that matter, where is the script?" I then pointed out that it was a bit unrealistic to hold us to a production schedule when we in fact hadn't even seen the script. I knew that we did not have a set design for *Perestroika,* and with no set, we could have no production schedule. Now, I was sure everyone already knew what I had been the one forced to point out, and so I expected from the others some reasonable acknowledgement of our predicament. However, instead of changing the schedule in light of the current circumstances, we all agreed to do our best to achieve the producers' goals. In the end, we still had to cancel performances—something I always knew would happen. Without real clarity on the physical production, it is very difficult to stay on schedule *or* on budget.

The 2006 Tony Award-winning production of *The Drowsy Chaperone*;
book by Bob Martin and Don McKellar; music and lyrics by Lisa Lambert
and Greg Morrison. Pictured is Trix the Aviatrix's Airplane,
built by Neil Mazzella's Hudson Scenic Studio, flying above the cast.
Photo by Joan Marcus, courtesy of SpotCo and the John Willis Theatre World/Screen World archive.

Before loading into the theatre, how the set is built, lights and sound prepped, and the costumes constructed, really can determine how much money is spent during the load-in. Yet the various aspects of the system we have in place to supervise and install these various elements does not always work in sync. For example, if the set isn't properly built, the installation can cost far more than it should. If it doesn't properly fit, the stagehands in the theatre will be paid a premium to rebuild it. And it is these different rates of pay that is at the heart of this disconnect. The crew that is directly responsible to the technical supervisor (and by extension, the show), is the production crew (often referred to as the *Pink Contract Crew* because of the color of the contract they sign once they begin work on the show). Its members supervise the various departments that are doing the actual work. The crews they are supervising are employed by the theatre owner, who has a contract with the local stage hands. Neither group will have an intimate knowledge of how the more intricate pieces of the set go together, thus requiring another supervisor, most likely from the shop that built the piece, in order to help assemble it. The parent union, IATSE, oversees all of these groups. The amazing part is that these varying groups work with differing pay scales, benefits, and working conditions. They are all there for the sole purpose of installing the show, yet how it gets installed is a negotiation among the production carpenter (directly responsible to the producer); the house carpenter (directly responsible for the local crew loading in the show); and the shop carpenter (who actually knows how the piece goes together). When the wardrobe crew and Equity members of the cast (among other groups) begin showing up at the theatre, the task of accommodating all the unions without entering a penalty phase (resulting in overtime, or worse—meal penalties), becomes impossible. The only way for a technical supervisor to make the right choice when confronted with varying costs and multiple solutions is to decide which of the master's interests—the designer's, director's, or the producer's—will add the most value to the production. Sometimes that decision takes tremendous compromise.

During the Washington, D.C. tryout of *Crazy For You*, director Mike Ockrent decided that he needed to add some pizzazz to the finale, ideally a *button*. He and set designer Robin Wagner came up with the idea that the leads would come up through the floor on an elevator. We quoted them a price of eleven thousand dollars for the elevator. Mike and Robin were told by the general manager that they had already maxed out their budget and that they didn't have another eleven thousand dollars to spend. Paul Gemignani, the musical director, even offered to leave one of the musicians from New York home and hire a local musician instead, thereby saving on housing and per diem costs, a savings that would allow for the cost of the elevator.

Working together on a show is always the best approach. General manager Albert Poland and I created the budget for *The Boy From Oz* five years before the show ever came to Broadway. The budget was based on the original production we had seen in Australia. But five years later we were doing the same show with a totally different creative team. Under the careful collaboration of the two original producers and the new creative team, we were able to guide the production through a budget that was essentially meant for a different show.

I don't have a road map to help navigate through the union rules, technical issues, design requirements, or schedules that make producing a new Broadway show hazardous, but if you put a team of talented people together that have their own priorities and respect those of the other members of the group, you at least have a chance of getting to opening night. Technical theatre has grown tremendously complex over the last twenty years. The introduction of computer control over every element of the production has called for more technologically skilled stagehands who can write code for computers, build and wire motors that fly cars, or raise large pieces of scenery through the floor. All of this is for a static industry that cannot increase seating capacity in the landmarked buildings in which they play. Managers still want to pay for one-set, two-character plays, but the twenty-first century allows for much more and the *commercial* theatre wants that technology just like every other segment of America. As a vendor of scenery and lights, as well as a supervisor of the installing of them, I have to realize that I will always be at the center of the tension between what one needs, what another wants, and what another will pay for.

Alan Schuster

Alan Schuster has been working in the theatre industry for more than thirty-five years, performing functions including stage hand, stage manager, house manager, general manager, theatre manager, theatre owner/operator, producer, writer, and even actor. He has also owned and operated Off-Broadway theatres, including three prominent Off-Broadway houses in New York City, a four-theatre complex in Chicago, and a 600-seat theatre in San Francisco.

In New York he was managing director of a Shakespeare touring company known as the Classic Theatre Company, a writer and director for the George Street Playhouse Children's Theatre, and in 1978 founded and served as President/CEO of Eastside Theatre Corporation and housed *Little Shop of Horrors*, one of the most successful Off-Broadway musicals ever produced.

Mr. Schuster produced the Broadway and London productions *Blues in the Night* (1982 Tony Award nominee for Best Musical and 1987 Olivier nominee for Best Musical), served as general manager of the Broadway production, and produced and general managed the two national touring companies. Off-Broadway shows produced and general managed by Mr. Schuster include *To Gillian on her 37th Birthday* (Oppenheimer Award), *The Garden of Earthly Delights* (Drama Desk Award Winner), *Angry Housewives* (New York and London*)*, *The Chosen, Bouncers, Key Exchange* (New York starring Brooke Adams and Los Angeles starring Kate Jackson), *Eden Court* (starring Ellen Barkin and Penny Marshall), *Bloolips* (OBIE Award-Winner), *Vita and Virginia* (starring Vanessa Redgrave and Eileen Atkins), Paul Rudnick's *Jeffrey* (Drama Desk Award nominee and Outer Critics Circle Award-Winner), David Mamet's *Oleanna* (London and two national tours, Drama Desk Award nominee and Olivier Award nominee), the Outer Critics Circle Award nominee *Jam on the Groove,* and *Moscow Stations,*

Marvin's Room (Drama Desk, OBIE, and Outer Critics Award Winner), and national tours of the Drama Desk Award-Winner *STOMP*— the most successful show in Off-Broadway history.

Mr. Schuster is the President and CEO of Union Square Theatre Management, which until 2000 and the inception of West 37th Group, LLC, operated the Union Square Theatre, the Minetta Lane Theatre, and the Orpheum Theatre in New York, The Royal George Theatre in Chicago, and Marines Memorial in San Francisco. He holds a Bachelor's Degree in History and Theatre from the University of Nebraska and is a member of the Players Club, the board of directors of The Atlantic Theatre Company, and was a past director of the League of Off-Broadway Theatres and Producers.

THINGS THAT HAVE BEEN DONE TO ME– CONFESSIONS OF A THEATRE LANDLORD

ALAN SCHUSTER
Managing Member, 37 ARTS

As I write this chapter I am holding in my hands a *license agreement* with one of our current Off-Broadway tenants. The agreement is twenty-three pages long. The first agreement I negotiated in 1978 was three pages long. The twenty-page difference is everything that has been done to me in the past twenty-eight years. The ability of human beings to figure out new ways to circumvent contracts has proved to be just as creative as the shows they want to put on our stages. I started in this business as an actor, then became a stage manager, a playwright, a director, and finally—when I had burned all my bridges—a landlord and producer.

I discovered my first theatre, the Orpheum (2nd Avenue between 7th Street and Saint Mark's Place), on my morning commute to my job as the producer of a children's theatre company at the George Street Playhouse in New Brunswick, New Jersey. I would drive from the East Village to the Holland Tunnel down 2nd Avenue, and one day there was this huge "For Sale" sign on the immense marquee that juts out of the Orpheum Theatre. I assumed the marquee and the theatre were proportional (they were not—*large* marquee; *small* theatre). The building was a shell and although we bought it for nothing, it took all of our income for the first two years to pay for the renovation. Although I have not been at the Orpheum for a number of years, while there I had the pleasure of *booking* one of the longest running shows in Off-Broadway history, *STOMP*, which began performances in 1994 and is still running. Previously for the Orpheum I had booked *Little Shop of Horrors*, which ran for five and a half years; *Oleanna*, which ran for a year and a half; and *Key Exchange*, which ran for fourteen months. So, the Orpheum has proven to be the most successful Off-Broadway theatre in New York even though it's a shoebox with seats. In 1984, I built the Minetta Lane Theatre, and have also run the Second Avenue Theatre, The Cherry Lane Theatre, and The Union Square Theatre in New York, as well as The Royal George Theatre in Chicago. Currently I am the manager of the three-theatre complex 37 ARTS, located at

450 West 37th Street, and I am pleased to be a co-owner there with Harriet Leve, Dan Markley, Kevin McCollum, and Jeffrey Seller.

The 1994 Alan Schuster Off-Broadway co-production of *Oleanna*, by David Mamet. Pictured are Rebecca Pidgeon as Carol and William H. Macy as John.
Photo by Brigitte Lacombe.

Let's go back to where we started—with me holding my license agreement. Why a license agreement and not a lease? We theatre landlords license you producers the use of the space for only specific periods of time, reserving the rest of the time for our own uses. So if I book an off-night concert or a TV commercial, the income is the theatre's, not the show's. Also, we control the front of house, box office, house management, ushers, technical directors, and janitors—they are all theatre employees. The ticket receipts are controlled by the theatre and are distributed to the production on a weekly basis, after deduction of all our costs. (That way we can assure ourselves of getting paid.)

My experience is primarily Off-Broadway, although I have produced a few Broadway shows. The major difference between Off-Broadway and Broadway is the cost of doing business, directly related to the Broadway union contracts and the lack of most of those contracts Off-Broadway. To be classified as an Off-Broadway theatre, the house has to be less than 500 seats and should be outside the *Broadway Box* (34th Street to 66th Street, between 6th and 9th Avenues). Why do shows go to Broadway if they are so much more expensive than Off-

Broadway? Size matters. Some shows need large numbers of seats in order to pay for a huge cast or major production costs. Off-Broadway can be a development stop, but cannot be the ultimate destination if your *break even* needs to be in the hundreds of thousand dollars per week. Some egos will not allow themselves to work Off-Broadway and some careers require the potential of a Tony Award, which we do not have Off-Broadway.

As you can see below I have included the cover of our license agreement. Let's go through each of the lines. The deal is as follows:

LICENSEE	Who are we dealing with: an LLC, an LP, or a Corporation? An unknown entity or an ongoing company?
PLAY	Obvious.
COMMENCEMENT DATE	The first date an activity begins, be it rehearsal, load in, or even first date the Box Office opens.
REHEARSAL/ LOAD IN PERIOD	Should be time restricted so that we can get to the increased performance Licensee Fee sooner.
REHEARSAL/LOAD IN FEE	Usually its one-third to one-half of weekly Licensee Fee, but can be negotiated based upon how hot the show is and the market condition Off-Broadway.
WEEKLY LICENSE FEE	There is a standard rack-rate that the theatre will use as a benchmark. Usually if a break is going to be given it is within the critical first six weeks when a show's fate is usually determined.
WEEKLY SERVICE FEE	The personnel package (usually not negotiable). Our package includes Box Office, House Management, Technical Director, and custodial services. Some packages include ushers some do not.
WEEKELY OVERAGE FEE	Our standard overage is 5% of the gross from dollar 1. Again if a break is to be given it is usually in the first six weeks.
SECURITY DEPOSIT	Usually four weeks of License Fee (rack rate).
RESTORATION CHARGE	Currently $1.25 paid by the patron (used to pay for and maintain our very expensive New York real estate)

STOP CLAUSE	Usually a percentage of the Gross potential usually around 35 percent of capacity. This clause allows a theatre to vacate a threatre if a show is limping along for a negotiated period of time. The clause is seldom exercised but psychologically important. There can be exclusionary periods within the language of the agreement. For example: the first six weeks are usually excluded and so are traditionally difficult periods such as 4th of July or post–Labor Day.
COMPUTERIZED TICKET CHARGES	These charges will be deducted from the Gross Box Office Receipts at the time of each performance via the Box Office Settlement.
MAINTANCE FEE	Weekly fee for use of the system (in our case Ticketmaster-there are several other systems in use, such as Telecharge).
PER TICKET CHARGE	The cost to the show of printing each ticket.

These are the specifics of a deal done in broad strokes. Lets look at two clauses in our agreements that deal with the specifics we have already discussed. The use of the space when there is not a performance, and the STOP CLAUSE.

The use of space is reserved rights, so Article 5 of our License agreement is titled RESERVED RIGHTS:

5. RESERVED RIGHTS BY LICENSOR:

A. Licensor reserves for itself the exclusive use of the Theatre at any time and at all times not herein expressly granted to Licensee.

B. Licensor further reserves, without limiting other uses, the right, upon giving not less than seven (7) days prior notice, to permit rehearsals of other productions, filming, television productions, recordings, or any other use with respect to any other attractions in the premises during the term hereof, without any reduction of the Licensee's weekly payments hereunder, provided that such rehearsals or other attractions do not interfere with Licensee's use of the premises and its sets, props, costumes, etc. In the event of the use of the premises during Licensee's term for any other use, Licensor shall be responsible for all costs and expenses incurred as a result thereof and Licensor shall require the presence of one of its representatives during such use. In the event that either the sound or lighting systems of the Play are used, Licensor shall require the use of the house electrician or production soundman as applicable. Licensor shall be responsible to see that the Licensee's setting is restored and its lights restored and refocused in their original condition, if so required. Licensee shall be reimbursed for the use of Licensee's electricity, lamps, natural gas, fuel oil, and any other costs as mutually agreed upon. Licensor will indemnify and hold Licensee harmless from and against any claim, action, loss, or liability resulting from the use of the Theatre by Licensor or by any other party than the Licensee. Licensor must obtain all necessary permissions for use of Licensees production elements (including lighting, but such approval not to be unreasonably withheld). Licensor further agrees to engage and pay Licensee's representative for any and all uses of the Theatre described above and to provide ample time for the restoration of all elements of the production.

Licensor further reserves the right to purchase at box office prices six (6) tickets for each performance (house seats). Said house seats shall be Row X; seats 1–6 of the orchestra section of the Theatre. One pair of unused said house seats shall be released 48 hours prior to the performance and one pair of unused said house seats shall be released 24 hours prior to the performance. Final pair will be released 1 half hour before the performance Licensor will also be entitled to four (4) complimentary admissions to any performance of the Play for which tickets have been issued as "paper." Licensor shall further be entitled to purchase at box office prices, ten (10) additional pairs of house seats for the official opening of the Play at the Theatre.
STOP CLAUSE is article 14 in our agreement:

14. STOP CLAUSE:

A. Licensee agrees to present the Play at the start of the Performance Period and thereafter for eight (8) performances during each week until the run of the Play is terminated in accordance with this Agreement. If the Gross Weekly Box Office Receipts shall be less than the Stop Clause Sum for any two (2) consecutive week periods, either party shall, by delivering Notice of Termination no later than two hours before the performance on the Second Monday following the Sunday of the second qualifying week, have the option to terminate the run of the Play. In such event the Term hereof shall end at the close of the evening performance on the second Sunday following the aforesaid notice (or if notice is delivered after the two-hour mark on Monday after the third Sunday). Notwithstanding the foregoing, neither week of such two (2) week period shall consist of: (i) the first four (4) full weeks of performances; (ii) the week following July 4th; (iii) the period commencing Labor Day through Yom Kippur; (iv) the period commencing Thanksgiving through Christmas; (v) the weeks containing Passover and Easter.

1. In the event that the Licensor exercises it's right to elect to terminate this Agreement based upon the provisions set forth in subparagraph A. of this paragraph and provided that Licensee has otherwise complied with all of the terms and conditions of this Agreement and is not in default hereunder, then the Security Deposit shall be applied against the Weekly License Fee for the final one (1) week of the Performance Period, and the balance of the Security Deposit shall be liquidated damages. Unless the production elects to run for four additional weeks, then the standard return of security deposit applies.

2. In the event that the Licensee exercises it's right to elect to terminate this Agreement based upon the provisions set forth in subparagraph A. of this paragraph and provided that Licensee has otherwise complied with all of the terms and conditions of this Agreement and is not in default hereunder, then the Security Deposit shall be applied against the Weekly License Fee for the final one (1) week of the Performance Period, and the balance of the Security Deposit shall be retained as liquidated damages, without prejudice to Licensor's additional rights and remedies hereunder.

B. Under no circumstances shall Licensee or anyone acting on Licensee's behalf be permitted to purchase tickets for the purpose of avoiding the provisions of this Paragraph, nor shall Licensor take any action to purposely reduce Gross Weekly Box office Receipts below the Stop Clause Sum.

That gives you an idea of the specifics within the agreement. The most important thing when negotiating with a landlord is your show. If it is a hot property, then you have the leverage. If it is unknown but has some exciting elements (i.e., a star, a famous playwright, or a major director), the leverage is still in your favor. Market conditions will always prevail. I will look for the best play (or musical) I can find, and actually read the scripts and see the shows if I can. I have held the theatre empty or worked to extend weak productions in order to get to a specific show. To quote a successful British playwright, "The play is the thing." If you have a great one, you *will* make the deal.

Mike Isaacson

With his producing partner Kristin Caskey, Mike Isaacson produced the Broadway, National Tour, and West End productions of *Thoroughly Modern Millie* (six 2002 Tony Awards including Best Musical); *One Flew Over the Cuckoo's Nest,* starring Gary Sinise (2001 Tony Award for Best Revival of a Play); and *'night Mother,* starring Edie Falco and Brenda Blethyn (2004). He also worked on the Broadway productions of Arthur Miller's *Death of a Salesman,* starring Brian Dennehy (four 1999 Tony Awards including Best Revival of a Play); *You're a Good Man, Charlie Brown* (two 1999 Tony Awards); and *Jekyll & Hyde* (also first national tour). Current projects including *Legally Blonde—The Musical*, directed and choreographed by Jerry Mitchell, set to open on Broadway in the spring of 2007, and the 2006 Richard Rodgers Award-winner *True Fans*, a musical about three friends biking across America.

Mr. Isaacson is chair of the Investment Committee of the Independent Presenters Network (IPN), which is a producer of the 2005-06 season production *The Color Purple*, as well as the 2005 Tony Award-winning Best Musical, *Monty Python's Spamalot*. Other IPN productions include the Broadway production and national tour of *Thoroughly Modern Millie; Dr. Dolittle*, starring Tommy Tune; *Bombay Dreams*; *Starlight Express;* and the London productions of *Thoroughly Modern Millie* and *Edward Scissorhands*.

Mr. Isaacson is responsible for selecting and negotiating for shows for the US Bank Broadway Series at the 4,100-seat Fox Theatre in St. Louis, Missouri. He also serves on the Executive Committee of The League of American Theatre Producers and Presenters. He has a BA in English as well as an MBA from Saint Louis University, where he has also taught.

THE ROAD NOT TAKEN

MIKE ISAACSON
Vice President of Programming/Producer, Fox Associates/Fox Theatricals

Within their tribe, Broadway *presenters*—the people and organizations who host *touring Broadway* shows—joke about the calls from New York producers inquiring, "What would America think of…?"

Actually, it's a very shrewd question.

As in New York, the primary ticket buyer for Broadway shows throughout the U.S. is a woman thirty-eight to fifty-four years old. But as the business of the road has become more sophisticated, and more data has been collected and exchanged, it's clear that regional, cultural, and economic realities can often impact a show's success. When *The Full Monty* toured, producers and presenters were surprised to find that the demand for tickets was milder than it had been in New York. The same result occurred with Andrew Lloyd Webber's London and Broadway hit *Sunset Boulevard*. Even rock sure smash New York and road hits such as *The Producers* and *Mamma Mia!* have found the occasional city where ticket sales were soft.

The opposite happens too. While the recent Broadway revival of *The Sound of Music* was a moderate success in New York, its subsequent tour starring Richard Chamberlain was a blockbuster. Similarly, there are shows—mostly musical revivals—that are produced solely to tour: *Annie*, *West Side Story*, and *Jesus Christ Superstar* have had very successful tours in the past few years. A rewritten and redesigned edition of the London stage musical *Dr. Dolittle* is touring starring Tommy Tune with no plan to play in New York.

For the 2004–05 season, the combined gross of all Broadway shows was $769 million; for touring Broadway it was $934 million. The myth is that a hit Broadway musical or play spawns a road company that sweeps through the provinces collecting buckets of easy cash. Like many elements of producing in the *commercial* theatre, myth and reality are far apart. Producing for the road is a highly complex endeavor, and a producer must take into account a variety of variables that if not smartly attended to, can result in the cash buckets sprouting leaks.

This chapter will have two parts: first, a primer on the structure of how the road operates, focusing on deal structure and management obligations; second, a loose discussion of the culture of the road and how that impacts what is produced and what sells. Because the majority of touring shows are musicals, discussions and examples will focus on them. In the past few years, one new play (if that) has toured, although in the world of *everything changes,* the 2006–2007 season saw four touring plays *(Doubt, 12 Angry Men, Legends!,* and *Who's Afraid of Virginia Woolf?).*

To begin, let's define the basic roles and responsibilities of the *presenter* and the *producer.* The producer provides a show with a rehearsed cast, complete sets, costumes, lighting, sound, and production team (stagehands, hair, wardrobe, stage, and company management); the *marketing* materials to sell the show; and transports the entire production in a timely basis to the presenter's theatre.

The presenter is responsible for promoting and selling the show to its local audience; providing a theatre and its administrative staff; hiring local stagehands, musicians, wardrobe, and hair personnel to support the production; and operating the theatre during the period the show is *booked* (handling all functions involved such as house management, ushers, security, box office, and programs).

As simple as these divisions may read, it's a highly interdependent and complex operation. The key to good road producing is to understand the entire world of presenting: how presenters sell, the level of talent they have administratively as well as backstage, what they need to satisfy their audiences, and their physical and financial parameters. Similarly, the key to being a successful presenter is to understand every aspect of the show on its way to your theatre: to whom it appeals; how it looks, travels, and plays; and the philosophy and management style of its creators and those producing it. The national presenting community is just as diverse and idiosyncratic as the New York producing community. It's foolish to think that all rules can apply to every market, every show, or every presenter. With different histories, economic structures (*for-profit* vs. *nonprofit*; *Independent Presenters Network (IPN)* or a *Live Nation* partner), and community and marketing obligations, there are always market-to-market variances that impact a show and how it is presented.

Now, if you've made it this far, but you're beginning to wonder what's on HBO, read the next paragraph because it contains the most important idea in this chapter.

Like all commercial endeavors, the producer–presenter relationship is ruled by the *risk/reward relationship,* i.e., for both parties, how much is each willing to risk (read: spend) in order to make a potential profit? Simple, right? Hardly. Determining which show is worth the risk for you, how much you're willing to risk for it, and how you can sell the show to measure your risk, is what a presenter does. Determining the value of your show—both from a cost as well as a perceived value perspective—is what a tour producer does. That written, there are three primary deals that are used to define the producer/presenter risk/reward relationship: (1) *Guarantee*, (2) *Four-Wall*, and (3) *Co-production*.

The Guarantee Deal

The most common deal today—the guarantee—developed because New York producers were tired of taking the huge financial risk of mounting a tour for presenters only to subsequently finding road sales that weren't good enough for the tour to continue. The presenters would lose minimally, but the producer massively. It also created chaos because presenters would occasionally announce a show that would never arrive, inspiring audience confusion and anger, and the panic of finding another show to fill the slot. The guarantee served to stabilize the business of touring Broadway, and arguably allowed for its growth into a consistent national enterprise.

To ensure stability for both parties, the guarantee model demands that the presenter put up a guaranteed amount of money for a performance week, thereby reducing the producer's risk and ensuring that the show will arrive. The presenter must pay the guarantee even if the box office receipts don't meet the required amount. What the guarantee buys, however, is only the show at the loading dock. After the guarantee, the presenter pays for three other categories of expenses for which the presenter is also *at risk*: (1) *advertising*; (2) local stagehands, wardrobe, and hair staff; and (3) in the case of a musical, local musicians. After those bills are paid, the presenter receives income to pay for theatre rent and administrative costs. Finally, should there be monies after all these bills are paid, the remaining amount splits between the producer and presenter.

Before we look at an example, there are two other concepts that affect how the money is divided in a guarantee deal. First, the presenter also gets a series of box office deductions *off the top*—these include a group sales commission, a *subscription* commission, and credit card processing deductions for box office, phone, remote, and Internet sales. The theory here is that these items are necessary business tools (and costs) that benefit both producer and presenter, and their payments can't be at risk—they are essential services to the ongoing enterprise of touring Broadway. They also help the presenter immediately measure the risk involved in a guarantee because after paying the guarantee, the presenter begins to "earn" money first.

The other elements off the top are: (1) local taxes, and (2) theatre restoration charges. The theatre restoration charge goes to the theatre (sometimes a presenter doesn't actually own the theatre), to help with the enormous physical upkeep they require. As with the Broadway theatres, many of the theatres throughout the U.S. are quite old. With these elements we get an important distinction: *Gross box office* "the gross"; versus *Net Adjusted Gross Box Office Receipts*—the "net gross." Generally, guarantees are a fixed amount plus a percentage of the net gross.

Before your head is spinning, below is a very basic example of a financial settlement using simple numbers. At the bottom of the chart, you see what both a presenter and producer, respectively, have made on an engagement. Suppose *Cops: The Musical*, is a touring Broadway show and to buy a week of it a presenter must pay $250 thousand plus 10 percent of the net gross, and the proposed split is 60 percent to the producer and 40 percent to the presenter. And let's believe that those dancing cops were a solid hit in Tulsa, Oklahoma for a week, and grossed $750 thousand

TULSA COPS SETTLEMENT–GUARANTEE DEAL MODEL		
Gross		$750,000
Taxes and Restoration		$30,000
Adjusted Gross		$720,000
Total Box Office Deductions/Commissions (10%)		$72,000
Net Adjusted Gross Box Office Receipts (NAGBOR)		$648,000
Producer Guarantee ($250,000 + 10% NAGBOR)		$314,800
Presenter Variable Expenses	Advertising	$100,000
	Stagehands	$60,000
	Musicians	$40,000
Presenter Fixed Expenses		$50,000
TOTAL EXPENSES		**$250,000**
Balance		$83,200
	Producer Split at 60%	$49,920
	Presenter Split at 40%	$33,280
Balance		$0
TOTAL TO PRODUCER ($314,800 + $49,920)		**$364,720**
TOTAL TO PRESENTER ($72,000 + $50,000 + $33,280)		**$155,280**

out of a potential one million dollars. The settlement is seen in the table *Tulsa COPS Settlement—Guarantee Deal Model*, using rounded, estimated numbers.

The Four-Wall Deal

The second construct, the four-wall, is used by producers who are extremely confident they have a very popular show. Shows that have used this model include *Mamma Mia!*, *The Lion King*, and *The Phantom of the Opera*. In this case, the producer offers much tighter terms, but in exchange, the presenter has no risk while the producer takes enormous risk. In the inverse of the guarantee, no matter how many tickets are sold, the presenter gets paid. Essentially the producer is renting the theatre, hence the term *four-wall*. Presenters receive their deductions (usually slightly reduced from the guarantee amount), their fixed expenses, and a much smaller percentage of the split. The producer pays all the advertising, stagehand, and musician costs.

But in a four-wall deal, something else important happens. In the case of a guarantee, the producer and presenter are in a partnership for the engagement, sharing the division of duties. A four-wall deal acknowledges the greater role to be played by the producer in the engagement, which can play out in a myriad of ways—control of marketing strategy, determination of advertising budget, and in the case of Disney's *The Lion King*, even more of a role in house management. A four-wall doesn't eliminate the partnership, but it certainly shifts its balance.

Let's say that *COPS* is a worldwide smash hit, and toured on a four-wall deal as shown the table *Tulsa COPS Settlement—Four-Wall Deal Model*. Note in the

TULSA COPS SETTLEMENT–FOUR-WALL DEAL MODEL	
Gross	$750,000
Taxes and Restoration	$30,000
Adjusted Gross	$720,000
Total Box Office Deductions/Commissions (6%)	$43,200
Net Adjusted Gross Box Office Receipts (NAGBOR)	$676,800
Presenter Fixed Expenses	$50,000
Balance	$626,800
Presenter Split at 5% of NAGBOR	$33,840
Balance	$592,960
TOTAL TO PRODUCER	**$592,960**
TOTAL TO PRESENTER ($43,200 + $50,000 + $33,840)	**$127,040**

table that the balance of the producer's take would ultimately be $392,960, as the producer is responsible for paying the advertising, stagehand, and musician bills ($200,000) in a four-wall. It should also be noted with hit shows of this magnitude, advertising costs are often half of what is needed for a guarantee show. Think about it—word of mouth is the cheapest form of advertising, and monster hits are made through word of mouth. It's interesting to note that in recent years, smash hit shows such as *Wicked* and *Spamalot* have modified their risk by going out with very high guarantees, but also receiving a few of the other standard four-wall terms.

The Co-production Deal

The final model, the co-production deal, tries to moderate the risk factor from both the producer's as well as the presenter's perspective. In a co-production, a group of presenters put up the financing for a tour in the form of either an investment, *advances* against the *guarantee*, or both. The producer's risk now greatly reduced, they offer very favorable terms for the presenter, usually in the form of a lower than usual guarantee and a much greater percentage of the upside. Using *COPS...*, see the table *Tulsa COPS Settlement—Co-Production Model* for how the results might appear.

Now a fair question to ask is "How is a producer supposed to know what is the best deal for their show?" Because a producer needs to (and should) spend the majority of their time producing the show, the presenter mostly communicates and negotiates with two critical people: the show's *booking* agent, and its *general manager*. These two also provide the producer with the knowledge and experience to determine which is the best financial model.

The booking agent is responsible for actually selling and *routing* the show (i.e., determining which cities the show will play in and when), negotiating all the terms with the presenter, and issuing the contract. While this may seem like a simple job, it is wildly complex, requiring a substantial body of knowledge and experience. Bad booking has destroyed more than a few tours. Mistakes such as terrible routing (closing in Buffalo, New York on Sunday night, and having to be in Denver, Colorado by Tuesday), misunderstood deals ("I'm sorry my fax is old, but I thought that $80,000 was $30,000 so that's all I'm paying"), or lack of knowledge about regional peccadilloes ("The Upper Peninsula of Michigan is sort of deserted in January...") Even the most innocent of miscalculations can cost a show tens of thousands of dollars.

The agent also serves as a critical conduit between the show and the presenter, feeding both with each other's information and insights that often help shape critical marketing, financial, and production decisions. They are often in effect translators, helping each side understand the other's business.

TULSA COPS SETTLEMENT–CO-PRODUCTION MODEL			
Gross			$750,000
Taxes and Restoration			$30,000
Adjusted Gross			$720,000
Total Box Office Deductions/Commissions (10% Estimated)			$72,000
Net Adjusted Gross Box Office Receipts (NAGBOR)			$648,000
Producer Guarantee ($200,000 + 10% NAGBOR)			$264,800
Presenter Variable Expenses		Advertising	$100,000
		Stagehands	$60,000
		Musicians	$40,000
Presenter Fixed Expenses			$50,000
TOTAL EXPENSES			**$250,000**
Balance			$133,200
		Producer Split at 50%	$66,600
		Presenter Split at 50%	$66,600
TOTAL TO PRODUCER			**$331,400**
TOTAL TO PRESENTER			**$188,600**

The tour's general manager is also (but not always) the show's Broadway general manager, so they begin their work for the touring production with many lessons learned, and communication with the show's artistic and production teams in place. For the tour, the general manager is responsible for all the accounting, box office, and financial transactions with the local presenter, as well as ensuring that the show is functioning on and off stage. They too have an enormous body of knowledge and history they need to know in order to make a tour function smoothly.

The general manager's first critical responsibility is to work with the show's artistic and production staff to determine how much the production will cost on a per-week basis. This input is immediately transferred to the booking agent to help determine the cost of the guarantee. Once this is determined (and it often takes months of work), the general manager works with the production staff to make the performing and moving of the show as smooth, simple, and cost-effective as possible. These decisions have a direct impact on the expenses the presenter will have to pay, and they are critical, particularly those about the set. Most road shows close in a city after a Sunday night performance, have to break down the sets, costumes, and lighting, get them in the trucks, and then get to the next city and set up in order to make an 8:00 p.m. Tuesday night opening. Along with cast size, the design and production of a touring set can make or break a show's profitability. In fact, in recent years it has been the rule, rather than the exception, that a touring set has to be modified during the life of its tour in order to make the economics more sound. Outside of a few blockbusters such as Disney's *The Lion King* and *The Phantom of the Opera*, almost all shows undergo some level of rethinking and redesigning before (and often during) a tour. More than ever there is extraordinary pressure on a show's scenic, costume, and sound designers to deliver the maximum amount of a Broadway production in the most efficient manner possible.

Even with the best booking agent, an experienced general manager, and a show that is a solid hit on Broadway, no one can absolutely predict that a show will have a lucrative tour, which brings us to the examination of the question of what factors go into figuring out what sells on the road? To assume anyone could absolutely answer the question of what sells on the road is ludicrous; like film, television, and popular music, touring Broadway is a cyclical, fickle, and arguably unpredictable business. Yet, there are two principles that are constantly discussed:

There are subscribers, and there are people... and they all need to buy tickets.

Most touring Broadway presenters sell annual subscription packages of shows. Once a year, they package anywhere from four to six shows, and sell them to their subscribers at a discount with guaranteed seating. The subscription model helps both the presenter and the producer by having a base of tickets sold before they go on sale to the general public. (And this is why presenters may take a percentage off the top—to help defray the cost of marketing to and servicing their subscribers.) Except for a handful of markets, no producer and presenter can make a profit without strong single tickets sales on top of subscription sales.

Here's the grand irony: while subscribers tend to be more interested in the newest shows, single ticket buyers may be more reluctant to buy something they are unfamiliar with. Yet, if you continually offer a series of *Cats*, *Annie*, and *Les Misérables* every year, you will quickly lose your subscribers, while still doing pretty well in single tickets. In the way a politician needs to cover his or her base but also reach out to others to get elected, the same holds with selling tickets to shows. Most presenters look for a blend of the new and the popular that audiences want to see again. They also try to identify shows that may appeal to their traditional Broadway buyer, as well as other constituencies. It's no secret that the extraordinary appeal that *RENT* and *Wicked* hold with younger audiences has been integral to their enormous financial success. A key responsibility for the presenter is to work with the producer as early as possible to begin to educate their market and their subscribers about an unfamiliar show, and to begin to identify segments in their community to whom the show will appeal.

The Mike Isaacson co-production of the 2002 Tony Award-winning
Thoroughly Modern Millie; book by Richard Morris and Dick Scanlan; new music by Jeanine Tesori; new lyrics by Dick Scanlan. Pictured is Sutton Foster as Millie.
Photo by Joan Marcus, courtesy of the John Willis Theatre World/Screen World Archive.

It's not easy. Recently, producers and presenters have been struggling to understand the bigger issue of how news about a Broadway show gets to audiences across the country. As newspapers continue to cut arts coverage, as the only national television programs that occasionally cover Broadway are *The Today Show* and *Good Morning, America*, and the tabloid and entertainment news culture essentially ignores Broadway, it is harder and harder to get news of a show beyond the core audience that follows theatre. (And we're not going to mention how radio has given up on Broadway; that's very old news.) While the Internet is providing interesting new opportunities, finding new methods to spread the word of Broadway is a top priority.

Stars sell, so a show needs a star. And if not a star, a name. And, if not a name, how about a title?

Yes, there will always be consistent smash hits. When you build them, they will come. Cameron Mackintosh practically bred them during the 1980s and 1990s: *Cats, Les Misérables, The Phantom of the Opera, Miss Saigon.* But many (perhaps even most) touring shows are not automatic smashes. They may be worthy, wonderful shows but audiences across the country may not have heard of them. One way to get attention for an unfamiliar show and make it an event worthy to a ticket buyer is to cast a star.

This is a tricky area to explore, because first, everyone has his or her own definition of a star—one man's Diana DeGarmo is another's Debbie Reynolds. You can also make the case that Hollywood and television aren't making the number of stars that they used to, or at the very least, in an era of the art of overexposure, being a star is something entirely different from what it used to be. But is there any doubt that if Julia Roberts toured in *Hedda Gabler*, there wouldn't be an empty seat?

But big Hollywood stars don't tour, and even the days of Broadway stars touring are also long gone. Except for Cherry Jones in *Doubt* and Bill Irwin in *Who's Afraid of Virginia Woolf,* when you survey the last decade of Tony Award–winning actors, not one toured in their show. When they do, it usually works; the excitement generated by a Broadway star can generate sales. When Tonya Pinkins repeated her extraordinary Broadway performance in *Caroline, or Change* in Los Angeles, the grosses were much higher than those in New York.

So if you can't get a Hollywood or a Broadway star, what do you do? There are many talented actors who are recognized by audiences, who may not be stars but their presence in a tour can add a spark that inspires ticket buying. In the business, they are known as *names*, and very often you'll hear, "That tour needs a name." Translation: A slight edge that will get the public interested and close the sale. When names tour, they receive great interest from local radio and television, and when they walk out on stage, there is a spark of communal recognition that goes through the audience. A name in a show elevates the production to an event, and people buy tickets for events. Recent examples of such strategies include Maureen McGovern as Marmee in *Little Women*, Molly Ringwald in *Sweet Charity*, and Joely Fisher in *Cabaret*. The Weisslers have been geniuses in this methodology by strategically placing names in their many international companies of *Chicago*.

Sometimes a show may sell based on its title alone, understanding it gives a buyer a familiarity that gets them interested. Certainly Disney has capitalized on this idea through their stage adaptations of their film phenomena *Beauty and the Beast* and *The Lion King*. Confounding all expectations, a stage version of the film and television show *Fame* toured quite successfully and continues to play in London's West End. *Jekyll & Hyde* sold quite well in its pre-Broadway tour, and its title certainly helped it with its four-year Broadway run. But there are popular titles that didn't draw. The tour of *Footloose* went out within two months of its Broadway opening, and the results were tepid. (For the record, it is now extremely popular with stock and amateur groups.) Even with its family-friendly title, the tour of *Dr. Dolittle* has proven a mild draw, as did the tour of the musical version of the Tom Hanks film *Big*.

The question of touring revivals of classic Broadway titles (*The King and I, Camelot*) is particularly vexing. To begin with, you have to ask the following: revival for whom? There are audience members for whom *Oklahoma!* was a seminal experience, while there are others for whom *Cats* is their defining musical. Understanding the current cultural placement of a title is the first key to assessing its potential. The Rodgers & Hammerstein titles are enormously popular with school and amateur groups, but does that then inspire or dissuade audiences in paying for a Broadway production? In some cities it may, in others it won't. There are certain A-List titles—*Annie, West Side Story, The Sound of Music*—that are the safest of bets, but even these can sometimes occasionally fail to draw. In recent years, revivals have been having a harder time selling tickets, but it remains to be seen if this is a cyclical or permanent trend.

✦

I will conclude by answering a question I'm often asked (because for Fox Associates and Fox Theatricals, I serve as both a presenter and a producer): What is the difference between a Broadway and a road audience? Talk to any actor who has toured, and you will hear the same thing from them all: There is something distinctive and wonderful about road audiences. In New York, with an amazing array of theatrical choices available every night, and twenty-seven Broadway theatres running eight shows a week, it is sometimes easy for the public (and, *ahem,* the critics) to become blasé about Broadway and the artists who work there and the worlds they create.

Not so on the road. Road audiences cherish the excitement of a Broadway show in a distinct way. They not only celebrate the art form, but there seems to be an extra glee, an added dose of sheer wonder that people are actually talented enough to be doing this, and that they are doing this for *us here and now.* It's really marvelous to witness, and arguably the greatest reward for any tour producer or presenter. (After the split, of course.)

Investing and Raising Capital

Do you know what the first and second rules of show business are?
(1) Never put your own money in the show,

and

(2) NEVER PUT YOUR OWN MONEY IN THE SHOW!

—MEL BROOKS (VIA MAX BIALYSTOCK),

The Producers

Steven Baruch

Steven Baruch was born in 1938 and graduated (magna cum laude and Phi Beta Kappa in his junior year), from Yale University in 1960. In addition to a lifelong career in real estate, he has produced or co-produced, among many others, *Penn and Teller, Driving Miss Daisy, Frankie and Johnny in the Clair de Lune, The Cocktail Hour, Love Letters, Song of Sinapore, Marvin's Room, Oleanna, Jeffrey, Later Life, Angels in America, Damn Yankees, Forever Tango, A Funny Thing Happened on the Way to the Forum, Smokey Joe's Café* (the longest running musical revue in Broadway history), *The Weir, The Mystery of Irma Vep, Swing!*, and the first ever Broadway revivals of *The Sound of Music* and *Little Shop of Horrors*. He is currently represented on Broadway by *The Producers* and *Hairspray*.

Mr. Baruch and his partners have produced two national tours and two Broadway engagements of *Penn and Teller* (in addition to its two Off-Broadway runs); national tours of *The Producers* (two tours out currently), *Hairspray* (one tour out currently), *Driving Miss Daisy, Angels in America, Smokey Joe's Cafe, Swing!, The Sound of Music*, and innumerable national tours of *Love Letters*. They have produced *Frankie and Johnny in the Clair de Lune* and *Oleanna* in London; *Smokey Joe's Café* in London, Australia, Europe, and the Far East; *The Cocktail Hour, Marvin's Room* and *Oleanna* in Washington, D.C.; and *Jeffrey* in San Francisco.

Mr. Baruch regularly serves as guest speaker at theatrical seminars and panels, has lectured on theatrical producing at Yale and at other colleges, and operates the Arts Theatre in London. His productions have won Pulitzer, Tony, OBIE, Drama Desk, Outer Critics Circle, Lucille Lortel, and Grammy Awards.

FINANCING COMMERCIAL THEATRE

STEVEN BARUCH
President, Scorpio Entertainment

Having graduated from Yale University as a philosophy major—and therefore prepared for absolutely nothing in the real world (or, arguably, for everything)—I spent the first quarter century of my working life as an executive in a publicly owned real estate company. One of my co-workers was Tom Viertel (our grandmothers were sisters, whatever that makes us), and neither of us had the slightest notion of ever becoming involved in theatre.

In 1984, when Tom visited the Summer Olympics in Los Angeles, his brother Jack—now creative director of Jujamcyn Theatres, but then the drama critic for *The Los Angeles Herald Examiner*—took Tom around to a few L.A. shows that he had loved and reviewed favorably. One of them was a bizarre, dark, and fascinating magic act performed by two young guys by the names of Penn & Teller. Tom fell in love, I went out and saw them and also fell in love, and together we determined to bring them to the New York *commercial* theatre.

We had never even considered producing a show, and the notion of putting what essentially seemed like a variety act into a legitimate Off-Broadway theatre seemed like an idea from Mars. But we talked to Penn & Teller about it and found that the rights to bring them to New York were held by an experienced producer from the *not-for-profit* world (Richard Frankel, who had recently served as managing director of the Circle Repertory Company,* and was making his first foray into commercial producing). We had never met, or even previously heard of Richard, but the three of us sat down together and forged a partnership to bring *Penn & Teller* to the West Side Arts Theatre on 43rd Street. The critics raved, audiences were thrilled, and we continued to produce *Penn & Teller* shows for the next seven years or so—on Broadway, Off-Broadway, and on *national tour*.

The three of us, along with Marc Routh who joined us shortly after we started and is now a full and equal fourth partner, have produced more than fifty-five

---

* Circle Repertory Company was one of the most celebrated Off-Broadway theatres in history, winning many Tony Awards and producing Pulitzer Prize-winning plays, and with alumni running the gamut from Olympia Dukakis to Mary-Louise Parker. They closed their doors in 1996 after twenty-seven years.

shows together over the last twenty years, without—I can't resist saying—a single tense moment or harsh word that I can remember.

Stimulated by our unexpected triumph with *Penn & Teller*, we proceeded to produce or co-produce a long string of small, classy, non-musical Off-Broadway shows, among them *Driving Miss Daisy*, *Frankie and Johnny in the Clair de Lune*, *The Cocktail Hour*, *Love Letters*, *Marvin's Room*, *Jeffrey*, *Oleanna*, and *Later Life*. Virtually all of the above were successful both artistically and financially. We were spoken of in some quarters as the "Kings of Off-Broadway," and were the subjects of lots of articles written in places like *The New York Times*, *Variety*, *Business Week*, and even as far away as *The Washington Post*. Now, of course, we've become megalomaniacs who produce huge Broadway musicals; but in those days, at least, we were calm, modest, and relatively rational.

The alliance with Richard was a terrific one for both sides, I think, because he had a lot of experience in producing shows (about which we knew nothing at that point), but he didn't quite know how to go about raising the capital required to put them on. Tom and I at least had a bevy of rich real estate friends. By the mid-1980s the economy was booming and real estate, particularly, was flying. Tom and I were also by that time among the leading converters of rental housing to cooperative ownership throughout the New York metropolitan area, and we effectively financed *Penn & Teller* by calling up a number of our real estate connections and getting each of them to put a little bit of money into the total $175 thousand that a small Off-Broadway show actually cost in those days.

By the end of the 1980s, the real estate boom was over, the co-op conversion business was extinct, and most of our real estate friends were broke or at least in big financial trouble (as were Tom and I). We eventually worked our way out of it quite nicely, but we had launched ourselves at just the right moment, and by the time things in our little real estate world had collapsed, we were well on our way to being recognized producers of Off-Broadway plays and musicals.

The notion of *capitalizing* a show by putting together a significant number of very small investors seemed like a good idea to us and became more and more doable as our reputation for producing successful financial results grew. I think it's fair to say that today the most unique thing about our producing operation is that we've stuck to that pattern; that is, we're among the few, if any, producers who are capitalizing even huge Broadway musicals by bringing together sometimes literally hundreds of ten-thousand-dollar investors.

I might mention at this point that we think of producing shows as being a serious business, and given the fact that both Tom and I come out of a business background—and that Richard's involvement as managing director of Circle Rep put him more on the business side of producing than the artistic one—it's clear that at least in terms of our early training and function, we've been more business people than show people. I think it's also fair to say that we have a pretty solid record of success in this irrational business, and that this track record is at least partly attributable to a businesslike approach to putting on shows.

Because the key to attracting investors is most fundamentally a record of success, a quick word about that track record, at least as of this writing. We're often asked to put numbers on how our shows have performed, and it's always been a bit of a puzzle to figure out a sensible way to quantify how a pile of completely unique, separate businesses have faired in the aggregate. The one standard that's made sense to us is to ask what an investor's annual rate of return would be if they had put ten thousand dollars into every show that we ever produced—the complete flops, the big hits, and everything in between? We actually do this precise calculation at the end of every year, and the number always hovers around forty percent. That is to say that if an investor had participated in every show that we ever produced, they would have achieved an internal return of about 40 percent per year over our entire twenty-year producing history.

We four partners make all significant and substantive decisions about our producing activities together, usually at seemingly endless four-way partners' meetings every Thursday afternoon. But each of us has our own area of concentration expertise and activity, and mine happens to be raising money to capitalize our productions.

I have a list of more than 900 people who have either invested with us in the past or have expressed a specific interest in doing so in the future. For the most part these people have come to us by word of mouth as our producing reputation has grown over the years, but I occasionally write letters just asking (in a very low-key, brief, and non-threatening way), if someone would be interested in principle in participating in this kind of activity. Some of these investors turn out to be quite wealthy and would be prepared to invest significant sums in a show that seems promising, but often we set a modest cap on these participations, and in fact looking back over the years there have been very few investments that have exceeded ten thousand dollars in any given show. We've discovered a number of advantages, as well as disadvantages, in financing commercial theatre projects in this fashion.

Let's start with the disadvantages. Needless to say, it takes a huge and constant effort—and lots and lots of time—to find, court, and maintain relationships with this large an investor pool. An article about me in *Crain's New York Business* not too long ago read, "Many of Baruch's colleagues applaud his group's strategy, but say they would never have the patience to follow it themselves."* The article went on to quote several prominent Broadway producers who said things like, "I don't even know that many people…I prefer the ease of dealing with a limited number of people who can afford greater risk." Another producer said, "I would rather have a group of fewer investors and pay proper attention to them" (presuming, obviously, that we don't pay proper attention to ours). Continuing, he said, "When plays—forget musicals—cost $1–2 million on average, it becomes simply too much. I find producing hard enough without having to deal with a group of fifty investors. It would drive me bananas, and I think most of us feel that way." And a third major producer player said, "Cobbling together small increments takes too much time…if you're going to do a production today you need to move quickly. It doesn't allow you two years to raise your capital." (I can't resist pointing out that our investors are sufficiently ready to go so that when we're set to raise several million dollars, we can do so within a couple of weeks.)

Another disadvantage—a problem with which most producers would have no sympathy, I know—is the possibility of becoming over-subscribed, particularly with smaller shows. With enough investors to capitalize a huge musical, you can imagine that the day you do a small Off-Broadway play, you end up with many more interested people than you have room for, and have to disappoint lots of precious investors. The way we handle this problem, incidentally, is to have a lottery. In other words, we put the names of every interested investor into a hat and simply pull out the number required to fill the *capitalization*. At least those who are left out have been treated fairly and seem to understand enough.

My personal feeling is that the advantages of financing shows in this manner far outweigh the disadvantages. For example, nobody commits suicide if we fail, because the stake simply isn't high enough to warrant self-destruction. Also, small investors have no credit, no power, no voice, and, perhaps most importantly, no sharing in the *general partners'* profit points. And we never become dependent on large players who might desert us if a show in which they have a major investment disappoints them.

A not insignificant (if seemingly technical) advantage of having many small investors is the willingness of such players to allow us to use their investments as so-called *preformation capital*. Under regulations that guide the capitalization process of theatrical ventures, every investor has the right to require a producer

---

* Miriam Kreinin Souccar, "Serious Showbiz," *Crain's New York Business*, June 18–24, 2001.

to raise every last penny of the needed capitalization before that investor's money can be used. The need to start spending substantial amounts on such things as sets and costumes early in the process means that unless they are independently wealthy, a producer simply must use investors' money long before the last dollar of capital arrives at the bank. Some investors, at least, need to be willing to let the producer use their money prior to full capitalization, thereby taking the risk that full amount might never be raised and the show never actually mounted. This is a risk for which there is no reward offered, so what's needed is a significant level of confidence in the producer (presumably based on a track record in which he has never failed to fully capitalize in the past), and an amount which, if lost for this reason, wouldn't be crippling to the investor. So here again, smaller investments are helpful to the producer.

Some people have suggested that there is another advantage to raising money the way I do: namely, the ability to meet wealthy women. (Actually, I've been happily married for over forty years, and I never would have thought of that on my own.) It was such a delicious notion that when Charles Osgood featured a discussion at Sardi's restaurant in New York with the producers of *The Producers* on his *CBS Sunday Morning* program, I couldn't resist telling the following short but true story to a national audience: "You'll recall that *The Producers* is about an unscrupulous producer who sleeps with hundreds of little old ladies to get them to put money into his shows. Well, one of my little old ladies called me the day after attending opening night of *The Producers* and said, 'There's definitely something missing in our relationship...'"*

There's little doubt that having developed this large investor "family" has been very helpful in enabling our partnership to successfully mount several significant shows a year (if, in any given year, that many shows seem worth producing). But unearthing those potential investors is only half the battle. Once they actually participate in a show, we feel it's vital to keep them informed and entertained. This just isn't a rational enough business to allow us or any producer to sit back and let the numbers speak for themselves. The enterprise simply has to be fun and exciting for a producer to reasonably expect an investor to come back show after show.

We really do bend over backward to make sure that we come as close to accomplishing this goal as we possibly can. I keep a continuous stream of letters to investors on every show—updating them on the latest news and gossip, sending them press notices from around the country (or world) that they probably haven't

---

* "The Producers of *The Producers*," interview by Charles Osgood, *CBS Sunday Morning*, May 13, 2001.

The Steven Baruch co-production of the
2004 Tony Award-winning *Hairspray*; book by Mark O'Donnell; music by
Marc Shaiman; lyrics by Scott Wittman and Marc Shaiman;
a Baruch-Viertel-Routh-Frankel Group co-production. Pictured is The Company.
Photo by Paul Kolnik.

seen, and sending along whatever financial information is available. I simply hate long vacuums between communications with investors.

Part of this *investor relations* enterprise, incidentally, is making sure that everyone is persuaded that whatever I say in these letters can be relied upon as truthful. As part of our effort to establish credibility, for example, I send participating investors every review from a show they're involved in (including the worst pans that may have appeared anywhere). Another example of bending over backward (to be ruthlessly honest) has to do with our need to provide our many investors with opening night tickets and party passes. I make sure that everybody's seating location expectations are as low as possible, writing everyone, for example, that they can expect to be sitting in the theatre with their backs pressed up against the balcony wall, and to be standing—not sitting—at the party trying to balance their plate of food. Usually these opening night attendees are pleasantly surprised, but at least I've established a certain level of honesty in their minds, and I assiduously try to maintain that impression in every letter or conversation with an investor. A good rule of thumb when talking or writing to an investor, is to try hard never to put a positive spin on anything that doesn't absolutely deserve it.

We spend a fair amount of money trying to make this experience fun for investors. For each of our shows, every investor gets a framed poster (either hand delivered, or if they're from out of town, shipped to their office), a cast album (if it's a musical), a souvenir book (which retails for at least ten dollars in the theatre), and other appropriate goodies, if available. Investors are usually given an opportunity to purchase a show jacket, just like the cast does and, of course, to arrange *house seats* for themselves or for anyone they know and like—or, if it's a bad show, for anyone they don't like—any time they wish. Occasionally, a backstage tour is arranged for an investor if it's a special occasion.

All of these perks are not only costly to us but also significantly time-consuming and require effort. Fortunately, people who want to invest in theatre tend to be pretty interesting people, at least in my experience, so I thoroughly enjoy my many conversations each day with current or prospective investors. Some of them turn out to be presidents of huge companies or hospitals or universities, and many of them, though not well known, have interesting business or recreational pursuits of various kinds. Some have turned out to be indicted criminals... but that's the kind of thing that keeps this job interesting.

I mentioned that I'm part of a four-member group in which each partner carries his own weight in one or another specific area involved in mounting the shows we produce. I must add that in my judgment, each of my partners performs his specialized functions absolutely superbly and the four of us, each with our special area of effort and expertise, form a fairly competent and experienced producing entity. It would be hard, I think, for a single producer to be able to carry on the kind of program we maintain without this kind of help. There's no doubt that I'm able to build a roster of investors and to relate to them on a regular basis principally because I have highly skilled partners who are performing, at a high level, the other necessary functions of producing in the commercial theatre. Hats off to all three of them and I can only hope that my contribution to the enterprise is the equivalent of theirs. I'd like to think that they believe it is.

Rodger Hess

Rodger Hess Productions Inc., founded in 1973, produces live theatrical events. Broadway: *Six Dance Lessons in Six Weeks, Wait Until Dark, 1776, Annie: 20th Anniversary Production, Joseph and the Amazing Technicolor Dreamcoat, Jelly's Last Jam, Leader of the Pack, The Five O'Clock Girl.* Off-Broadway: *My Old Lady, Water Coolers, Cowgirls, Fallen Angels, Potholes, Blame it on the Movies, How I Got That Story*; Touring: *Six Dance Lessons in Six Weeks, Swing, Finian's Rainbow, Annie, A Chorus Line, Evita, Elvis: A Musical Celebration, Run For Your Wife,* and *Nintendo World Championships.*

Mr. Hess created and produced the worldwide touring shows starring the Warner Bros. and DC Comics, Inc. cartoon characters including *Bugs Bunny Follies,* and *Bugs Bunny Meets the Superheroes, Bugs Bunny in Space, Bugs Bunny Sports Spectacular, Bugs Bunny Circus.* Mr. Hess has written numerous articles for publications including *The New York Times, New York,* and *How About A Little Action?* (betting games in golf, distributed by *The Booklegger*). Mr. Hess serves on the board of the Manhattan Theatre Club, the executive committee of the Maltz Jupiter Theatre, the advisory board of Theatreworks USA, and is a governor of the League of American Theatres and Producers. Mr. Hess is on the advisory board of SCAN-NY, an inner city settlement house provider, and is past co-chairman of The Associates, Mt. Sinai Hospital New York, and the Contemporary Action Committee of the American Jewish Committee.

DISPOSING OF DISPOSABLE INCOME

RODGER HESS
President, Rodger Hess Productions

As of this writing I have produced or co-produced approximately twenty-five shows. They were staged On Broadway, Off-Broadway, and in arenas as well as convention centers. They appeared on *tour* in the United States, Canada, Central America, South America, Australia, Spain, and England. They have been performed in English, Spanish, and Portuguese. They all had one thing in common—they had to be funded. I look forward to sharing with you the fundraising lessons I learned and mistakes that I made. I hope what follows will make your journey more profitable.

I am going to make two assumptions about you: First, you are not independently wealthy or if you happen to be, you do not wish to put all of your money *at risk*; and second, you do not employ sales people to raise money for you and are apprehensive about your ability to do so on your own.

There are two basic types of *offerings* for raising money: *public* and *private.* Within those categories there are two basic entities that can make either of those offerings: a *limited partnership* or a *limited liability company.* In a public offering (rarely used), you can advertise for investors and must be approved by the Securities and Exchange Commission. In a *private offering* (most widely used), you cannot advertise but you are exempt from registering with the Securities and Exchange Commission. One of the most compelling reasons to use a limited partnership or limited liability company is that the concentration of authority is with you, the *general partner* of a limited partnership, or the *managing member* of a limited liability company, whereas in a corporation your authority is shared with the stockholders.

In both public and private offerings there have been a few unsuccessful attempts to raise money for a *blind pool.* In a blind pool a large sum of money is raised that can be put into a number of shows to be selected by the general partner or managing member. The investors have no advance knowledge of the shows in which their money will be invested.

LLC/LP is the limited liability company and the limited partnership—the most widely used vehicles for raising money. The differences between the two will not affect the fundraising information to follow. For simplicity I will use terms associated with a limited partnership.

In a limited partnership the producers, for the most part, are referred to as the general partners. The investors are referred to as *limited partners*. I say for the most part because some investors who put in a substantial amount of money negotiate to have their name on the same line as the producers but they are not considered general partners. The basic difference between the general partners and the limited partners is that the general partners make all the financial and creative decisions of the partnership. In a limited partnership their financial exposure is *unlimited* should the project go over budget or a lawsuit be instituted for whatever reason. In a limited liability company the parties with decisional authority are called the managing members. Their liability is *limited* but the filing fees are often more expensive. In a limited partnership or LLC the investor is only exposed up to the limit of his or her investment.

Both vehicles pay the investors back first out of profits (return of capital). After the return of capital, the net profits are split between the investors and the producers on a 50/50 basis. For example, let's say an investor puts $100 thousand in a production *capitalized* at one million dollars. His percentage of the capitalization therefore is ten percent. From the first one million dollars of profits the investor will receive 10 percent (one hundred thousand dollars). From the next one million dollars of net profits, the investor will receive fifty thousand dollars, since he is now sharing the net profits with the producers on a 50/50 basis. There are variations in these scenarios as there are in most deals. In England, for example, the sharing is generally 60 percent for the investor and 40 percent for the producer. You will note that I have used the terms profits and *net profits*. Prior to the return of the capital it took to mount the show the money returned is out of the weekly profits, or *operating profits*. Once *recoupment* has been reached the monies then distributed are referred to as net profits. Once recoupment has been reached some entities such as the *general manager* and or star(s), among others, negotiate a share of the profits to be deducted *off the top* from 100 percent of the net profits. The amount remaining to be distributed is therefore referred to as *adjusted net profits*. For example, let's say recoupment has been reached in our one million dollar show. Our star has negotiated for 2.5 percent of net profits off the top. From the one million dollars of net profits, twenty-five thousand dollars goes to the star. The general partners and limited partners will split the remaining $975 thousand on a 50/50 basis. The $975 thousand is the amount of the adjusted net profits.

When you create a limited partnership, your *lawyer* will have to prepare a *private placement memorandum, a limited partnership agreement*, and *subscription documents*. The private placement memorandum can be lengthy and sets forth all the information about the project including among others, the risk factors, the units being offered, descriptions of the general partners, agreements relating to the play, use of proceeds, estimated weekly budget, tax matters, rights of general and limited partners, share of losses between general and limited partners, termination of the partnership, financial reports, other financing, who may invest, the budget, biographies of the creative people involved, a description of the show, the areas in which the investors participate and the risks involved, and so on. The risks involved are in **bold type** which will no doubt unnerve you.

Under the limited partnership you can raise money from an unlimited number of *accredited investors*. An accredited investor is one whose individual net worth, or joint net worth with spouse, at the time of investment exceeds one million dollars. Real estate can be counted for purposes of determining net worth. A person who had an individual income in excess of $200 thousand in each of the two most recent calendar years, or joint income with spouse in excess of $300 thousand in each of those years, and who reasonably expects an income in excess of such amounts in the current calendar year, is also an accredited investor.

There are other entities that can invest which have their own set of definitions to qualify as an accredited investor, such as a trust, a tax exempt organization, and a corporation, but let's stick to private individuals (if all of the owners of a corporation, partnership, or limited liability company are themselves accredited investors then the entity is automatically accredited). A principal of the general partners is automatically an accredited investor even if he or she does not meet the financial criteria.

You can use a limited partnership agreement and subscription document and avoid the private placement memorandum if your budget is one million dollars or less, or if all the investors are accredited. You are always limited to accepting money from thirty-five or fewer non-accredited investors to add to your accredited ones.

If your offering is subject to New York law, the subscription documents need to be filled out by your investor. It will request the method of ownership (i.e., an individual, husband and wife, joint tenants or tenants in common, corporation, partnership, and limited liability company), among others. It will also ask the investor to fill in the amount their investment, address, social security number, and so on.

The subscription documents will also ask your investor if the money invested can be used immediately—waiving any refund, not waiving any refund, or not authorizing immediate use of the funds. Money raised cannot be spent until the minimum amount of the capital necessary (as stated in the papers) to produce the show has been obtained.

Why would an investor allow the use of their investment if the partnership has not been formed? In principle, an investor would not want to put his or her money at risk (to be spent) prior to full capitalization but there are reasons why investors allow the *up front* use of their money (use the investment prior to capitalization). For example, if the investor has confidence that the project will get off the ground, and knows that the producer has expended his or her own money for years in pulling the project together, allowing the producer the up front use of investor's money is a courtesy. I have invested in a number of Cameron Mackintosh shows, producer extraordinaire of such shows as *Cats*, *Les Misérables*, *Miss Saigon*, and *Phantom of the Opera*, to name only a few. I know that he has spent his own money in developing these shows and I know the shows for which he is seeking funds will be produced; therefore, I have no problem with allowing him the use of my investment prior to the completion of the partnership.

There are situations where you can get an extra benefit for the use of your up front monies. As you can imagine, you will need to spend thousands of dollars to develop a show before you go out to raise money. You will need to *option* a property, hire a lawyer, create artwork, and produce workshops and *readings*. All of this takes capital or front money. In New York there has been a law limiting the number of front money investors to four. It is unclear whether any amendment to Federal Securities Law has eliminated this limitation, but I feel it is still prudent to comply. In return for the use of their money up front, investors are entitled to receive an amount equal to what their investment bears to the aggregate from the limited partners' side of the profits. They are also entitled to money from your side (i.e., the general partner's share of profits). There are a variety of formulas that can be used but let's say for someone putting up 10 percent front money you give them a *one for two*. This means that in our one million dollar show an investor who has given you one hundred thousand dollars for use up front will receive 5 percent of the net profits from the limited partners side (i.e., 10 percent of the fifty percent to which all investors are entitled, for having provided 10 percent of the aggregate amount provided by all investors) and 2.5 percent (1 percent of the producer's net profits for every 2 percent in which the investor is entitled from the investors' net profits) from the general partners' share of net profits.

It is important for you to understand the private placement memorandum. Investors will undoubtedly ask you questions about the contents. You will not likely be expected to answer tax questions. You can recommend that they seek tax advice from their accountants. Under the current tax code *passive loss* from a theatrical investment can only be deducted from a *passive gain*. A passive investment is one in which you have no control over the management of the enterprise (stocks, bonds, etc.).

At the beginning of my career I was asked many questions about the investment documents. I intuited that potential investors were checking out my knowledge of the business. You will find, I believe, that most of the investors are investing in you. They should know that you don't know if the show is going to be a success. Therefore do not use any puffery. You can convey excitement about the property, the creative staff (director, choreographer, set-light-costume designer, etc.), the cast, the potential for *subsidiary rights* income and, most importantly, why you believe in the project. You should never guarantee success or make unsubstantiated claims—most theatrical investments are unsuccessful.

It is important for you to tell your potential new investors that investing in the theatre is very risky and that they should be prepared for the total loss of their investment. The private placement memorandum will tell them the same thing in **bold type** so you may gain some honesty points for being up front.

People invest in the theatre for a variety of reasons. Broadway theatre owners might invest in the show to insure that the property is performed in one of their houses. *Presenters* may invest if they believe that ultimately the show will tour *on the road* and they wish to ensure their participation. Movie companies might invest for obvious reasons. Civilians, often referred to as *angels*, invest for the excitement of being involved on Broadway. Do not underestimate this. Broadway has sex appeal for a number of investors. They love to go backstage, meet the performers, attend the opening night, and be brought up to date with *publicity*, newspaper articles, and reviews. Keep in touch with them as often as you can. Send them the show poster, the script (if it exists), and the cast recording—if there is one. Investors appreciate being kept in the loop. They also love to be able to call your office for *house seats* (orchestra section seats controlled by the producer) to any of your Broadway shows. I produced a musical about Elvis Presley. It was *booked* on the road with *guarantees* for at least forty weeks. That meant that the investors were guaranteed a return on their investment unless no one wanted to see the show—an unlikely event. We had not scheduled the show for New York because we were not sure the critics would embrace the music or subject matter. Many investors passed on the opportunity because there was no guarantee that the show would play New York. They preferred to be at risk in a Broadway venture than to invest in a show that on paper guaranteed a better chance at recoupment. I was amazed but it taught me how appealing it is for some to be involved on Broadway.

Most investors will ask where their money will be used, in what areas of income they participate, when the money is required and, if the show is successful, how long it will take before they get their money back. With respect to the areas in which the investors participate, your contract with the author will give you the right to share in the author's subsidiary income provided you have produced the show on the road or in New York for a negotiated number of performances. Subsidiary income is generated from stock and amateur performances, *second-class productions*, movie sales, and from foreign productions. Under the APC (Approved Production Contract of the Dramatists Guild)—the document which sets forth most of the basic deal points between a producer and author—if the author of a musical is a guild member, the producer has the right to choose among

The Rodger Hess co-production of the 1992
Tony Award-winning *Jelly's Last Jam*; music by Jelly Roll Morton;
additional music by Luther Henderson; lyrics by Susan Birkenhead. Pictured are
(center) Savion Glover as Young Jelly and (right) Gregory Hines as Jelly Roll Morton.
Photo courtesy of and ©Martha Swope.

three different sets of percentages and durations of participation for each type of exploitation (there are four sets for a non-musical play). Under the APC for foreign productions, the producer's share of the author's income is twenty-five percent, revivals twenty percent. Under the APC, the producer's share in the author's motion picture income lasts the term of the author's copyright. Some budgets included in the offering documents have a recoupment schedule based on a variety of percentage of capacities.

The strategies used for fundraising can vary depending upon the nature of the show. As corny as it sounds I have always followed two principals with respect to the daunting task of raising money for a show: (1) the harder you work the luckier you get, and (2) just do it.

Pueblo was my first show. It was based on a true incident surrounding the capture of the USS Navy vessel *Pueblo* by North Korea in 1968. The captain and the crew were released after a year when the United States admitted that the USS *Pueblo* was indeed a spy ship. The play received offers from the Mark Taper Forum in Los Angeles and the Arena Stage in Washington, D.C. I *licensed* it to the Arena Stage and began my first fundraising efforts. Their production gave me an opportunity to preview the show to potential investors. *The Pueblo* received wonderful reviews. It became clear that a polemic with a cast of forty-plus could never recoup on Broadway. I stopped trying to raise the money. ABC-TV acquired the rights to produce the show on television and the star, Hal Holbrook, received an Emmy Award for his performance. I learned that despite good intentions to the contrary, *it's the budget, stupid. Pueblo* took so much of my time that I had to get a job. I went to work for the Licensing Corporation of America, which represented the licensing rights to a variety of properties including the Warner Bros. and DC Comics, Inc. cartoon characters. I approached them with the idea of building sets of costumes that could be worn by actors representing their various cartoon characters such as Bugs Bunny, Daffy Duck, Porky Pig, Elmer Fudd, Road Runner, Wile E. Coyote, as well as Batman, Robin, Wonder Woman, and The Joker, among others. They agreed. I produced a number of small shows featuring the various properties that were performed at shopping centers, state fairs and amusement parks, among other places. I then strung together a number of these small productions into a large one called *The Bugs Bunny Follies* that opened at the Westchester Premiere Theatre. The show was a success and LCA allowed me to create my own company representing the rights to the Warner Bros. and DC Comics, Inc. cartoon characters. *The Bugs Bunny Follies* attracted people from Madison Square Garden, who had wanted to enter the family show touring business. They financed the next five productions, which were performed throughout the world in arenas and theatres in several foreign languages. The tours lasted for eight years. I was paid a weekly fee by Madison Square Garden plus a percentage of the profits and was able to operate as an *independent* producer.

These six shows that I produced at the beginning of my career, all of which were funded by others, and five of the six paid me a fee and a percentage of the profits. I cite these examples to illustrate that not all of your projects need to take the customary financing route.

Evita and the *Nintendo World Championships* were two projects that took another funding route. I acquired the rights to produce *Evita* in South America. While I started the traditional funding route of calling people who I thought might be interested in the project, various promoters in South America, desirous of being the presenters in their local markets, offered *advances* to secure their position. The advances totaled an amount close to the amount we needed to fund the show. The advances would be just that—an offset against what we would have normally charged them to bring the show to their country under their auspices. The danger of using advances is that if the show—for whatever reason—is cancelled and you don't show up, you must repay the money advanced. Fortunately this did not happen with *Evita* and we played every market with a show capitalized, for the most part, with promoter advances.

I co-produced the *Nintendo World Championships*. This was a tour that showcased Nintendo products, had an entertainment component and a competition with an entrance fee, and quite substantial prizes for the winners. It was scheduled to tour thirty cities and play in convention centers. My partners were able to secure advances from five corporate sponsors, the totality of which added up to the amount we needed to fund the show. Again, the downside was if the tour folded, we would owe the sponsors the money committed. The tour played every market. I grant you these are non-traditional ways to fund projects but, as you can see, they do exist and they do happen.

Let's return to Elvis. As he lived in Memphis, Tennessee, I surmised there would be a number of people there who would have a special interest in investing in the show. I talked to a friend of mine in the area who gave me a list of potential investors. I booked a restaurant and invited them. The authors had created a series of storyboards with colorful graphics, which explained the arc of the show. I wrote out what I wanted to say and then memorized it. The conclusion of my presentation and the actual show ended with the death of Elvis. By the time I got to this point I was in tears. I was so invested in the concept and moved by the subject matter that I couldn't help myself. It happened every time I made this presentation. I am not suggesting a similar route but being passionate about what you are selling will have a positive effect.

What about the shows that fail? Will those investors ever invest with you again? I have found that if you produce a well-directed, well-cast, handsome-looking production, and if you keep your investors in the loop every step of the way, many will return.

I had an interesting situation with *Finian's Rainbow*. I intended to bring it to Broadway. I knew people loved the score. I arranged a series of *backer's auditions* consisting of three actors singing the score and I described the scenes that preceded the songs. I was able to raise the money and *enhance* two *out-of-town* productions. This means that I found several theatres interested in presenting the show but not on a Broadway scale. I made up the difference between their budget and mine with enhancement money. I was unhappy with the production and felt that it would not succeed on Broadway. Since I believed my investors had invested in the potential Broadway opportunity, I gave them their money back and took the hit for the enhancement money. Legally, I didn't have to and most of them were shocked to get their money back. Over half of them said to put them down for my next show.

These dog and pony shows, or backers' auditions, are a relatively inexpensive way to showcase your product. Actors are happy to do them for the experience and a shot at being in the show if it moves forward. You can pay them a modest honorarium for their work. Full-blown workshops and staged readings are another route but they are more expensive than hiring actors to read the play in someone's apartment. Many of these are accompanied by set models and costume sketches.

It helps to have partners at the beginning of a project who share your interest in the show. It will alleviate you from having to raise all of the money. I would suggest you do not attempt to produce a revival on your first outing. If you are unsuccessful in raising the money, the authors stand to lose their income from stock, amateur, and foreign productions during the time you are fundraising. This is because you will need to have the licensing agency which licenses the show (grants organizations the right to present/produce the show) curtail their efforts so as not to dilute the value of your forthcoming production. The authors (to protect themselves from the possibility of your not raising the money), will expect to receive a healthy advance if they allow you to option their property at all.

No matter what method you choose to market your material to potential investors, never lose sight of the fact that most of them will be investing in you.

Apart from the unusual situations, you will have to raise the money the old-fashioned way (i.e., you will have to call friends, relatives, and acquaintances). You might want to peruse the names of benefactors of *nonprofit* arts organizations—they will be listed in the donor section of their programs. Most investors are wealthy and have discretionary income. Their names appear in a variety of publications and lists. Ferret them out and make cold calls and/or send letters describing your project. The letters must have a legal, fundraising disclaimer. Your attorney can give you the wording. If you are not prepared for rejections, disinterest, and downright rude reactions, pick another profession.

To be successful at fundraising, as I have stated before, you must believe in the project and the creative people associated with it. It is important to network at every opportunity and let people know what you do for a living. Most people are fascinated with the business. You never know when someone will say, "Please let me know about your project—I might be interested in investing."

Building a Team

A producer is a banker,
a cheerleader, and a fireman.

—AMY DANIS

George Allison Elmer

ILLUSTRATION BY DOUG GERBINO

George Allison Elmer was a theatrical producer and general manager, retiring in March 2004. He continues to act as a commercial theatre management consultant.

Mr. Elmer has produced theatre pieces, industrials, special events, and charity benefits.

He was managing director of the nonprofit Broadway theatre, producing company, and acting school, Circle in the Square (1993–1995); managing director of The Philadelphia Theatre Company (1978–1979 season); co-producing director of Merry Enterprises Theatre (1972–1976); and has optioned and developed more than a dozen plays and musicals.

Among other productions, he has general managed: *Duet* at The Greenwich Street Theatre, *The Countess* at the Lamb's Theatre; *Doctor, Doctor!* at the Players Theatre; *Remembrance* at the John Houseman Theatre; *Ruthless* at the Players Theatre; *Cut the Ribbons* (also executive producer) at the Westside Theatre (Downstairs); the revival of *The Rothchilds* at Circle in the Square (Downtown); *Quiet on the Set* at the Orpheum Theatre; *Spare Parts* at Circle in the Square (Downtown); the Broadway musical *The Prince of Central Park* at the Belasco Theatre; *Other People's Money* at the Minetta Lane Theatre; Circle in the Square's Broadway presentation of the Gate Theatre of Dublin's production of *Juno and the Paycock* at the John Golden Theatre; *Hair for the Next Generation* at the United Nations General Assembly; Steinway and Sons *Celebration* at Carnegie Hall; the commercial Off-Broadway run of *The Garden of Earthly Delights*, for Music Theatre Group/Lennox Arts Center, at the Minetta Lane Theatre; the Broadway production of *The Musical Comedy Murders of 1940* at the Longacre Theatre; *Inner Voices* for the 1986 Spoleto Festival at the Dock Street Theatre; and *Nite Club Confidential* at The Ballroom.

Mr. Elmer worked with Dorothy Olim Associates, Inc. as associate general manager and company manager (1982–1986), during which time that firm provided theatrical general management services to more than twenty-five productions presented on Broadway, Off-Broadway and out-of-town. He also worked with the press agent offices of Seymour Krawitz and Frank Goodman.

Mr. Elmer has been the general manager of Theatre Four, the Astor Place Theatre, the Jack Lawrence Theatre, and the Audrey Wood Theatre. He was also house manager of the Martin Beck Theatre and the Eugene O'Neill Theatre.

He holds a BFA in Theatre from Virginia Commonwealth University (formerly Richmond Professional Institute).

DEVELOPING A THEATRICAL PROPERTY

GEORGE ALLISON ELMER
General Manager

There are several motivations for wanting to develop a theatrical property (which I will refer to as a *play* or *production*). This chapter is intended for the individual whose ambition is to facilitate taking a play from its current draft form to the realization of a script that is deemed ready for *commercial* production, with the desire to be the producer of that commercial production. However, those wishing to simply allow the playwright to hear the current draft form of the play or organize a *reading* to solicit potential producer interest are encouraged to read the entire chapter to understand the options available to them and the limitations and/or obligations that are associated with each option.

There are two definitions of *development* commonly used in the American theatre industry. The first definition is *refining a dramatic text*. That is, assisting the playwright with developing the play from its current draft form to a script that is deemed ready for commercial production, and is the one on which I will focus. The second definition is *fundraising*. In the *nonprofit* arena, the person responsible for soliciting grants, contributions, and other fundraising activities usually has the title of Director of Development, and is the head of the institution's Development Department. In the commercial theatre arena, development in this sense is *seeking interest from potential producers, co-producers, associate producers, and/or investors*. It is important to remember this when using the words *development, develop,* and *developmental*, so that appropriate supporting language can be employed to clarify the usage.

If it is your sole intention to seek interest from potential investors, then you should retain a practicing *theatrical attorney* to advise you on: the documentation required for the type and level of funding you are seeking; and what you must say, may say, and can't say in connection with the documentation. If you do not have in-depth knowledge of the current commercial theatre arena and/or budgeting skills, you should engage a *general manager*. And, if you intend to use professional actors, you should get a copy of the appropriate (Broadway or Off-Broadway)

Backers' Audition Code from Actors' Equity Association. This chapter does not address *backers' auditions* directly.

Now, before going on, I want to address the qualifications that I believe are necessary to contemplate facilitating the development of a play and producing one or more developmental production(s) of a play: a reasonable amount of intelligence and the capability of learning as you go; self assurance; a reasonable amount of people skills; an appreciation of theatre; a genuine desire to acquire knowledge about all aspects of the business of show business and who does what, where, when, and why; capital resources (either one's own or accessible from others); and the determination to see the play (theatrical property) of *your choice* come to life on the stage.

Never forget that every seasoned producer began as a tyro.

A producer becomes the producer of a play when the live stage performance rights (see *Option Agreement*) are acquired from the playwright. In order to realize a production of the play, the producer must provide and/or acquire the required financing. Everything else, except determining who to engage for delegation, can be delegated.

Some scripts grabbed me all at once and I immediately envisioned them in production and determined the appropriate commercial *venue* (i.e., no development needed).

However, when I found a script that intrigued me, before I contacted the playwright, I would invite a few actor friends to sit in my living room and give the play a *cold* (unrehearsed) *reading* (I call this an *informal reading*), for one or two of my mentors (not potential backers) and myself, after which we would discuss the play, its merits and its potential (usually with beverages and snacks— if not a meal). Sometimes I found that I had to do this twice to make certain that the script just didn't have it or that I wanted to continue. When I was satisfied that I didn't have just a passing interest, but that I was acquiring a passion for the potential of the play, I then mulled over my developmental and commercial production options (the beginning of long term strategic planning). I also made a list of the directors that I thought were approachable for both the developmental process and the ultimate commercial production of the play. (I never liked the idea of planning to switch horses midstream.)

Presuming that I didn't already have the information, I then contacted the playwright to determine the history of the play (readings, other developmental presentations, productions, and/or publication) and what, if any, rights in the play were outstanding. If the play was unencumbered (or I did not find the outstanding rights counterproductive), I expressed my interest in producing the play (no specifics), and if the playwright responded positively, I made an appointment to meet (presuming that we didn't know each other) and begin to get to know each other and make my preliminary *pitch*.

When I met with the playwright, I would have prepared an oral resume that focused on my business and theatre-related background. I tried to find out the playwright's educational and vocational background, what other plays they had written, and their production history, if any. Based on their responses, when appropriate, I tried to determine how frequently they attended theatrical productions and over what period of time, and their knowledge of both landmark plays and productions. I also asked if they were a member of the Dramatists Guild. Whenever appropriate, I inquired about people we may have known, and made appropriate comments on interests we had, in common. Only after this "getting to know you" did I begin to discuss my interest in the play, my feelings about the current draft of the script, and my intentions. My objective was to determine if the playwright agreed with my assessments and would welcome (or at least agree) to further development of the current draft of the play and was interested in pursuing my (generally outlined) game plan. If all went well, before making arrangements for our next meeting, I would ask if they had representation (an agent or attorney).

Before I put time and money into pursuing the first step of my plan, I would firm up my strategic planning (both short-term and long-range) in order to determine the nature and extent of the rights I wanted to secure in the *option agreement*, with particular attention to the time I believed would be necessary to realize each step of the plan (including reasonable wiggle room).

Although I have embarked on the development of a play with a simple rights agreement allowing only for a reading and/or showcase production of the play with a *first right of good faith negotiation* provision for a full commercial option agreement, I don't recommend this approach. I believe it is far better to enter into an all-encompassing option agreement that allows for all potential levels of development prior to the commercial exploitation of the play, with the payments due to the playwright being proportionate to the production level.

For example: "One hundred dollars and other good and valuable services" for the right to present up to five *public readings* and five backers' audition readings (*private readings* [limited to myself, the playwright and potential actors and directors, unless otherwise agreed to by the playwright] are without any payment required); One thousand dollar advance against royalties (of five percent, increasing to 6 percent at 125 percent of *recoupment*) for the first year of the Off-Broadway option (which includes all customary additional terms and conditions—including exclusive performance rights for the U.S. and Canada and a reasonable *subsidiary rights* participation schedule), which must be paid within one year and prior to the first rehearsal for a fully staged production (i.e., Showcase or institutional theatre production) and renewed annually for an additional one thousand dollar advance against royalties until the Off-Broadway production begins rehearsals; $250 for an Equity Showcase production (with no royalty, but a stipulations that if any performing actor receives greater compensation, then the playwright will receive the same greater amount as the actor); $500 for an Equity Mini-Contract production (with a modest royalty); "what is normally paid" for a *regional* theatre production; and for a Broadway production, if the playwright was a member of the Guild, "the then applicable minimum terms and conditions of the Dramatists' Guild's Approved Production Contract" (APC), or, if not a Guild member, the equivalent of the minimum terms of the APC for advances and royalties, without reference to the APC or the Guild; with the same terms applying to similar productions in other territories (outside the U.S. and Canada).

I believe that both the producer and the playwright enjoy a far richer and productive relationship with this approach. If you agree with me, you should retain a practicing theatrical attorney to devise the option agreement and assist you with any negotiation that may ensue.

It should be noted that before one acquires the knowledge and skills to feel secure about producing on one's own, a theatrical general manager should be sought out and engaged as a mentor and consultant to advise and assist in the developmental process. It is advisable to do this prior to the initial meeting with the playwright (and certainly before discussing acquiring the desired rights in the play). The process of acquiring the rights generally takes between four and ten weeks.

While developing a play, the union of jurisdiction for performers is Actors' Equity Association (A.E.A. or Equity). For commercial productions of the play that meet the criteria for other genres, for instance, for a musical review, I could engage the cast under an American Guild of Variety Artists (A.G.V.A.) Contract; or for an "opera" or "song and dance (with no dialogue) show," I could engage the cast under an American Guild of Musical Artists (A.G.M.A.) Contract. The union of jurisdiction for Directors and Choreographers is the Society of Stage Directors and Choreographers (SSDC).

For the director, I would pre-negotiate the essential terms and conditions for all anticipated subsequent production possibilities (fee; and royalties and advance against royalties, where appropriate, more often than not expressed as a percentage of "the then current minimums") *billing, house seats*, and everything else that is required to be set forth in a Rider, or would be in excess of the applicable contractual minimums) and set them out in a Letter of Agreement. Only when the development of the play progressed to a level requiring a contract would I then deal with SSDC. I would take the same approach with any designer(s) that was deemed necessary.

As I stated before, as I embarked on developing a play, I would begin to lay out my short term and long range strategic planning. I would read and make sure that I understood the current version of the various Equity guidelines, codes, agreements, and contracts that I felt I might be working under. Unlike the bad old days when I had to physically go to the Equity offices to get a copy of the current document, today I can go on the internet, type in http://www.actorsequity.org, then click on Document Library, and then click on Codes or Agreements, depending on what I am looking for. Under Codes, I can click on, view, and download the Showcase NYC (Basic) Code and the Showcase Application (Basic); under Agreements, I can find every multi-employer collectively bargained and promulgated contract that Equity has to offer, any of which can be clicked on and then viewed and downloaded. However, as of the end of 2004, neither the Equity Staged Reading Guidelines nor the Equity Staged Readings Contract was available. Neither was the Equity Workshop Agreement. (And it probably never will be, as it is deemed a *special contract*—although there are a number of provisions that are generic, each workshop contract is negotiated to meet the particular needs of the process the producer wishes to follow and the rates and some conditions will be determined by those requirements.) So the bad old days aren't entirely gone. There are periods when a particular code or contract is in flux, particularly a collective bargaining agreement between the expiration date and the time at which the language for the negotiated changes are finalized, and any code or promulgated contract that is subordinate to it; therefore, always confirm the effective termination date of the document.

At this point I need to point out that it is important to understand how Equity is structured and operates. The union is governed by the Equity Council, of whom members are elected by the membership. The Equity Council is the supreme body which concerns itself with union-wide (national) issues and hires the chief operating officer, the executive director. In its wisdom, the Equity Council divided the country into three jurisdictions: Eastern, Central, and Western. Each jurisdiction has a regional board (for New York, the Eastern Regional Board), which together make up the Equity Council. Each regional board delegates routine matters to the various committees, which in turn work with one or more business representatives, who are the liaison between the committee and the producers. Each committee is chaired by a member of the regional board. The regional board also hires the executive staff for its region, to which it delegates specific duties (including administrative oversight of the business representatives) and authorities, the exercise of which they report to the regional board. There is a committee and business representative(s) for each Equity guideline, code, and contract, as well as other areas of specific concern, such as the Equal Employment Opportunity Committee, Performers with Disabilities Committee, Chorus Affairs Committee, Stage Management Committee, etc. Any one business representative may work with more than one committee.

Whenever I made application for the use of an Equity guidelines, code, or the Mini-Contract, I would first contact the appropriate business representative to get a copy of the then current document and application form. If I was not fully conversant with the document, I would find the time to read through it and familiarize myself with the particulars, and if it was a new or updated version, I would make note of any changes from its predecessor. Before completing the application, I would discuss the options and limitations inherent in the current documentation with the director and any co-producers I had on the project (and the producer when I was a management consultant), and determine which available options should be elected and if there were any concessions (an elimination [waiver] of, addition to, or alternative to a term or condition) to the limitations imposed by Equity that should be requested for this particular production.

I would then submit the application form with the elected options to the business representative, and they in turn would check Equity's records for any information regarding prior relations in connection with the play (and the Defaulting Employer List) and, if there was nothing amiss, I would be given *Equity Approval.*

If I also requested one or more concession(s), rarely did they have the authority to grant it without first taking it to the committee (or, when time was a factor, at least the chair of the committee, who may have the authority to approve or may allow telephone polling of the committee members before the next scheduled meeting). Depending on the nature of a concession request, after being presented to the committee, it may then have to be approved by another committee (for instance, if the concession impacts on the stage managers they would want the Equity Stage Management Committee to also give approval). Most Equity committees meet once a month, and some bi-weekly. Once the concession request was approved by the committee, it was referred to one or more of the executive staff for review and approval. If the concession I requested was novel (i.e., no one has requested it before), if the committee didn't reject it out of hand, they would put it on the agenda for the next meeting of the regional board, who in turn may want to refer it to the Equity Council. So, this process could take several weeks to several months.

Just because I wanted a concession, no matter how well reasoned from my perspective, didn't mean I would get it. For the most part it has been my experience that the business representatives and committees operate on a *past practices* basis. However, even where there had been a number of approvals granted to a given concession request, the past practice of approving those concession requests did not ensure that my concession request would be approved.

While on the subject of union jurisdiction, if the genre of the play is a musical, musical review, or opera, or otherwise requires the engagement of a musician, any member of the American Federation of Musicians (Local 802 in New York) who provides services for music preparation (orchestrations, arrangements, copying), auditions, rehearsals, or performances of the play, has an entitlement to union dictated minimum compensation and union benefits. Traditionally Local 802 has not pursued services provided by the composer, unless the composer has requested them to do so. Tread carefully in these waters.

There are two primary reasons to give serious consideration to going the non-union route, particularly in the early stages of developing the play: artistic and budgetary. In regard to readings, Equity requires me to work under their Staged Reading Guidelines, which I can use only once (without a concession). Any additional readings must be under their Staged Reading Contract (which you will see below is far more expensive, including the posting of a security bond). Once I have committed to a reading under the Equity Staged Reading Guidelines, if thereafter I elect to develop the play non-union (i.e., not subscribing to Equity's Staged Reading Contract or Showcase Code, etc.) I will be subject to being placed on Equity's *Defaulting Employer's List*, which effectively bars me from subscribing to any Equity guidelines, code, or contract until I have satisfied Equity with settlement of all outstanding claims and/or providing a security bond in an amount satisfactory to Equity, determined in its sole discretion.

If I want to mount a developmental production with rehearsals, direction, and costumes, etc., if I use any union members I must use the Equity Showcase

Code; but if I go non-union I do not have to limit the ticket price, the performance schedule, or the number of performances I can give, I don't have to adhere to a *most favored nations* compensation and can pay my director, designers, and production staff without effecting what I pay the cast. And Equity requires that rehearsals and presentations for readings and Showcase productions must be given in spaces that meet Equity's promulgated Safe and Sanitary Rules, which may rule out using many apartment living rooms for readings, and many rehearsal and performance spaces that I could otherwise consider for a developmental production.

The informal reading that I mentioned above (inviting a few actor friends to give the play a cold reading) is also outside union jurisdiction as long as I inform each actor that I invite that is a union member that it is a private informal reading and I have no intention of informing Equity now or in the future; it is not an audition but a favor; it is a cold reading, for me and one or two of my advisors just to hear the words; the playwright will not be present; they don't have to read the script before the reading if they don't want to; there will be no rehearsal or any imposed stop and repeats; and it will not be recorded. Of course I also tell them that there will be food and beverages. I emphasize that these actors are friends, not strangers or passing acquaintances. Although I do believe in gender-specific *casting*, they do not have to be right for the role they are reading, just be able to read and enunciate and not try to give a performance. The cost to me was the food and beverages and I would always offer to reimburse the actors for their transportation costs (because I wanted to, not because they asked or I was required to).

For other readings I may want to arrange for the playwright (and the director or prospective director, if any) and myself to hear the play, where I do not want to be under union jurisdiction, I explore the opportunities that may be available at acting schools, play reading groups, and nonprofit theatre companies. If this does not prove successful, I network through my friends and acquaintances for non-union actors (and ask the playwright to do the same, if so inclined). The playwright and I (and the director, once engaged) will cast the roles as close to the characters as feasible. If I am successful in finding an acting school, play reading group, or nonprofit theatre company, more often than not they have an appropriate space at little or no cost. If I am not successful, I find the least expensive rehearsal hall or meeting room available for the desired time. During the course of the reading, the cast may be asked to stop and repeat a section with some direction being given by the playwright and/or director. When the reading is over, the cast is thanked, paid the agreed upon stipend—sometimes just reimbursement of transportation costs plus ten dollars, but more often twenty-five dollars without the reimbursement (in 2003), and sent on their way. Circumstances will dictate whether I then take the playwright (and the director, or prospective director, if any) somewhere (preferably private and without distraction) or schedule a meeting or phone conversation for the earliest mutually available time, to discuss what each of us feels works and isn't working.

There could be a drawback to acting schools, play reading groups, and nonprofit theatre companies, as they usually include a discussion of the script by all participants following the reading. Particularly in the early stages of the play's development, many playwrights take what is said very seriously and do not have the faculty to understand that most of the comments, no matter how well meant or strongly supported by others, are coming from the perspective of *the play I think you should write,* not the play that you are supporting the playwright in achieving. These discussion sessions sometimes knocked the playwright off track to the point that I lost my interest in continuing and dropped the project altogether. Where there wasn't a requirement for such a session, I never asked (or allow the playwright or director to ask) any of the cast their opinion of their role, any other role or the play.

Sooner or later (I hope) the playwright will bring the current draft of the play to the point that we want to have the play get a proper reading to find out how it plays to an audience. I rarely did this until I had a director attached to the project. The director, playwright and I would discuss ideal casting for each role (i.e., create a *casting breakdown*, with character descriptions and the desired actor traits) and the appropriateness of any of the actors we had used before. Then the director (and playwright, if so inclined) and I networked through our friends and acquaintances. On several occasions I consulted with a casting director. The director, playwright, and I would cast the roles as close to the characters as feasible.

If I wanted to continue non-union, I would place a casting notice on the bulletin boards of professional acting schools with the heading "NON-UNION ACTORS SOUGHT FOR READING" (I never placed a casting ad in *Back Stage* or other trade publication—it puts up all sorts of red flags). I booked an appropriate space and invited designers, stage managers, and others that we were considering; prospective co-producers, venue operators, *marketing* mavens, a few friends and their adult family members, and acquaintances that I knew to be avid theatre-goers that were both intelligent and articulate. I consciously avoided inviting prospective investors beyond anyone that had already provided financial support (*seed money* or *front money*). I always tried to have a full cast rehearsal reading several days before, and another the evening before an afternoon reading or the afternoon of an evening reading. Generally, I provided catering both before and after the reading. I would pay the cast the agreed upon stipend, (in 2003, generally seventy-five dollars [twenty-five dollars for each of the 3 calls]) before the reading and tell them that they need not stay for the post-reading social. During the post-reading social, the playwright, director, and I would stay together (so we all hear the same *what was said by whom, in what context, and what was their agenda*) and I would have made plans for us to get together (usually the next day) to discuss the effectiveness of the current draft of the play, the audience reactions during the reading, and the reactions of those that spoke to us after the reading and *where do we go from here.*

Anywhere in the process, as the play developed, I may have had to re-think my game plan. Occasionally it would be revealed that the playwright just didn't understand his characters in a dramatic context (usually these were plays that I came to learn were autobiographical or plays written about acquaintances, relatives, co-workers, etc., where the playwright couldn't get beyond the characters they knew, with all the limitations of knowledge that comes with limited observation). When this proved to be the case, I would be devastated, but knew it was time to throw in the towel. Sometimes reading just didn't work (a key actor not showing up, the playwright not being present—injured, sick, in a snit from a rehearsal, etc.—very inclement weather, a transit strike), and another unanticipated reading had to be organized. Sometimes a reading would reveal that what we thought would play just didn't make it from the page to the voicing of the words, and intricate rewrites were in order (same thoughts, new words, attention to rhythms), before the next reading. And some readings proved so productive and rewarding that the next step in my planning was no longer necessary.

Once the script arrived at a place where I, the playwright, and the director believed the story being told by the playwright (or the rhythms and arc of a non-linear piece—a revue or new vaudevillian presentation or such) was not entirely *there yet* (i.e., not quite ready for prime time) but needed a fully staged production to achieve the necessary further refinement, I had to determine if this should be approached as a non-union *downtown underground* production, a New York Showcase, or a similar production under another territorial specific agreement such as the Hollywood Area Theatre (Los Angeles ninety-nine seat Waiver) Agreement or the Chicago Area Theatre Agreement, the Mini-Contract, a regional theatre's second stage production, or an Equity Workshop production.

Sometimes available funding was the determining factor but for the most part it was what I thought was needed. If I didn't have the financial resources on hand, I had to go back to begging to get what I needed.

If I thought I had a Broadway-worthy property but did not have the resources to pursue a Broadway production and couldn't get the necessary interest to co-produce the project from any of the established Broadway producers, I would try to get the production placed at a New York City institutional theatre, where, if it got all the breaks, it could get the attention it deserved and make the move to the Great White Way.

A word of caution! On two occasions I agreed to allow the playwright to develop a script with a community theatre. In theory, it's not a bad idea. In neither case was it productive. Although there are many very good actors in community theatres across the country, there are few, if any, community theatres that have all good (much less very good) actors, and casting is done more for organizational policies and politics than for art. Very few of those community theatre actors proved nimble enough to absorb and realize script changes in a short period of time. Both of those productions cost me money, time, and deep emotional distress.

Remember, if you still have the passion—if at first you don't succeed, try, try again!

BUDGETS, CRITICAL PATH, AND CASH FLOW ANALYSIS

The budgets for each phase of the development of a play, the *critical path* and the *cash flow analysis* are totally interrelated and interdependent. Because "time is money" is as true in the theatrical production business as it is in any other enterprise, I strongly recommend that all three be completed before the budget stating the total *capitalization* is finalized. I have often found budgeting errors and critical path omissions when I would do the cash flow analysis, which is an expression of when what portion of the amount budgeted for each line item will be spent, based on the dates derived from the critical path.

In order to determine how much money I will have to raise to produce a given play, a budget must be devised. In order to accurately assess the expenses to be incurred, my long term strategic planning needs to be reduced to a critical path. And in order to know how much of the total funding needs to be available at any given time, a cash flow analysis will be needed. Compiling these is usually the domain of a general manager and are not skills that must be acquired in order to be a producer. But understanding them and their applications is a valuable asset for any producer. The general manager may extract many things from reading the script but is not a mind reader. The producer must share his or her plans as fully as possible (and respond to probing questions) in order to have the most accurate assessments of his or her financial needs and the sequence of events that is going to be the most cost effective. Any omission(s) can cause serious repercussions (artistic and financial). Paying attention to every detail of a production's needs and related requirements is the key to developing the most accurate budgetary calculations.

Before the early-to-mid 1980s, everyone did everything with a legal pad, a calculator, and a typewriter. In this day and age personal computers have become indispensable and the budget, critical path, and cash flow analysis are all laid out on spreadsheets. Each phase of the construction of each of these spreadsheets should be prominently dated "As At:" until finalized.

LONG TERM STRATEGIC PLANNING

For example, suppose I have found a script that I want to produce. After serious consideration, I decide that the ideal venue for the highest potential rewards (artistic and commercial) would be a 399-seat Off-Broadway Theatre. I then mull over the probable track for developing the script to maximize its assets in order to help the playwright tell the story in the most direct and entertaining way. I project that once I acquire the rights to the play I will organize an informal reading. I imagine that I should allow for two more readings and that I may have to hold two backers' auditions to raise the front money needed to do a Showcase production, which, if all goes well, I will extend under the Equity Mini-Contract while I raise the money for the Off-Broadway production.

BUDGETS

I will need several budgets. First, one for all the pre-production expenses I believe I will incur, giving practical consideration for, among other items: the attorney's retainer and disbursements; the initial and subsequent payments to the playwright for the production rights; the general manager's initial payment; script reproduction; the costs associated with readings and backers' auditions (cast reimbursements and stipends, space rental, food, and beverages); director's payment(s); insurance premiums; perhaps a casting director's fee; costs of reproducing the *offering materials*; and my own out-of-pocket expenses (phone, transportation, meetings at restaurants, etc.). Second, a budget for the envisioned Showcase (or other fully staged) production, with a break-out of the direct

Showcase production expenses and the preliminary costs and payments to be charged against the subsequent Off-Broadway production budget (for instance, the director and designers will do the Showcase on a most favored nations bases with the actors, but may require the first installment on their Off-Broadway fees; fully realized costumes, props, set dressing and furnishings that are intended to be utilized for the Off-Broadway production; press agent related expenses; and, if a musical, music preparation costs). Remember, the Showcase budget must be submitted to Equity before they will approve the use of the Showcase Code and must conform to the limitations imposed by the Code. Also, to the extent they are included in the producer's long-range strategic plan, a budget for the allowed extension (four performances) of the Showcase production, and a budget for further extension of the production under an Equity Mini-Contract. Finally, a budget for the expenses of the Off-Broadway production, which enfolds all the anticipated net developmental costs and expenses.

Some of the costs set forth in the first budget (pre-production expenses) may be enfolded in the second budget (Showcase production) leaving a net cost that is less than the total of both; just as all of the costs incurred in the development of the play (except those directly related to fundraising, which by law cannot be charged to the investors), off-set by box office income, will be enfolded into the commercial production budget, which will express the total funding being sought for the entire journey from securing the rights to producing and sustaining the desired commercial production (the total *capitalization*).

Once these budgets had been finalized and the offering materials were issued, any internal budget changes were reflected in the *working budget*. Expenses in excess of what was initially budgeted would have the effect of reducing the contingency fund aspect of the general reserve (and if depleted, then the general reserve itself) and any savings would have the effect of increasing the *general reserve*.

With each revision of the critical path, there would usually be a revision of the working budget.

Budget templates can be found in a number of sources. The most readily available are in the book *From Option to Opening* by Donald Farber. All templates, no matter what the source, are generic and should be thought of only as a starting point. No two productions have the same budget. In order to be effective, each budget must be crafted for a specific play with a specific target venue and projected production dates, and reflect all of the needs of the play inherent in the script, the applicable union minimums and the going rate for non-union positions, and the producer's prerogatives regarding artistic staff, casting (including understudy assignments), the duration of rehearsals and previews, the desired level of the production values, *advertising* and marketing, and any number of other considerations, not the least of which is a realistically adequate general reserve fund.

I have never finalized a budget without first laying out a critical path and then a cash flow analysis. In every instance I have discovered errors I had made and time duration impacts on the costs and expenses to be anticipated (among other considerations beyond anticipated cost-of-living increases, union minimums, theatre costs, and advertising rates increase annually, each on their own cycle and at their own rate of increase).

As a producer, as I worked with my general manager toward finalizing the Off-Broadway budget, I never hesitated to ask questions about any line item or related production track consideration that concerned me: What makes this line item so high? Does this line item take into consideration the need for *x?* Do you remember the conversation with *y* that I told you about—is it reflected in the applicable line items? When I was general managing for another producer, I would review each line item, and for each one that was not a pro-forma calculation (such as union benefits or payroll taxes), I would review all the internals it included and ask the producer if there was anything else they could think of that might have an impact (positive or negative) on that line item.

It has been my hard and steadfast rule to never budget *fat* (excess) into a line item. I always tried to project what I should reasonably expect to pay for what I believed I would require, be it the scenery, the director's fee, and advance, the initial and weekly payments on the insurance premiums, or the opening night party and gifts. Producing a play costs too much as it is. Over budgeting can result in a capitalization that cannot find its funding. And if the capitalization is unduly increased, the investor pool is unnecessarily diluted. What I have done, and recommend to others to do as well, is provide a Production Contingency line item within the Reserve Funds. As a rule, I used a figure, rounded to the nearest thousand dollars, that represented somewhere between 2.5–3.5 percent of the pre-reserves total, depending on the physical production demands of the script and my confidence in meeting my initial critical path schedule. Aside from production date slippage (that would cause me to pass the annual date of increases in union contract minimums, *The New York Times* advertising rates, etc.), with tight budgeting I want to provide allowance for, among the other concerns I may have, budgeting scenery costs before there is a design, the scenic designer's fee before one is engaged, and what the actual costs of the insurance premiums will be at an unknown future date. I also want to give myself some degree of flexibility for unforeseen circumstances. For instance, it has been my experience that when negotiating to go to contract with a theatre that was *dark* (no current show running), the owner/operator would demand (i.e., make this a deal-breaking condition) that I use the theatre for rehearsals for more rent that I had budgeted for rehearsal space. Another concern comes from my personal experience when I was the general manager on *Other People's Money* by Jerry Sterner. The script called for no sound whatsoever. The play was given a developmental production at American Stage Company which—without any sound effects—was very well received. Subsequently, the play was produced at the Hartford Stage Company. The artistic director, Mark Lamos, engaged David Budries to design sound for the production. In my opinion, a stroke of genius—as the sound he created was so integral to the script that thereafter, I couldn't imagine a production of the play without it. The budget for the Off-Broadway production did not include a line item for a sound designer. Without the production contingency line item to absorb this unanticipated expense the general reserve fund (which is relied upon to cover weekly *operating losses* after opening until *the gross weekly box office receipts* catch up with the running costs) would have been imperiled.

CURRENT TITLE: **TOM'S MIDLIFE CRISIS** AS AT: 3/30/04

A.E.A. Showcase Code Production Budget (Rehearsals & Performances) For A 74-Seat Theatre 4 Weeks Rehearsal 12 Performances Over 3 Weeks	Projected Production Dates
	Rehearsals Commence: 8/9/04
	First Performance: 9/9/04
	Final Performance: 9/26/04

PHYSICAL PRODUCTION

Scenery Construction, Painting & Flameproofing	1,200
Scenic Rentals (Soft Goods, Flameproofed)	0
Props, Set Dressing & Furnishings—Purchase & Fabricate	500
Props, Set Dressing & Furnishings—Rentals	0
Props—Perishable	40
Costumes—Purchase, Alter, Etc.	700
Costume Rentals	0
Costume Rentals/Purchases for Cast	300
Shoes—Purchase	75
Shoe & Boot Rental	0
Shoe Rentals/Purchases from Cast	50
Lighting Equipment Rental	500
Lighting Equipment Supplies	350
Sound Equipment Rental	250
Sound Equipment Supplies	50
Sound Recording	100
Musical Instruments & Stands Rental	0
Theatre Preperation	160
Take-In, Hang & Focus Crew	1,200
Work Calls	200
Take-Out Crew	560
Local Carting & Trucking [In and Out]	600
	6,835

ARTISTIC STAFF COMPENSATION

	Number of persons	Days	Rate	Total
Director	1	36	$4.00	144
Assistant to Director	0			0
Choreographer	0			0
Assistant to Choreographer	0			0
Scenic Designer	1	8	$4.00	32
Assistants Scenic Designer	0			0
Costume Designer	1	24	$4.00	96
Assistants Costume Designer	0			0
Lighting Designer	1	8	$4.00	32
Assistants Lighting Designer	1	12	$4.00	48
Sound Designer	1	8	$4.00	32
Assistants Sound Designer	0			0
Production Manager	0			0
Musical Director	0			0
Orchestrations, Arrangements & Copying, etc.	0			0
				384

CAST & STAFF COSTS [Remember "Most Favored Nations" Condition]

Cast	3	36	$4.00	432
Understudies	0		$4.00	0
Recorded Voices	0		$4.00	0
Stage Manager	1	41	$4.00	164
Assistant Stage Manager(s)	0		$4.00	0
Assistant Stage Manager/Under Study	0		$4.00	0
Musical Director/Leader	0			0
Musician(s)	0			0
Synthesizer Premium(s)	0			0
Rehearsal Pianists	0			0
Electrician	1	20	$4.00	80
Follow Spot Operator(s)	0			0
Sound Operator [See Stage Manager]	0		$4.00	0
Stage Crew	2	16	$4.00	128
Wardrobe	1	16	$4.00	64

Production Assistant(s)	0		$4.00	0
House Manager	1	13	$4.00	52
Box Office	1	13	$4.00	52
Ticket-Taker & Ushers [See House Manager]	0			0
Porter (Janitor)	0			0

972

PROMOTION, PUBLICITY & ADVERTISING

	Cost per unit	units	total
Print & Other Paid Advertising			0
Direct Mail Advertising	$0.55	800	440
Posters	$2.50	100	250
Discount Coupons, etc.			0
Signs & Boards	[Computer Generated In-House]		0
Flyers & Distribution	$0.15	1,000	150
Logo Design & Related Art Work	[Computer Generated In-House]		0
Mechanical & Production Expenses			0
Photographer & Photo Reproduction			200
Special Promotion			0

1,040

THEATRE

		Cost per unit	units	total
Rent	Weekly Rehearsal Rental Rate	2000	1 week*	2,000
	Weekly Performance Rental Rate	2500	3 weeks*	7,500
Box Office	Preliminary			0
	Performances			0
House Staff [House Manager, Technician &/or Porter]				0
Ushers (Volunteers)				0
Utilities, Telephone & Sanitary Supplies		900	1	900
Public Liability Insurance - 90% projected attendance		$0.25 per capita charge	888[†]	200
Payroll Taxes, Benefits and Employer Liabilities			0	0
Administrative Charge				0
Other Reimbursable Expenses				25

10,625

ADMINISTRATIVE & GENERAL			
Production Rights (Playwright)			250
Script Reproduction	$0.06	Pages: 72 Copies: 20	86
Preliminary Administrative Expenses			0
Casting & Audition Expenses [Space Rental]			160
Rehearsal Halls (weekly rental)	$960	3.7 weeks	3,520
Postage, Telephone & Messenger, Etc.			125
Non-Original Music Performance Rights			0
Union Pension Fund Payments			0
Union Health Insurance Payments			0
Payroll Taxes			0
Computer Payroll Expenses			0
Employer Insurances (WC & Dis./Liability)			0
Insurance (General Liability & Volunteer Accident)			1,500
Opening Night Expenses (Gifts, Party)			300
Wrap Party			300
Programs	$0.40	888†	355
Wardrobe Supplies & Costume Cleaning		[3 week run]	150
Stage Manager's Expenses			100
Departmental Expenses			150
Inspections & Permits [Open Flame?]			0
Miscellaneous			250
			7,247

ESTIMATED TOTAL DIRECT PRODUCTION EXPENSES	27,102

DEPOSITS	Theatre – Security Deposit	1,000
BONDS	Actors' Equity Association	0
	A. F. of M. Local 802	0
	S.S.D.C.	0
TOTAL ESTIMATED PRODUCTION DISBURSEMENTS		28,102

RESERVES	Production Contingency	0
	General Operating Reserve	0

TOTAL ESTIMATED PRODUCTION CAPITAL REQUIREMENTS	**$28,102**

TOTAL ESTIMATED PRODUCTION CAPITALIZATION	$28,102

ESTIMATED POTENTIAL GROSS RECEIPTS:			
Seating Capacity	74		
Performances	12		
Ticket Price	$15.00		
GROSS POTENTIAL:		$13,320	

ESTIMATED ANTICIPATED GROSS RECEIPTS:			
Est. Average Paid Tix	$12.80		
Projected Paid Attend.	80%		
		$9,093	

RETURN OF THEATRE DEPOSIT	**$1,000**	

PROJECTED NET PROFIT/(LOSS):		**($18,009)**

Notes & Comments:

See Showcase Extension Budget

See Schedule of Off-Broadway Pre-Pays

Please be advised that this is a full disclosure budget for the producer's use only. The budget to be submitted to equity should not include any line item with a zero expense ($0.00), or any notes or comments. No reference should be made to the expenses anticipated for an extension; or for any "Off-Broadway pre-pays."

The report of expenses to be submitted to equity should be in the same line item format; with any unanticipated expense that does not logically fall into a line item given its own line item and noted as ["unanticipated expense"].

The attendance and income report to be submitted to equity should be by performance, with number of paid attend., box office income; tdf vouchers value; number of comps.; total income for performance; and a cover sheet showing total of all performances.

If the showcase is extended, the expenses for those performances should be listed separately and a separate attendance and income cover sheet submitted.

* Required to be Prepaid
† Seats x Performances x % of attendance

CURRENT TITLE: **TOM'S MIDLIFE CRISIS** AS AT: 3/30/04

A.E.A. Showcase Code Production
For a 74-Seat Theatre
Budget Addendum
4-Performance Extension

PHYSICAL PRODUCTION

Scenic Rentals (Soft Goods)	0
Props, Set Dressing & Furnishings—Rentals	0
Props—Perishable	10
Costume Rentals	0
Costume Rentals from Cast	0
Shoe & Boot Rental	0
Shoe Rentals from Cast	0
Lighting Equipment Rental	125
Lighting Equipment Supplies	0
Sound Equipment Rental	63
Musical Instruments & Stands Rental	0
	198

CAST & STAFF COSTS

	Number of persons	Rate per person	Total
Cast	3	$40	120
Understudies	0	$40	0
Stage Manager	1	$40	40
Assistant Stage Manager(s)	0	$40	0
Assistant Stage Manager/Understudy	0	$40	0
Musical Director/Leader	0		0
Musician(s)	0		0
Synthesizer Premium(s)	0		0
Electrician	1	$40	40
Follow Spot Operator(s)	0		0
Sound Operator	0		0
Stage Crew	2	$40	80
Wardrobe	1	$40	40
Production Assistant(s)	0		0
House Manager	1	$40	40

Box Office	1	$40	40
Ticket-Taker & Ushers	0		0
Porter (Janitor)	0		0
			400

PROMOTION, PUBLICITY & ADVERTISING

	Cost per unit	Units	Total
Flyers & Distribution	$0.15	1,000	150
			150

THEATRE

Rent			2,500
Box Office			0
House Staff (House Manager, Technician &/or Porter)			0
Ushers			0
Utilities, Telephone & Sanitary Supplies			200
Public Liability Insurance- 97.5% Projected Attendance	296	$0.25	72
Payroll Taxes, Benefits and Employer Liabilities			0
Administrative Charge			0
Other Reimbursable Expenses			0
			2,772

ADMINISTRATIVE & GENERAL

Postage, Telephone & Messenger, etc.			30
Non-Original Music Performance Rights			0
Union Pension Fund Payments			0
Union Health Insurance Payments			0
Payroll Taxes			0
Computer Payroll Expenses			0
Employer Insurances (WC & Dis./Liability)			0
Insurance (General Liability & Volunteer Accident) Under Min. Premium			0
Programs	289	$0.40	115
Wardrobe Supplies & Costume Cleaning			25

Stage Manager's Expenses		50
Departmental Expenses		25
		245

ESTIMATED TOTAL PRODUCTION EXTENSION COSTS	3,765

ESTIMATED POTENTIAL GROSS RECEIPTS		
Seating Capacity	74	
Performances	4	
Ticket Price	$15.00	
		$4,440

ESTIMATED ANTICIPATED GROSS RECEIPTS			
Average Paid Ticket	$13.85		
Projected Paid Attendence	93%		
		$3,792	

PROJECTED NET PROFIT/(LOSS)		$27

Notes and comments:

The Box Office Income from the Initial 12 performances will finance the Extension. No additional Capital will be required.

CURRENT TITLE: TOM'S MIDLIFE CRISIS AS AT: 3/30/04

A.E.A. Showcase Code Production
Budget addendum
Schedule of pre-pays against Off-Broadway production budget

PHYSICAL PRODUCTION	Against Line Item	Against Dev. Exp.
Scenery Construction, Painting & Flameproofing	1,000	0
Props, Set Dressing & Furnishings - Purchase & Fabricate	1,200	0
Costumes - Purchase, Alter, Etc.	450	0
Shoes - Purchase	150	0
Sound Recording	400	0
	3,200	0

STAFF COMPENSATION		
Director	2,500	0
Assistant to Director	0	0
Choreographer	0	0
Assistant to Choreographer	0	0
Scenic Designer	1,000	0
Assistants Scenic Designer	0	0
Costume Designer	1,000	0
Assistants Costume Designer	0	0
Lighting Designer	1,000	0
Assistants Lighting Designer	0	700
Sound Designer	1,000	0
Assistants Sound Designer	0	0
Production Manager	0	750
Musical Director	0	0
Orchestrations, Arrangements & Copying, Etc.	0	0
Casting Director	2,000	0
Commercial Management Consultant [G.M.]	2,000	0
Legal	1,000	0
Accounting	750	0
	12,250	1,450

CAST & STAFF COSTS

Recorded Voices	0	0
Stage Manager	0	1,000
Musical Director/Leader	0	0
Audition & Rehearsal Pianists	0	0
Company Manager	0	0
Production Assistant(s)	0	0
	0	**1,000**

PROMOTION, PUBLICITY & ADVERTISING

Logo Design & Related Art Work	500	0	
Press Agent	2,000	0	P & H
Press Agent Office & Expenses	350	0	
Photographer (Not Photo Reproduction)	250	0	
	3,100	**0**	

ADMINISTRATIVE & GENERAL

Producer's Administrative Expenses	0	0
Commercial Management Consultant Office & Expenses	0	400
Casting & Audition Expenses	240	0
Rehearsal Halls	0	0
Postage, Telephone & Messenger, Etc.	375	0
Non-Original Music Performance Rights	0	0
Union Pension Fund Payments	0	0
Union Health Insurance Payments	0	0
Payroll Taxes	0	0
Employer Insurances (WC & Dis./Liability)	0	0
Insurance (General Liability)	0	0
Legal Disbursements	150	0
	765	**400**

ADVANCES (NON-RETURNABLE) AND/OR ROYALTIES

Devisor(s) and/or Author(s)	1,000	0
Composer(s) & Lyricist(s)	0	0
Underlying Rights	0	0
Non-Original Music	0	0
Director	0	0
Choreographer	0	0
	1,000	0

Total Pre-Pays Against O-B'WAY LINE ITEM EXPENSES:	20,315
Total Pre-Pays Against DEVELOPMENTAL EXPENSES:	2,850
TOTAL "PRE-PAYS AGAINST OFF-BROADWAY"	**23,165**

TOTAL ESTIMATED SHOWCASE DIRECT PRODUCTION DISBURSEMENTS	28,102
TOTAL ESTIMATED SHOWCASE PRODUCTION EXTENSION COSTS	3,765
TOTAL ESTIMATED SHOWCASE & RELATED EXPENDITURES	**$55,032**

TOTAL PROJECTED SHOWCASE PRODUCTION INCOME	9,093
TOTAL PROJECTED SHOWCASE EXTENSION INCOME	3,792
TOTAL PROJECTED SHOWCASE BOX OFFICE INCOME	**$12,885**

PROJECTED NET SHOWCASE & RELATED COSTS:	**$42,147**
IF NO EXTENSION - EXPENDITURES BEFORE INCOME OFF-SET	**51,167**

CURRENT TITLE: **TOM'S MIDLIFE CRISIS** AS AT: 3/30/04
Production budget
A.E.A. Mini contract
Direct roll-over from A.E.A. Showcase code production
For a 74-seat theatre

TAKEN INTO CONSIDERATION:	
0.0	WEEKS REHEARSAL IN STUDIO
0.0	WEEK(S) REHEARSAL IN THEATRE
0.0	WEEK(S) PREVIEWS

PHYSICAL PRODUCTION

Scenery Construction, Painting & Flameproofing			0
Scenic Rentals (Soft Goods, Flameproofed)			0
Props, Set Dressing & Furnishings - Purchase & Fabricate			0
Props, Set Dressing & Furnishings - Rentals			0
Costumes & Shoes (Understudies)			1,100
Lighting Equipment Rental	0.0	200	0
Lighting Perishables (Supplies)			350
Sound Equipment Rental & Supplies			0
Sound Recording & Design Expenses			0
Theatre Preparation			0
Take-In, Hang & Focus Crews			0
Work Calls			300
Local Carting & Trucking			0
			1,750

STAFF COMPENSATION

Director	1	3,500
Assistant to Director		0
Scenic Designer	1	1,000
Assistants Scenic Designer		0
Costume Designer	1	1,000
Assistants Costume Designer		0
Lighting Designer	1	1,000
Asst. Lighting Designer		0
Sound Designer		1,000
Assistants Sound Designer		0

Production Manager		0
Composer (Original Music)	Per Agreement	1,000
Casting Director		0
Producer(s)		0
Commercial Management Consultant		0
Legal		1,000
Accounting	(See ... & WEEKLY FEES)	0
		9,500

REHEARSAL & PREVIEW SALARIES & WEEKLY FEES

			#	weeks	rate	
Cast	-Rehearsals	Minimum	3	0.0	322	0
	- Previews	Minimum	3	0.0	410	0
Understudies	(Rehearse - Wk. #3 + 4)		2	0.0	322	0
Stage Manager	Rehearsals		1	1.2	400	467
	Previews		1	0.0	480	0
If Operating Lights			1	0.0	70	0
If Operating Sound			1	0.0	70	0
Assistant Stage Mgr.	Rehearsals		1	0.3	346	115
	Previews		1	0.0	440	0
A. S. M./Under Study	Rehearsals		0	0.3	367	0
	Previews		0	0.0	461	0
- If A.S.M. Wardrobe			1	0.0	140	0
Rehearsal Overtime				per hr.	17	0
A.E.A. Sick (Not Vacation) Pay	ACCRUAL					18
Electrician	1 = if S.M.		0	0.0	370	0
Sound Operator	1= if S.M		0	0.0	315	0
Stage Crew			0	0.0	210	0
Wardrobe	1= if A.S.M		0	0.0	350	0
Stage Crew & Wardrobe	Rehearsals & Over Time					0
General Manager			1	2.0	200	400
Company Manager			1	1.0	400	400
Press Agent (See PROMOTION, etc.)			0			
Production Assistants			0			
Producer(s)			1	2.0	0	0
Accountant			1	1.0	100	100
						1,500

PROMOTION, PUBLICITY & ADVERTISING				
Print & Paid Advertising				24,000
Broadcast Media Paid Advertising				0
Direct Mail Advertising				600
Window Cards				0
Signs & Boards	(Computer Generated In-House)			0
Flyers & Distribution				400
Logo Design & Related Art Work	(Computer Generated In-House)			0
Mechanical & Production Expenses				1,000
Photographer & Photo Reproduction				0
Press Agent Office & Expenses				0
Press Agent/ Marketing	4.0		600	2,400
Opening Night Press Expenses				0
Marketing/Sponsorship	0.0		0	0
Marketing/Trade	4.0		400	1,600
Special Promotion				0
				30,000

THEATRE				
Rent	Rehearsal	0.0	2,000	0
	Previews	0.0	2,500	0
Box Office	- Preliminary		$10/hr.	150
	- Previews	0.0	$10/hr.	210	0
House Staff (House Manager & Porter)	0.0	$10/hr.	400	0
Ushers- Volunteers, if any			0	0
Utilities (Con Ed)	0.0		150	0
Telephone (Incl. installation)	0.0		38	338
Sanitary Supplies	0.0			0
Carting (Refuse pick-up)	0.0		50	0
Public Liability Insurance	0.0	500	$0.25	0
Payroll Taxes and Employer Liabilities		17.50%	150	26
Administrative Charge	0.0			0
Other Reimbursable Expenses				0
				514

ADMINISTRATIVE & GENERAL

	EPA&I Only	Space Rental	@ Theatre	
Script Reproduction				0
Preliminary Administrative Expenses				0
Casting & Audition Expenses				0
Rehearsal Halls				0
Producer Office Expense				0
General Manager Office Expense				0
Postage, Telephone & Messenger, Etc.				250
Non-Original Music Performance Rights				0
Local Transportation				0
Union Pension Fund Payments				328
Union Health Insurance Payments				742
Payroll Taxes & Employer Insurances & Liabilities		17.5%	11,550	2,021
Computer Payroll Supplies				35
Insurance (General Liability)	0.0		125	0
Legal Disbursements				0
Opening Night Expenses				2,500
Programs	1.0	500	$0.60	300
Wardrobe Supplies & Costume Cleaning	1.0	90	20	110
Departmental Expenses				50
Inspections & Permits				0
Miscellaneous				400
				6,736

ESTIMATED TOTAL DIRECT PRODUCTION EXPENSES	50,000

ADVANCES (NON-RETURNABLE, BUT RECOVERABLE)

Author	500
Composer	0
Director	0
Theatre	3,500
	4,000

DEPOSITS	
Theatre (Closing Costs)	1,500
	1,500

BONDS	
Actors' Equity Association	8,135
	8,135

TOTAL ESTIMATED PRODUCTION DISBURSEMENTS	63,635

RESERVES		
Production Contingency	3.14%	2,000
General Operating Reserve		34,365
Post-Opening Advertising Support	"Quote Ads"	20,000
		56,365

TOTAL ESTIMATED ADDITIONAL PRODUCTION CAPITALIZATION	**120,000**

PROJECTED PRODUCTION DATES:	
Rehearsals Commence:	Roll-over from Showcase
Previews Commence:	Oct. 5, 2004
Official Press Opening:	Oct. 7, 2004
Initial Run (6 Wks.) to:	Nov. 14, 2004
Max Run (13 Wks.) to:	Jan. 2, 2005

Notes & Comments

The intention is to finance both the Equity Approved Showcase Code Production and the "Roll-Over" to an Equity Mini-Contract with a combination of "Front Money" and "Pre-formation Use" investment in the Off-Broadway Production.

If that proves problematic, I will create a LPA or LLC specifically for the Mini-Contract Production, which will state: a) NO HOPE OF RETURN OF INVESTMENT, unless; b) a subsequent Off-Broadway production is realized, which will enfold the investors hereunder at their respective full dollar amount of investment, it being understood that the net costs of the Mini-Contract Production will be included in the Capitalization of said Off-Broadway production.

As incentive for investing in the Mini-Contract production, I will give them an additional "taste" from Producer's share of profits from the Off-Broadway production.

CURRENT TITLE: **TOM'S MIDLIFE CRISIS** As At: 3/30/04
WEEKLY OPERATING EXPENSES
A.E.A. Mini contract
For a 74-seat theatre

SALARIES & WEEKLY FEES

Cast *Minimum	3	420.00	1,260
Understudies (after 2 wks.Reh.)	2	420.00	840
Stage Manager	1	520.00	520
- If Operating Lights	1	70.00	70
- If Operating Sound	1	70.00	70
Assistant Stage Manager(s)	1	445.00	445
Assistant Stage Manager/UnderStudy	0	466.00	0
- If A.S.M. Wardrobe	1	140.00	140
A.E.A. Sick (Not Vacation) Pay (ACCRUAL)	3.125%	3,345.00	105
Electrician	1	= if S.M.	0
Sound Operator	1	= if S.M.	0
Stage Crew			0
Wardrobe	1	= if A.S.M.	0
General Manager	1	200.00	200
Company Manager	1	520.00	520
Press Agent	(See PROMOTION, etc.)		0
Production Assistants	0	0.00	0
Producer(s)	1	0.00	0
Accountant/Bookkeeper	1	100.00	100

* at GWBOR $13,650 - $15,000	**4,270**

PROMOTION, PUBLICITY & ADVERTISING

Print & Paid Advertising	3,000
Broadcast Media Paid Advertising	0
Flyers & Distribution	350
Mechanical & Production Expenses	150
Press Agent/ Marketing	600
Marketing/Sponsorship	0
Marketing/Trade	400
Special Promotion	0
	4,500

THEATRE

Rent			2,500
Box Office			210
House Staff (House Manager & Porter)			400
Ushers- Volunteers, if any			0
Utilities			150
Telephone			38
Sanitary Supplies			20
Carting (Refuse pick-up)			50
Public Liability Insurance	500	0.25	132
Payroll Taxes, Benefits and Employer Liabilities	17.50%	610	107
Administrative Charge			0
Other Reimbursable Expenses			0
			3,606

ADMINISTRATIVE & GENERAL

Producer Office Expense			0
General Manager Office Expense			0
Postage, Telephone & Messenger, Etc.			25
Local Transportation			0
Union Pension Fund Payments			289
Union Health Insurance Payments			864
Payroll Taxes	17.5%	4,170	730
Computer Payroll Expenses	(In House - Quick Books) - Supplies		35
Insurance			125
Programs	500	$0.60	300
Rentals - Scenic (Soft Goods)			0
Props			0
Lighting			200
Sound			0
Costume Cleaning			125
Departmental Expenses	(Lamp & Gel replacements, etc.)		50
Miscellaneous			25
			2,768

TOTAL ESTIMATED DIRECT WEEKLY OPERATING EXPENSES	**$15,144**

ROYALTIES

	At Gross of $16,650	
Author	5.00%	833
Director	2.00%	333
Producer	2.00%	333
Other:	0.00%	0
TOTAL ROYALTIES	9.00%	1,499

THEATRE PARTICIPATION

From 1st Dollar of GWBOR	0.00%	0
		0

TOTAL ESTIMATED WEEKLY OPERATING EXPENSES BASED ON GROSS WEEKLY BOX OFFICE RECEIPTS OF $16,650	(BREAK EVEN)	**16,643**

WITH MINIMUM ROYALTY POOL GUARANTEES				
Total Estimated Direct Weekly Operating Expenses				15,144
Estimated Minimum Royalty Pool Guarantees		9.00	$70	630
Estimated Theatre Participation	0.0%	$15,774		0

TOTAL ESTIMATED WEEKLY OPERATING EXPENSES (BREAK EVEN) WITH MINIMUM ROYALTY POOL GUARANTEES	**15,774**

RECAP		
WITH:	$45.00	Top Ticket
	$30.00	Lowest Ticket
Projected:	$38.25	Average Ticket Net

ESTIMATED WEEKLY POTENTIAL GROSS RECEIPTS AT CAPACITY (74 SEATS)	19,814

ESTIMATED WEEKLY EXPENSES AT CAPACITY	17,627

ESTIMATED WEEKLY OPERATING PROFIT AT CAPACITY	2,186

WITH FULL ROYALTIES PAID - EST. BREAK EVEN PT.	84.0% OF POTENTIAL CAPACITY

WITH ROYALTY POOL–EST. BREAK EVEN POINT	79.6% OF POTENTIAL CAPACITY

CRITICAL PATH

The critical path is a sequential listing of each and every aspect of a production laid out on a time line, with awareness of what needs to be accomplished before something else can occur and the latest date by which something must be done without causing a delay (which, if missed, would have a negative artistic impact on the production and/or negative financial impact on the budget). It isn't just the obvious flow of "casting must precede first rehearsal," but that the Equity Producer's Questionnaire (Bonding Application) must be submitted—before the Equity bond can be posted—before contract forms can be prepared and issued, and takes into consideration the time it should reasonably take to accomplish those actions), and then the delivery of the contracts (providing a reasonable amount of time for them to be signed and returned). Just as important is the requirement that the date of the first rehearsal and the date the first paid public performance must be on the Equity contracts, which means that the theatre agreement must be finalized before the Equity Bonding Application can be completed. Although the exact time frame can not be known, an experienced producer and/or the general manager can make a reasonable estimate of the elapsed time between auditions and the completion of negotiations for the cast. It is out of the critical path that the production schedule is derived. My critical paths were always laid out: first by consecutive months, with the time period of each phase (preliminary, private readings, public readings, backers' auditions) sketched in so they could be easily moved in blocks; and then, as the rehearsals for the first development production approached, by consecutive weeks (with the heading "week ending" and the date of the Sunday of each week), all without dates until the initial compilation was completed, and only then was the date of securing the rights laid in as the anchor and the ensuing dates determined. Then holidays, and my prior commitments could be inserted and any necessary adjustment made. As I assembled the artistic staff, all of their prior commitments and other conflicts could be inserted and the appropriate adjustments made and taken into consideration when making a future revision.

Every aspect of each step along the way needed to be plotted. I found it easier to do this by starting at the end and working toward the beginning. In this example, the "end" was the Off-Broadway production and the "beginning" was acquiring the rights. I had a good idea of when the rights would be secured and what I found out was the earliest time frame of the realization of my desired Off-Broadway production. Among the most important things to be ascertained was when the Off-Broadway Theatre contract had to be signed (and I must note that it was that projected date that most often was not realized and put my critical path in a holding pattern, while I waited for an appropriate theatre to become available).

While I'm on the subject of the theatre contract, the theatre operator requires a lot of specific production information. Among the most important are the dates of the *take-in*, the *first preview*, and the *official press opening*. Sometimes, particularly when more than one production wants the theatre, in the negotiation the production's schedule is as important to theatre operator as the *weekly license fee* (rent) is to the producer. In these negotiations, time is of the essence. With a well-reasoned critical path, the producer can easily and quickly ascertain the possibility of the dates the theatre desires (demands), and if not possible, what adjustments in the schedule can be made, to make a counter-offer. Keep in mind that the agreed upon schedule will be memorialized (with other information provided) in the *theatre license agreement* as the "Producer's Representations," and missing any one of the dates may cause a default, which could give the theatre operator the right to terminate the agreement.

A good critical path will allow for all contingencies that one should anticipate with any given track (wiggle room). If a contingency entry is not needed, then it can be removed and the schedule of that track may be accelerated depending on its relationship to other related or dependent track activities. Nothing should be assumed in the interim between two entries of a common track. For instance, for the scenic design, the scheduling of *scenic design approval meeting* cannot occur before the theatre contract is executed, as no two theatres have the same *stage foot print* (width, depth, height to the grid, wing space, proscenium opening or sight lines), and reasonable time must be allowed for the scenic designer to digest the input of the director and producer as it applies to the specific theatre in which the play will be presented. It should not be assumed that the designs initially submitted by the designer at the scheduled design approval meeting will be approved. If they are, great! However, in my experience, far more often than not the director and/or the producer (or the costume and/or lighting designer) would suggest, request, and/or demand changes (occasionally, a wholesale rethink), and another meeting was necessary for the approval. Reasonable time must be allowed for the designer to accomplish changes, but it must fit into the overall scheduling needs of the production. Following approval of the designs, a *bid session* must be scheduled, but it must allow the scenic designer reasonable time to prepare and reproduce the working drawings. Following the bid session, reasonable time must be allowed for the scenic shops to make their calculations, speak with the scenic designer about methods of construction and acceptable substitute materials, etc., before submitting their bids. It should be anticipated that the bids could be beyond budgetary consideration and for that reason a *scenic design re-hash meeting* should be scheduled before *award scenic construction contract*. Then a reasonable allotment of time must be given for the shop to construct, flameproof, and paint the scenery (without incurring overtime) before *take-in* is scheduled.

Although the process of creating a critical path is very clinical, as it evolved I would get a feel for the journey I would be taking. Many of the considerations were no-brainers while others were intricate and had to be scheduled with surgical precision. Also, as more people and activities became involved, the more specificity needed to be applied. I should note that the most significant and useful aspect of a well-developed critical path is placing various production meetings. Initially, the necessary meeting between the producer and director don't have to be on specific dates but rather within a defined window of opportunity. However, subsequent meetings that include prospective designers— and then the designated designers— and then the contracted designers would have more and more tightly defined time frames.

There should be nothing in a critical path that is casual or dispensable, i.e., that missing would not negatively impact the production and no other entry relied on its achievement. These kinds of entries may be made for notation purposes, but should be noted as *perhaps* or *nice if.* Also, there should not be tracking of minutia that can be assumed as the day-to-day duties of a particular person or department.

As it evolved, the critical path for a production of a play would become an organic thing. As circumstances along the way dictated, it would be revised. For instance, I may have wanted to shorten it if I found that I did not need all the readings I projected; and it would have to expand if I hadn't achieved the fundraising necessary to proceed at a given point. Also, as I would rethink my plan as each step was realized (or missed), or when I changed my mind about any phase that I had previously anticipated, the critical path had to be amended to reflect that change. For instance, if instead of a Showcase, I agreed to the first full production of the play being staged by an institutional theatre, the expenses to be incurred by me in connection with that production were usually different than the costs of the Showcase. As the time frame of that production was dictated by the institutional theatre, it was invariably different from the production dates in my critical path, and often created a time delay, so I had to determine what the timing and cost impacts on any of the subsequent steps of my plan would be.

It was also possible that other considerations, outside of my control, would dictate revisions. Typically, the director's availability for a reading or casting or other critical point of collaboration; theatre availability; waiting for the availability of a key actor; a disaster, newspaper or transit strike, or other socio-economic occurrence. The critical path provided me with an indispensable tool to make certain that I informed everyone that was on board, or in the negotiation pipeline at a given time, of the impacts that a necessitated change would have on them and in turn they could inform me of any conflicts that the change created for them.

CURRENT TITLE: **TOM'S MIDLIFE CRISIS**

PRODUCER'S DIARY AS AT: 3/30/04
[Includes Critical Path Achieved and Noted]

ACTUAL DATES			Out-of-Pocket Development Expense	Fee Paymt.
NOVEMBER	11/1/03	Read Script		
	11/8/03	Made 6 copies of script	$26.00	
	11/22/03	Private Reading w/Lunch– Robt. T. good choice for "TOM"	$32.85	
	11/23/03	Typed-up Notes on Script		
	11/24/03	Tel. w/Attorney		
	11/24/03	Tel. w/G.M.		
	11/26/03	Began Laying out prelim. Long Range Plan (L.R.P.)		
	11/27/03	THANKSGIVING		
	11/28/03	Consulted with Fred V.		
	11/30/03	Finish Rough-out of L.R.P.		

DECEMBER	12/1/03	Tel. w/Playwright (Peter P.)		
	12/8/03	Met w/G.M. - a.o.k. Fee: $2,000	$8.50	
	12/11/03	Met wPlaywright - he seems to get it, we'll see.		
	12/15/03	Met wAttorney Fee: $4,000	$12.00	
	12/17/03	Tel. w/Director A, delivered script	$10.50	
	12/20/03	Tel. Response from Director A - "Not for me."		
	12/22/03	Tel. w/Director B, delivered script	$6.50	
	12/23/03	Tel. Response from Director B - "Let's meet."		
	12/25/03	CHRISTMAS		
	12/27/03	Met w/Dir. B, discussed Script & Long Range Plan	$45.00	
	12/29/03	Tel. Response from Director B - "Let's meet."		

JANUARY	1/3/04	Met w/Dir. B, discussed Long Range Plan & his proposed deal.	$43.75	
	1/4/04	Revised Long Range Plan		
	1/7/04	Met w/Dir. B, re: Revised Long Range Plan & counter-deal.	$65.00	
	1/8/04	Tel. Response from Director B: Ken D. - "Let's go." - Agent: Bob D.		
	1/8/04	Tel. w/Peter P.; Tel. w/Ken D. [both x2]		
	1/15/04	Met w/Peter P. & Ken D - all systems GO!	$82.50	
	1/16/04	Tel. w/Bob D.; e-mail to Bob D.		
	1/18/04	Met wPeter P. - Script Notes, Dir., Plan & Deal a.o.k. - No Agent.	$35.00	
	1/19/04	Check to Attorney		$4,000
	1/19/04	Check to G.M.		$2,000
	1/20/04	Tel. w/Attorney - don't push Agent on Playwright - suggest Attorney		
	1/21/04	e-Mail deal points to Attorney (Playwright & Director) cc: G.M.		
	1/24/04	Tel. from Bob D.; tel. to Attorney (o-o-t Per Diem over Union Min.)		
	1/26/04	Met w/Attorney & G.M. - Proposed Agreements revised	$14.00	
	1/28/04	Attorney Faxed proposed Dir. Agreement to Bob D.		
	1/30/04	Met wPeter P. - gave and reviewed Agreement	$37.50	

FEBRUARY	2/2/04	Tel. w/Bob D.; e-mail from Bob D. - fwd. to Attorney & G.M.		
	2/3/04	Tel. from Attorney; tel. w/Bob D.; e-mail to Bob D. cc: Attny & GM		
	2/5/04	Set-up Pvt. Reading - Robt. T. will do TOM again		
	2/6/04	Delivered Revised Agreement to Duva	$12.00	
	2/6/04	Received signed Agreement from Peter P. (w/very nice note)		
	2/7/04	Tel. w/ Ken D. re: SM: Bill McC. - he doesn't know him - set up meeting		
	2/9/04	Tel. w/Henry R., Fred V., Jeff R., Bill McC.		
	2/13/04	Received signed Agreement from Ken D.		
	2/15/04	Pvt. Reading w/lunch (Peter P., Ken D. & Fred. V. attended)	$45.50	
	2/16/04	Dinner Meet w/Peter P. & Ken D. re: Script & Robt. T.	$85.00	
	2/19/04	Met w/Ken D. & Bill McC.	$56.00	
	2/20/04	Tel. from Ken D. - Bill McC. o.k.; discussed Reading dates		
	2/22/04	Tel. from Ken D. - Casting AGNES & BARBARA		
	2/23/04	Got re-writes from Peter P. (he gave copy to Ken D.)		
	2/24/04	Tel. w/ Ken D. - he likes re-writes & can get M.R. to read AGNES		
	2/24/04	Tel w/Peter P. - M.R. o.k.; no thoughts on BARBARA		
	2/24/04	Tel w/Ken D. & Peter P. re: Casting Director - Judy H. all agreed		
	2/24/04	Tel. w/Judy H. - meet on 27th @ 6:30		
	2/27/04	Met w/Judy H. (w/P.P. & K.D.) re; Casting role of BARBARA	$45.50	
	2/29/04	Tel. w/Judy H. Fee: $1,000		

MARCH	3/4/04	Check to J.H.		$1,000
	3/8/06	Reserve Space for Reading 3/21, 3/22 & 3/24		
	3/9/04	Casting session & Meet w/Peter P. & Ken D. after	$61.00	
	3/10/04	Tel. - Connie W. agreed to read BARBARA; Tel. P.P. & K.D.		
	3/11/04	Calls to organize Public Reading for 3/22 @ 3:00pm		
	3/12/04	Confirmed Space for Reading #1 - 3/22		
	3/15/04	Booked Space for Reading #1	$240.00	
	3/17/04	ST. PATRICK'S DAY		
	3/18/04	Met w/ Ken D., Peter P., Bill McC. & Fred V.	$156.00	
	3/20/04	Rehearsal		$44.00
	3/22/04	Public Reading (#1)	$375.00	
	3/23/04	Met w/Peter P. & Ken D. re: reactions and thoughts	$52.00	
	3/24/04	All agreed need another Public Reading - tent. in 4 wks.		
	3/24/04	Tel. w/Judy H. re: re-cast TOM & AGNES		
	3/30/04	Finished revisions of L.R.P., Laid-out Critical Path		

TOTAL OUT OF POCKET TO DATE:	$1,591.10	
TOTAL FEES PAID TO DATE:		$7,000.00
TOTAL EXPENSES PAID TO DATE:		$8,591.10

CURRENT TITLE: **TOM'S MIDLIFE CRISIS**

CRITICAL PATH (BASED ON CURRENT LONG RANGE PLAN) AS AT: 3/30/04

PROJECTED DATES				
MONTH	DAY	DATE	STATUS	TASKS/ TO DO
APRIL		4/1/04		Casting session @ Judy H.
		4/3/04		Re-writes from Peter P.
		4/5/04		Organize Public Reading #2 for 4/22
		4/6/04		PASSOVER
		4/7/04		Book space for 4/22 Reading
		4/10/04		Commit to Schedule for Backers' Auditions
		4/11/04		EASTER SUNDAY
		4/12/04		Call Press Agent re: B.A.s
		4/22/04		Public Reading (#2)
Re-Commit		4/26/04	BEGIN	Check Availability of Showcase Theatres
MAY		5/3/04	Latest	Meet w/Ken D. re: Designers, etc.
		5/4/04		Invite Designer Candidates to B.A.s
		5/10/04	Earliest	Backers' Aud. #1
		5/26/04	Latest	Backers' Aud. #2
		5/28/04		Leave for Springfield
		5/31/04		MEMORIAL DAY
JUNE		6/1/04		Return to NYC
Re-Commit		6/2/04	Latest	Evaluate Position– Revise L.R.P. accordingly
		6/3/04	Begin	Ascertain Availability of Showcase Theatres
		6/3/04		Call Peter P., Ken D. & Press Agent
		6/4/04	Begin	Negotiation with Showcase Theatre
		6/4/04		Offers to Designers (Qualified)
		6/11/04	Latest	Production Meeting– Director's Concept & Expectations
		6/14/04		Engage Designers
		6/15/04		Go to Alternate Designers, if necessary
		6/18/04	Latest	Tentitively Book Showcase Theatre
		6/23/04	Latest	Full Production Meeting
		6/29/04		Preliminary Design Production Meeting
JULY		7/1/04		Leave for Lake w/HB+KG
		7/6/04		Return to NYC

		7/8/04	Latest	Scenic Design for Approval
		7/9/04		Scene Design Re-Hash Session
		7/16/04	Latest	Approved Scenic Design
		7/19/04	Latest	A.E.A. Showcase Application
			Latest	Production Manager designated
		7/23/04	Latest	A.E.A. Approval secured
				Working Scenic Drawings
			Latest	Confirm Booking of Showcase Theatre
			If Needed	Call Judy H. re: Auditions
			If Needed	Book Audition Space
			If Needed	Book Rehearsal Space 8/9 - 8/28
			Latest	Book Studio Space for Rehearsals 8/31- 9/3 (?)
		7/24/04		Prod. Meet - Lighting & Sound
		7/26/04		*Scenic Bid Session
		7/28/04	Latest	Costume Designs for Approval
		7/29/04		*Scenic Bids In
		7/30/04	Latest	Call Insurance Broker for current options & Initiate for 1st Audition/Reherarsal
AUGUST		8/1/04		Review and Amend C.P.
	M	8/2/04		Confirm 1st Reh. w/everyone– re: Meet & Greet
				Costume Designs Re-Hash
	Tu	8/3/04	Latest	
	W	8/4/04		Act on Scenic Design Execution requirements
	Th	8/5/04		Sound Spec's. out for Bid
		8/5/04		Lighting Spec's. out for Bid
		8/5/04		Wardrobe Supervisor Designated
	F	8/6/04		Award Scene Shop Contract
	Sa	8/7/04	Latest	Costume Designs Approved
	Su	8/8/04		
	M	8/9/04	Target	First Rehearsal & Costume Measuring
	Tu	8/10/04		Rehearsal
	W	8/11/04		Rehearsal
				Sound Bids In
	Th	8/12/04		Rehearsal
				Lighting Bids In

	F	8/13/04		Rehearsal
	Sa	8/14/04		Rehearsal
	Su	8/15/04		Day Off
			Latest	Production Crew Designated
	M	8/16/04		Rehearsal
				Sound Re-Hash
	Tu	8/17/04		Rehearsal
				Lighting Re-Hash
	W	8/18/04		Rehearsal
	Th	8/19/04		Rehearsal
	F	8/20/04		Rehearsal
				Award Sound Shop Contract
	Sa	8/21/04		Rehearsal--Full Run Thru
	Su	8/22/04		Day Off
				Sound Recording Completed
	M	8/23/04		Rehearsal
				Award Lighting Shop Contract
	Tu	8/24/04		Rehearsal
				Costume Fittings - A
	W	8/25/04		Rehearsal
	Th	8/26/04		Rehearsal
	F	8/27/04		Rehearsal
				Costume Fittings - B
	Sa	8/28/04		Rehearsal--Full Run Thru x 2
	Su	8/29/04		Cast Day Off
	M	8/30/04		Rehearsal
				Load-In Set & Lights
				Assemble Set
	Tu	8/31/04		Rehearsal
				Focus & Cue Lights
				Load-In Sound & Costumes
				Install Sound & Test
SEPTEMBER	W	9/1/04		Rehearsal
				(3 Hrs. quiet for Sound EQ.)
				Dry Tech Lighting
	Th	9/2/04		Rehearsal
				Dry Tech Lighting; Set Sound Cue Levels; Full Dry Tech

	F	9/3/04		Rehearsal
				Work Calls, Adjustments, etc.
	Sa	9/4/04		Cue to Cue 12- 4; 5:30 - 7:30
	Su	9/5/04		TechRunThrus 11-4; 5:30-6:30
	M	9/6/04		LABOR DAY
				Cast Day Off
				Re-Focus & touch-up
				(3 hrs. quiet for Sound EQ.)
	Tu	9/7/04		Full Run Thru -- 8 out of 9 Hrs.
	W	9/8/04		Rehearsal & Invited Dress -- 8 out of 9 Hrs.
	Th	9/9/04	Target	Reh. & 1st Performance -- 8 out of 9 Hrs.
	F	9/10/04		
	Sa	9/11/04		
	Su	9/12/04		
	M	9/13/04		
	Tu	9/14/04		
	W	9/15/04		E-ROSH H.
	Th	9/16/04		
	F	9/17/04		
	Sa	9/18/04		
	Su	9/19/04		
	M	9/20/04	Latest	to Decide on Extension
	Tu	9/21/04	Latest	Commit to Mini - Expedite AEA App., PQ, etc. - Additional Theatre Deposit
	W	9/22/04		
	Th	9/23/04		Identify Co. Mgr.
	F	9/24/04		E-YOM K.
	Sa	9/25/04		
	Su	9/26/04		end 3 wk. run - ?
	M	9/27/04		Co. Mgr. Engaged/Begins
	Tu	9/28/04		
	W	9/29/04		
	Th	9/30/04		
OCTOBER	F	10/1/04		
	Sa	10/2/04		
	Su	10/3/04		end 4 wk. run - ?
	M	10/4/04		
	Tu	10/5/04		8:00 - 1st Mini- performance

	W	10/6/04		8:00pm
	Th	10/7/04		6:45pm PRESS
	F	10/8/04		8:00pm PRESS
	Sa	10/9/04		2:30pm & 8:00pm PRESS
	Su	10/10/04		2:30pm PRESS
	M	10/11/04		Day Off (COLUMBUS DAY)
	Tu	10/12/04		***Continue Mini until ... 1/2 or OB Th.***
			Latest	Interest Calls to O-B Theatre Operators
	Tu	10/19/04		
	Tu	10/26/04		
	Tu	11/2/04		Post Provisional Closing Notice— If Capitalization is Not in Sight
	Tu	11/9/04		
NOVEMBER				
	Su	11/14/04		Close Mini - If Capitalization is Not in Sight
	Th	11/25/04		THANKSGIVING
	Su	11/28/04		Evaluate Closing Options (2 wks. Notice to A.E.A.)
DECEMBER				
	Tu	12/7/04		Check-in with O-B Theatre Operators re: Availability
	Su	12/19/04		Potential Closing of Mini-
	Tu	12/21/04		Follow-up with O-B Theatre Operators re: Availability
	W	12/22/04		Personal Conflict (NO BUSINESS)
	Th	12/23/04		Follow-up w/O-B Theatre Operators
	F	12/24/04		CHRISTMAS EVE
	Sa	12/25/04		CHRISTMAS
	F	12/31/04		NEW YEARS EVE
JANUARY	Sa	1/1/05		NEW YEARS DAY
	Su	1/2/05	Latest	Closing of Mini-
	M	1/3/05	Latest	Commence Off-Broadway Theatre Negotiation

CONTINGENCIES

9/22/04 IF MINI'S A GO
EPAs for Replacement and U/S?
Scenic, Prop, Costume Upgrades?
Scenic, Costume, Lighting, Sound Improvements?

MINI-CONTRACT PRODUCTION TRACK

w/e 10/10	Wk. 1	
w/e 10/17	Wk. 2	
w/e 10/24	Wk. 3	
w/e 10/31	Wk. 4	
w/e 11/7	Wk. 5	
w/e 11/14	Wk. 6	Potential Closing #1
w/e 11/21	Wk. 7	+ $20 AEA Longevity Raise
w/e 11/28	Wk. 8	
w/e 12/5	Wk. 9	
w/e 12/12	Wk. 10	
w/e 12/19	Wk. 11	Potential Closing #2
w/e 12/26	Wk. 12	
w/e 1/2	Wk. 13	+ $20 AEA Longevity Raise

IDEAL TRANSFER PRODUCTION TRACK

Week	Date			
WEEK: -8 (w/e 1/16)	1/10/05	A.E.A. Cast Breakdown approved by all		
		A.E.A. Cast Breakdown submitted to Equity & Breakdown Service		
		All O-B Designer Contracts out		
		Prod. Meet re: Production Vision (Dir, all Designers, PSM, GM, designated Co. Mgr.)		
		PSM mutual letter of commitment executed		
		Met w/P.A. & Advert. - campaign presentations		
WEEK: -7 (w/e 1/23)	1/17/05	All Designer Contract Received (signed)		
		A.E.A. Bond Posted		
		INSURANCE IN PLACE		
		Artistic Production Meeting (Show & Tell)		
		Sides for Auditions Prepared		
WEEK: -6 (w/e 1/30)	1/24/05	E.P.As.	Scenic Design for Approval	
		Agency Submissions	Approved Scenic Design	
		Call Backs		
WEEK: -5 (w/e 2/6)	1/31/05	Casting Offers out	Working Scenic Drawings	
			Scenic Bid Session	
		Casting Completed	Production Manager designated	
			Costume Designs for Approval	
			Scenic Bids In	
		All Equity Contracts out	Scene Design Re-Hash	
			Lighting & Sound Meeting	
			Approved Costume Designs	
			Wardrobe Supervisor Designated	
			Lighting Spec's. out for Bid	
			Sound Spec's. out for Bid	
WEEK: -4	2/7/05	Company Manager on	Costume Measuring	Award Scene Shop Contract
Tuesday	2/8/05		Lighting Bids In	
Wednesday	2/9/05		Sound Bids In	
Thursday	2/10/05		Lighting Re-Hash	

Friday	2/11/05		Sound Re-Hash
Saturday	2/12/05		
Sunday	2/13/05		

WEEK: -3	2/14/05	P.S.M. Pre-Production week	
Tuesday	2/15/05		Award Lighting Shop Contract
Wednesday	2/16/05		Award Sound Shop Contract
Thursday	2/17/05		
Friday	2/18/05		Production Crew Designated
Saturday	2/19/05	Asst.Stage Mgr. on - Tape Stage	
Sunday	2/20/05		

WEEK: -2	2/21/05	Rehearsal	
Tuesday	2/22/05	Rehearsal	Costume Fittings - A
Wednesday	2/23/05	Rehearsal	
Thursday	2/24/05	Rehearsal	Full Run Thru
Friday	2/25/05	Rehearsal	Costume Fittings - B
Saturday	2/26/05	Rehearsal	Full Run Thru x 2
Sunday	2/27/05	DAY OFF	

WEEK: -1	2/28/05	Rehearsal in Studio		Take-In Set & Lights	
Tuesday	3/1/05	Rehearsal in Studio	Take-In & Focus	Load-In Sound & Costumes	
Wednesday	3/2/05	Rehearsal in Studio		Focus & Cue Lights	
Thursday	3/3/05	Rehearsal in Studio	Dry Tech	(3 hrs. quiet for Sound EQ.)	
Friday	3/4/05	Rehearsal in Theatre		Tech w/Cast	
Saturday	3/5/05	Rehearsal in Theatre	Tech Run Thru	(3 hrs. quiet for Sound EQ.)	
Sunday	3/6/05	Rehearsal in Theatre		Full Run Thru	

Monday	3/7/05	Rehearsal & Invited Dress
Tuesday	3/8/05	Rehearsal & 1st Preview
Wednesday	3/9/05	Rehearsal & Preview (No Mat.)
Thursday	3/10/05	Rehearsal & Preview
Friday	3/11/05	Rehearsal & Preview
Saturday	3/12/05	Previews Mat. & Eve.
Sunday	3/13/05	DAY OFF
Monday	3/14/05	Rehearsal & Preview

Tuesday	3/15/05	Rehearsal & Preview
Wednesday	3/16/05	Previews Mat. & Eve.
Thursday	3/17/05	Rehearsal & Opening Night
Friday	3/18/05	DAY OFF
Saturday	3/19/05	Mat. & Eve. Perfs.
Sunday	3/20/05	Mat. Perf.

Monday	3/21/05	DAY OFF
Tuesday	3/22/05	8:00
Wednesday	3/23/05	2:00 & 8:00
Thursday	3/24/05	8:00
Friday	3/25/05	8:00
Saturday	3/26/05	2:00 & 8:00
Sunday	3/27/05	3:00

CASH FLOW ANALYSIS

The cash flow analysis, prohibitively expansive to be included herein, is an extension of both the budget and the critical path. Once the budget and critical path were finalized, then it was just a matter of assigning the appropriate portion of each budget line item to a given week based on the critical path. For example, *engage scenic designer* required the initial fee payment and, if on a union contract, the pension and health benefits; *approve scenic design* triggered the next installment of the designer's fee, and prompted *scenic bid session* followed by *award scenic construction contract,* which triggered the initial payment on the scenery line item.

I would begin preparing the cash flow analysis template, which would encompass each phase of the development of a play—from securing the rights and the first private reading through the last developmental production (i.e., until the capitalization was raised for the commercial production), by copying the budget line item titles (but not any Reserve line items). In those cases where a line item was the total of several considerations I would create a break-out of each aspect (for example, under union Pensions I would breakout Director, each of the Designers, Cast, Stage Managers, Understudies, and any other employees under union contract [this way I would save a lot of time by just writing the formula of each union's applicable benefit rates referenced to the applicable line item]. Under THEATRE, Box Office, I would eliminate one of the two Box Office lines (Preliminary & Performance) and title the remaining one just Box Office and under House Staff, I would make a line item for each of the House Managers, Technicians, and Porters. If I were not working on a musical, I would expunge all of the Musical related line items, from Musical Instruments and Stands Rental, through the BOND for A.F. of M. Local 802. I would also expunge any other line items that I knew would never come into consideration for any production of a particular play, such as Follow Spot Operator(s). But I would not expunge those that could conceivably evolve as the play was developed, such as Props—perishable or Recorded Voices where none were required by the current draft of the script. And I would not expunge the redundant listings of House Manager, Box Office, and Porter under both Cast and Staff Costs and THEATRE until the last developmental production theatre agreement was signed and I knew whether one or more of those positions came with the theatre and which, if any, would be my responsibility.

Just as the critical path is laid out first by the time period of a phase (preliminary, private readings, public readings, backers' auditions) and then, as the first development production approaches, in weeks, so is the cash flow analysis. However, where the critical path weekly headings are usually "week ending" (w/e), because funds need to be on hand from the beginning of each week, I recommend that the weekly headings for the cash flow analysis be "week of" (w/o) with the date of the Monday of each week. Each revision of the critical path would necessitate a revision of the cash flow analysis, whether or not it caused a revision of the budget.

Most producers do not engage an accountant to perform periodic bookkeeping for the developmental expenses incurred. They do it themselves or have an assistant do it. Usually a producer will make a weak attempt at best to keep track of their own out-of-pocket expenses. The cost of transportation, restaurant meetings, postage, photocopying, and similar expenses can become sizable over time. One way to keep track is using the critical path to note the expenses incurred in connection with each activity as they occur, and then they can easily be transferred to the cash flow analysis.

DEVELOPMENTAL PRESENTATION/PRODUCTION ELECTIVES

The various options that I consider for the development of a play begin with the consideration of working outside the jurisdiction of the performer's unions (*non-union*). I can do this only if I do not intend to engage any Actors (the word "Actor" with a capital "A" is all-inclusive of the membership of *Actors' Equity*

Association ["A.E.A." or "Equity"]: Actors, Stage Managers, Understudies, Chorus Performers and Swings) who are a member of any of the Associated Actors and Artistes of America (the "four As,") affiliate unions, which most notably include Equity, Screen Actors Guild, American Federation of Television and Radio Artists, American Guild of Musical Artists and American Guild of Variety Artists, even if they are on *honorary withdrawal* ("union member"). If I do intend to engage any union member(s), then I must work under the jurisdiction of Equity. An exception to this is developing the play in an accredited school with their students without any outside (non-enrolled) union members, even if some of the students are union members.

Equity requires that an application be made requesting permission to use their Staged Reading Guidelines, Staged Reading Contract, Showcase Code, Mini-Contract, and Workshop Agreement/Contract, with each application requiring specific information relevant to the production.

READINGS

Both the Equity Staged Reading Guidelines and the Equity Staged Reading Contract strictly enforce: for invited audiences only; NO admission may be charged, NO advertising; Book in hand, NO memorization; NO choreography; NO scenery; NO props; NO costumes, NO wigs and NO make-up; and NO recording of any kind. And when they say no, they mean NO!

Equity Staged Reading Guidelines

Promulgated by Equity, these guidelines currently* cover all rehearsals and up to a maximum of three readings within a fourteen-day period. "There may be only one use of the Staged Reading Guidelines per project without the express written permission of Equity." For up to a total of fifteen hours of service (twenty hours for musicals), "such times to be at the Actor's convenience," there is no specified minimum compensation, only reimbursement for the Actors' actual transportation expenses. "Hours" are determined on a daily basis for all hours *and parts thereof* from "time called" to "time released" (excluding a meal break not exceeding one and a half hours, which must be taken to avoid working more than five consecutive hours). If fifteen hours is exceeded, then, for up to a maximum of twenty-nine hours, all Actors must be paid a minimum "stipend" of one hundred

---

* All rates are as of December 31, 2004, unless noted otherwise. Always verify current rates and conditions with the appropriate business representative at Actors' Equity Association, 165 W. 46th St., New York, NY 10036 (212) 869-8530. Drop in or call and ask the receptionist or switchboard operator for the business representative for the guidelines, code, agreement or contract you are interested in.

dolllars and reimbursement of their transportation costs. If twenty-nine hours is exceeded, then the Equity Staged Reading Contract (see page XXX) automatically applies [retro-actively to the first Actor's call]. The Staged Reading Guidelines allows only "minimum staging," which, at most, allows for the actors to enter from off-stage or rise from a seat at the side of the stage, deliver their dialogue at a designated place (standing or sitting) and exit off-stage or return to a seat at the side of the stage and sit, not interactive blocking. It also requires that all rehearsal and performance spaces be wheelchair accessible (unless the space has been "grandfathered" by Equity). Non-union actors may be engaged but do not qualify for membership by virtue of the engagement. Non-Resident Aliens may not be engaged. Any Actor may withdraw from participation at any time without notice. Insurance is not specifically required.

While on the subject of insurance, whenever I engage one or more actors (whether or not they are going to be paid), I am technically their employer in the eyes of New York State. I am responsible for them from the time they arrive at the "place of employment" to the time of their departure from the premises (and if they are going straight home, then to the time they arrive at their domicile). Over the years I have become very knowledgeable about Small Business Laws, Federal and New York State Labor and Employment Laws, and the nature, scope, and cost of the various insurance coverage potentials that are available to me and the ones I must have or may want to consider. Even with this acquired knowledge, I still consult with my attorney and insurance broker to make sure that nothing has changed, and when there have been changes, to become familiar with them. I strongly recommend that anyone pursuing the development of a play speak to their attorney and an insurance broker about their potential liabilities, contractual requirements and statutory mandated coverages.

Equity Staged Reading Contract

A *Special Agreement* promulgated by Equity, covers all rehearsals and presentations within a two-week period, and allows for only "minimum blocking, which will not interfere with the Actor's ability to refer to the script." Through October 23, 2005, the minimum weekly salaries are: $437 for Actors; $524 for the Stage Manager (who shall be paid for no less than three days of pre-production work, pro-rated at one-sixth per day); and $481 for an Assistant Stage Manager. Each work week is limited to thirty cumulative hours. Overtime (except for Stage Managers) is permitted only with the prior written consent of Equity, and when permitted is at the current* Off-Broadway rate: seventeen dollars per hour or part thereof. Any actor or stage manager who is non-Equity must be treated the same as an Equity member and may become a member of Equity. The producer may elect either a six-day work week of a maximum of five hours per day; or a five-day work week of six out of seven and a half hours per day, but may not mix. The producer must provide Equity with a schedule of the presentations when making application for the contract. Although not stated in the contract, Equity limits the number of presentations that may be given, but has allowed more than three for which they negotiated additional compensation for the Actors. A full security bond must be posted before individual contracts can be issued. All Actors receive conversion and contingent rights(*buyout*) if not offered their role or function for a subsequent contract production or the play is produced in another medium, which is more thoroughly addressed under Showcase Productions, see page XXX). Pension (8%) and Health at the Off-Broadway rate, currently $131.50* per Actor per week (including the Stage Manager's pre-production work) apply. [If the first week begins on other than a Monday or Tuesday (or Wednesday, if a five-day work week), there will be a third week of Health payments due, whether or not the Actors actually work in that week.] Payroll taxes apply, including employer's contributions for Unemployment Insurance, Social Security, and Medicare.

Rule 18 of the current* Equity Staged Reading Contract states: "All other terms and conditions of the AGREEMENT GOVERNING EMPLOYMENT OFF-BROADWAY, including provisions for arbitration of any dispute arising hereunder, shall apply at the discretion of Equity as though set forth herein." It should be noted that, among other provisions, Rule 41 of the current* Off-Broadway Agreement provides that any Actor may, at any time after signing the Equity Stage Reading Contract, with two days prior written notice of more remunerative employment in the entertainment industry, take an unpaid leave of absence of one or two days during the rehearsal period prior to the technical rehearsal.

If I were ever to use the Equity Staged Reading Contract, and did not have a business entity already set up, I would shop around for a *paymaster service,* that would act as the *employer of record* so I wouldn't have to create a business entity (for which I would have to pay a lawyer, pay a filing fee and open a bank account, file Federal, State and Local tax returns and pay annual corporate or unincorporated business taxes for the business entity, and make all the payroll tax filings) and have to get Liability insurance (for which there is a minimum annual premium), and Workers' Compensation and Disability insurance (for which there are minimum

* See footnote page 255.

quarterly premiums). And, if I didn't have the knowledge, ability and time necessary to take care of the calculations and required filings myself, I would have to engage an accountant. A *paymaster service* eliminates the need for me to create a business

entity and fulfills all these needs for which I will pay a flat rate charge and/or a percentage of the total payroll expenses (depends on which paymaster service, the number of checks each week and the gross weekly payroll expenses) which in the aggregate will usually be significantly less than I would otherwise end up paying, and without the aggravation.

The producer of a play is the employer of everyone engaged in connection with the production of the play, except those rendering services as an *independent contractor*, the determination of which is very specifically defined by State Employment Law. Whenever I engage someone to work on a play with me (other than Actors and Stage Managers), who will be receiving a fee (i.e., no payroll tax deductions will be made) and I believe qualifies as an independent contractor (for instance, the director, any designers, consultants, press, and marketing people, whose work is not "under my direct supervision"), I state in the letter of agreement between us that we mutually acknowledge that the services to be rendered are those of an independent contractor. This will effectively reduce my payroll tax liabilities and Workers' Compensation and Disability premiums.

When reading an Equity code or contract, there are two things in particular that I look for. First, the effective expiration date. Then to see if there is a reference to another contract, such as Rule 18 of the current* Equity Staged Reading Contract: "All other terms and conditions of the AGREEMENT GOVERNING EMPLOYMENT OFF-BROADWAY, including provisions for arbitration of any dispute arising hereunder, shall apply at the discretion of Equity as though set forth herein."

SHOWCASE PRODUCTIONS

There are two Equity Showcase Codes, both promulgated by Equity: one for Seasonal Institutional producing companies (which I will not address); and one for *one shot* producers, THE BASIC SHOWCASE CODE (NEW YORK CITY), which the current* rules allow for up to twelve performances to be given within a four-week period with a maximum of four consecutive weeks of rehearsal (six-day week, six hours per day [except the last three days may be eight hours] with a one-hour meal break after no more than five hours), which must be scheduled

---

* See footnote page 246.

according to the availability of the Actors. The production is to be presented in a theatre with a seating capacity of less than one hundred. The Actors receive minimum public transportation reimbursement only, except that there is a "most favored nations" provision that requires the producer to pay the Actors the same amount that is paid to anyone engaged in any capacity for the production (the director, choreographer, musicians, designers, et al.). An additional four performances may be added for which the Actors are to be paid a stipend of ten dollars per performance. Ticket prices are limited to fifteen dollars* and TDF vouchers must be accepted. The producer is required to obtain volunteer accident insurance prior to any interviews or auditions. Rehearsals after the first paid public performance are subject to the consent of the Actors involved, scheduled to the availability of the Actors, are limited to 3 hours on non-performance days, and on a performance day the total rehearsal and performance time (measured from the half hour call), but not including the 1 hour meal break, cannot exceed 6 hours. Once a play is presented under the Showcase Code, it may not be presented under the Showcase Code again for one year. The production may not be recorded in any way at any time until twenty-six weeks after the closing. An Actor may leave the production at any time without prior notice.

The application for an Equity Showcase Code (which must be made no less than fourteen days prior to the first rehearsal) requires, among other things: the name of the theatre; the proposed rehearsal and performance schedule; a statement of financial backing, the budget (which must be under twenty thousand dollars); and detailed supporting documentation. And within ten days following the final performance, the producer is required to submit a statement of actual expenses, income and attendance.

All of the Equity Actors may be entitled to conversion rights—in the event of a subsequent production under an Equity Contract, they must either be given a bona fide offer to perform their role or function or paid a buyout. The specific time frame that these rights pertain will depend on which contract (Production, Off-Broadway, L.O.R.T., etc.) the subsequent production is produced. However, as long as the producer notifies the subsequent producing interests and Equity of the Showcase Code production, in writing prior to the beginning of casting for the subsequent production, the producer shall have no obligation to the Actors— it becomes the sole obligation of the subsequent producing interests.

The Equity Actors also may be entitled to subsidiary rights—in the event of a subsequent production in another medium (motion picture, television, video,

---

* By March, 2006, the maximum ticket price had increased to eighteen dollars.

etc.) for which the rights were acquired within four years following the final performance of the Showcase Code production, unless the Actor is engaged to perform their identical role or function in the media production, they are entitled to a buyout, to be paid from up to a maximum of 50 percent of the Showcase producer's total proceeds derived from participation in the author's subsequent *disposition* and/or *exploitation* of the play ("Subsidiary Rights participation"), if any.

Non-Union actors may be engaged for an Equity Showcase production but may not gain membership as a result of the engagement and do not have Conversion or Subsidiary rights or "most favored nations" entitlement. *Non-resident Aliens may not be engaged.*

EQUITY WORKSHOP AGREEMENT/CONTRACT

This is intended to be used by a producer that is developing a script from an idea or re-shaping and extensively rewriting a script and relying on the active participation of the Actors in the process.

Equity requires the producer and author to sign an Agreement assigning the Actors engaged for a Workshop production a royalty to be derived from *all* subsequent productions and other exploitation of the play. Each Workshop Contract is negotiated between Equity and the producer and individually crafted by Equity to meet the Producer's stated requirements. The minimum salary for Actors will depend on the number of rehearsal days per week (five or six) elected by the producer, the overall duration of the Workshop production and any unpaid breaks. The number of presentations ("attended rehearsals") and the total number of invited audience is limited.

MINI-CONTRACT

The Equity Mini-Contract is promulgated by Equity. It was originally devised as a means of extending a Showcase production with some possibility of commercial viability. Although it is still used for that purpose, a number of producers have been allowed to use it without first doing a Showcase production. This contract is a set of modifications to the Off-Broadway Contract. It applies to theatres with a seating capacity of less than one hundred, requires posting a bond and submitting box office Statements weekly.

The Mini-Contract currently* allows up to seven performances per week. Rehearsals are limited to a maximum of four consecutive weeks, six days each

* See footnote page 246.

week, six hours per day, with a one and a half hour meal break after no more than five hours; except during the week prior to, and the week of, the first paid public performance there may be two ten-out-of-eleven-and-a-half-hour days, but the work week may not exceed thirty-nine hours and on a performance day the rehearsal may not exceed five hours. Musical productions are allowed an initial fifth week of rehearsals limited to vocal rehearsals only, five hours per day for five days. In the second week of performances, rehearsal is limited to a total of eight hours with no more than three hours on any one day, for which the Actors are paid seventeen dollars per hour or part thereof. Thereafter rehearsals are limited to five hours per week. However, rehearsal is permitted in lieu of a performance, but only for the duration of time established from the half hour call to curtain down. And up to three hours of overtime is permitted weekly, for which the Actors are paid thirty-four dollars per hour or part thereof.

All roles except star and bit parts must have an understudy. Understudies are required to be engaged no later than the beginning of the third performance week. For announced Limited Run productions the Understudies do not have to be engaged until the beginning of the seventh performance week. A performing Actor may understudy up to three roles, a general understudy may cover up to five roles.

Currently* minimum weekly salaries are determined by the seating capacity of the theatre: up to 50 seats, 51–75 seats and 76–99 seats. For rehearsals, Performing Actors and Understudies receive $303, $322 or $343; Stage Managers receive $390, $401 or $419; and Assistant Stage Managers receive $328, $347 or $368. For performances, there is a sliding scale based on gross weekly box office receipts with increases beginning at $9.1 thousand and when more than $15 thousand, escalating to the Off-Broadway category "A" minimums, currently* $493 for performing actors. There are also "longevity" increases of twenty dollars per week at the seventh performance week and again at the thirteenth performance week. However, if any Actor receives a weekly salary greater than the Off-Broadway "E" category minimum, currently* $857, then the minimum for all Actors will be the Off-Broadway category "A" minimum (if this is going to be the case, it is advisable to use the Off-Broadway (category "A") Contract from the outset). Also, the Off-Broadway category "A" minimum salaries will apply after eighteen performance weeks (and the bond needs to be increased). Whenever the Mini-Contract production is going to continue running beyond eighteen performance weeks, four weeks beforehand it is advisable to request a conversion to the Off-

* See footnote page 246.

Broadway (category "A") Contract effective the beginning of the nineteenth week, to post the increase in the Bond and issue Off-Broadway contracts to the Actors. Among other benefits, this will allow an eight-performance week.

All Actors are entitled to conversion and contingent Rights, Pension (8%), Health at the Off-Broadway rate, currently* $131.50 per Actor per week (including the Stage Manager's pre-production work) and 1 week of Vacation after twenty-five weeks of employment. Payroll taxes apply, including employer's contributions for Unemployment Insurance, Social Security, and Medicare.

Any non-Union Actor engaged must become a member of Equity. **No Non-resident Alien may be engaged.**

OFF-BROADWAY

Equity and The League of Off-Broadway Theatres and Producers negotiate the Agreement and Rules Governing Employment under the Off-Broadway Agreement. The current* Agreement sets forth seventy-four Rules in ninety-four pages and expires on October 23, 2005. Off-Broadway is divided into 5 categories: "A" applies to theatres with up to 199 seats; "B" for seating of 200–250; "C" for seating of 251–299; "D" for seating of 300–350; and "E" for seating of 351–499. The current* minimum weekly salary for actors range from $493 for category "A" to $857 for category "E." Category "A" salaries are on a sliding scale based on Gross Weekly Box Office Receipts and cap at $556 when the Gross exceeds $60,683.

---

* See footnote page 246.

A.E.A. CONDITIONS & RATES FOR DEVELOPMENTAL PRODUCTIONS

	STAGED READING GUIDELINES	STAGED READING CONTRACT	APPROVED SHOWCASE CODE	MINI-CONTRACT	OFF-B'WAY CATGRY. "A"
Max. Reh. Period	2 - 4 Days	2 Wks.	4 Wks.	4 Wks. (Mus. + 1)	5 Wks.
Reh. Days/Wk.	(Maximum of)	6 (or 5)	6	6	6
Reh. Hrs./Day	15 Hrs. Drama	5 (or 6)	6 + Last 3 = 8	6 of 7.5	7 of 8.5 (LAST + 3: 10 OUT OF 11.5)
Max. Reh. Hrs./Wk.	(20 Hrs. Musical)	30 Hrs.	36 (42 Last Wk.)	36 (39 Last Wk.)	42 (58 Last wk.)
Actor $/Wk. Min.	Rehearsal & up to 3 Read's NO PAY	437	0	*303 / 322 / 343	493
SM $/Wk. Min.		524	0	*390 / 401 / 419	581 / 591
ASM $/Wk. Min.		481	0	*328 / 347 / 368	528
Sliding Scale	n/a	n/a	n/a	Yes - To O-B "A"	YES ["A" Only]
Longevity Increase	n/a	n/a	n/a	$20 @ Wks. 7 & 13	YES
Reimbursement	Actual Exp.	Actual Exp.	$3/Day + Exp.	NO	NO
Favorded Nations	n/a	NO	YES !	NO	NO
Non-Pro's.	O.K.	O.K.	O.K.	NO	NO
Make Member	NO	YES	NO	YES	YES
Payroll Tax	NO	YES	NO	YES	YES
Pension	NO	8%	NO	8%	8%
Health	NO	YES	NO	YES	YES
Bond	NO	YES	NO	YES	YES
Insurance	Qualified NO	YES	YES	YES	YES
Unemployment	NO	YES	NO	YES	YES
Max. Run	3 Perf's.	12 Perf's.	*12 Perf's. IN Up to 4 Wks.	18 Wks. = O-B "A"	OPEN-ENDED
Perf's/Wk.	n/a	6		7	8
Max. Audience	Invited/NoLimit	Invited/NoLimit	99 Seats	*99 Seats	199 Seats

	STAGED READING GUIDELINES	STAGED READING CONTRACT	APPROVED SHOWCASE CODE	MINI-CONTRACT	OFF-B'WAY CATGRY. "A"
Max. Ticket $	No Charge	No Charge	$15 + TDF V.	NO LIMITS	NO LIMITS
Buy-Out	NO	YES	YES	YES	YES
M.P. Rights	NO	YES	YES	YES	YES
w/AEA Approval	Provisional	YES	YES	YES	NO
Budget Limit	NO	NONE	$20,000	NONE	NONE
			*includes 4 Perfs. Ext.	*- 50 / 51- 75 / 76 -	

ALL THINGS ARE NEGOTIABLE—ALMOST ALWAYS (SOMETIMES).

The above chart is provided as a guide to the Actors' Equity Association conditions for their Staged Reading Guidelines and Contract, Basic Showcase Code (NYC), Mini-Contract, and Off-Broadway Contract (Category "A") that were in effect at the end of December 2004.

Some of the headings in the left hand column are in short hand. The full titles are:

Maximum rehearsal period

Rehearsal days per week

Rehearsal hours per day

Maximum rehearsal hours per week

Minimum Weekly Compensation for Actors

Minimum Weekly Compensation for Stage Managers

Minimum Weekly Compensation for Assistant Stage Managers

Sliding Scale (Based on Gross Weekly Box Office Receipts)

Longevity Increases

Reimbursement

"Most Favored Nations" condition imposed

Non-Professionals (i.e., an Actor who is not a member of any of the 4 A's unions)

Make a member of AEA (non-Union actors must/may join Equity)

Payroll taxes applicable

Pension contribution applicable

Health (sometimes referred to as "Welfare") contribution applicable

Security Agreement and Bond

Insurance required

Unemployment applicable

Maximum run

Maximum performances per week

Maximum audience (per performance)

Maximum ticket price

Contingent rights with Buy-Out if not offered same role or function

Motion Picture rights

A.E.A. Approval required

Budget Limitations

I couldn't possibly responsibly outline the significant terms and conditions within the confines of this chapter. I urge anyone who is going to pursue developmental productions to get their own copy and make notes while reading it. However, I will point out that Rule 41 of the Off-Broadway Agreement provides that an Actor may, in order to accept more remunerative employment in the entertainment industry, take an unpaid leave of absence of one or two days with two days prior written notice; or up to three weeks with nine days prior written notice, or terminate their employment with twelve days prior written notice.

If after having read an Equity guidelines, code, agreement, or contract, you find that one or more of the provisions make it prohibitive for your intended use, do not presume that you should not continue to pursue it. Approach the appropriate Equity business representative and explain what the issue is. Equity has a long history of allowing concessions (waiver or modification of a Rule) but you should anticipate Equity wanting quid pro quo for the concession, if granted.

For Fred, with all my admiration and respect.

Now, get those angels into rehearsal!

Roger Alan Gindi

Roger Alan Gindi is the head of the Gindi Theatrical Management, which is a theatrical producing and general management firm. During the 2004–05 season he produced a tour of *Tea at Five* and Jay Johnson in his critically acclaimed show, *The Two and Only*, which he will be producing on Broadway in Fall 2006. He recently managed Whoopi Goldberg and Charles S. Dutton in August Wilson's *Ma Rainey's Black Bottom* on Broadway, as well as *Jolson and Company, Blue Burning, Class Mothers '68*, and *Heat Lightning* Off-Broadway. The previous season he was represented by the Off-Broadway productions of *Thunder Knocking on the Door* and *Endpapers*; and the season before that he was represented on Broadway by both August Wilson's *King Headley II* and *The Gathering*, and by *I Sing!* and *If It Was Easy* Off-Broadway. He was a producer of *Maybe Baby It's You* and *Shakespeare's R&J*, the hit four-man adaptation of *Romeo and Juliet* Off-Broadway. He was general manager for August Wilson's award-winning *Jitney* and supervisor of its London production at the Royal National Theatre, followed by a tour of Seattle and San Francisco. He was general manager of *Nunsense A-Men!* Off-Broadway and the hip-hop musical *Jam on the Groove* on an international tour. He was general manager of *Warp, The Amazing Metrano*, Dan Butler's one-man play *The Only Thing Worse You Could Have Told Me…* and *Lust* (the musical). He was also general manager of both of Dan Goggin's hit musicals, *Nunsense* and *Nunsense II: The Sequel*, the Broadway engagement of Famous People Players in *A Little More Magic*, and David Mamet's controversial hit Off-Broadway play *Oleanna*, as well its national tour. Also on Broadway, Mr. Gindi served as producer of Abraham Tetenbaum's *Crazy He Calls Me*, starring Polly Draper and Barry Miller, the associate producer of Alan Ayckbourn's *A Small Family Business*, and general manager of Richard Baer's Broadway Alliance comedy, *Mixed Emotions*, starring

Katherine Helmond and Harold Gould. Off-Broadway he was general manager of the *Cover of Life*, *Smiling Through*, *The Destiny of Me*, *Raft of the Medusa*, *Balancing Act*, *Loose Lips*, and the workshop production of *Cristobal Colon*. Mr. Gindi was general manager of *A Change in the Heir*, a new Broadway musical at the Edison Theatre. Additionally, he general managed the Broadway Alliance production of *Our Country's Good*, which was nominated for six Tony Awards including Best Play. He has also served as theatrical manager for the past three *Victoria's Secret* fashion shows.

For the past twenty years, Mr. Gindi has been general manager of the long-running musical comedy *Nunsense* and its offspring. *Nunsense* has been performed in hundreds of theatres of all sizes across the country and around the world and was recently on a highly successful national tour. To date, *Nunsense* has returned a profit in excess of 2,750% on its original investment.

Mr. Gindi is currently working with several producers on shows planned for Broadway and Off-Broadway next season, including *Princesses*, a new Broadway musical comedy; and *Deep Song*, a flamenco-infused musical inspired by the life and works of Federico Garcia Lorca.

Mr. Gindi began working independently as a general manager in 1982 with *It's Better with a Band* at Sardi's. He has served in that capacity for numerous showcase productions and workshops, one of which became *Nunsense*. He has been involved in theatrical management since 1973. He spent eight years with the New York Shakespeare Festival serving as company manager on such shows as *Runaways*, *For Colored Girls...*, *A Chorus Line*, and *I'm Getting My Act Together...*, including their Public Theatre runs as well as their commercial transfers Off- and on Broadway. In 1981, with the commercial transfer of *March of the Falsettos* from Playwrights Horizons, Mr. Gindi began his association with Gatchell and Neufeld, Ltd., where he worked as company manager on numerous shows including *Beyond Therapy*, *Hurlyburly*, *Song & Dance*, *Smile*, *Cats*, and *Starlight Express*.

I'M NOT A [INSERT PROFESSION HERE], BUT I PLAY ONE IN THE THEATRE

ROGER ALAN GINDI
President, Gindi Theatrical Management

When asked, "What does an Off-Broadway *general manager* do?" I often reply, half-jokingly, "Just say no." I spend a lot of time telling designers, directors, and even producers, "No, we can't afford that."

A *lawyer* for a producer, who was about to engage my services as a general manager, once asked me to add a job description to the standard contract for my services. Here's the paragraph we mutually negotiated; it has stayed a part of my contract for over fifteen years:

> Gindi Theatrical Management will cause Roger Alan Gindi to perform to the best of his ability and with all due diligence the services of a General Manager for a first rate production in connection with all presentations of the Play produced by Producer. These duties include, but are not limited to, working in conjunction with the Producer and the production attorneys on authors' options, financing documents and budgets, negotiating and administering contracts for actors, directors, designers, theatre, advising on publicity and advertising layout, working in conjunction with the production accountants on production and operating statements, assigning and administering house seats, paying bills (to the extent of available funds provided by Producer), assisting Producer with all routine and customary financial matters with respect to the play, maintaining records and files of the above, and generally being available as consultant to the Producer.

Much of this needs no elucidation, but I will try to clarify where I feel necessary. Many of the producers I work with—though far from all of them—are relatively inexperienced and need a general manager to take them through the process of producing a play. In many cases, these are the same concerns as I have whether I manage a Broadway or Off-Broadway production; the difference being that on Broadway there is often more leeway because the *capitalization* is many times that of one Off-Broadway.

Generally, the producer will have already identified an already-written script that he wishes to produce. On much rarer occasion the producer will have an idea for a play or musical and I will assist in finding the writer(s) who can best turn the idea into a script. Either way it will require a negotiation with the author's representative (either lawyer or agent) on the *option* or *commissioning document*. Usually it is the producer's attorney who leads this negotiation, but a general manager's input is vital to the process because many issues will arise that are outside the purview of legal counsel. For example, will we require a royalty pool and if so what will the parameters be? This is something that requires ballpark budgets at least for production and operating costs—more about that later—and what the production requires (or at least can be lived with). How can we make the production attractive to investors in terms of recoupment and possible profit while properly compensating the author (and other creative personnel) for their work? Although there are basic parameters of royalties and alternative royalty formulas, each production will have different needs and the option will reflect these. Among other issues for the option would be what kind of author's *billing* would be appropriate, how much (if any) per diem living expense the author should receive when away from his home town, what participation the producers (and their investors) will have in the *subsidiary rights* in the play, and to whom and how many *house seats* or opening night tickets will be made available. Sometimes the author wants something and on behalf of the producer I just say no, although sometimes I suggest to the producer that saying yes will serve him better in the long run.

Before the producer's attorney can create *offering documents* for the investors, a budget is required that will show how the capitalization will be spent, how much it will cost each week to operate the show, and how the production might *recoup* the capitalization at various levels of box office capacity. I had had a couple of shows where the producer informed me that offering papers had already been issued based on figures they felt could be raised, and I had to *back into the budget* (adjust line items so that the total capitalization was the same as in the offering papers). In one case, I was able to do this. In another, the producer had devised a capitalization so low it would have been impossible to produce the show, so we had to issue revised offering papers even though they had already received signed papers and checks from a few investors. It is therefore wise to have a general manager retained prior to issuing offering papers.

It is important that each step in the production process be done with the idea of what will be best for the investors. I try to keep our production and running costs as low as possible in an attempt to accelerate return of the investors' investment, but many times I have to remind a producer that we cannot be penny wise and pound foolish. We have to be responsible and always accountable in the long term for the decisions made.

Many of the line items in a budget will be simple math. For example, rehearsal salary is almost always at the applicable Actors' Equity (AEA) minimum salary, so the line item for actors' salaries will be

$$(\text{The number of actors}) \times (\text{the number of weeks of rehearsal}) \times (\text{the AEA minimum})$$
$$= \text{total amount of weekly rehearsal salary}$$

Other items require knowledge of past practice (sometimes combined with union regulations). Among them:

What will the fees for the director or designers be? This will be based on their experience and the scope of the production.

What should the physical production (sets, props, costumes, lighting and sound equipment) cost for the production? I will have to balance the practical needs of the script with the desires of the director and designers and a proper amount relative to the size other theatre involved and its gross and sales potential.

How much *advertising* should we budget before we start running? How much while running? These will be based on theatre size and what we feel we have to sell—a show with no *names* (well-known actors) might spend less *up front* and anticipate spending more once the reviews come in.

How much reserve do we think is necessary to be part of the capitalization? On *Oleanna*, an Off-Broadway two-character one-set play by David Mamet, I budgeted about $100 thousand in reserve for preview and *operating losses*. However, the initial demand for tickets was so high that we started making an *operating profit* from the first performance and were able to return 25 percent of the capitalization on opening night. Other shows have not been as lucky and have had to take *priority loans* (non-recourse loans that are returned to the lenders prior to the return of any capital to the investors) to keep the show running, despite a generous reserve in the capitalization.

The Roger Gindi Off-Broadway co-production of the
1998 Lucille Lortel Award-winning *Shakespeare's R&J*. Pictured are
Greg Shamie as Romeo and Daniel J. Shore as Juliet.
Photo by Carol Rosegg, courtesy of the John Willis Theatre World/Screen World Archive.

Once the budget has been created (often negotiated between myself and the producer, balancing the pragmatic with the ideal), I must then negotiate with the various people (usually through their agents or attorneys), and endeavor to keep within budget. Generally I hope to pay no more than is in the budget; sometimes I am able to negotiate way below the budgeted amount and sometimes the representative has higher figures in mind. On rare occasion, I must just say no and we move on to a second choice of director, actor, designer, and so forth; sometimes the producer and I will determine that paying more than we had budgeted is necessary for the good of the production.

Negotiation is a fine art. I try to initially make a fair offer in the lower end of the range where I hope to end up; making too lowball an offer may set up an antagonistic relationship that could eventually lead to a higher final figure when the representative digs his heels in for a fight. I try to keep each negotiation distinct, not allowing my past experience with the agent in question to color my position on the new project. If an agent and I ever get into a heated argument, I believe that we each know we are only riled up about the specific issues at hand, and the next day we could be very cordial negotiating about a different client in a different production. Such is the small world of *commercial* producing.

When we ultimately come to terms, contracts must be written. Even today, with the technological help of being able to Cut and Paste together a contract, each document must be looked at as unique to the specific circumstance and production. Quickly using boilerplate language can create some humorous papers. On a recent musical, although both his attorney and I had gone over the contract several times, a lighting designer came to me with his unsigned contract chuckling that he thought his billing probably should not read "Scenic Design by..." Although I had performed a Find and Replace function in my word processing to change "Lighting" to "Scenic" throughout his contract, I failed to catch them all. I try to have the major contracts (theatre, author, and director) vetted by the production attorneys; on others I only consult them when I have a specific concern.

Like the old advertisement with a man wearing surgical mask who says, "I'm not a doctor but I play one on TV," I'm not a lawyer (or accountant, advertising executive, or theatre critic), but I play all those roles when giving the producer advice about his production. Years of experience in the business give a general manager a great deal of knowledge about many areas. It is a situation where being a jack of all trades and having a little knowledge in a lot of areas can actually be a good thing, saving the producer a lot of time and money in seeking advice from an attorney or accountant. In fact, in today's producing environment, it is often the general manger who is the constant, full-time, and seasoned professional on the management team. Today it takes multiple producers to finance and mount one show, and many of these producers do not always work full time in the field. They remain at other, more lucrative professions and produce as a second career. The general manager has therefore become a central clearinghouse for the group of producers and it is even becoming possible for a group of producers to have one producer as executive in charge of assigning that task to a general manger.

Three things for a producer or producing team to remember when "casting" a general manager:

1. Look for transparency, trust, and candidness in the relationship. The producer needs to needs to hear the good, the bad, and the ugly from the general manager and must have expertise and communication in the relationship. And, the general manager has to feel the same about the producer.
2. Get a general manager early in the process and before a capitalization total has been determined.
3. Expect a general manager to challenge, ask good questions, give opinions, and in the end, support your decisions (as long as they are legal, in good faith with investors, and proper according to contracts agreed upon).

…and don't feel so bad when your general manager just says no.

Jason Baruch

Jason Baruch, a graduate of New York University School of Law, is a partner at the law firm Franklin, Weinrib, Rudell, & Vassallo, P.C., where he represents clients in the areas of theatre, publishing, television, motion pictures, new media, and music. Jason has served as production counsel for such stage productions as *The Producers* (Broadway, national tours, Canada, Australia, U.K. and other foreign productions), Sarah Jones' *bridge & tunnel*, *On Golden Pond*, *Dame Edna: Back With A Vengeance*, *Death of a Salesman*, *Dance of Death*, *The Price*, *Dirty Blonde*, and *The Exonerated*. Jason has also served as legal counsel to regional and developmental theatres around the country, including Signature Theatre in Virginia, Denver Center for the Performing Arts, and The Culture Project, and he represents dramatists such as Pulitzer Prize and Tony Award-winner Douglas Wright, author of *Quills* and *I Am My Own Wife*. He currently serves a chairman of the Theatre and Performing Arts Committee of the Entertainment, Arts, Sports Law Section of the New York State Bar Association, and is on the Board of Directors of HERE Center for the Performing Arts in New York. Jason organizes and participates in numerous panels and lectures on the subject of theatre and was the lawyer-teacher for the Commercial Theater Institute's 2006 intensive twelve-week course.

Jason received his undergraduate degree from Yale University. Prior to joining the firm in 1997, Jason clerked for The Honorable Ruggero J. Aldisert of the U.S. Court of Appeals for the Third Circuit, was a litigation associate at Simpson Thacher & Bartlett in New York, and received a Masters of Laws (LL.M) from the University of Hong Kong. He is admitted to the bar in both California and New York State.

THE ARRANGED MARRIAGE BETWEEN NOT-FOR-PROFIT THEATRE COMPANIES AND COMMERCIAL PRODUCERS

JASON BARUCH
Partner at Franklin, Weinrib, Rudell, & Vassallo, P.C.

THE INTRODUCTION

In my law practice, I have the privilege of representing successful *commercial* producers, brilliant playwrights (sometimes referred to as *authors* in this article), and resourceful *not-for-profit* theatre companies (NFPs) all over the country. These clients all have different interests and needs, and I find myself wearing a number of different hats on a daily basis. I like to think that the broad range of my theatre work has given me some measure of insight into the relationships among these different clients.

While a great deal of my time is spent negotiating production contracts between commercial producers and authors, I am also called upon frequently either to prepare (when I represent the NFP) or to negotiate (when I represent the author) *developmental* theatre production agreements between authors and NFPs, as well as *enhancement* agreements between NFPs and commercial producers. It is this three-way dance among the author, NFP, and commercial producer—and more specifically the tango between the NFP and commercial producer—that is the subject of this chapter.

THE SET UP

In order to discuss the sometimes uneasy alliance between the *for-profit* and not-for-profit theatre worlds, a little background about developmental theatre agreements (that is, the agreement an author enters into with an NFP interested in developing the author's piece), and how they are structured, will be helpful. The basic developmental theatre agreement between the author and the NFP has the NFP bearing the costs of developing and mounting a new play or musical. The developmental process may involve *staged* or *informal readings* and, ultimately, fully staged performances before a paying audience, a portion of the audience for which may be comprised of *subscribers* of the NFP. In consideration for developing a new work, the NFP will ask that the author guarantee the NFP future *billing* credit plus some sort of ongoing financial participation.

The financial participation typically takes the form of a percentage of *gross weekly box office receipts* (GWBOR) from future commercial performances plus a percentage of the *net profits* of any commercial entity formed to produce the play. It would not be uncommon, for example, for a NFP to request 1 percent of GWBOR and 5 percent of the net profits. Some of the more influential NFPs, particularly what I will call the Manhattan-based (super-NFPs), might demand as much as 2 percent of GWBOR and 10 percent of the net profits in connection with third-party commercial *transfers* of plays they have developed. The right of the NFP to share in future income usually *sunsets* if the author does not enter into a production contract with a commercial producer within a certain period of time, such as three years after the close of the NFP's production. The theory here is if a commercial producer shows interest in the work, say, eight years after the close of the NFP's production, that interest probably was not sparked by the NFP's production, and the NFP should benefit financially only if its developmental efforts were the proximate cause of a commercial production. (A less common variation of the gross/net participation might have the NFP, instead of sharing in *gross* and net *profits* from a commercial production, simply being treated as an investor in the commercial production to the tune of the NFP's developmental production costs. For example, if the NFP spends $400 thousand to mount a new musical, which is then produced on Broadway for $8 million, the NFP will be deemed to have invested 5 percent of the capital of the commercial production.)

But what if there is no commercial production that results from the NFP's presentation of the play? What if, for example, the play lives a vibrant (and possibly even profitable) life in *regional* productions, without the benefit of a commercial run? Most developmental theatre agreements with authors have a built-in contingency plan along the following lines: If there is no commercial producer to assume the gross and net profit obligation to the NFP then, in lieu of the foregoing, the author agrees to pay the NFP a percentage of the income the author receives from all sources in connection with the author's *exploitation of rights* in the play. This percentage might be as high as 10 percent of the author's income (generally net of agency commissions), but more typically around five percent. Occasionally, an NFP will ask for both a gross/net participation from future commercial productions *and* a percentage of the author proceeds, although this is a point that is (or should be) vigorously debated by the author's representatives. In addition, from the author's perspective, the developmental theatre agreements should contain an additional clause whereby the NFP agrees to reduce its contractual share of gross and net profits by a certain amount, by as much as one-half, if a second developmental production is required and the second NFP requires an ongoing financial participation. In this case, the first developmental production yields a work that apparently is "not ready for prime time" and, in order to render the work suitable for commercial production, further development (*capitalized* by a new NFP) is required.

A different, and increasingly common, spin on the ongoing participation theme will have the NFP requesting the exclusive right to effectuate a commercial transfer of the play, by itself or with co-producers, within a certain period following the close of the developmental production. Ever since *A Chorus Line* was transferred from The Public Theatre in 1975 to the Shubert (filling The Public's coffers with more than $25 million), NFPs no doubt dream of a similar destiny, and many endeavor to provide for that right contractually in their agreements

The Company of the 1976 Tony Award-winning production of *A Chorus Line*;
book by James Kirkwood and Nicholas Dante; music by Marvin Hamlisch;
lyrics by Edward Kleban, which eventually transferred from The Public Theatre to the
Shubert in 1975, becoming one of the longest running shows on Broadway.
Photo by Martha Swope, courtesy of the John Willis Theatre World/Screen World Archive.

with authors. The terms of the commercial transfer will either be spelled out in the developmental theatre agreement itself or negotiated in good faith if and when the NFP elects to exercise its commercial *option*. In this situation, where the NFP actually succeeds in mounting a commercial production, the terms set forth in the commercial production contract generally supersede the gross/net formula or the author proceeds formula set forth above. What is often vexing to authors, however, is that many of the NFPs requesting the right to transfer the play have little or no experience, and perhaps no interest or capability, in producing commercially. We are not talking about the super-NFPs like Manhattan Theatre Club, but rather the smaller NFPs, most with no track records for producing commercially. Often this negotiated exclusive right to transfer serves the primary function of putting the NFP in the driver's seat in controlling the negotiation of commercial stage rights to third-party producers and, consequently, cutting the best possible financial deal for the NFP if the play is a hit. If an NFP produces a phenomenal critical and financial success and producers are knocking down the doors to transfer the play to the commercial stage, the NFP that has carved out for itself the exclusive right to produce or co-produce the play commercially will find itself in a position of leverage.

Some of my clients have expressed to me their belief that it is inappropriate for NFPs to demand any ongoing financial stake, be it from the authors or from future producers. Their position is that NFPs are financed by public funding and tax-deductible contributions, and their mission is to help authors bring new works to the stage, not to exact a pound of flesh from authors or to financially encumber the property if the result of the developmental process is a commercially viable play. While I understand that point of view, in my experience a modest future participation by the NFP, particularly one that will be assumed by a third-party commercial producer, is not out of line and does not create significant obstacles for future exploitation.

Assuming the propriety of an NFP asking for a future financial stake in a property, we must examine the myriad of factors relevant to determining whether the financial participation requested is reasonable or not. One factor relates to the extent of the development by the NFP. It makes sense that a theatre company that has nurtured a new work—from its moment of inception, through countless drafts, readings, workshops, and stage productions—is deserving of a greater future financial interest than a theatre that essentially was handed a finished product (perhaps already developed elsewhere). Another relevant question is the degree of the financial commitment by the NFP to the development of the work:

from an author's perspective, having to pay 5 to 10 percent of the author's income from future exploitations of the author's play is an easier pill to swallow when the theatre company has invested hundreds and thousands of dollars from its annual budget on the production of a play as opposed to a theatre company that has kicked five thousand dollars into a small production. Similarly, the size and scope of the developmental production may be relevant: Needless to say, an eight-week subscription run of a play in a 400-seat theatre will have more of an impact on the future value of a play than a six-performance run of a play in a forty-nine seat theatre, and it will be easier for a NFP to justify a greater ongoing participation in the former scenario. Of course, the reputation of the developmental theatre itself plays an important role, both in what is appropriate for the NFP to request and its ability to get what it wants. Some regional theatres with excellent reputations as Broadway *feeders* will have an easier time persuading an author to commit to a meaningful future participation than a wonderful but obscure theatre company that has never presented a play that went on to be a commercial success.

Interestingly, many of the smaller NFP theatre companies I represent are concerned more with billing than anything else. Financial participation takes a back seat to recognition to these organizations (which may explain while some are struggling to meet payroll on a weekly basis). Being credited as an originating home for a commercially successful project is an invaluable *marketing* tool for raising awareness of the NFP, as well for their managing and artistic directors, who are often credited along with the theatre company. In a perfect world, this broader recognition can increase the subscriber base and traffic to the theatre and boost fundraising potential. It might also attract higher profile artists interested in showcasing their work. The sort of credit negotiated depends on the nature of the NFP involvement. An eventual move to a commercial theatre within a certain number of years following the close of the NFP production could result in a simple "Originally Produced at ABC Theatre Company" credit somewhere at the bottom of the title page, a fraction of the size of the credit accorded the commercial producers. If, however, the commercial production is essentially transferred *en toto* from the NFP, a more meaningful credit might be negotiated such as an above-the-title credit along the following lines: "X, Y and Z Commercial Producers present ABC Theatre Company's Production of…" In figuring out what sort of transfer merits such a prominent credit for the NFP, a typical rule of thumb is this: If the transferred production uses the same direction, at least two of the three principal designers and at least half of the original cast, it is the developmental theatre's production of the work. In my experience, most authors and commercial producers do not begrudge the originating theatre its credit, although size and placement of that credit can often be the subject of protracted negotiation.

THE THIRD SIDE OF THE TRIANGLE

The reality is that many plays developed by NFPs already have commercial producers *attached*. These commercial producers find it far less risky to develop a property in the relative safety of the not-for-profit world. They have, in most cases, already acquired commercial stage rights from the author pursuant to a production contract. That contract almost always requires the author to hold back or "freeze" non-commercial production rights while the commercial producer retains commercial production rights). The commercial producers then temporarily waive their exclusive stage rights for the purposes of allowing the NFP to premiere the play. For reasons relating to the not-for-profit status of the theatre company (an area more dear to the accountants and not, therefore, a focus of this piece), the commercial theatre producer cannot be the producer of, or exert control over, the not-for-profit production. However, the commercial producer can and does enhance the NFP production financially.

A typical example of how this could work follows. A commercial producer acquires the rights to a new musical from an author. The estimated production budget for a Broadway production might be $12 million. A reasonably sophisticated pre-Broadway production could be presented at an NFP theatre for $1.2 million. In addition to allowing the parties to see how the play goes over with audiences (some of whom may be subscribers, thereby ensuring at least minimal attendance), the NFP production will generate reusable tangible assets, such as set elements, costumes, and props. The problem is the NFP theatre in question has a maximum per play production budget of $500 thousand. In this hypothetical, the commercial producer might enhance the developmental production by an additional $700 thousand. While this is still a substantial investment, it is an effective method of managing risk. Rather than being forced to raise $12 million for an unproven show that could bomb on Broadway on opening night, the commercial producer has the opportunity, for the relative bargain price of $700 thousand, to give the work a test run before paying objective audiences (i.e., not an invited crowd of industry insiders and relatives of the cast). This would take the form of a polished professional production largely funded by the NFP, which will reap assets that can be used by the commercial producer should a commercial transfer be appropriate). The NFP, in turn, gets the advantage of premiering a high-profile show that will bring in audiences and, perhaps, increase the theatre's subscriber (and donation) base in the future. Moreover, as previously noted, the theatre will strike a deal with the commercial producer that allows the theatre to share in the gross box office and net profits generated by the commercial producer's exploitation of rights in the play, including the Broadway production and future *touring* or *sit-down* productions.

Some commercial producers have *first look deals* with NFPs, domestically or abroad, where, in consideration of a financial contribution by the commercial producer to the theatre company, the commercial producer has the first right to effectuate a commercial transfer. One major Broadway producer, for example, has a special relationship with the National Theatre of Great Britain which gives the commercial producer the right to move to Broadway plays presented by the National Theatre.

Whether all of foregoing effectively makes the NFP a research and development arm of the commercial producer and, if so, whether there is anything wrong with that sort of relationship, is what will be explored next.

THE GRIPES

Although most of my author clients are thrilled to have any theatre company interested in developing their plays, I hear a familiar refrain from others. NFPs, the authors argue (as do a few commercial producer clients), have a mandate to support playwrights and foster the art form. As previously noted, they are not commercial theatre producers, and their mission is not to profit from their productions or transfer their productions to Broadway. They enjoy significant tax benefits and subsist on donations and grants. The gripe is that when an NFP requires a percentage of a playwright's future income from subsequent productions for helping develop a piece, that theatre company is betraying its mission. Similarly, I have heard on more than one occasion, when a theatre festival demands a percentage of future box office and/or author income for what in most cases amounts to the furnishing of a *venue* and certain group marketing initiatives, it is not so much supporting new artists as investing in them with the hope of some financial return while potentially making the now financially encumbered property less attractive to commercial producers (who, all things being equal, would rather not produce a work that arrives with substantial monetary obligations to third parties attached).

On the other side of the issue, most of the NFPs I represent survive, barely, on donations and grants, with annual budgets of far less than one million dollars. Their productions in general are not intended to turn a profit; indeed it is an impossibility for many to ever *break even* under a "perfect storm" of favorable circumstances (e.g., a renowned playwright, enjoying rave reviews, and a standing room only run). What I hear from my NFP clients is this: "Why shouldn't our struggling little theatre company enjoy some contingent benefit from developing a new work should that work attain a measure of financial success? If we develop the next *Avenue Q*, *Vagina Monologues*, or *RENT*, why shouldn't we replenish our coffers and have the opportunity to reinvest this income into the theatre company? In our shop, the successful works essentially subsidize the other good work we do which, in a world where donations and grants inadequately subsidize our enterprise, could be the difference between existence and insolvency. In any event, we generally are not assessing the playwrights, but rather asking that the future commercial producer bear the payment obligation to us." I have a certain amount of empathy for this position. It is true that NFPs enjoy tax exempt status, the benefit of donations and the other perquisites of being a 501(c)(3) organization (e.g., less expensive postage, better deals with publications in connection with advertisements, etc.). But at the same time I have observed that fundraising itself, in the form of grant writing and outreach to private donors, is an excruciatingly time-consuming and expensive process. Many NFPs have staff members devoted solely to the task of grant writing and private fundraising, and this in an environment of diminishing governmental support. Of every dollar spent by a typical NFP, I am told, barely half comes from the box office. The majority of NFPs, according to the Theatre Communications Group, lose money.

I am also told by my NFP clients that it is particularly disheartening to nurture an artist and a project from infancy, at times even commissioning the artist to create the work in the first place (one theatre company I have represented even experimented with giving their resident artists health insurance), only to hand over the reigns to another producer that will transfer the production and, inevitably, grab the glory. When a commercial success emerges from the developmental process and the NFP theatre has not negotiated a financial participation, the potential for bad feelings is great. Not surprisingly, many of the NFPs I represent are so poorly funded, and sometimes inexperienced, that they really have no idea what to ask for in their author agreements (or, if applicable, enhancement agreements), and no counsel to guide them. My advice to the young NFPs is to make the investment in procuring professional representation in creating form agreements, which can act as the template for future contracts. If you can get an experienced *entertainment lawyer* on your board of directors (which is really just code for free legal advice, of course), do it. The same goes for accountants and other professionals. If it means paying a representative to work through the basic structure of your various agreements, I believe (at the risk of sounding self-serving) that this is money well spent.

Finally, most of the commercial producers I represent do not begrudge an NFP a reasonable ongoing financial participation for having developed a work. The more the NFP requires, however, the more encumbered the property becomes and, therefore, the potentially less attractive it becomes to the commercial producer that, with its investors, ultimately will have to bear the financial burden to the NFP. Commercial theatre producers by and large understand the invaluable service the NFPs provide in developing new product—and new product is the lifeblood of commercial theatre. They also know that in a world of escalating production costs it often is not economically viable to nurture a new project from square one for the commercial stage. This explains why so many of the dramatic plays and musicals on Broadway have their origins in the not-for-profit world.

To be sure, some producers have bypassed the NFP route altogether. In the process they have sacrificed the benefits of spreading the risk (read: cost) of having an NFP produce the initial production, but they have also reigned in creative control of the process and eliminated the continuing financial obligation to the NFP. This does not mean that these producers have elected to open cold on Broadway—this is rarely done, and almost always at the peril of the commercial producer. Instead, these commercial producers mount an *out-of-town tryout*, *four-walling* the production in a venue outside of New York before bringing it to the Great White Way. This was recently done with tremendous success by the producers of *The Producers*, *Hairspray* and *Wicked* at The Cadillac Theatre, Fifth Avenue, and The Curran Theatre, respectively. This gave the producers an opportunity to see how the show works before a paying audience and gauge the impressions of some of the non-New York critics, and to tinker with the production before its Broadway transfer. The risk in this approach, however, is that a failure out-of-town could spell a financial disaster.

THE STATE OF NOT-FOR-PROFIT THEATRE TODAY: A MARRIAGE BORN OF NECESSITY

The relevance of NFP theatre cannot be understated. In the past fifty years, NFP *resident* theatres have grown from a modest collective of stages in big cities to a network of more than 1,200 theatres. All but three of the last thirty-three Pulitzer Prize-winners for Drama originated at regional theatres, nurtured in the not-for-profit community. Many of these plays had successful commercial runs (e.g., *Doubt, Proof,* and *RENT*), and most arguably would not have seen the commercial light of day if not nurtured through an NFP's developmental process. It is this assumption that is used to justify coordination between NFPs and commercial producers: a mutually beneficial relationship is forged when two different communities with differing motivations and objectives can, together, accomplish what neither of them could accomplish on its own.

At the same time, as the embrace between the commercial producers and NFPs tightens, so too do concerns that the world of not-for-profit theatre is losing its way, and forsaking its roots as a vital resource to support new and emerging artists and bring to audiences important—but not necessarily economically viable—works. By getting into bed with the commercial producers, the argument goes, the NFPs are encouraged to develop properties that have a possibility of financial reward, and these theatre companies then fail in their purported mission to introduce challenging works on stage.

La Jolla Playhouse ("LJP") in Southern California is an interesting example of the intersection. LJP was the birthplace of *The Who's Tommy, Big River,* and the current Broadway hit *Jersey Boys,* among other wonderful projects. The artistic director of LJP is a founding member of an organization known as the Dodgers, a major commercial producer, as is the head of Jujamcyn, a major Broadway theatre owner. The Dodgers eventually transferred all three musicals to Broadway houses owned by Jujamcyn, highlighting the choreographed dance that can take place between not-for-profit and commercial interests. And like the Old Globe Theatre's production of *The Full Monty* (enhanced with funds from the film company Fox Searchlight), it is difficult to argue that these productions were anything other than Broadway tryouts. Whether this illustrates a disconcerting muddying of lines, or instead demonstrates an admirable, or at least necessary, cross-pollination of two worlds (a cross-pollination that has given bloom to a finely honed gem enjoyed by a wide swathe of theatregoers and which, in the process, has funded the operations of an NFP and has given financial nourishment to commercial theatre producers arguably immersed in an economically irrational business), is a matter of debate. Whether this growing interconnectedness comes at the cost of the NFP theatre developing other challenging and possibly non-commercial works is hard to say, but it is naïve to think an NFP theatre has no interest (or should have no interest, for that matter) in benefiting from a financially successful and widely seen production.

Rocco Landesman, head of the aforementioned Jujamcyn, wrote an essay entitled "A Vital Movement Has Lost Its Way," published in the June 4, 2000,

Arts & Leisure section of *The New York Times*, which has been oft repeated in the theatre community. In the essay, Mr. Landesman talks about the Roundabout Theatre Company, one of the super-NFPs I have referred to occasionally, and the success its artistic director Todd Haimes has had in bringing readily consumable quality theatrical fare to a broad audience: "It would, I suppose, be hyperbolic to say that Todd Haimes has had a more pernicious influence on the English-speaking theatre than anyone since Oliver Cromwell (and it wouldn't be nice, either, since Mr. Haimes is a personable and honorable man), but it can be reasonably argued that the forces of the marketplace through the years have been just as effective a censor as government edicts." I view Mr. Landesman's statement as a well-intentioned provocation—with perhaps a modest infusion of mea culpa—for those of us who care about theatre to evaluate what effect this marriage of art (in theory, the province of the NFPs) and commerce (in theory, the province of the commercial producer) has had on the theatre industry in general and the creative works (or product) it births in particular.

THE SUPER-NFPS: SINGLE AND LOVIN' IT

Which brings us, finally, to the super-NFPs like the Roundabout Theatre Company, Manhattan Theatre Company ("MTC"), and Lincoln Center Theatre ("LCT"). Up until now I have devoted most of my attention to the hungry little NFPs (many of whom I represent and/or on whose boards I have sat). The super-NFPs are interesting hybrids. Like other NFPs, government, foundation, and corporate funding support them. They have budgets in the tens of millions of dollars. They have the cushion of substantial subscriber bases of tens of thousands of theatregoers, which ensures a minimum attendance for their productions. They enjoy substantially lower operating costs during their subscription runs, and have further negotiated a number of concessions for the post-subscription commercial runs. They do not need to worry about repaying investors. To top it off, they can earn additional revenue by selling corporate naming rights (so now you can watch a Tony Award-winning Roundabout production in the American Airlines Theatre—formerly the Selwyn Theatre—enjoying an agreeable Sauvignon Blanc and Oreo® cookie in the Nabisco Lounge). All of this arguably puts the super-NFPs at a competitive advantage over commercial producers. Moreover, in their developmental theatre agreements and enhancement agreement, they are able to exact the largest continuing financial participations (i.e., gross and net profits) of any NFPs should they not move forward with commercial production of a property developed by them.

What really sets the super-NFPs apart from their NFP brethren, however, is the fact that they also happen to operate out of Broadway houses: LCT out of the Vivian Beaumont Theatre, the Roundabout out of the American Airlines Theatre, and MTC out of the Biltmore Theatre. The super-NFPs are unique because they actually compete with Broadway producers. Because they present their works in Broadway houses, they are eligible for Antoinette Perry ("Tony") awards. LCT snatched the Best Musical Tony Award from commercial producers in 2000 with its production of *Contact*. Most recently, in the 2005 Tony Awards, LCT's production of *Light In The Piazza* won six Tony Awards. This is not an academic matter—commercial producers are now vying for the most coveted theatre awards, and audience dollars, with the super-NFPs. These are not struggling downtown theatre companies with $300 thousand budgets constantly behind on their rent founded by recent college graduates who also take tickets and serve beer out of a makeshift concession stand. These are huge organizations, run by wealthy and well-connected boards. They have tens of thousands of subscribers, budgets of tens of millions of dollars. And they operate out of Broadway houses— not to mention on the *road*, with Roundabout having recently announced that it will produce its first national tour, its successful Tony-nominated New York production of *Twelve Angry Men*, commencing September 2006.

Whether these super-NFPs serve a critical function in producing high quality theatre that would not otherwise have been produced by commercial producers who must answer to investors expecting a return, or act as merely a different type of commercial producer with certain features of a NFP, is the real question. What is not in question is the fact that these super-NFPs are a vital and likely permanent part of the Manhattan theatre landscape.

CONCLUSION

The First American Congress of Theatre (FACT), the brainchild of Broadway producer Alexander H. Cohen, took place at Princeton University from June 2 through June 5, 1974, for the purposes of resuscitating a very ill (terminally ill, some thought at the time) commercial theatre industry. It was followed twenty-six years later by the Second American Congress of Theatre—Act II (ACT II), which took place at Harvard University from June 16 through June 18, 2000, and explored the relationship between the for-profit and not-for-profit worlds of theatre, and how they could help each other nurture an atmosphere in which new and exciting theatrical works could blossom, artistically and financially.

At FACT, Mr. Cohen warned in his keynote address: "Broadway, Off-Broadway, nonprofit, professional, experimental—we all work under a sword of Damocles. The sword has different edges for all of us, but it is the same sword, and it is high time that we began to design a common shield."* In the intervening twenty-six years before ACT II, the for-profit and not-for-profit worlds have forged an alliance of sorts. The industry began to recognize that the commercial theatre world and the NFP world together could achieve certain objectives that neither could achieve on its own. What came out of ACT II was the sense by some that the alliance requires further refinement in order to better protect both worlds from the edge of the sword, but a sense by others that the alliance had already become too strong, the ties between two worlds too entangled and the final product too compromised.

Most new dramas these days do not have a third act, perhaps an acknowledgment of our collective diminishing attention spans. If the theatre community can continue to focus its attention on this complex interdependence between the commercial theatre world and the not-for-profit theatre world, it will be interesting to see what Act III brings. And hopefully we won't have to wait another twenty-six years to find out.

---

* From *ACT TWO —Creating Partnerships and Setting Agendas for the Future of The American Theater, a Report on the Second American Congress of Theater (June 16–18, 2000),* prepared by Jeremy Gerard, The League of American Theatres and Producers and Theatre Communications Group, 2002.

Ben Feldman

Ben Feldman has been practicing at the firm of Epstein, Levinsohn, Bodine, Hurwitz & Weinstein since 2002 and became a partner on July 1, 2006. He focuses his practice in matters concerning theatre and independent film. Mr. Feldman also provides counsel in the areas of art, book publishing, and television. His varied clientele consist of film and theatre producers (including film production companies and regional theatres), network sitcom television leads, Manhattan art galleries, publicists, New York stage venue owners, major motion picture distributors, talent agencies, writers, and even the puppet designers and builders of the one of the most popular stage musicals of recent memory. He has secured the film rights for stories appearing in publications ranging from *The New York Times* to *Vanity Fair* and the live musical stage rights to numerous novels and popular films. He has completed book deals with major publishing houses and has acted as production counsel on a number of independent films including two that have received national theatrical release since 2004. Also in his film practice, he represented more documentaries at the 2004 Sundance Film Festival than any other attorney, and as a producer rep he sold one, in an unprecedented deal, to a national broadcast network for prime time exhibition. He subsequently sold two additional films at the Tribeca Festival later that same year, in the spring of 2004, and represented four movies as both production counsel and producer rep at that festival in 2006. Ben represents two Oscar-nominated director–producers and a third whose work was acknowledged with the Grand Jury Prize at Sundance. Mr. Feldman's work as a theatrical attorney has been acknowledged at the Tony Awards ceremony twice in this century, more than any other attorney. His clients have been recognized in such categories as Best Revival of a Play (producer), Best Actress in a Play, Best Orchestrations, Best Score, and Best Book of a Musical. He has represented either the producers or authors of at least one winner of major New York theatrical festivals (Fringe, NYMTF, or NAMT) during each of the last five years. All of these productions have moved on Broadway or Off-Broadway.

In addition to his legal practice, Mr. Feldman also serves as a member of the board of directors of the Hourglass Group and of the New Festival Inc., sponsor of the New York Gay and Lesbian Film Festival. As a producer himself, Mr. Feldman has presented *The Cutting Room*, a short film featuring Kate Hudson, and the commercial run of *The Stand In*, a play developed by Naked Angels and later optioned by Miramax. He is an associate producer of *Another Gay Movie* (Tribeca Film Festival, 2006). Finally, Ben is also a writer who's work has been produced at the La Jolla Playhouse. He was commissioned by major film studios to write the librettos of two musicals to be based on major motion pictures.

Mr. Feldman became affiliated with Epstein, Levinsohn, Bodine, Hurwitz & Weinstein, LLP, in 2002. Formerly, he was affiliated with the law firms of Parker, Chapin, Flattau & Klimpl, LLP, and Kaufmann, Feiner, Yamin, Gildin & Robbins, LLP. Mr. Feldman was admitted to the New York Bar in 1999. He received his J.D. from New York University School of Law, where he won the ASCAP Copyright Law Prize and the school's Moot Court Oral Argument Competition. He is a summa cum laude graduate of Yale College.

NOTES FROM THE TRENCHES OF A YOUNG (WELL, UNDER 40) THEATRICAL ATTORNEY

BEN FELDMAN
Partner at Epstein, Levinsohn, Bodine, Hurwitz, & Weinstein, LLP

It was the start of 2001 and I was in St. Barthes. A rented villa with a pool. A gorgeous view. Everyone around was rich and beautiful. I have never been rich or beautiful, but I have (a) a way of using dark colors to my advantage; and (b) a partner who is a travel professional and gets me trips like this virtually for free. It was Christmas, a very spiritual time of year for me. Not because of Jesus or anything (check out my last name), but rather because the holiday offered the only fourteen-day period of the year during which the entertainment industry sort of shuts down. After twelve months of round the clock work, I would finally have some free time. I decided I would use the break to become a perfect person. I would finally shed those forty extra pounds that had been plaguing me since 1979. I would dutifully return every e-mail I had failed to answer since, well, since the invention of e-mail. I would learn wine tasting, photography, and yoga. I would become well-rounded. And tan, which can make anyone look better (as long as you don't get skin cancer).

Life was good, except for the fact that I had to do daily battle with a very aggressive, petite woman for time on the island's only Stairmaster. One day as I tried to stare her down when she passed the one-hour mark, I realized that she was Holly Hunter.

But then a call came in (which was weird in itself, as it's sort of impossible to reach people in the French West Indies). On the other line were two clients: one was a location scout for *Law and Order* who lived in Brooklyn; and the other was a word processor. They had written a musical, and a producer was interested but the deal presented to them was, I felt, substandard, and I let that be known. I believed strongly that given the terms, my clients should have politely passed. I felt that their talent would allow them other opportunities in the future were this deal not to work out.

"Ben," one of them said, "the producers are threatening to pull the plug." "Fine," I said, "then that's the way it has to be."

But against my advice, my clients, afraid of losing what they felt at the time to be their only chance for production, acquiesced and signed. It was a good thing they didn't listen to me. That show was *Urinetown*, and the production became one of the most beloved and respected to hit Broadway in years. Thanks to doing the opposite of what I said, my clients went on to win Tony Awards for Best Score and Best Book of a Musical.

The reason I stay in this business is because of what I learn from my clients—the advice and counsel they end up giving *me*. Every deal is fresh for me, because in each one I will learn something or meet someone new in the theatre. Really I should pay my clients, because each of them affords me greater expertise, and entrenches me deeper into a close-knit clique of people worldwide: theatre professionals.

I believe that a need to spend one's life in the theatre—whether you are a make-up artist in Tulsa, an acting teacher in Connecticut, or a *theatrical lawyer*—is an unexplainable, intractable quality you're born with. So here we are, this group of weirdos, stuck with each other for life. I am grateful that theatre law gives me the chance to make a living doing that. For that reason, the best advice I could give anyone is to handle yourself with grace; you will certainly meet up with the people on the other side of the table again.

Come to think of it, the theatre is full of fun little mantras to live by. A smart producer does not invest his own money in a show. In this business, you can make a killing, but not a living. And don't put money into a show that (choose one): (a) you don't feel passionately about; (b) does not have a producer or director with a previous hit on their resume; or (c) doesn't have a recognizably famous title or star. But these clichés are meaningless. They won't speak to your specific experience embarking on a career in the live stage business. There is too much risk, too many variables that can make a project go wrong, and too little evidence about how the public will treat a given entertainment product. So the one constant you're left with are your relationships—the team of people surrounding you. This particular combination of individuals—their skills, their successes, their connections, and their support of you—this more than anything will be the constant that can define your career. It will come closer than anything to being the crystal ball we all wish for, and it will bring you the greatest joy. When my firm made me partner, the first person I called was Tovah Feldshuh. Not because she was a client, but because her husband is the best attorney in town and I wanted his advice on how to negotiate my deal.

Life is sort of a war. For instance, when I visit my mom in Florida, I like to use the Stairmasters that they have at the nearby fancy Ritz Carlton condos (there's more than one, and Holly doesn't frequent Sarasota, Florida). To get the guest pass I need, I got *Jersey Boys house seats* for a doctor my parents know who lives at the Ritz. To get the house seats, I helped the assistant director with her

The 2002 Tony Award-winning production of *Urinetown*, which garnered the Tony Award for Best Book for Greg Kotis, and Best Original Musical Score for Greg Kotis and Mark Hollman, both of whom are clients of Ben Feldman, Esq. Pictured are Jennifer Laura Thompson as Hope (top), and Nancy Opel as Penelope Pennywise (front), with members of The Company.
Photo by Joan Marcus, courtesy of the John Willis Theatre World/Screen World Archive.

deal, which was hard because the director she works for had previously done me the great favor of producing and directing a musical I co-wrote, at the La Jolla Playhouse. This was thanks to the great work of William Morris; the musical's agent there has spent years developing this piece for no pay, even though, at this writing, I am negotiating against William Morris on three other deals. No problem—what I'm paid to do is negotiate, and that verb has a broader meaning. It refers to the ability to navigate a complicated terrain of interconnected people. This is what you're going to have to master as well, regardless of whether or not you pursue the law.

It's not always easy. Every time *Avenue Q* opens in a new city I am invariably accused of endangering the production when I tell the producers how much it will cost to build the puppets. (I have actually received numerous e-mails from Cameron Mackintosh's people telling me how desperately poor he is. I came close to mortgaging my one bedroom apartment to help him out.) So many times I've wanted to tell them how much I love the show—how I've seen it six times, how I will give my first-born the middle name "The," in honor of Lucy T. Slut—the funniest name in Broadway history.

Lucy's just the most recent in a long line of women I've adored on stage. Growing up, watching the Tony Awards on TV was the highlight of my year back in suburban Worcester, Massachusetts. The night Angela Lansbury performed "The Worst Pies In London" was the highlight of my life. I felt that theatre was a world of sophisticates and my heroes were the stage personae that inhabited it. (Little did I know I would one night stay at the office past 9:00 p.m. arguing that a client of mine should be able to keep her undergarments after the close of her one-person show). As I child I looked up to Evita—not really the true Eva Peron, more the theatrical version of her as manifested by Patti LuPone (and to think I was shocked when my mother figured out I was gay). But it was in the movie theatre that I decided to be an entertainment lawyer. The film was *The Player*, starring Tim Robbins. His attorney was the character everyone depended on to make things right; he was like a god. Plus he had a gorgeous home and a great pool. I wanted to be involved in live stage productions, but I also wanted a doorman and air conditioning.

In law school, it became quickly apparent to me that it was virtually impossible to get a job practicing in the theatre. Talk about a small bar. There are less than forty people who do it. I sometimes feel like a 17th-century silversmith in Amsterdam who has just finished his apprenticeship. At the time, one of the top theatre lawyers in town took a shine to a Broadway chorus boy. I told the attorney I'd fix him up with the chorus boy if he gave me employment. He did, and I orchestrated a couple of dates. I hate to admit this, but the chorus boy was my boyfriend at the time; we had been together for five years. Basically, I sold him into white slavery so I could get a summer internship. Amazingly, I think of myself not as a pimp, but rather as a nice Jewish boy from a good family who likes to help people make connections. O.K.—I'm being a bit funny for effect (and libel expertise inspires me to state the following): The truth is our relationship was near the end anyway. And that attorney (who is still the best artist rep in town, in my opinion) is actually a relationship-oriented sweetheart so it would not have been slavery. And "chorus boy" is a diminutive way of describing my ex (and current best friend), who has conceived of (or helped re-write) no less than two musicals opening on Broadway this season alone.

I suppose if there's a point to this rambling, self-conscious mess of an essay (apart from my obsession with Stairmasters, which you'd have too if you were inching towards a size 40 waist), it's that it's the people around you that make the difference. Some would argue it's the project, others the money, and I can't say they're wrong. I can only tell you that in my experience, people are the asset, and the greatest talent to develop is the ability to navigate relationships. Some of my happiest moments have been acting as advocate for the young producers that make up my clients. Ars Nova is an unprecedented *venue* that has nurtured relationships with young artists who think outside of the box. As a result, it has a loyal audience that knows they can get something there unavailable anywhere else in the theatre. David Binder's record breaking *A Raisin in the Sun* wasn't just an artistic and *commercial* triumph—it was also the triumph of a personality who had to spend years putting together a team that would satisfy the various *approval rights* of director, stars, and the Lorraine Hansberry estate.

Perhaps because I don't have actual, literal children of my own, I think of my clients embarking on their careers as producers like family. Like my own mother, I'm the type that likes to be available; far from being hard to reach, I might call you at two o'clock in the morning worried about how much a star is asking for. And over the years, from where I sit, I have seen patterns emerge. This perspective does not make me a producer by any means, but it may make me able to offer little tidbits of advice.

First, don't start working on something without a contract. This means, don't start developing a play or *attaching* a director until you have *optioned* it; don't start raising money without the *associate producer* agreement signed; don't use a director for a *reading* assuming you'll work out the details later. This seems obvious to the point of being patronizing, but it is astounding how many people break this rule—not because they're naïve but rather because time becomes too short to delay a work's development with time-consuming contracts. A corollary to this rule is another oft-broken one, which is that you are never too close to someone to have a contract. I don't care if you're developing a play based on your father's experience in a Japanese internment camp so as to honor his experience— get dad to give you exclusive rights in writing.

Another fun tidbit to remember is that there is an *x factor* in this business. I suppose when the makers of Oreo® cookies came out with their product they could try it out on a bunch of kids so as to determine how delicious they were. In the theatre, nothing is predictable. A show that's a hit in Chicago may tank in New York, even with the same creative team. Why? Are people here that much different? Who knows? Maybe they are. A show with bad reviews can be a hit. Elvis Presley, long dead, still attracts hundreds of thousands of visitors to his residence each year; but the musical with his incredibly popular songs did not *recoup* among Broadway theatre audiences. Why? I don't know—there is no accounting for the public's taste at any given time and anyone who tells you differently is lying to you. Learn to live with risk. Start thinking of yourself as a gambler.

Getting back to relationships, I always say the most important one is with your investors. It's great to make money, but probably more important is to give your investors a good deal—and a good time—because the long term goal is to be able to have them in your stable for the next time. Some people are very aggressive when they enter into contracts. They want to get the most that they can from the party on the other side. But you know what I think? I think a contract is a living, breathing thing, almost like a child that the signing parties birth together. It's something that should be thought of as a long term, active organism. It needs to work, not just now, but years down the line, for both sides, if the parties are going to collaborate successfully. As an example, the agreements for a current musical, the immensely fun *I Love You Because* Off-Broadway, weren't just put away in a drawer. They provide the roadmap for how we determine what obligations (to the author, the orchestrator, even the costume designer) need to be assumed by our licensees in Korea. You start charting this course once the negotiations begin. As such, I don't believe in representing people by screaming, swearing, or issuing threats. Remember when you hire an attorney that they represent you, who you are, what you want, and that they cannot act beyond your approval. They are your face to the world, and you are responsible for them and how they act. The buck stops with you. Don't assume that because they occupy a different human body you have carte blanche to be obnoxious through them. After college and before law school, I spent two years as the assistant to Daryl Roth, who has gone on to produce more plays that have won Pulitzers than, I believe, any carbon-based life form. One day she told me that it's good to be shrewd, but also to remember to write thank you notes.

I would say don't jump into things too quickly. For your first project, don't try to produce a Broadway musical. Become an associate producer; work under the tutelage of someone who's done it before. You won't have final say, but you'll have a discreet, doable set of obligations—a finite amount of money to raise within a given period of time. Or: produce an Off-Off Broadway one-person show. Or: if you have a musical (or even a play), don't open it in New York, London, or Las Vegas. Try San Jose or Portland. Find a *nonprofit* eager for *enhancement* and let the work have some initial breathing room. New York can be a very high stakes place with little opportunity for a second chance. And while you'll have to give up some power (and an ongoing interest) to another entity, you'll have the preparation necessary to give your all to the next, bigger step. You'll gain the ability to fail and still remain in the game. Also, I would not want to end this piece without mentioning the incredible opportunities that—especially recently—are afforded by these musical theatre festivals: The National Alliance, the New York Musical Theatre Festival, and The Fringe. Whether you are an author looking for a producer, or a producer looking for regional or financial partners, you now have an inexpensive way of exposing a new (musical) work to a relatively guaranteed and pinpointed market. This is amazing news when you think of the fact that there are many musicals written. Because they are so expensive, time consuming, and risky, it is hard to get them considered seriously by any given potential partner, let alone a lot at once.

In order to get a fair deal for yourself, be prepared to (politely) walk away if the terms are not to your liking. If you lose this ability, you forfeit the leverage necessary to make sure you get all that's coming to you. I still feel this way, despite my advice on *Urinetown*. It also helps, even if you do hire a lawyer, to understand the important parts of a contract, and which are especially important to you. The most important provisions concern rights. These usually break down into media (do you want rights other than live stage, like film? Did you remember to get *ancillary rights* such as merchandising and cast album? Or attendant rights such as the ability to use *names* in *advertising*?), time (how long do you have rights, and what do you have to do to maintain them?), and territory (is there a reason you feel it necessary to acquire rights in Belgium? Do you have friends there?)

Money—how revenue will be allocated is important but also something most people intrinsically know to be concerned with anyway. But equally important for your own career development is credit. Will you be credited in advertising? What about on versions of the work in other media? Can others be credited if you are not, in a given instance? Should you be concerned with size, placement, or type (*billing* block style vs. artwork) either as concepts in and of themselves or as points or comparison with others? Sometimes the most important issue to consider is *approval rights*. Are others accorded the authority to slow down your progress and put your investor's funding at risk because they don't like the dance arranger you've chosen? Who makes decisions, and how are disputes to be resolved? Services are a concept you may forget to think about. Are you being obligated to perform certain tasks, or do you require that of the others? Is their compensation related to the engagement to contribute work? Then there are overriding concepts that you might consider with respect to everything in the contract. One is *favored nations*—are others being treated better than you, in any way? This is important for artists to consider, especially, but even as a producer, you will want to know, for instance, that a nonprofit theatre did not ask for less money from the musical that was enhanced there last season.

People always speak of trying to get new and different audiences into the theatre and new trends (like the *jukebox musical*), but there is something relatively constant about the theatre business. I mean, there's always going to be a certain type of person that enjoys the theatre. Meanwhile, the audiovisual world is in flux. Network television shows are suffering as new modes of transmission allow viewers greater choice as to what can be shown on (or through) their TV sets. Fewer people actually go to the theatres to see movies (many get their entertainment through a cell phone). Yet the theatre business remains relatively stable. Why shouldn't it? It's been that way for many, many centuries, and there is something about the act of gathering to share the collective experience of seeing actors perform live that is irreplaceable and necessary in every culture. There's business to do among those who can stay in the game, despite the uncertainty surrounding any given production. I find that Pepsid AC helps with the stress. As do visits to the Stairmaster. And good friends.

Advertising, Marketing, and Publicity

Theatre is about an ass in every seat, every night.

—MIKE TODD

Adrian Bryan-Brown

Adrian Bryan-Brown is a partner in the theatrical public relations firm, Boneau/Bryan-Brown, Inc. Born in Oxford, England, raised in London and New York, and armed with a degree in Zoology from the University of London, Adrian Bryan-Brown began serving as a publicist in the late 1970s with the independent press agent Susan Bloch. Joining the Association of Theatrical Press Agents and Managers (ATPAM) in 1983, he subsequently worked with Josh Ellis at Solters, Roskin, and Friedman, and in 1991 formed Boneau/Bryan-Brown, Inc. with Chris Boneau. Adrian has represented more than 200 productions On and Off-Broadway, on national tour, and in Europe.

TOO MUCH IS NOT ENOUGH– THEATRICAL PUBLIC RELATIONS IN THE AGE OF THE BLACKBERRY™

ADRIAN BRYAN-BROWN
Partner, Boneau/Bryan-Brown

On any given day you might find yourself:

- Impersonating the voice of a celebrity who was unable to do an unimportant phone interview at the last minute
- Waking up at 3:00 a.m. to call an actor in London because that's when she wanted to discuss a *publicity* schedule, only to be told when the call is made to call back later
- Using a pencil eraser to retouch an unattractive photograph of an actor before sending them a photocopy of a newspaper clipping
- Giving up your cell phone for twenty-four hours so an actor can do an interview from an untraceable phone number and not personally have to pay for the call
- Stopping traffic by lying down so a chorus line of tap dancers could be seen relocating to a new theatre for the benefit of television news cameras

It's very hard in a few pages to convey everything a theatrical *press agent* does. While many producers and managers make the first call of the day to their press agent, others seem to be confused about the role of the *flak* and don't quite know how they fit in.

The basic function of the press agent has not changed. We serve as a conduit for genuine news about a production, supplying the press and the public with topical information through access to the various elements that go into the creation and maintenance of a show. What has developed recently is the remarkable explosion in opportunities for publicizing the theatre. In a world no longer dominated by print and broadcast media alone, we can now directly grab attention through the Internet and an ever-evolving universe of wireless personal devices.

The publicity strategy begins with a timeline (following intensive research) that outlines a series of news announcements, the distribution of press materials (including photography and video), the invitation of the press and critics to see the show, the news event of the opening, and the aggressive follow-up that will keep the show top-of-mind with the press, the Broadway fan, and occasional theatregoer for hopefully many years to come.

Rather than go through the steps of the campaign, which will—to some degree—always follow a variation of the above, I would like to outline some of the exciting challenges that we face in working with the media to sell tickets.

Over the past twenty years, an average of thirty-six shows have opened each season on Broadway. Roughly one in five will become a hit (defined as a show that makes back it's initial investment).

The average life span of a successful show has increased. Longer runs are also required for shows to *recoup* their financing, and a greater ingenuity in all aspects of *marketing* is necessary to keep productions profitable from week to week.

The pressure to keep a show running falls to the three key areas of marketing: *advertising*, promotion (usually called marketing in theatre), and publicity. All are quite distinct in style and function, yet all are symbiotic and share the same unsolvable dilemma—no matter how inspired or creative the marketing campaign is, nothing can ultimately suppress negative word of mouth and make someone buy a ticket to a bad show! Intelligent and creative marketing can: catapult an O.K. show into a mega hit; accelerate the popular experience of an intimate show into a solid success; and give renewed strength and stamina to a long-running Broadway landmark.

Public relations, press relations, media relations, press representation: in the theatrical world, they all means the same thing, and the terms are pretty interchangeable. Publicity implies a campaign involving a measurable amount of exposure for a project (i.e., a newspaper or magazine article, or a segment on a television program). *Public Relations* is a more encompassing term including an educational aspect directed at both the consumer (ticket buyer in theatre terms) and the press (editors, reporters, critics, etc.), leading to tangible publicity and hopefully increased sales!

Many theatrical producers (and others) mistakenly believe that public relations is free advertising. It isn't. So what are the distinctions? Public relations is an effort to focus newsworthy media attention and editorial on a particular product, show, or institution. Advertising is buying the attention in a guaranteed, precise, and targeted way. Promotion (a.k.a. marketing) is using the assets of a show to barter for additional exposure and further raise awareness. Public relations tends to be relatively inexpensive compared to the cost of advertising and most marketing, and has the credibility of editorial endorsement; people believe what they read in the papers and are skeptical of adjacent advertising.

When the Broadway cast of the musical *Titanic* appeared on *The Rosie O'Donnell Show*, the stirring performance and lavish words of praise from Rosie led to a boost in ticket sales, countering the mostly negative reviews the show had received from the Broadway newspaper critics. More recently, an extended cast appearance by *The Color Purple* on *The Oprah Winfrey Show* (who is also a producer of the musical), led to more than one million dollars in single ticket sales in the days following. The national appearances (which still carried production costs for the performers, dressers, and other show crew members), were more effective than a typical thirty-second TV commercial might have been, and cheaper when you consider the cost of making the commercial and subsequent residuals that would have to be paid to actors, musicians, and others to run the spot.

You can never guarantee the impact of any public relations effort. A favorable review or feature in a newspaper may be buried by the placement of a bigger news story. The feature story may even be bumped for breaking news. There may be negative aspects to the editorial piece that are beyond your control that might possibly hurt ticket sales. Knowing when to pass on doing a story is also important. Much of public relations is about gauging the variables and judging what makes the most sense for your show at a particular time. (You don't have to set up an interview just because the press asks for it.)

Advertising is precise. You can spend a little over one hundred thousand dollars to take a full-page color ad for a Broadway show in the *Arts and Leisure* section of *The New York Times* on a specific Sunday. You won't know exactly on which page it will run, but experience will tell you that it will be somewhere near the front of the section, close to theatre editorial copy. You have complete control on the information in the advertisement and you can be as aggressive as you want in telling a theatregoer about your production, using quotes from reviews and other details that might promote a sale. You also know from research that you are reaching a lot of potential ticket buyers by advertising that particular paper.

In the *commercial* theatre, the marketing effort compliments both press and advertising by using the currency of the show (tickets, cast recordings, and other merchandise), in a trade to get additional visibility through giveaways, contests, trade for advertising space, or endorsement. Sometimes the show is so in demand that a radio station or magazine might give free attention in the form of advertising space in exchange for time just to have an association with the production, or to get access to buy tickets to the show. Usually it is a trade of some kind. The role is further expanded in the institutional, *not-for-profit* theatre world, where marketing includes audience development through *subscription* and other loyalty campaigns.

Ideally, a theatrical press agent starts working on a project as soon as the producer acquires a script and a *general manager*. The potential audience is anyone with the money to buy a ticket. No show is for everyone, but you should work hard to ensure that anyone who might be interested in it, hears about it; and you can endeavor to make anyone who sees the show leaves as its ambassador.

Don't presume any particular group of people won't be potential buyers. However, before spending a lot of time, money, and energy going after a specialized audience, make sure that you have a clear strategy to get through to the committed theatregoer who is going to be more likely to buy a ticket (as well as knows *how* to buy one!) Occasional theatregoers are not only intimidated by the price of a Broadway ticket, but they are often confused about where and how to buy a ticket.

What are some of the assets that a show can identify to wage an effective publicity campaign?

Fun and Stars

Audiences want reinforcement that they are going to have a good time. They don't want to see a downer. *Casting* the right star is one way to protect a production from negative criticism and, as importantly, counteract negative or missing word of mouth. Are the stars big enough to carry a show? Do they match the project? Can you use stories in the press to explain the seeming disconnect of a TV sitcom star appearing in a Eugene O'Neill play?

Recognition and Accessibility

"What is it about?" Theatregoers are eager for information. The show could be adapted from a beloved movie, or the story of a famous person, or it could written by a popular author (Neil Simon or Andrew Lloyd Webber; or it could feature the popular music of John Lennon, ABBA, Johnny Cash, or The Four Seasons). Can you get a story about how a new musical is truly original? Does the story have international appeal? Do you need to understand English to enjoy the show? Is the show appropriate for all ages? Does it have a short running time?

Pricing and Scheduling

There is no price resistance on Broadway. We know we can't give away a ticket to a bad show, yet if a production is hot, people will pay *premium* prices, especially for special limited events or hot new shows in their first few months. Is the press aware of early curtains and additional matinees scheduled to appeal to family audiences?

Competition and Environment

There has never been more competition (or distraction) for our time. A single Broadway show is not just competing with dozens of other theatrical attractions, but numerous other forms of entertainment that fill up entertainment sections of newspapers that we would like to be championing the theatre!

Once established, these assets can be used in the press campaign which should be continuously re-thought and reassessed as more information is acquired in the changing environment. The role of the press agent is to play the part of the educator, informing the media and the public about a show. We can't do this by our word of mouth alone. Reaching ticket buyers individually is obviously impractical. We need to find envoys who can take the information and pass on a winning story. Trusted envoys in the media include Oprah Winfrey, whose endorsement of *The Color Purple* has made the show a huge popular success; Rosie O'Donnell, whose enthusiasm and support of Broadway musicals when she hosted a daytime talk show was known for being able to close a sale; WOR Radio's Joan Hamburg, whose audience is an exact match with the average Broadway ticket buyer; among numerous others in different media. They connect with their viewers, listeners, or readers, and make them feel good about going to theatre.

Another important emissary is the local critic who has seen a show in London (or anywhere else for that matter), and liked it. Not only do they create a buzz about an incoming show early, but they rarely change their opinion about the show when it arrives on Broadway.

The process of show publicity is always evolving. More and more people are using the Internet to get information about the theatre, and most of them start—not surprisingly—with a Google search. More immediate than newsprint and broadcast, information needs to be refreshed on the Internet constantly to keep a show at the top of the search lists. Combined with periodic feature stories in newspapers and magazines, we supply a constant flow of items that were once only used in newspaper columns to wire services like the Associated Press, and websites on the Internet that carry theatre news, www.broadway.com, www.playbill.com, www.theatermania.com, www.broadwayworld.com, etc.

We need to keep parceling out interesting facts about a show. This can be record weekly grosses; cast changes; performance schedule changes; winning awards; famous people visiting backstage; charitable events the cast is involved in; links to stories that have run in traditional media; or alerts to inform when the cast is performing a song on a television show.

For the right show, it can be effective and appropriate at some point in the campaign to generate news in the form of a stunt. These kind of fabricated event are usually very low on the news radar; fires, traffic reports, and weather are much bigger local TV stories. It is very important to schedule your event when you think you have the best shot of getting the press there; late morning works best because you can make very early morning reminder calls to the press, and if you have actors or stars involved, they don't have to get up early. The later in the day the event, the tougher it is to get coverage because news crews are at the end of their shifts and returning to hand over video for the evening broadcasts.

To safeguard your coverage from other news events that you make not even be aware of, you should make sure you hire a photographer who can service photographs of the event to the wire services and other media. And if you can afford it, you should also hire an experienced video crew who can cover the event, make quick copies of the footage, and service it to television news stations, distribution services, and websites that are often eager for content. In the next few years, we will be servicing news video by e-mail in the same way that we now take e-mailing still photography around for granted.

Sometimes stunts can take on a life of their own and build into a bigger story. In 1982, The Helen Hayes Theatre was demolished to make way for the Marriott Marquis Hotel in Times Square. A year later, out of respect for the legendary actress (who was still very much alive), it was decided to rename the Little Theatre on West 44th Street in Ms. Hayes' honor. In 1987, to drum up publicity for Larry Shue's *The Nerd* (I never really understood the connection!) a ceremony was planned to put Helen Hayes' footprints in cement (á la Grauman's Chinese Theatre on Hollywood Boulevard), on the sidewalk outside the building.

A special event was arranged with the cast members of *The Nerd*, lead by Mark Hamill and director Charles Nelson Reilly, surrounding Ms. Hayes as she delicately stepped into a tray of cement, leaving tiny footprints along with the star's autograph. The plan was to place the cement tablet in the sidewalk once it was dry and set. However, during the hoopla of the event, the block of cement disappeared! It had literally vanished. The lobby and basement of the theatre were checked—not a trace. Sheepishly we told the press—in all honesty—that the footprints had vanished. "Fifty pounds of concrete possibly stolen by a crazed fan!" The story of the missing footprints ran in *Newsweek* and was picked up

The 1982 Tony–nominated production of Shelagh Delaney's *A Taste of Honey*, the first Broadway show for which Adrian Bryan-Brown served as publicist. Pictured are Tom Wright as The Boy, Amanda Plummer as Jo, and Keith Reddin as Geoffrey.

Photo by Donna Svennevik, courtesy of the John Willis Theatre World/Screen World Archive.

by wire services, which gave the story international attention. The Helen Hayes Theatre and *The Nerd* got far more media space than the originally planned stunt would ever have received.

When one of the members of the Helen Hayes Theatre house staff admitted that they had taken the cement block to the alley next door to the theatre to dry undisturbed, we decided that it would spoil the fun to say the footprints had been recovered, so miraculously the "spare footprints that had been made by Miss Hayes as a back-up in case the cement did not set properly," were placed in the sidewalk.

The memorial eventually suffered the same fate as the first Helen Hayes Theatre. After a few months it was decided to remove the footprints from the sidewalk. I suppose there was concern that people might trip on them (and sue *The Nerd* or Ms. Hayes herself!) The impressions were replaced by a brass plaque in the sidewalk which bore the etched outline of Helen Hayes' shoes. A short time later the sleek and potentially slippery metal surface was removed and the sidewalk returned to its original state.

In moments of desperation, a producer may appeal to the press agent to generate *any* publicity to sell tickets. From experience, we know that any publicity does not always result in ticket sales.

In May 1991, playwright Paul Rudnick's Broadway debut, *I Hate Hamlet,* had just opened at the Walter Kerr Theatre. Starring British actor Nicol Williamson as the ghost of John Barrymore, the comedy also featured Evan Handler (who would become recognized internationally as Harry, Charlotte's boyfriend, on *Sex in the City*), as a struggling young actor making his debut as Hamlet on stage. In the Saturday, May 4, 1991, edition of the *New York Post*, a front page headline screamed BWAY SWORDPLAY TURNS REAL. Featuring photos of the two actors, the cover had a small inset box that read "To act or not to act. 'I Hate Hamlet' actor Evan Handler…had no trouble answering that question when co-star Nicol Williamson…smacked him on the rear end with his sword. Handler left the stage in the middle of the first act. See page 5."

Despite becoming worldwide news and a talking point on late night television shows everywhere, there was no change in ticket sales. In fact, they went down. Mr. Handler never returned to the show and the production closed a few weeks later. You couldn't ask for more "noise," but it did not make people interested in seeing the show.

Theatrical public relations is never dull; is always challenging; and is limited only by your imagination and by the numbers of hours of sleep you need.

Nancy Coyne

Nancy Coyne is the CEO of Serino Coyne Inc., the largest theatrical advertising agency in America, recently acquired by OMNICOM.

She represents the Broadway and touring productions of *Beauty and the Beast, bridge & tunnel, Hairspray, Jersey Boys, Mamma Mia!, Monty Python's Spamalot, The Light in the Piazza, The Lion King, The Odd Couple, The Phantom of the Opera, The Producers, The 25th Annual Putnam County Spelling Bee, Tarzan, The Wedding Singer, Three Days of Rain, Wicked,* as well as Lincoln Center Theatre, and American Express Gold Card Events.

Upcoming projects include *A Chorus Line, Curtains, Legends, Mary Poppins,* and *The Two and Only.* Ms. Coyne serves on the board of The Actors' Fund of America and has taught entertainment marketing at the Yale Drama School for the past fifteen years.

WHY BROADWAY IS BOOMING

NANCY COYNE (A CONVERSATION WITH)
CEO, Serino Coyne

BEN HODGES: Can you tell me a little about how you got into *advertising* Broadway?

NANCY COYNE: Well, I came to New York when I got married and I toyed with being an actress for about a minute and a half. I got my first "Leave your picture" with *The Man Outside* and I thought, "I don't want to do this." This is all about rejection. I better do something that is a little more up my alley—which I decided was writing, and specifically writing advertising. My husband was in advertising at the time and it seemed like fun. I went to work at a radio station where I wrote all of the copy for all of their clients, most of whom were too small use large agencies. The radio station was WRVR, which was a jazz station, and one of the clients was an ad agency called Blaine Thompson, that promoted Broadway shows. They were in the habit of just sending us a fact sheet, rather than produced radio spots, hoping that the deejay would read a live sixty-second spot on the air that would then sell tickets. So they would send us a list of the shows and the quotes from critics of the shows, the facts about who was starring in them, and the ticket prices—just literally a fact sheet; except most of my deejays at WRVR were not good readers. So it fell upon me to turn these fact sheets into radio spots. Since I had a library and some good voices to work with, I made produced spots. And pretty soon some of the shows that I was doing commercials for on WRVR asked if they could use the commercials on other radio stations. I said, "Actually, no, because I am being paid by the station, but if you would like to pay me to write spots for you, I would be happy to do it." So I had a little freelance business going writing radio commercials for Broadway shows. One day the agency offered me a job and I jumped at it because it combined two things that I loved—advertising and theatre. It couldn't have been more perfect when I went to work at that agency, Blaine Thompson. I really felt like I had died and gone to heaven. It was the best, best, best thing that ever happened to me.

HODGES: So, coming directly from an advertising world, how do you think that world has changed with respect to how you have chosen to advertise theatre then, and now?

COYNE: Well, I came not only from advertising, but I also came from radio. I have a profound respect for words and a profound respect for radio as a medium in that it has a great deal in common with the theatre and it asks the audience to use its imagination. It doesn't spoon feed you things as film and television do. It doesn't give you the whole picture. We will get into this later, but the use of television to advertise Broadway shows is very akin to putting a free sample of a detergent in the mail and sending it to you. It's "Try this little bit. If you like this little bit, we are sure you will want to buy the whole thing." So for me, radio is the ability to paint a picture using words and the music. I loved it. To this day I still think radio is a very important tool for selling the theatre, because it asks the audience with *these few words* and *this little bit of music* to envision the show.

HODGES: A "cooler" medium than television would be.

COYNE: Think about it—it is more interactive, which is what theatre is. The first interactive art form, if you will.

HODGES: So it sounds like from the outset you had a very minimalist approach to...

COYNE: Well, I believe that you can take every show on Broadway and sell it in sixty seconds or thirty, and that is a minimalist approach.

HODGES: So talking about advertising or *marketing* a Broadway show—whether it is radio, television, or another medium—how has it changed?

COYNE: It is interesting, as the world has changed. I have been doing this for thirty years now, and the world around me has changed dramatically. But the product that I sell is exactly the same as it was when I went into the business. It is a show that starts at 8:00 p.m. and is over by 10:00 p.m. or 10:30 p.m. (if you are lucky) [*Laughs.*]. There are one or maybe two intermissions; it takes place in a handful of theatres in New York City eight times a week—no more, no less; it is the same as it was one hundred years ago. The world has changed very dramatically and so we have many more avenues through which to tell people about theatre, but at the end of the day what people rely on when they plunk down one hundred dollars for a theatre ticket is someone's recommendation. It is usually someone they know, and it is someone very personal and someone who can assure them that it is worth the money.

HODGES: Considering that people *do* have choices, one of the reasons that I wanted to do this book is that there are people like me who work Off-Off-Broadway and in *regional* theatres across the country, who are doing multiple jobs, among them advertising and marketing.

COYNE: Right.

HODGES: They've got a limited budget, so whether it be a regional or a Broadway production, how do you gauge where to place your resources, depending on what might be going on in relation to *that* show in *that* climate, at *that* time?

COYNE: That is a great question. I taught at Yale for many years and what I taught was the trick of knowing your audience. My customer—my consumer base—is the people out there in the dark. The producers worry about what happens from the footlights *back*. I worry about what happens from the footlights *forward*. So I know that the very best I can do is to get the right people into the theatre first. The people who will love the show most are the people who will talk about it the most. So it is very helpful to know who you are talking to. You need to know them by name. You need to know what they like, where they go, what they do, and know, for sure, that they have some friends that they will talk to about this. It's really a matter of getting that first crowd in first. *Not* going for people who are too expensive to reach. It is the *low hanging fruit principle*, and we have to get those people in because they are the ones that start to spread the word. It's interesting. When we do focus groups, in every one there is a person who says, "Everyone in my crowd trusts me. I go to everything and I tell everybody else." People know that person. She is out there (and she is always a *she*). I mean in New York, she is. She is always a she. In fact she is always a she across the country. It is a woman, usually between forty-five and fifty, and depending upon the market, maybe between forty-five and fifty-five. She comes from a reasonably affluent household, and she is interested in the arts, and she has a lot of friends who trust her opinion.

HODGES: How much do you make a determination or expect that woman's taste or preferences to change? Is it season to season? Is it show to show? When you talk about doing focus groups and research, how often do you feel that you need to do that to keep up with what may be this woman's changing tastes?

COYNE: Well, we don't do focus groups to find out she wants; we do focus groups to find out how what we are promising matches what she wants. In some instances, all you have to do is put a star in a show. You put Julia Roberts in

Three Days of Rain and this woman is satisfied. She doesn't need any more information than that. You put Reba McEntire in *Annie Get Your Gun* and you have given her enough information. In some instances she will need another piece of information. For a limited time she can get a discount to the show and those two pieces of information combine sell the ticket and you're done. Then you have to put on a good show, because you have got to expect that what she comes in for she will get, to the degree that she is going to go out and talk about it.

HODGES: It's interesting because stars sell shows and clearly with the world getting smaller, that must have become even more of a selling point than it was in the 1970s or 1980s.

COYNE: It's been that way since the beginning of time, and that is why they call them star *vehicles*. A star vehicle was always a play that you could bet on selling because a star would want to do that role. Star vehicles are just solid theatre. I'm sure in Shakespeare's day (I don't know who they were), but I'm sure that there were actors that people wanted to see more than other actors. And the fact remains that the first question people ask is "Who's in it?" and the second question is "What's it about?" If who's in it is satisfactorily answered, they don't care what it is about. I venture to say no one buying tickets to *Three Days of Rain* has the vaguest idea what it is about.

HODGES: So given the product hasn't really changed, and the selling points of the product haven't necessarily changed, then what you are telling me is that it's the media through which it can be advertised that have changed?

COYNE: Vastly, and the biggest change is now the proliferation of media; how many ways we have to tell people. It is really quite astonishing in as much as we have a somewhat limited budget. If only we had more money (and we would have more money if there wasn't a ceiling on how many tickets can be sold—an interesting thing about theatre as opposed to film). Think about it, when they get ready to advertise a film that have the film *in the can* to work with. They can cut it up and make an infinite number of different commercials. Then they have a huge budget, because the number of showings of that film in the number of theatres is virtually limitless. The length that the film can stay in the theatre is limitless. Then they have the *ancillary rights* in DVD sales and before that, rentals; and before that, pay-per-view on television. They can make their money back, so their advertising budgets are gigantic compared to that in the theatre, because at the end of every week we have only been able to play eight performances, and we have only been able to sell eight times the seating capacity and that is the ceiling. At the end of every week we have to reconcile our numbers, so that leaves you with an incontestable amount of money compared to what a movie has. And then compare that to what McDonald's has! My favorite point to make is when you think about the New York marketplace and you think about advertising on television or radio (or anywhere), I'm spending money in the same market as McDonald's. But they are selling a product that costs one dollar and it is available on every street corner virtually at any time of the day or night (and you do have to eat). I am selling a product that costs one hundred dollars and it is only available eight times a week, at times that are not convenient for you, at a theatre that is definitely not convenient to where you live or work. And you don't have to go to the theatre. I have so much less money to do my job with, but the difference is that when I do it—when I get you there—you will talk about it and you are not going to talk tomorrow to people about the hamburger you grabbed for dinner last night. Theatre is special and therefore it requires that you talk about it. That's why we exist and that is why we can do our job with the limited dollars we have.

HODGES: One of the most surprising things I have read from the other contributors' pieces, is that of Roche Schulfer of the Goodman Theatre. Schulfer says that compared to other industries, theatre is incredibly undercapitalized. We tend to only see the very few examples of the most *capitalized* part.

COYNE: Unbelievably so. When a new show opens, that is the equivalent in another industry of a new product introduction into the New York market. Do you know the monies that are allocated by normal advertising agencies to do that job? And yet I am expected to get this product on the lips of everybody in Manhattan in a very short period of time with a fraction of the money necessary. It can be done because when it works it is *so* noteworthy, it is *so* press worthy, it is *so* special, that people talk.

HODGES: Let's consider for a moment that all playing fields are level—whether it be Omaha or New York—and talk about how you make a way in a crowded marketplace. Or, budgets that were limited in such a way that your creativity is tested by the demands put on it.

COYNE: Well, the greatest challenge that anyone has is to market a show that didn't receive good reviews. That is a challenge that we all have faced and the biggest problem there is, even if you think of the reviewers as I do as just a handful of opinions, nonetheless they are the beginning of word of mouth. So chances are no one will read all the fifteen critics (or in a smaller market *both* critics—they'll just read one). So one person has told them to *skip it*. Television

is very effective at countering a bad review. Radio is very effective. *Jekyll &*
Hyde is a good example. It opened to negative reviews, but the producers were
committed to keeping it going until we could make a television commercial.
We made a television commercial that capitalized on the genre. I think what
sold *Jekyll and Hyde* for the next three years was that TV commercial and the
realization that *Jekyll and Hyde* was the only sort of *horror musical* on Broadway.
So if that is the kind of thing that you like, this was the show that you needed to
see. We overcame the challenge by selling the very specific genre of the show.

HODGES: Let's talk about television commercials for a moment. I am from a small
town in East Tennessee, and now suddenly we see every local dermatologist
hawking eyelid surgery on television because of the advent of *commercial*
programming through cable channels. From what I understand, conventional
wisdom had it that the television commercial in the New York market was no
longer effective, and that seems to have changed recently. But I think your
comments will also have resonance elsewhere.

COYNE: It is coming back. One of the things that is interesting (and I believe
that we do this intuitively), is that you can't treat all shows the same; every one
is different. There are some that are better served by television and some that
are better served by radio. It depends upon the strength of the show. But, if
you have a show that is visually breathtaking, it does you a disservice to only
be on the radio. You want people to get a glimpse of it. The big change that
happened was—with the proliferation of channels—you could no longer reach
the tipping point as easily as you could in the 1970s and '80s. When I first
went to work on Broadway, it was to do television commercials and we were
instantly successful. But, in those day you could buy a thirty-second spot on
channels 2, 4, 7, 5, 9, 11 at 11:15 p.m. and you had 80 percent of the population
covered by buying six spots. The next day you saw an effect at the box office. It
was so efficient it took our breath away. And it worked so amazingly well that
for a time it was what theatre advertising became. It became about making
great television commercials. Then what happened was cable television came
along and now people were watching one hundred channels (or more like one
thousand these days), and you could no longer reach everybody with one spot.
So you had to be more and more careful and more and more selective, which
goes back to the issue that I talked about earlier—targeting. You need to know
to whom you are speaking. If you are speaking to women of a certain age
or demographic, you have to be very careful about what you are buying. You
can't buy just the news, which was what we used to do. We bought the news

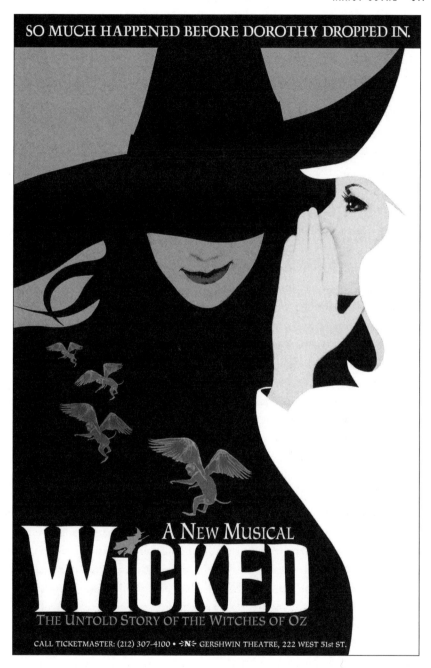

Key art from the 2004 Tony Award-winning production of *Wicked*;
Mark Platt, producer; Design by Trailer Park, Inc.; Jeff Bacon, creative director.
Courtesy of Serino Coyne and Universal Studios.

at 11:00 p.m. and we got everybody. It doesn't happen that way anymore. So it is a much more difficult game than it was in the '70s and '80s because of cable. But, it does offer you the opportunity to narrowly target. It's a balancing act. We have so much media to consider, that you really need to take your small budget, (fifty to sixty thousand dollars) and divide it over: print (which has become newspaper, which has become less important) the Internet (which has become more important), Radio, Television, and Outdoor. Tourists are a different breed. Sixty-four percent of the Broadway audience is sometimes from *out-of-town*. You don't reach them the same way that you reach a person who lives here. So a bus going by or a billboard in Times Square is critical to getting the word out that this is an important show to see.

HODGES: Let's talk about those aspects of advertising, because I do think they apply everywhere in the country, and possibly even the world. As to changes since 9/11, do you think they are permanent? And what are those changes?

COYNE: There were two effects of 9/11 in the theatre: one was negative, obviously. People don't plan as far in advance as they used to and I don't think they will ever go back. I think our naiveté, if you will, about how long we are going to be here is gone forever. People don't take things for granted the way they did including the fact that they will be here next month or next year to see *The Lion King*. If they can't get tickets now, then they will see something that they can see tonight. So the *advances* are not what they once were. They *are* coming back. There are creeping back, but the ability to plan way out in front—I don't think it will ever be what it was before 9/11. The positive side, I think, is that it's becoming more and more important for people to gather with other people and to not isolate themselves in a room with a video game, computer, television, or a DVD player. I think the act of congregating to sit in the dark to watch live theatre has become somehow infinitely more important to us. That's what we saw in the aftermath of 9/11. People came back to the theatre before they went back shopping or to restaurants. In many, many interviews we did with people coming out of the theatre, they said that it seemed to them like "the right thing to do." It felt like the right place to be. I think the isolationism that happens is because of computers. E-mailing someone rather than speaking to them directly is something that the theatre effectively combats. It asks you to sit in the dark and have the same feelings as the person sitting next to you at the same moment in time. I think that is something that we cherish more than we once did. The success of the theatre is numbers. I don't know what they are like across the country because Broadway is my primary market. But, what I

Disney's *The Lion King* poster artwork.
Courtesy of Buena Vista Theatrical Productions, Ltd. and ©Disney.

see here is healthy. It's people being respectful of the theatre and what it can do, and how it can make you feel and the fact that it is the communal experience and not a singular experience. I think that is great!

HODGES: You know I like the tone of this conversation because it has to do with theory and really giving people a landscape from which they consider aspects like direct mail versus e-mail and so I think this is a great take on this subject. What kind of qualities does a producer need to have to be able to help you do your job the best you can?

COYNE: Decisiveness. If I could pick one quality that I like in a producer, it is someone who knows what they want and stays with it—isn't swayed by others who come up with something, whether it is on the stage, or the page for an ad, and has the courage to back it.

HODGES: What if someone is inexperienced and doesn't know where to invest their advertising resources?

COYNE: I think if someone is inexperienced, the best decisions they can make are who they trust. I think people should rely on their instincts. I have rarely made an instinctive decision that I regretted. The ones that I have regretted have been labored, intelligent, and thought out. My instinctive decisions are my best and my most theatrical, and I think a good thing for producers to realize is that the gut that brought them to the theatre in the first place will tell them what to do. They need to follow that. That is what *live* is all about, isn't it? Live is a choice you make and it is not the economically sound choice. Think about it—if you were approaching this purely as a businessperson, you would never go into a business where there were a fixed number of units you could manufacturer. But that is what we have in the theatre. We have only so many seats, only so many performances. If you were a businessperson, you would make movies or DVDs or something that could be mass-produced ad infinitum. So somebody who is in the theatre is here for a different reason. They are here because they have a love of this peculiar art form that is live. That happens between 8:00 p.m. and 10:30 p.m. and that will never be duplicated again in exactly the same way. So right off the bat, you are special. Stick with all the things that make you special. Forget all the things that make you like everybody else and go with the things that may you unique. That is how we try to strategize with every show. We try to find what makes it different. What makes it different from every other show on Broadway? What makes it worthy of two hours of your time and one hundred dollars of your money? That is the question that we ask. I think a producer has to ask himself the same thing. What is it about the show that I am about to produce that makes me capable of saying "Give me one hundred dollars to see it." What do I love about it? What do I want to capture? What do I want to tell people? I love listening to people at intermission—I really do. I sometimes think that I am not a copywriter as much as I am a good listener. Because I hear the copy—I just hear them say it. When a show hits a nerve, you will hear people say the most wonderful things. I remember a focus group that we did once (I can't remember the show actually), but it was about the theatrical experience. It addressed the point that the new audience that I am most interested in is family audience. (Not just because I handle Disney, but because I watched Times Square and 42nd Street change and I watched the change in the people who were walking up and down the street.) If you told me twenty-five years ago that there would be little girls in patent leather shoes all over Broadway, I would have said, "What?" But, they are here now and at one focus group a parent said, after taking her children to a show, that the best part was the ride home. We asked why. She said it was because they were all talking about the same thing. She said that usually they have such different experiences and they're talking about *their* shows and *their* video games, and she said this time on the ride home they they were all talking about the show they had just seen. It is a transformative experience. From my soap box, I think personally that going to the theatre is right up there with literacy in terms of a child's development and how they develop an imagination. When you give them a film in which every special effect is done to simulate reality, they don't have to imagine anything. But a child is capable of imaging that a cardboard stick is a tree—you just have to ask them. That is what theatre does—it asks you to play along and kids who go to the theatre are smarter than kids that who don't. That is all there is to it.

HODGES: Well you've led me into my next question. My regular gig is editing *Theatre World*, and I have seen very clearly in black and white the scarcity of new plays being produced annually. There's almost a complete absence of plays with more than four characters being produced anywhere On of Off-Broadway (other than a *nonprofit*). And because people may have more trouble marketing a play than a musical, what would you to say to people who are faced with the choice—be it a *resident* theatre or nonprofit, in New York or otherwise—of having to cater to people who may only be expecting entertainment in the form of spectacle, rather than something that the directors may want to produce for other reasons?

COYNE: Well, I don't do very many plays and I don't do any Off-Broadway and I don't do much in the way of regional theatre. I care about it, but I don't do it for business reasons. If I didn't run a business, and if I were to have a personal interest in Off-Broadway and nonprofit and the straight play, I would first of all work on calling Off-Broadway something other than Off-Broadway. I don't think you should ever define something by what it is not. Call it "Neighborhood Theatre" and make your constituency your neighborhood. Try to work out a different set of union rules so "Neighborhood Theatre" could be cheaper. If a musical is one hundred dollars a ticket a play should be fifty dollars—that is what I believe. I don't think the Broadway theatres can support the fifty dollars ticket anymore (except for discounted musicals and only then in part of the house). I see Off-Broadway—or in my vision "Neighborhood Theatre"—as owning the plays. They wouldn't be for tourists—tourists don't go Off-Broadway. They would be for the *intelligentia* of New York. That is how I would start to segregate the two. Does that make any sense?

HODGES: Absolutely. I don't know if these are trade secrets, but I am very curious as to how much discussion among your employees goes into how you find out what the next trends are going to be. Talking about trend research and focus groups, how much of that is a part of what you do overall, and how do you plan that kind of thing?

COYNE: Well, I'll tell you a lot of it has to do with budgetary concerns.

HODGES: So it is show specific.

COYNE: It is much more show specific than trend specific. We can't afford to do research that is independent. We rely on The League for some information about where our audience is and what we are doing, but when I say instincts never leads you wrong, we have one hundred people here who go to the theatre all the time. We talk to the people sitting to the right of us; to the left of us; we talk to each other a lot; we read a lot; and we care passionately. So everything we do is informed and made better by the fact that we have so few dollars with which to do so—we have to make sure we don't waste any. I am part of a very large agency now, Omnicom, and I have many, many chances to connect with my fellow CEOs from other agencies and what I am constantly struck by is how much more involved with our *products* we are. We know every day how many tickets are sold to our shows and how many tickets are sold to other shows that we don't handle. We have a completely imbedded relationship with all of our producers and that is not something that most agencies have with their clients. So in that respect, we are almost like their in-house marketing department to some degree. We are unbelievably close to what we sell and it is one of the reasons that people are happy working here because they feel very responsible. We have a couple of shows right now where we monitor the direct mail results everyday. We know how many tickets were sold every day. That kind of response makes you feel very attached to a show, very much a booster, and not just an employee. It's an interesting field because no one would go into producing shows if it were just for the money. No one would go into advertising them either for the money. There would be many easier things to do than this. But, the upside is that you are connected at all times to the product and to the result of your efforts and that's what people seem to get a kick out of in their work—the notion that they make a difference. I have never felt like I didn't make a difference; that the agency didn't make a difference, and I think that is how we are able to keep on doing what we are doing. I think it is true of theatre across the country. People who work to sell it feel uniformly good about what they do.

HODGES: If I am Off-Off Broadway—because that is what we call it until we come up with a better name! [*laughs*], and I have five thousand dollars, some people say direct mail is what I should spend it on. Some people say an e-mail blast—*that* is what to spend it on. Some would say to hire a *publicist* as they will get the critics there and they, in turn, will get the people there. Is there a way to quantify that?

COYNE: Well, the most efficient thing to do is an e-mail blast because you can purchase a list of people who want to hear, who have *asked* to hear about new shows. You give them a price point and enough information that's valid and appealing, and you will have a response that more than pays for the cost. There is nothing else that you can do that will have a return on the investment of five thousand dollars that is as quantifiable as an e-mail blast.

HODGES: You have given us a wonderfully theoretical take on advertising.

COYNE: I like the theory of it. I had this class from North Carolina that came and we talked about the theory of advertising and how to isolate the salient points. I said it is the most fun you can have without a client in the room—to talk about it purely. You don't have to think about "Well *he* likes blue, and *he* likes radio, and *he* doesn't like anything that has to do with *that*." The theory behind it is fascinating.

HODGES: So, one last question—weren't you behind the original *The Elephant Man* campaign which Fred spoke of often and has become the stuff of legend?

COYNE: Yes.

HODGES: Could you just tell me about this? Fred talked about this and I never got the whole story. What was the thing about?

COYNE: It was one of the first times that a play successfully advertised on television because usually plays don't have enough money to go on television. They could go on television but they couldn't buy enough spots to make a difference. So *The Elephant Man* won the Tony and it had a little burst of money that poured into the box office. The producer Liz McCann decided she wanted to try and to do a television commercial, and we were very fortunate. The logo for *The Elephant Man* was a little orange elephant man with a very, very big round head—it was a very graphic representation. It looked like the medallion on the Tony, so we took the Tony and we asked a couple of people some questions like, "Do you know what the Tony is?" And they didn't. What we had been doing all those years was saying, "Come see the Tony-winning play…." So we thought maybe they don't know that the Tony is to the theatre what the Oscar is to film and what the Emmy is to television. So we just took the Tony, and shot it straight on, but we spun the medallion. We spun the medallion and the voice over said, "In television it is the Emmy, in film it is the Oscar, and on Broadway it is the Tony…and only one play wins. This year the play is *The Elephant Man.*" As the medallion slows down it turns into a logo. We pulled back and it the ad read "Winner of the Tony Award for Best Play. That was it. But, it had a noticeable effect.

HODGES: So that is the whole story. Now I've gotten it. Thank you, Nancy.

COYNE: Thank you.

Jim Edwards

Jim Edwards, from the start of his career, has always worked in entertainment marketing. At Grey Advertising, he initially worked on the Warner Bros. Films and ABC-TV Prime Time accounts before he entered the world of theatre advertising in 1986. Since then, he has participated on the ad campaigns of many productions including *M. Butterfly, Other People's Money, The Who's Tommy, Grease, RENT, Chicago, Wit, Copenhagen, Avenue Q,* and *The Color Purple.* In 1997, SpotCo, the newest and fastest growing advertising agency in the Broadway industry, was founded and Jim has been there from the start. He is a graduate of Wilkes University and Ohio University. Jim lives in Brooklyn, New York.

ADVERTISING TO PRODUCERS–ADVERTISING TO AUDIENCES

JIM EDWARDS
SpotCo

M. Butterfly, the 1988 Tony Award-winner for Best Play, was the first Broadway show I worked on as a theatre *advertising* account executive. I had been working at Grey Advertising for about six years on national accounts such as Warner Bros. movies and ABC-TV Prime Time, but the powers that be wanted to add theatre to our roster of entertainment clients. Jeff Ash, who had worked in theatrical advertising his whole professional life, joined Grey to help us build the theatre division. His father was one of the original innovators in the business of theatre advertising and is credited for creating the directory of Broadway and Off-Broadway show listings that runs in *The New York Times* every day.

Stuart Ostrow, a long time friend of Jeff Ash and his father, was producing *M. Butterfly* and hired Grey to handle the show. At the time, I had no idea how courageous a feat Mr. Ostrow was taking on by bringing this new play to Broadway. Based on a true story about a diplomat who has an affair with a Chinese opera singer/spy for years but doesn't realize his lover is a man, it was written by an unknown and first-time Broadway playwright named David Henry Hwang, and starred John Lithgow (before he had gained fame in *3rd Rock from the Sun*). I also didn't realize what a leap of faith Mr. Ostrow was taking by hiring Grey to give his show an identity and to position it within the marketplace as none us, except for Jeff, had ever done this before. It was an incredible learning experience, exciting as well as thrilling, and soon into it I knew that I never wanted to work on anything else but live theatre for the rest of my advertising career.

Seventeen years later I'm still at it, working as director of account services at SpotCo, the newest of the ad agencies in our industry. While the business of *marketing* shows continues to evolve, many aspects never change. Part of my job is to continually monitor and analyze how shows are sold: what works, what doesn't, what are the trends, who can break out from the pack and succeed, who can't and why, and to synthesize all that information and apply it to each new show we are assigned.

Ad agencies have a unique vantage point in our industry and the smart producers will use that to their advantage. To understand, let's say there are one hundred active producers at any given moment on Broadway. Producers hire a *general manager*, a *press agent*, and an advertising agency. And while there are roughly twenty general managers and ten press offices working at any given time on Broadway, there are only three advertising agencies.

The Coca-Cola Company and PepsiCo would never be at the same ad agency, but shows on Broadway can't afford that same luxury. Due to the size of their ad budgets and the very narrow focus we market within, it is actually beneficial for many shows to be handled under one roof. The current ad agencies are well-organized and set up with an infrastructure to work on several shows at once. It also gives the ad agencies a wealth of information on trends within the industry as well as the exceptions to them. Without giving away other shows' specific marketing strategies before they are unveiled, the ad agency can guide a seasoned or novice producer through the latest ways to effectively and efficiently sell his or her show based on our current (and recent past) list of shows.

Where does it begin? In most instances, it is simply a phone call. A veteran producer will call up the ad agency and say, for example, "We're bringing *The Miracle Worker—The Musical*, starring Cher and Dakota Fanning, to Broadway. Start thinking of ideas." It's rare that we actually pitch a show. (A *pitch* is a presentation of creative and strategic ideas to the client at the ad agency's expense in order to win the account.) The reason is that most of our new shows are being produced by either clients we are currently working with or have worked with in the recent past. They know what we are capable of and how we approach a project. They like what we do and/or enjoy working with us. So, we're hired.

For new producers it can be tricky. If you are a producer with no track record and you want to bring what you believe is the next Pulitzer Prize-winning play to Broadway, I suggest you look at the ad campaigns of shows similar to yours and define what you liked about those ad campaigns and, of course, what you didn't. Find out who handled the advertising and first request a meeting. Many new producers will call us and ask us to pitch for their business. We often ask a few questions first. For example, is that producer fully *capitalized* yet? (If there is no money in the bank account, we'll pass on the business. Many theatrical ad agencies have gone out of business due to producers who can't pay their bills on failed shows.) Do they have a Broadway theatre with a confirmed booking? Who is their general manager? Basically, we're trying to verify the credibility of the project. If it is something that looks real (meaning the show and its producer have credibility on several fronts), and if it is a project that interests the ad agency, we would first suggest a meet and greet meeting to find out more about the project from the producer. At this meeting both the ad agency and the producer are getting a feel for each other. What's their sensibility? What's the balance between enthusiasm and pragmatism for the project? Are they nice enough where we would all want to sit around a conference room table for the next couple of years if the show is a hit? From there, it can go to a pitch, but usually the ad agency is hired from that initial meeting.

Once the agency is hired, we ask more questions. If the show currently exists and we've seen it in an *out-of-town* engagement, we'll want to know how much of the show is going to stay exactly as we saw it and what's going to change. The producer spends more time with the show than anyone on his marketing team. We'll pick their brains as to how audiences are responding to certain elements within the show.

If there is nothing but a script, we'll talk to the playwright or director and sometimes even the designers for their take on the look and feel of the show. These conversations are often very helpful and all of this is part of the process.

Then we start our work. We all may brainstorm initially, and by that I mean representatives from the design department, copy department, possibly broadcast production department, and the account team handling the show. Basically, we try to define the unique aspects of the show, define who the target audience is, and then determine, within the budget parameters given, what's the best way to reach that target demographic. More often than not, a Broadway show will be targeted at the traditional theatregoer (a woman usually fifty years of age or more who has made theatregoing part of her leisure activities). Since most shows are aimed at the same demographic, it is also our responsibility to differentiate the show from all the others—in other words, know our competition and how to separate us from it.

Positioning a show within the marketplace is something we do well at SpotCo and it starts at the top. Our creative director of the agency, Drew Hodges, is also the president and owner of the company. Drew first owned his own design firm working with a wide range of clients, but mostly centered in the entertainment world. After he created the campaigns for *RENT* and *Chicago*, more and more producers were seeking his expertise and he decided to move away from being a design shop to a full-fledged advertising agency. His involvement is imprinted on every show SpotCo handles. His goal is to be innovative without throwing the rulebook out the window. How can we position each new show creatively and uniquely without forgetting the information the ticket buyer wants to know? That's the challenge.

What *does* the ticket buyer want to know? After many years of attending focus groups, talking to the operators at Telecharge.com and Ticketmaster (official ticket sources for most of New York City's theatres), or just deliberately eavesdropping on conversations in the theatre, here's what they want to know:

1. What's the show about?
2. Who is in it?
3. How much are tickets?
4. Where am I going to sit?

The ad agency very rarely can answer the last question for the consumer. That is done at the point of purchase. Our job is to best answer the first three questions so that the fourth question isn't an obstacle. We want them to see the show so badly they don't care where they sit.

It's really the first two questions that are the most important: What is it about and who is in it? The answer to those questions really indicates how commercial the project is. A production of *Annie Get Your Gun,* starring Bernadette Peters doesn't really need much explanation. An Off-Broadway show called *De La Guarda* (an Argentinean performance art group where 90 percent of the action takes place over a standing audience) needs to impart more information in its marketing materials. Vanessa Redgrave and Brian Dennehy in a limited engagement revival of *Long Day's Journey Into Night* is a pretty *commercial* production. The ticket buyer doesn't care how much a ticket is and would probably sit in the ladies room as long as they could hear.

But a play about a German transvestite living through World War II, the rise and fall of communism, and starring one actor the general public has never heard of, is a marketing challenge. *I Am My Own Wife* originally opened at Playwrights Horizons to excellent reviews. But when Drew and I saw the play at the request of the producers who intended to move it to Broadway, the theatre was only two-thirds full. If a highly acclaimed play cannot sell out at a small Off-Broadway house, how can we sell tickets to the same production in a *venue* two to three times larger? Despite these obstacles, the producers (David Richenthal and Tony and Charlene Marshall), wanted to produce a show that interested them a great deal and bring it to a larger audience. They also wanted to support the creative team of playwright Doug Wright, director Moises Kaufman, and actor Jefferson Mays.

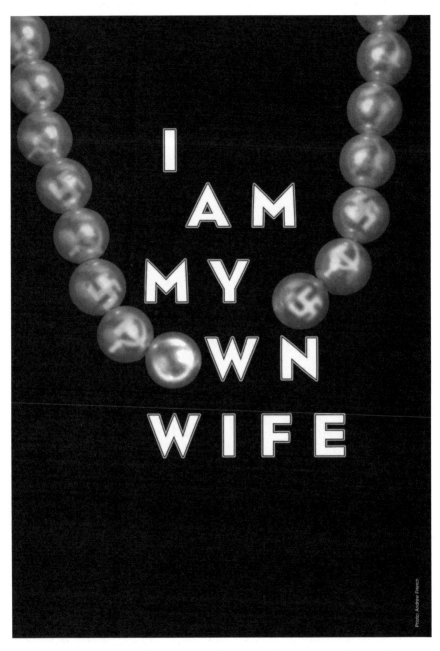

Key art from the Pulitzer Prize and Tony Award-winning production of
I Am My Own Wife; Drew Hodges, creative director; Gail Anderson, art director.
Courtesy of SpotCo.

Coming up with the artwork for this show was a long process. How do we tell potential audiences what this play is about? Do we include Nazi and Communist symbols? A photograph of our actor no one knows in costume would be very off-putting, in or out of context from the show. After many, many designs we came up with a look that featured a string of pearls with swastika and hammer and cycle symbols "ghosted" in each pearl. Instead of an all-purpose copy line to give a sense of the story and show, we used a review quote from the Playwrights Horizons' production. The *key art* (the graphic image and title treatment used in ads, posters, flyers and mailings) then positioned the show within the Broadway marketplace. But we knew no one would come based on that information alone. Why would they? When launching most shows, we use direct response (direct mail and e-mail blasts) to close early sales and help build an *advance* prior to starting performances. For *I Am My Own Wife*, direct response was the only method that would sell tickets before we were re-reviewed as a Broadway show. In a direct mail piece or e-mail blast you have more real estate than a print ad to tell the show's story. You are able to go into more detail about the pedigree of those involved. Also, several review quotes with more detail can be included. But most importantly, we offered tickets at a discount. The thought is that when our woman of fifty-plus years opens her mailbox and receives our direct mail piece, we answer all her questions about the show and top it off with an offer for her to see it at 35 percent less than everyone else. We want her to think to herself, "Who is better than me? I'm going to see this great play *and* at a discount!"

The unfortunate part is that we send out so many direct mailings and e-mail blasts that our early audience is now well trained. They will see an announcement ad and wait for the mail to arrive inviting them to see our show at a discount. Clearly a show starring Nathan Lane and Matthew Broderick won't offer any discounts, but most shows do. The trick is to determine if your show should do a direct response effort and then, if so, what level of discount to use. This is easier said then done and we don't always get it right. (When I say *we*, I'm referring to the marketing team, which includes the producer, general manager, press agent, and ad agency, who all pipe in with ideas on what the discount should be. The producer and general manager want to get the highest price per ticket so they can meet weekly running costs at the theatre and maybe even make a profit. I am often recommending a lower price based on what other shows are offering and the success—or failure—of what those shows have sold. Sometimes I win the debate and sometimes I lose.)

With *I Am My Own Wife* on Broadway, it didn't matter. Yes, we sold some tickets through direct response, but audiences were indifferent or wanted to know more. When the play was reopened, the first five paragraphs of the review in *The New York Times* talked about the craziness of bringing this production to Broadway. It was actually a rave but read like a bad review. You unfortunately had to keep reading to realize it was positive. Our post opening day *wrap*, in terms of gross ticket sales, wasn't as strong as it should have been. What finally seemed to put this show on the right track, however, was a feature article about Wright, Kaufman, and Mays.* It spoke of the initial collaboration between the writer, director, and actor that made this production such a unique theatrical event. Ticket sales started to rise because the team worked together. The press agent for the show, Richard Kornberg and Associates, got that article placed, and the ad agency kept fanning the flames to position the play as worthy of attention. More direct response efforts went out and this time, more people bought tickets.

Then the award season started. *I Am My Own Wife* won the Pulitzer Prize for Drama. Our job was to herald the production as the "Best Play in Town!" The show was nominated for every Best Play award available and every time the producers showed up at an award show, they took home the top honor. It was our job to let ticket buyers know this play was the undisputed champ. The show ran for almost a year on Broadway, *toured* the country, and was produced in London. And it all could have easily ended at Playwrights Horizons if it wasn't for the courage of the producers and their trust in letting us do our job. Our best work always happens when a producer takes us on as a marketing partner and not "the ad agency with those huge invoices I hate paying."

The best example of an ad agency and client relationship based on trust and empowerment would be our work on the Tony Award-winning musical *Avenue Q*. I was the first person from our office to see it at a *reading*. I liked it very much and assumed they were going to try to produce it Off-Broadway. It played like an adult version of *Sesame Street* with puppets and humans telling the story together. It had adult themes and language but had an underlying sweetness to it that made it all the more appealing. It wasn't for little kids but it wasn't raunchy or obscene. The show went Off-Broadway to the Vineyard Theatre as part of its subscription season. If it was well received, Jeffrey Seller, Kevin McCollum, and Robyn Goodman would move it to a small Broadway theatre. The Gulf War had been initiated the night before the review came out. People weren't going to the Arts section with any sense of urgency that day, but it was a good review and

---

* Jesse McKinley, "Putting a Guy Into a Frock Takes Teamwork," *The New York Times*, December 17, 2003.

the producers gave us the green light to start working on a campaign for a Broadway transfer.

How do you sell a Broadway musical with puppets? How do you let people know it isn't for kids but that they don't have to be afraid of its mature language and plot? How do you let people know this is a full-fledged Broadway musical worthy of top dollar ticket price? This campaign was one of three steps forward and then always one or two back. We made assumptions that were wrong. We learned from those mistakes. We then responded to those mistakes. This process happened several times.

Jeffrey, Kevin, and Robyn hired Sam Rudy Media Relations for press, TMG (The Marketing Group) for promotions and special events, and SpotCo for advertising. Ad meetings were conducted in a spirit that no idea was a bad one. Everyone at the table could contribute and respond. And the producers led with confidence while never surrendering to panic or anxiety because they simply believed in their show. As good as this sounds, it is often the exception to how Broadway business is conducted, rather than the rule.

They let each of us do our jobs and empowered us in such a way that we all did some of our best work. It really just came down to trust. From the ad agency's point of view, the launch was very frustrating. After the initial ad materials were made, we soon learned that many adult theatregoers were out-and-out bigots when it came to puppets. We couldn't give the tickets away. The show opened with about a $500 thousand advance (ticket sales for future performances). This is an incredibly low and scary figure. Everyone would have felt a lot better if the advance was at least three to four times larger.

The show opened in the middle of summer—the first musical of the season and almost a full year before the next Tony Awards. Again, we received good reviews—*great*, in fact—but the post opening day sales were not going to break any records. It was going to be a very slow build. The more the show performed, the more the advance grew, but did I mention that it was *s-l-o-w*?

One idea that we came up with that helped position the show as a real live Broadway musical—one worthy of your attention and dollars—was to run an ad every time a new musical opened, welcoming the newcomer to the street. Suddenly, *Avenue Q* became the host, the elder statesman, the de facto emcee of the theatre community, positioning us within the industry as a formidable musical equal to our competition. (Some producers of new plays not selected for inclusion in this campaign actually complained to us asking why *Avenue Q* didn't target their shows when they opened.)

Poster art for the 2004 Tony Award-winning production of *Avenue Q*
Drew Hodges, creative director; Drew Hodges; Gail Anderson, art director.
Courtesy of SpotCo.

When the award season came around, we took a bold move and played off the presidential election that was happening at the time. From the moment the Tony Award nominations were announced until the week before the awards were presented, our message was dressed in a political theme. Print ads were created to look like "I like Ike" ads from the 1950s. Buttons were created with slogans like "America's Counting on Q!" "Yes Q Can!" "Don't Suck Vote Q," and "Putting Broadway First!" The theatre's front of house displays were dressed in bunting and everything was red, white, and blue. No one gave us a shot in hell to win the Tony Award for Best Musical, but Jeffrey, Kevin, and Robyn all agreed that even if we lost it was all worth it because the show had totally reinvented itself and after a year's run, it was getting more and more attention on Broadway.

I'll never forget the moment the 2004 Tony Award for Best Musical was given. Nathan Lane was the presenter and when he opened the envelope and his mouth started to pronounce the "*Av*" in "*Av-enue Q*," it was unbelievable. As an ad guy, I felt like we had certainly contributed to the show's winning achievement, but it was really because the producers knew how to lead, empower, and inspire.

The ad agency is only as good as the client allows. Our work on *Avenue Q* was a joint effort between everyone who came to those weekly ad meetings. And that's how it should be.

Barbara Eliran

Barbara Eliran has served as director of advertising for Madison Square Garden, San Francisco's American Conservatory Theatre, and in a smaller capacity for one of the nation's premiere arts complexes, the John F. Kennedy Center for the Performing Arts in Washington, D.C.

An expert in media planning and negotiation, a former ATPAM press agent, brings her public relations and promotional background, along with over thirty years of experience in leisure industry marketing, to the entertainment industry.

She has been responsible for the planning, creation, and execution of the marketing campaigns for hundreds of both Broadway and Off-Broadway productions plus a wide range of cultural presentations including such highlights as Leonard Bernstein's Mass and *Pavarotti in Concert*. On the opposite side of the spectrum, she guided campaigns for the New York Rangers, the New York Knicks, and the World Wrestling Federation. Specialty marketing has included her work for restaurants, hotels, and travel destinations.

TOP BILLING: THEATRICAL ADVERTISING

BARBARA ELIRAN (A CONVERSATION WITH)
CEO, Eliran Murphy Group

BARBARA ELIRAN: First, I'd like to dedicate this chapter to Fred Vogel. Fred didn't talk about it often—only in the last five years or so did he mention it when he introduced me as I began a CTI seminar—but he gave me my very first job in the *commercial* theatre when he hired me as the receptionist for Brownstone Associates, a small theatrical *advertising* agency on West 44th Street in New York. The agency was owned by Fred Segal (the brother of actor George). It was in the heyday of Off-Broadway—Norman Mailer, Rip Torn, and Jean Claude VanItalie are a few *names* to sprinkle to set the era. Tiny Brownstone consisted of Fred Segal, Fred Vogel, another account executive, a couple of absolutely wonderful artists, and at the reception desk—yours truly.

Things move very quickly in our business, and very shortly thereafter, the fabulous Mr. Vogel left to move on, the other lovely account executive announced her pregnancy, and I was anointed the sole account executive for Brownstone. Thus began a career that has been, for over thirty-five years, one of the major loves of my life and a career that I clearly learned from the bottom up.

Fast-forward to March 2006, and Eliran Murphy Group (EMG)—which I co-own with my business partner, Ann Murphy. It has been in existence for fifteen and a half years and is one of the three major advertising agencies specializing in this particular niche world of theatrical advertising. Let me say here that I think EMG is perhaps different from our two competitors in the market place, SpotCo and Serino Coyne, in that in addition to commercial theatre both Broadway and Off-Broadway, we service the largest number of *resident not-for-profit* theatres here in New York City. These include Roundabout Theatre Company, Playwrights Horizons, Theatre For A New Audience, and NY Theatre Workshop, to name but a few. In addition to theatre, however, we also do the advertising for many of the city's cultural institutions—New York City Opera, The Chamber Music Society of Lincoln Center, the American Museum of Natural History, the Whitney Museum, and Channel 13 (WNET), among many others. The array of both commercial product and cultural institutions puts us in the unique position of reaching the lion's share of patrons who frequent the arts.

In many ways, the business is quite similar to what it was thirty-five years ago, and in many important ways, it now faces the challenges of an industry that has entered the twenty-first century. It is an industry that competes neck-and-neck for the individual with leisure time and disposable income.

Advertising for the commercial theatre is not rocket science, and it's not neurosurgery, and as I said previously, there are three agencies that do this work. I believe the differences end up being about the creative process and perhaps the personalities.

I'd like to give you my definition of entertainment and cultural advertising: it's that which you pay for, dollar for dollar. You see an ad in *The New York Times*, you hear a radio commercial, you see a TV spot, you notice a billboard, or you receive a piece of mail, or an e-mail—all of the above comprise paid advertising. There are four broad categories in what I call *theatrical advertising*: (1) print, (2) broadcast, (3) outdoor, and (4) direct response.

Once you have figured out which of those four categories are in your *marketing* scope, then the next steps become about the budget and about the creative. Now, the budget is the meat and potatoes, and it's the portion that the producers, *general managers*, and the people who are watching the dollars are very concerned with. So, you kind of break it down; how are you going to spend the funds allocated to advertise the show, and what mediums are you going to use? What proportion of the dollars is going to be spent in the various segmentations? And then the BIG issue that everybody talks about is the creative. It's the one image that—in the mind of the public—sums up everything that people see on stage for two to three hours. What is that image? It's critical and there is no science to it. It becomes extremely subjective. I remember I worked with David Merrick years ago, and there was something wonderful about the autonomy of working with a man who made a decision—perhaps a decision you didn't like—but he made it instantly. Today there are fifteen, sixteen, seventeen, or eighteen people who sit around a conference room table for an artwork presentation, and the decision is often made by consensus. I'm not necessarily sure that consensus makes for the strongest piece of art.

At any rate I wanted to talk about how we here at Eliran Murphy go about the creative process. Ann Murphy, our creative director, spearheads the process. A new show comes in and Ann and I will read the script (and listen to music if it exists). If the producer so desires their involvement, Ann will speak with the playwright and the director and perhaps the set designer. (Producers determine who they want involved in this process. Sometimes producers will say, "Gee, it's not really the director's decision," and then they pick a piece of art and the director says, "Absolutely not, that's not my show," and then you end up going back to the drawing board.) We will have a conversation with the producing team as it's important for us to hear about how they envision representing the show. We want to hear about what they don't like. For example, as an illustration, I often say, "If you don't like purple, tell us, and we will make sure that we don't show you a color palette of purple." We want to hear about what they *do* like. If the producing team has a vision of exactly what they are looking for, this is the time to tell us. Don't make us guess. On the other hand if there is no set idea, that's fabulous. This gives EMG the best opportunity to make a brilliant creative presentation. Next we have a briefing with our copywriters and all of our at directors. (We have six on staff.) At this session, Ann comprehensively briefs the art directors. From all of the conversations discussed above, Ann distills the salient information. She will have certain ideas that she wants explored and will assign that to several of the art directors. Then a date for the first *internal* review is set and the art directors are given scripts, any other pertinent information, and CDs if music is available. Ann will also decide if this project warrants additional art director input—perhaps a specific illustration style—in which case an outside illustrator will be asked to sketch.

And now the magic begins—the creative people are creating! We next meet on *internal* day for the first look. Perhaps at this juncture there will be twenty-five or thirty sketches, concepts, ideas to look at. Each piece is reviewed and discussed. Decisions are made about inclusion in the presentation, changes that need to be made to the piece, perhaps a new direction that needs to be explored, and ultimately picking the best of the ideas that will be shown in the final presentation. How many pieces are shown in the final presentation? Sometimes as few as three and often as many as fifteen. It is very much a determination about showing a wide range of options. Because we think that there is not only *one* way. That is very much the philosophy here at Eliran Murphy Group. Our philosophy is to show a wide range of *creatives*, so that we have a spectrum to look at. We are happy to make a recommendation when asked. If we are showing ten pieces and we think two are extraordinary, of course, we will say that. If we are showing five pieces and we think one is *the* one, we will very much say that we think it's the strongest one.

Now comes show time—presentation day. Producers, general managers, *press agents*, and the marketing people are generally all present at the artwork presentation. The presentation consists of the selected concepts shown in color on boards that are window card size (fourteen inches wide by twenty-two inches high). We also do what we call *takedowns* to show what it would look like when this art runs in black and white (because the first question that anybody who has been in the business asks is, "We love this, but how is it going to translate to small units in the newspaper?"). And then the process begins. Sometimes, when we're really lucky, everyone at the meeting agrees and says, "Yes, this is the piece of art—we love it. We're sold. This is the one that we want. Thank you, it is fabulous!" More often it's, "What a great presentation—we've narrowed it down to three pieces, and we would like you to go back to the drawing board. We would like to see *Atwork A*, but we would like to see three different color palettes, perhaps a bigger type face, and perhaps you can remove this, and we would like to see several variations on *Presentations D* and *H*." Then we'll set a date—perhaps a week or ten days later—to come back and look at the variations.

I'm including an illustration (see pages 341–344) of how the process worked on *Pacific Overtures*. Roundabout Theatre Company produced a Broadway production of Sondheim's *Pacific Overtures* in the fall of 2004 at Studio 54. It was directed by a Japanese director and had a decidedly different take on the original production. Four pieces were in the final selection, including the wonderful piece, designed by our Senior Art Director Sean Keepers, that was chosen to represent the production.

BEN HODGES: How far in advance will you begin working with producers?

ELIRAN: It very much depends on how far out their financing is in place. Are they able to pay for this piece of art? We charge a creative fee of $7,500 for Broadway show art, and we charge $3,500 for an Off-Broadway piece of art. Additionally some outside expenses can come into play—a photo shoot, an illustration, *rights* to use images used in the *concept* process. Generally if the decision is to have a photo shoot, the production needs to be cast. Perhaps a producer has a property *optioned* and they're planning to produce it in three years, but currently want art for press packets and an image that will help with raising money. We certainly need to be compensated for our part of it at the time that we are doing it. We are not going to be able to wait until they ultimately raise the money. It is an important consideration. And particularly in the Off-Broadway arena, many people have properties that they have optioned and some of them never get produced.

Four Pieces from the Final Selection Process of the Poster for Pacific Overtures

Image of boat is a woodblock print by an unknown artist circa 1854.
Sean Keepers, art director, Eliran Murphy Group.

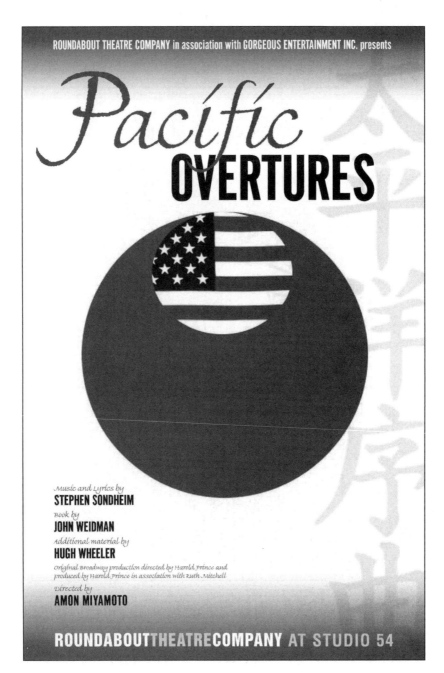

One of four final selections of the poster for *Pacific Overtures*.
Sean Keepers, art director, Eliran Murphy Group.

Artwork from poster created for New National Theatre production in Tokyo, Japan; used by permission. Janice Brunell, art director, Eliran Murphy Group.

The winning selection of the poster for the Broadway revival of *Pacific Overtures*.
Sean Keepers, art director, Eliran Murphy Group.

HODGES: Will you join a production in advance of an *out-of-town tryout*, or is it always when they are coming to New York?

ELIRAN: If they ask us to come up with a logo for an out-of-town tryout, we will do that. Sure.

HODGES: Moving to the differences between nonprofit and *for-profit* productions, how do they differ with respect to the strategies that you may come up with?

ELIRAN: I don't think that they differ necessarily in the strategy of what the ultimate piece of art is. I do think that they very much differ in terms of who we are pleasing. In the not-for-profit world, often playwrights and directors are very much involved. So in some cases it happens as I just said previously—you have a conversation with the director, and you have a conversation with the playwright, and many times they're present at the presentation, because it is their vision. How do they see their play? That happens certainly for Roundabout Theatre Company and Playwright Horizons. In other not-for-profit and most commercial productions, the determination is made that the artistic, executive, and marketing directors are going to select the artwork. Obviously in the commercial context it will be the producers. If it is a producer who's been producing for thirty years, this is an individual that knows the game and how he is going to go. He is going to make the decision. I previously used David Merrick as that example. It will work again in this discussion. He wasn't going to listen to others' business opinions; he knew what he wanted and that was how it was going to be—good, bad, or indifferent. That sort of decision making rarely happens now.

HODGES: So let's move past pre-production into opening. How would your strategy differ between a show that opens well with the critics and one that is panned? Is that as important as it once was?

ELIRAN: Interesting, as I think one of the things that has really changed a lot over the years is production photography. There was a time when a logo was chosen for the show and for the life of the show that is all you saw. Production photography was used for press purposes only—it wasn't used that much in advertising. Now, however, because of star *billing* and the importance of pushing those tickets and pushing them very quickly, if you look in the paper you'll notice how many ads are photographs of the people in the show. Fortunes are spent on those. We have done photo shoots that are very, very expensive, depending upon who the actor or actress is, and which photographer you use. Often times the actor will want to use a very celebrity photographer, so we will do that in order get a shot (as apposed to an illustration or a logo).

Sometimes we will do a logo and then the show will open and we will switch to production photography. The logo will be the typeface and perhaps if there was an illustration that went with it, the illustration will go by the wayside and now you will be using photographs. That happens quite a bit as well.

HODGES: If a show doesn't happen to open well but the money is in place to keep it running in hopes of turning around, what kind of adjustments or considerations will you make to try to hit a different audience, or to try to build an audience, when one is not generated from the reviews?

ELIRAN: I think it is rather complicated. If you're looking at the Broadway audience, 60 percent of that audience is a tourist audience. That's a big number. Particularly for the musicals, that means you are going to try and get the tourist either before they come to New York or you're going to spend the advertising dollars trying to reach them while they're here. Whether that means a tourist publication, the back of a bus, or perhaps television that is within the hotel, those are some of the ways to reach the tourist market. If you are talking about a show that has the segmentation of audience here in New York, for example, if it's a specific ethnic segmentation, perhaps then it wouldn't come down to the image, but rather where you spend your dollars. If you are going to make a radio buy, you're going to pick radio stations that target the audience that you are trying to reach. If you are going to make a television buy, television is a very broad medium so that becomes a much wider range. But, you asked me about segmenting and trying to reach specific audiences, and the advertising dollars often dictate what and where that is going to be. Nobody ever has enough money to advertise in the New York market. We're in the most crowded entertainment environment certainly in the country—and perhaps in the world. There are so many choices that people have to make. I am always fond of saying that nobody opens a newspaper and says, "Gee, I want to go to the show that is in a 199-seat house, versus a show that is in an 1,800-seat theatre." The public is not conscious of this, so you need to be as impressive and make as strong of an impact when you've got 100–200 seats as you do as when you have 1,800 seats. You are still vying for the very same ticket buyers; it is just that you need so many more of them when you are going for a Broadway show. The poor guy who is in a small theatre really pays the price for that—because he is still going for that big audience, and it has to stand out. Very difficult. There is never enough money to do an adequate job—*never*. Prices go up every single year, as do ticket prices. The advertising part of the component of a budget is astronomical. Particularly on the small end, there is just not enough money to get on people's radar.

We have a show that is just about to celebrate its tenth anniversary, *I Love You, You're Perfect, Now Change*. We opened ten years ago this August, and I always hypothesize that if you walked outside on the street and you stopped twenty people and you said, "*I Love You, You're Perfect, Now Change*," you would be lucky if two of them knew what you were talking about. That is a show that has been running for *ten years* in an Off-Broadway environment. So, you're not on everybody's radar. Now if you stop twenty people in front of this building and talked to them today about *The Pajama Game*, I would say to you that 80 percent of them would know that Harry Connick, Jr. is starring in *The Pajama Game*. It just opened last week, and they would know about that because it has been everywhere, because it is supported not only with advertising, but also with extraordinary reviews and by the press. So we have a big challenge there if you are talking about commercial theatre in the Off-Broadway landscape. It is very difficult to make your mark. Very difficult.

HODGES: So whether it is a show like *I Love You, You're Perfect, Now Change*, or maybe you have another example, how has the environment in the city changed since 9/11?

ELIRAN: I really can only speak for the theatre, but there was a time when people were willing to purchase their tickets way in *advance*. I think 9/11 changed all that. Perhaps it was just individuals thinking that they didn't know where we were going to be in the world, so why in God's name would they buy a ticket six months out? Therefore, the timeframe of the ticket-buying pattern has shortened significantly, unless you have a superstar, or unless you are able to convey to the public that if they do not buy this ticket now they will not get a seat. The savvy theatregoers know that they can get a seat. Additionally, I think that when we talk about the savvy theatregoer, (we're talking about the multi-buyer here—the person who goes to theatre more than once a year). I always say that when we're trying to advertise for a new show, if someone has gone to the theatre eight times this year, they're most likely to go a ninth. On the other hand, if someone hasn't gone to the theatre at all this year, or if they have only gone once and it was to a big musical, it is quite unlikely that they are going to purchase a ticket to an Off-Broadway show. So the more the person goes, the more likely that they're going to go and embrace something new. The less frequently they go, the more mass appeal the show has to be for them to purchase a ticket. Again, it is only those shows to which people think they can't get a ticket which they will buy in advance. Have we changed our advertising due to that? Absolutely. Before 9/11 we might have advertised six months or eight months before a show arrived to try to garner an advance sale. We don't do that very much anymore. It has to be pretty close in. There are some other costs involved. You know, it is the cost of opening a box office. There are *service charges* that are levied by Telecharge or Ticketmaster. Some people like to go to the box office so that they don't have to pay that service charge and opening a box office costs money. If there's someone sitting in that box office for six months before a show opens, you have to pay them. So everything is much more condensed at this point.

HODGES: Having worked in an Off-Broadway theatre and Off-Off Broadway theatre in this city, and also in the *regional* theatre, I know that very often most of the staff is working for nothing. What advertising budget you *do* have may be less than fifty thousand dollars or even five thousand dollars. How do you gauge where you're going to put your resources? How do you prioritize them based on what market you may or may not have? I've had people—all well intentioned—but adamantly saying to me everything from "e-mailing is the way to go," to "Direct mail is the way to go," to, "Pay your publicist because they are going to get the critics there." Is there a way to evaluate—especially if you are not familiar with your market, how to get that kind of information before you spend the resources?

ELIRAN: I think you have to ask a question of your budget: must every dollar be traceable? And if that is the case, then that pretty much tells you that the effort that you're going to make that will track a response is either a direct response mail effort, or an Internet-based direct response. Those are really the only two ways in which sales efforts are directly trackable. It may cost five thousand dollars for a direct mail effort or an e-mail effort and the yield may be thirty-five thousand dollars, or the yield may be eight thousand dollars. And the same would be true for a direct mailer if you were going to mail one hundred thousand pieces or 200 thousand pieces. We can say what a good return would be, we can say what a bad return would be, and we can tell you what it's going to cost and that that percentage has changed. In the old days you got a 1 percent return. You are lucky if you get a 1 percent return on most things. We always tell people that on direct response (either e-mailed, or an actual direct mail piece), you are sending a *dedicated message* to the consumer. So if you are mailing one hundred thousand pieces and let's say you sell one thousand tickets from the piece, then that means ninety-nine thousand additional people have received a dedicated message in their home or on their computer about a particular property. Perhaps only a very small segment has purchased at this time, but it is one impression that you have made, and it's great because it is a dedicated impression. It's not an impression that you are sharing with everybody else. So it's the one component that really is traceable. You can put ads on radio and television and it is very unlikely that one spot runs and causes the phones to light up; it doesn't really happen. You can run a radio campaign and at the end of the week you can say, "Gee, our wraps have gone up, it must have been the radio," but can you really pinpoint it? Absolutely not. I'm fond of saying that nobody has ever filled out a survey as to why they purchased the ticket and said it was because they saw a sign on the back of the bus. [*Laughs.*] So that is what I am talking about—the components of an advertising campaign. Those which we can trace directly are those direct response efforts. If you need to track directly, then you will only be able to use direct response. If your budget is limited, then perhaps that is all you need to do, because dollar for dollar you need to spend *this much* and you need to get *that much* back. The more money you have, the broader the campaign becomes. So then you start doing things that are about impressions, be it a billboard, a side of a bus, a phone kiosk, or all of those wonderful outdoor advertising vehicles (which are a terrific way to create an awareness of your property).

HODGES: Can you tell us about focus groups or research? Because that is something that can be inexpensive for people who are not in New York City, and possibly even if they are.

ELIRAN: We do focus groups to test artwork to see which concept or treatment tests better. Focus groups are not inexpensive, therefore, they would probably only be used for pre-New York or open-ended runs. It wouldn't be cost efficient to test very limited engagements.

HODGES: I only have one more question: If you were going to paint a portrait of a producer, which would not simply make your job easier [*laughs*], but what kind of qualities would they have? What traits would help a producer accomplish what's in the best interest of their show?

ELIRAN: I think it is a really good question. From my vantage point, I think it needs to be a person who is able to make a decision. A person who is confident in their product, confident in their ability, confident enough to be a leader. I think that there certainly has been a change in the landscape of who is producing these days, and so many people come to the table, which is wonderful. We embrace anybody who wants to be part of the commercial theatre. It is an industry that's very welcoming to people who have no prior experience. I can't think of too many other businesses where—armed with some money—you can suddenly be embraced and you're sitting at the table with a group of seasoned producers, and perhaps a noted director, and start out as an *associate producer,* work your way up, and suddenly you're a producer. That first stage, of course, is about raising money. So many decisions need to be made, and they can often be painful decisions. We talked before about a consensus—we need to have a producer who is forceful, who could live with their convictions and say, "This is the way I want to go. I feel that this is how I want to market this property," and go with it. The forces, the pressures are so severe that producers often feel that they must take some sort of immediate action. A good example is if you take an opening ad and it doesn't sell. The first phone call is that the advertising doesn't work. "Let's change the ad. It didn't sell." Well, what were the expectations? We try here very much to manage expectations. If you place an announcement ad in the paper, are you putting the ad in the paper because traditionally you feel you need to for the cast, or because you've got producers who want to see their name in the paper? Is it because the press agent feels that you need to begin to build some awareness so that on the press side they can begin to get interviews? There are many reasons for taking an opening ad, and there are instances where the ad will not sell any tickets. But, you as a producer would have to make that decision taking into consideration that costs are very expensive; today, a full-page color ad in *The New York Times* is $107 thousand for one ad.

HODGES: I would imagine that to change your mind is not only disadvantageous, but expensive, and changes the message you're trying to present.

ELIRAN: I think what happens is that when something doesn't work as well as we think that it should, the first issue is that people have concerns. It certainly is the case after a show is up and running. As a producer, once the show has been frozen and it has been reviewed and it's playing eight performances a week (save for *casting* changes which one can make along the way), there really are only two things that you can affect: You can affect the advertising and perhaps you think you can affect the press. The play is written. It has been directed. The costumes are ready. Everything is there. So the only area that you can hope to affect is how the public is responding to the message that you are sending out there. That can be a very tense time. Remember, you've gone through previews, you got the show up, and the critics have come. Let's talk about a property in which there are mixed reviews—now what? Now we have to spend advertising dollars, right? And when the advertising doesn't work, well, the thinking is "Let's change the advertising; let's change the image." It happens a lot. "The radio spot was on last week, it didn't do anything." But maybe it only ran twenty times; maybe it needs to have more frequency. The idea of change is certainly one that we don't necessarily advocate because people need to see the image and hear it over and over and over again. Remember, we talked at the beginning about how crowded the environment is. Now, *you* may eat, sleep and drink theatre, and *I* may eat, sleep, and drink theatre, but there is a whole world of people who take advantage of other entertainment options, be it television, movies, concerts. We eat, sleep and drink this product, but the public doesn't do that. They really don't. So to change an image and not to let the impression of the same image work over and over and over again, is probably not very advisable. Although, people do that.

HODGES: I would imagine—not ever having been your client—that you must have become a therapist quite often to producers in various situations. How often are you involved in helping people to decide when it is better to cut their losses?

ELIRAN: If asked? [*Laughs.*] That is an interesting thing. With most shows there are two ways you can come to New York and try and make yourself critic-proof. One way would be perhaps to spend $3–5 million dollars in the market place to try to pre-sell a show so that regardless of what the critics say, at least you have a strong base. On the other hand, if you don't have enough money, how in God's name are you going to pre-sell it? Many people *capitalize* and budget and they mount the show and then they're totally dependent upon the reviews. And if the reviews are horrible, the show will close. I've had them close the same night, I've had them close in a week, or they make a go—a fight—for it. You can survive. The biggest thing in the end is when you finish with all these beautiful pieces of art and logos and great advertising campaigns, there is one thing that ultimately sells a show and it is *word of mouth.* If the word of mouth is not positive, the show will not survive. You can have the greatest advertising campaign in the world and if the public is only lukewarm, or mildly interested in the product, it won't make it. Those shows that succeed do so because the public likes them. Now, if they like them, and if they read a good review, that helps them to like it even more, but certainly there are many shows where critics have given shows wonderful reviews and the public just didn't respond to them. Either they are too erudite, or they are too "in" for the general public—it happens all the time. You can't give those tickets away if the public doesn't want them.

HODGES: Conventional wisdom says that musicals can survive even without favorable reviews, but not so with a play?

ELIRAN: I think that's right. Absolutely.

HODGES: Thank you, Barbara.

ELIRAN: Thank you.

Shara Victoria Mendelson

Shara Victoria Mendelson is President of Plum Benefits. Established in 1998, Plum Benefits is a direct marketing company that promotes entertainment events to an untapped corporate audience. Leveraging established relationships with over twenty-five thousand corporations, the company delivers invaluable exposure and measurable ticket sales within a controlled environment to its entertainment partners. To its corporate clients, Plum Benefits is an easy, cost-free employee benefit service that employees appreciate because it maximizes entertainment options while saving them time and money. Plum Benefits delivers consistent results and reliable service. Before founding the company, Shara began her career at Grey Advertising in account services. Shara is a 1995 graduate of Middlebury College. Shara also serves on the board of The New Group, a nonprofit theatre company in New York City.

PASSION

SHARA VICTORIA MENDELSON (A CONVERSATION WITH)
President, Plum Benefits

SHARA VICTORIA MENDELSON: Would you like me to start with my history?

BEN HODGES: Sure. What's your background and how did you get into this business?

MENDELSON: Do you know? I'm just curious. Do you remember?

HODGES: I do. [*Laughs.*] Our readers don't.

MENDELSON: So many people in the theatre have come from theatrical backgrounds. Their families were in the business; they were theatre lovers as children; they had been on stage at some point. I always get that question as to whether or not I was an actor and I quickly say, "Absolutely not!" I am in unbelievable awe of everyone on stage and that is why I should remain behind it—it's important to know your strengths and, in this case, your weaknesses! Instead, I fell in love with the theatre as an adult. I use that word *love* on purpose because this is a business built on passion. In fact, I think "Passion" is the appropriate title for this chapter.

My theatrical career began as a result of pure misery in my first position out of school. Perhaps I was no different than most recent college grads. I was idealistic and ambitious, but I was disappointed in my first job…I had this coveted job in the account department of a major *advertising* agency, but I had no mentors, I was not assigned to stimulating projects and, worse, the work environment was far from passionate.

When I am not excited about what I am doing, I tend to look for something challenging, something new that I have never done before. For me, that turned out to be the theatre. It happens that my father had recently become involved with a *nonprofit* theatre company, The New Group, and had invited me to stuff envelopes on the weekends. My perspective had always been limited to that of an audience member. For the first time, I was curious about how a production actually came to be. That is, basically, how it all started.

The theatre company was located in an old building. The offices were not glamorous, to say the least! Donated furniture, old equipment…not much color. The only staff members were the executive producer, the artistic director, and an assistant. The rest of us were volunteers. Everyone had been involved in theatre since they could remember. I was definitely the odd man out. But I related to one thing: their need for passion. These were struggling actors and playwrights, all working two jobs at least, but no one complained during all those hours stuffing mail. They were working toward something they believed in and, in that way, their space was alive! I knew I wanted to support them. The question was how.

It was somewhat ridiculous at twenty-three years old. I had, for all practical purposes, no experience. My liberal arts education had provided few real skills and my ten months in advertising consisted mostly of copying tapes. But I was motivated! After contacting every alumnus from my college remotely involved in the arts and sending out my resume anywhere and everywhere in the creative fields, I began learning about the theatre industry. And then I got lucky. The New Group was *transferring* their latest production to a *commercial venue* and I was given the opportunity to meet the producers taking the show to its new home. Upon learning of my background, and after a bit of personal salesmanship, they invited to me to a meeting with the advertising agency handling the campaigns for the commercial run.

From the back of a large conference room I listened. The producers, *general management*, *press agents*, and advertising execs were reviewing everything from the lists for a direct mail piece to the *key artwork* for the print campaign. Several things stood out. First, the budgets. At my job, the product I was assigned to was a kids' beverage that advertised only four months out of the year, but the monies allocated reached over $20 million. For this Off-Broadway show, the numbers were in the tens of thousands of dollars for a direct effort. Such limited budgets obviously demanded tremendous creativity and strict monitoring of return on investment. There is little room for error in this business. Second, the *marketing* strategy. At my agency, directives came from the company that manufactured the product. Their marketing department, filled with MBA grads, created the *brand* strategy that was then handed off to the advertising agency responsible for implementing the advertising campaigns. In the theatre, it seemed, the advertising agency controlled everything from direct mail to media buys to promotions and more. There was less focus on *umbrella* marketing, and the directives did not relate back to the financial models.

Several hours later (you know those meetings), the meeting ended. But I was just beginning! I quit my job just three weeks later. The producers of the commercial transfer hired me as a *marketing consultant*! And my new purpose was to create cost effective marketing efforts for the theatre industry. That was 1996.

I immediately started doing research at the New York Public Library for the Performing Arts at Lincoln Center (which wasn't online at that point) to learn what theatrical marketing consisted of historically. When I did that run in their database, only one article came up with the words *theatrical marketing*. It was a piece about Susan Lee and the League of American Theatres and Producers' efforts at that time. I called her up and we had a wonderful conversation. I discovered that she and Jed Bernstein had the goal of presenting the theatre as a brand. During my time at the ad agency, all initiatives stemmed from brand development. I had been exposed to this process, from research and positioning, to name generation and tag line creation, to design. Susan absolutely inspired me to apply this experience and I became obsessed with just getting the word out there.

HODGES: When you say theatre wasn't being sold as a brand, you mean the industry itself, as well as each individual show?

MENDELSON: At the time I began, neither Broadway, nor the individual shows were being positioned as brands. Jed and Susan were, to my knowledge, pioneers. Then, on an individual show basis, over the course of the next five years, things started to grow. I believe some of this growth was a direct response to large companies like Disney and Livent driving stakes in Times Square. Entities like these had marketing savvy. The pressure caused the rest of the industry to step it up. So Broadway began to see itself as a category, just like the beverage industry I had been exposed to in my days in the Account Department. Individual shows were products that needed to have clear brand positioning to differentiate themselves from other shows, their competition. From a management standpoint, new companies like The Marketing Group were founded, producers started hiring marketing directors and the advertising agencies were expanding their services to meet similar needs. Umbrella marketing efforts were developed and began to include new media beyond traditional advertising (TV, radio, outdoor, and print), press and promotion. The theatre was just getting its feet wet in e-mail response marketing and web marketing, for example.

HODGES: So marketing in the theatre, as you see it, was in its infancy?

MENDELSON: In some ways it still is. The financials are very difficult and that means limited resources. But marketing strategy is done much more proactively

The 1995 OBIE Award-winning production of Mike Leigh's *Ecstasy*, produced
Off-Broadway by The New Group. The experience of Shara Mendelson's father,
Michael Mendelson, of seeing this production and her own subsequent volunteering
for the company in 1996 led to the founding of Mendelson's theatrical and corporate
marketing firm, Plum Benefits. Pictured are Caroline Seymour as Jean, Patrick
Fitzgerald as Mick, Jared Harris as Len, and Marian Quinn as Dawn.
Photo by Ron Reeves.

and new mediums are being used and return on investment is definitely on
everyone's mind in a bigger way. It is an extremely exciting time! Again, this
is where passion comes in. There is so much opportunity for growth in this
industry!

Remember, I am personally an example. I was never truly aware of my
interest in theatre, but then I fell in love through a random experience, and if
I can fall in love with it, then I believe there are a lot of other people out there
who can. The major goal is to build new audiences. Rather than competing
with all these other unbelievably intelligent, successful people—advertising
agencies, group sales agents, promotional, and marketing agencies—you have
to ask yourself, what can I do to create an increase in that theatregoing pie, an
increase in that market place and an increase in the number of attendees?

In the beginning, I did the most ridiculous things to accomplish that goal.
It's embarrassing looking back on it! I was getting up on buses to speak about
the shows I was representing. I was flirting with the doormen [*laughs*] on Park
Avenue. This was actually very successful [*laughs*] because that target audience
has money, and the doormen would put flyers in all of the building's mailboxes.
So, you know—silly, silly things. The planning and the results were minimal.
But then I tried something different.

Since the only experience I had was in corporate America, I decided to call a few companies. My thought was, if I got connected to a Human Resources executive and offered her (it's usually a her) really good seats at a slight discount, maybe she would distribute an e-mail (e-mail was relatively new at that time) or pass out flyers to all of that company's employees telling them about the show. Well, that was the beginning. If I remember correctly, JP Morgan was my first client.

More tickets were sold from that call than from anything previously done. Definitely more than from the bus lectures. Remember, when you have limited resources (e.g., time and money), you must look at return on investment. There was no denying that this corporate call was returning. For goodness sake, it was free! The producer loved that! [*Laughs.*]

Initially, my company had an unsophisticated business plan. I grabbed the yellow pages and thought, "O.K., any company that is in large font and bold must be the bigger opportunity." I just got on phone, and started calling with the goal of getting as many companies to agree to the distribution of the Broadway offers as possible.

The phone calls never stopped. My company, Plum Benefits (founded as SVM), is now clearly defined as a direct marketing company that promotes entertainment (Broadway and beyond) to an untapped corporate audience. We have relationships with over twenty-five thousand corporations and, as our tag line says, *We put butts in seats.* But my entire team, now growing past twenty employees, is still on the phones all day either acquiring new corporations or maintaining relationships with current corporate clients. You see, much more than the luck of stumbling upon a viable idea, much more than intelligence or good decisions, it takes a lot of hard work to see results. That is the be all and end all of any entrepreneurial business, and the entire theatrical industry is made up of this spirit.

It's back to passion—starting with the belief that theatre—Broadway and Off-Broadway, *regional* and local—is something that should, that *needs* to exist. Whether viewed from the perspective of entertainment, of education, or of transformative personal experience, the theatre is an important and necessary part of our lives. From a business standpoint, this is the conviction that drives you to maximize existing audiences and build new ones. What's exciting to me are the potential media still to be developed whether by current industry executives or by new theatre professionals yet to arrive. We have not yet reached our marketing potential. Opportunities exist.

It is important to point out that Plum Benefits is only one part of an overall marketing mix, a very specific corporate medium. I think there are more Plum Benefits concepts out there. If you can find a new way of communicating, there are many markets that could be encouraged to come to the theatre. I would love to see more new, growing businesses driven by the passion and hard work that unites everyone involved in the theatrical community.

HODGES: But beyond the hard work, what has made this marketing effort unique and successful?

MENDELSON: If I were to say why we have been successful (beyond our passion, our work ethic, and the fact that we tapped into a new corporate marketplace), I would talk about *yield management*, sometimes known as revenue management. It is the process of understanding, anticipating, and reacting to consumer behavior in order to maximize revenue. It can be used to smooth the demand pattern. In peak season, the shows can increase revenues by increasing the fare on its tickets and in low season, it can increase capacity by offering low prices. Industries that use yield management typically have computer systems to measure supply and demand and generate variable price points. You are most familiar with this in the airline ticket industry, no doubt. But in the theatre industry, or in entertainment ticketing in general, no such system exists. The challenge is that there are several disjointed parties, who each play an essential role in the sale of a Broadway ticket. There are the producers who own this event, who rent a venue from a theatre owner, who has long-term agreements with ticketing agencies that fulfill the tickets. In addition, you have all these people charged with selling the show—marketing, advertising, promotions. But there is not a system that connects all the data and measures supply and demand patterns to arm us with the information we need to make good pricing recommendations.

Of course, when I began, I was young, so I was not afraid of these challenges! There had to be a soft way around them if the concrete numbers could not be had. It began with analyzing sales patterns to determine my theatrical clients' needs. Look at your numbers diligently! What are they telling you? Are you sold strong in the next few weeks, but advanced buys for two months out are weak? Are weekdays struggling, but weekends doing well? Is the average number of tickets sold per order two, or four? The answers to these simple questions could be the beginning of determining strategy to meet specific goals. If you need to build sales months out, your goal is to increase the *advance*. If you need to improve weekday sales, your strategy may be to support Tuesday-Thursday

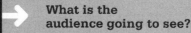

copy strategy

Define
the production

What is the audience going to see?
· Summarize the story
· Identify musical or play
· Clarify comedy, drama or mystery
· Label new show or revival

Communicate
the emotional experience

How will the audience feel?
· Laugh out loud funny
· Romantic and touching
· Smart and thought provoking
· Familiar and nostalgic

Target
specific demographics

What type of audience will the show appeal to?
· Family friendly
· 20-30 year olds
· Couples and dates
· Group and office outings
· Diverse ethnic audiences

Highlight
additional qualities

How does the audience perceive value?
· Elaborate sets
· Lavish costumes
· Impressive choreography
· Dinner or drinks included
· Convenient curtain time

Stimulate
point of purchase

Why should the audience buy tickets now?
· Anticipated hit
· Limited run
· Last chance
· Special occasions and holidays
· Great for gifts

plumbenefits™
we put butts in seats

media and timing strategy

	Goal	Solution
Prior to Previews	· Generate Buzz · Push Advance Sales	· Build exposure to establish brand awareness with advertising and press · Develop private offers which stimulate purchases for preview performances, while protecting full price tickets after opening
During Previews	· Stimulate Word of Mouth · Push Immediate Sales	· Continue advertising and press to increase consumer awareness · Take advantage of controlled promotions that target purchases during previews and create sense of urgency
Post Opening Strong Reviews	· Maintain Brand · Capitalize on Sales	· Leverage critical success in advertising and press to maximize full price sales · Analyze sales trends to determine which specific performances could benefit from exclusive incentives
Post Opening Weak Reviews	· Expand Audience · Maximize Revenue	· Reach out to new audiences rather than relying on traditional theatergoers who tend to read reviews · Take advantage of variable pricing and consider promotions to include less private mediums, provided that results are measurable
During Sold-Out Run	· Sustain Sold-Out Perception · Extend Advance	· Further demand by supporting successful brand through advertising campaign · Promotions focus on full price and premium tickets to build revenue for future performances

plumbenefits™
we put butts in seats

ticketing strategy

Analyze sales

to determine your needs
· Last minute buys or advance purchases
· Immediate sales vs. future performances
· Weekday vs. weekend trends
· Average number of tickets per order

Develop strategy

to reach your goal
· Push previews
· Build advance
· Support Tuesdays-Thursdays
· Encourage "mini-groups"

Direct consumers

with several price points
· Greater incentive for previews
· Series of purchase by dates offering
· increased savings
· Best value on weekdays
· Better deal for multiple ticket buys

Evaluate results

to measure success
· Determine consumer's response to offer
· Assess goal attainment

Revise strategy

as your needs change
. Anticipate difficult months and create special seasonal offers
. Increase ticket prices and limit availability as demand grows and show begins to sell out

plumbenefits™
we put butts in seats

performances. If you see your average number of tickets per order is unusually high, you may choose to encourage *mini-groups.*

Once you decide on a strategy, then you can implement pricing structures to encourage the consumer to purchase according to your needs. Let me offer a few examples showing the power of just two price points: If a purchase is made for a weekday performance then the consumer could be offered 20 percent off the regular price, but if they want a weekend performance, they will only receive 10 percent off the full price ticket. This is a very common offer strategy for many of my clients. Another strategy may come from a typical pattern for a family show, where the number of tickets per order are higher than average. In this scenario, the dual price points can encourage a mini-group. If the consumer purchases one to three tickets they will pay one price per ticket, but if they purchase four or more, the price per ticket offered will go down. So, in practical terms, that mother with two kids is now going to react and say to her children, "Ooo—grab another friend, bring them along." The effect? An increase in the number of tickets sold because a natural sales pattern was encouraged further. In both these scenarios, the results will stimulate sales where the show needs them most. Not all sales will be pushed into these purchase patterns, but more people will be in seats, spreading more word of mouth, and the incremental increase in sales will increase revenue for the production.

Let me relate the hypothetical history of a show throughout its lifecycle for better understanding. Suppose a show begins selling tickets two months prior to coming to Broadway. If it is an unknown quantity (a new play, no stars, etc.), public awareness will be little to none out of the gate. Since demand is low, pricing can be manipulated to increase sales. A targeted discount for preview performances only, can stimulate demand by creating a sense of urgency. At the same time, the perceived value of the show can be protected by adding a *fence*, such as a "purchase by" date. In that case, the consumer understands that if they don't purchase by that date, the price will go up. If the offers are promoted correctly, in controlled mediums with effective reach, supply (the number of seats) will go down and demand will increase. Then a show can begin increasing price points for performances following previews.

Still, there may be new patterns that show other weaknesses. In a second stage strategy, you may implement a weekday versus weekend incentive to stimulate purchases for mid week performances. A fence or an end date could be used again to create that sense of urgency and clarify to the consumer that the value of the full price ticket is maintained. During any stage, seasonality can affect strategy as well. Even if a show has effectively used marketing and pricing to increase demand, the winter months may change that pattern. Proactively promoting special winter opportunities can buffer declining sales January through March, for example. Once again, the consumer must understand that prices will pick up in the spring, so as to maintain the perceived value of the show. Eventually, demand may be so high and supply so low that a show is Sold Out. Many factors outside of marketing and pricing, such as star *casting*, limited runs, unusual word of mouth, or reviews can affect whether this happens early in a show's run or later. But when it does, you have the option of going into what the industry now calls the *premium market*. All that means is that you can raise your tickets beyond what you deemed your full price initially. Brokers have been taking advantage of the economics of the situation for years, and I am thrilled to see producers owning this, so they can take the revenue they deserve which is often going into other pockets. Of course, this is a new concept and people are tentative. In fact they are tentative with the concept of yield management as a whole.

HODGES: By *people*, you mean producers?

MENDELSON: Not just producers, but the industry in general. And I am sensitive to that. Change is exciting because it presents new opportunities, but it is also scary because the risks are unknown. New ideas can create questions, even conflict. I am well aware that some of the concepts are not very popular. For one, the analysis of sales data is sometimes difficult to accomplish because that information is not shared readily. Few people have access to reports, and there is concern about the leak of those numbers. I think it is essential for any marketing partner to ensure confidentiality. My only goal in looking at the numbers is to help a show improve them. That has to be clear to create comfort with the flow of information. An additional challenge is that, from a technology standpoint, different promotions mean more programming. The more sophisticated the pricing structures, the greater the need for increased technology. The development of such software takes time and money and we currently have some limitations. The good news is that the fulfillment systems have improved substantially in recent years to accommodate the growth in coding different price points, among other things. Finally, I think the greatest hesitation in variable pricing is the concern that the theatre will become a discount-driven industry and the value of the full-price ticket will be destroyed. This is a valid concern and it speaks to something I have consistently mentioned alongside any pricing strategy: maintaining the perceived value of the show by carefully choosing the media in which incentives are promoted.

Personally, I do not support *public* discounting. Rather, I have seen long-term results gained by strategically placing different prices in controlled environments. For instance, because Plum Benefits is positioned as a private employee benefit service, only corporate employees receive our offers. Our website is password protected and only accessible from a corporate domain. In fact, we are so determined to remove our offers from the public arena that we do research weekly to find out if any of our offers have been posted on line. If so, we take immediate steps to get the offers down and keep control in the hands of the show. When discounts are promoted publicly, the consumer may believe that there is little value in the ticket and, by extension, that the production itself has no value. It is very difficult to rebuild your ticket price if you are discounting publicly from the beginning. If you choose targeted media, we have found that you can then—as the demand increases—raise that price point, because you actually haven't affected the consumers overall perceived value of the product, of the actual show. Does that make sense?

HODGES: It does. Am I right in assuming then, that that strategy is based on a finite number of discounted tickets?

MENDELSON: You are on to something important in yield management. There are a finite number of tickets. Not specifically discount, full, or premium, but tickets (or seats) *are* limited, as you say. To create a successful variable pricing structure, several factors must be present, including perishable inventory and limited capacity.

But we could talk about ticketing forever! Beyond the controlled media and the pricing strategy implemented, descriptive copy communicating the benefits of the live production is also essential to successful response marketing—especially when it comes to building new audiences. Many of us assume that everyone knows Broadway, but in truth, few people out there know much about Broadway at all. For instance, consumers are not familiar with directors' names or even some of the most renowned actors on stage. So when we use these facts from a show to attract buyers, we are often speaking a language most don't understand. They are, in turn, alienated and that is the last thing you want to make a newcomer feel. Instead, our copy should welcome them! We need to smile when they come to our door and say to them "Don't worry. We know that this is intimidating, but you are going to have a great time." At the end of the day, that's the selling point for a new consumer—a great night of entertainment that could be life changing. I mean isn't our passion for the theatre about the fact that it really can do that?

Here are some immediate suggestions to keep in mind when targeting new audiences. First, ask yourself if the copy defines the production. Simply identify the fact that it is a musical or a play. Clarify that it is a comedy, a drama, or a mystery. Communicate if it's a new show or a revival. These are just a few hints that can give a consumer an understanding of what they may expect. This clarification will help them feel comfortable, breaking down one barrier. Second, see if you communicate the emotional experience well. Live performance is so unique because you feel so intensely. Use that uniqueness to attract new buyers. Let them know...will they be laughing? Thinking? Feeling romantic? Touched? This will help a buyer relate to the show. Finally, target specific demographics. Whether this is a family friendly production or something for twenty-year-olds. Whether it's a great show for couples or African-Americans. Let the target know this is a show for them through the tone of the copy. Be respectful that there are very different types of people who are interested in a variety of productions and theatre can offer each a wonderful experience. There are many more people interested in going to Broadway. We just have to talk to them.

HODGES: Are we not speaking to them because of the material we are producing, or because of the way in which it is marketed?

MENDELSON: That is a very interesting question. There is an ongoing debate about the cause of the theatre's limited audience. Are the shows relevant to only one or two target markets—the dedicated theatregoer and the tourist—or are current marketing strategies limited? I think it is a combination of the content and the marketing. As I have said, I believe there are new audiences to tap. Obviously, when a show is created that has diverse appeal, there is a natural opportunity to attract a new audience. The marketing effort for such a show will be targeted to that audience. Whether it has, for example, African-American or Latino appeal will inform the positioning of the show, the media buys for the ad campaign, potential press opportunities, and even pricing. But, I believe that with innovative marketing even traditional Broadway productions can tap into new audiences as well. For instance, if we are going to get to a younger audience or maybe encourage that once a year buyer to purchase multiple times annually, we can choose atypical marketing media that target new audiences, create descriptive copy that speaks to them in their own language, and consider price points within their reach. Of course, this is risky. Huge risks are involved with even the most bankable Broadway enterprise. Developing shows based on material not typically seen on the stage and attempting new marketing techniques present additional risks. So it is understandable that there would be resistance to innovation. But there are examples of success stories, and it is exciting to witness those successes in theatre because it emphasizes the potential of new audiences and the continued development of passionate theatregoers. I look forward to more of this in the future!

HODGES: O.K., so let's take a scenario that as a producer, you have a big hit, and as price point is a very important consideration, with respect to that, what is the best way to market a hit? I know you don't do umbrella marketing campaigns, but how would you use that information to do what you do?

MENDELSON: When demand is very high and so little supply exists, the value of just getting access into that event skyrockets. Think concerts and sporting events. People are willing to pay premium. We mentioned this market earlier in our discussion as one that is just emerging in the industry. It is also important to remember that the lifetime of Sold Out status is finite, as well. So maintaining a presence on a marketing level, whether that be in advertising mediums or direct response mediums like Plum Benefits, is important. One day that show is going to come down and you're going to start having to do creative things again. I would save as much money as possible during the good times. I would try to ride that wave as long as possible. But be prepared, rather than surprised, for that moment when you are going to have to start adjusting those price points. When that show is not flying anymore, you don't want it to hit you in the face. Things that I have heard again and again are, "This show is definitely going to be a hit," or "After those reviews, we are invincible!" My experience has taught me to be realistic and because my commitment is to ensure my clients are making money, I often celebrate good times, but quickly prepare for the next stage. I like planning. I like being prepared because I want to make sure that the production is getting every boost that it can, no matter where it is in its lifecycle. Preparation is potentially the only thing in our control. *Assume* you are *not* going to get great reviews. *Assume* that you are not going to be a Sold Out hit. *Assume* the best of times are not going to last. Instead, put in place plans that are going to be smarter than banking on things that are totally out of your control.

HODGES: And the opposite: a show to which the producers are incredibly dedicated and have the money to run it for a certain period of time—maybe through the first six months of the actors' contracts—but the reviews are horrible. How do we bolster the show?

MENDELSON: My answer is a continuation of my last response-I am going to start sounding repetitive! Of course, there is no denying that reviews still play a role in the potential success of a production. But I think marketing today is much better equipped to direct the success of a show, rather than simply relying on great reviews. If a marketing campaign is truly initiated, from branding and pricing strategy to media choices and content, and if reasonable financial support and planning is in place, then there is an opportunity to rely less on reviews. Being proactive is essential. Bolstering preview performances with your target audience will help spread positive word of mouth early. And when the reviews do come out, there has to be a plan in place to deal with any outcome. Plan A for great reviews, Plan B for mixed, and Plan C for the tough ones. Plan B and C may include targeted discounts. Emotional reactions, while totally understandable, will not lead to good decisions. So avoid them by planning. And if difficult decisions need to be made, due to financial hardships sustained from reviews or otherwise, try to make them quickly. Hopefully, as we continue to increase the sophistication of our marketing efforts, fewer producers will be faced with this decision. We all know what a difficult business this is. It is the passion that keeps us coming back.

HODGES: I was reviewing CTI seminar tapes from the mid-1980s, and the Internet wasn't even a concept in those discussions—like television in the early 1940s. How much of what you do is based on projections of how media may evolve?

MENDELSON: Plum Benefits is not a new media company and my expertise is not in the ever changing world of technology. With that said, my business could never have gotten started without technology. The development of the web and e-mail allowed me to create a cost-effective marketing medium. Our business, like every business today, must stay current about the available technological resources in order to remain efficient and successful. The theatre is just beginning to take advantage of web marketing, but is less active in other available media. This could be a reflection of our traditional audiences, our limited budgets, or just habit. Other industries, especially those driven by a younger male consumer, must remain attuned to the latest in order to be competitive. I expect we will see more use of new media on Broadway as the theatre audience develops and theatrical marketing continues to evolve.

HODGES: If you are a small theatre, a community theatre, or a smaller regional theatre with a small budget and limited personnel, how do you accurately measure cost effectiveness? How do you market the return on your investment with respect to those different aspects?

MENDELSON: It's no different than any other business. Analyze your profit and loss statements regularly. To determine the cost effectiveness of your marketing efforts, specifically review the return on investment of your marketing/advertising/promotions line items.

Throughout the entire lifespan of a show, you should review income and expense patterns, even in immeasurable media, to assess the success of your efforts. For instance, your income can be looked at from the different sales channels (e.g., phones, box office, Internet). Your expenses can be broken out by media (such as TV, radio, print, outdoor, and web) and your different marketing efforts. If you look at your spending and your sales revenue side by side, you will begin to see a pattern. When you launch a campaign for a new show, for instance, you should see a correlating increase in ticket sales following the drop of the launch ads. With direct response efforts such Plum Benefits, you can measure return on investment more easily. These efforts should be coded, no matter what the price point, so that when a purchase occurs, they can be attributed to a specific direct effort. Once you understand which direct response efforts are returning the greatest, put more of your resources, both time and money, behind those efforts and eliminate the less successful ones from your marketing agenda. Remember, this type of analysis must be consistent and regular to ensure that the best plans are created, the best decisions are made, and the best results are realized! Don't hesitate to look at your numbers, the answers are there!

HODGES: As we know, in small theatres many times people are functioning as actors, directors, producers, and advertising and marketing persons all at the same time (I know, I've done it, even though I had a six-figure budget), but one of the reasons I wanted to do this book was that I wanted to get people in areas (geographic as well as artistic), ideas and information they could use to till their respective soils. And as much as you are embodying a revolutionary concept in New York, what you are talking about in many ways will be even more so in other parts of the country and world—especially the forward thinking with respect to trends. How would you share this with interested people in this in other areas of the country. How they should best go about it?

MENDELSON: Well, first, I think the concepts of pricing strategy and copy strategy that we have covered today can be applied anywhere. Second, I think the sales analysis and focus on return on investment is applicable in any business. Finally, I think it comes back to passion. Be creative! If your company's resources are limited, or if little theatrical marketing exists in your area, perhaps there are opportunities elsewhere. Read and listen and learn to what other local businesses are doing and see their if methods are applicable to your theatrical company's goals. Something may transfer from one industry to another. I think the fact that I came from outside the industry helped me bring something new and creative to the mix. While it is a real pleasure to be integrated into the theatrical community now after so many years, I force myself to think like an outsider in certain ways. To learn marketing techniques beyond Broadway. To continue to experience new things, so that I can bring them back to the theatre, my passion.

When I think of the people who influenced me, they consistently encouraged passion and the development of new ideas. They believed it would result in progress. They supported me through all the times I was being questioned and they pushed me to continue working hard. Without them, I could never have built this resource on behalf of the theatre industry. My father, Michael Mendelson, and Fred Vogel were two of my greatest role models. In their absence, I believe it is now my responsibility to support.

Glossary

abc's. *Advertisements* in daily newspapers that alphabetically list the productions running in a geographical area.

accredited investor. When used in the context of a private (as opposed to that of a trust, tax-exempt organization, or corporation), an individual whose net worth or joint net worth with spouse (including real estate), at the time of investment, exceeds one million dollars; or an individual who had an individual income in excess of $200 thousand in each of the two most recent calendar years or joint income with spouse in excess of $300 thousand in each of those years; and who reasonably expects an income in excess of such amounts in the current calendar year. Contrast *non-accredited investor.*

adjusted net profits. Upon *recoupment*, what remains for distribution to *investors* after any monies have been deducted by entities such as a *general manager* or stars, or others, from *net profits*, if share(s) to be done so is/are negotiated.

advance. (1) Any sum under the amount needed to *capitalize* a production, which can be used toward the actualization of that production. In a *producer–presenter* arrangement, an amount supplied to the *producer* by a *presenter* in order to help secure the eventual production in the *presenter's* theatre. The danger of using *advances* is that if the production—for whatever reason—is cancelled and you don't show up, you must repay the money *advanced*. (2) Money taken in for tickets prior to actual performance date. This also includes promises to buy.

advance man. Person who goes ahead of a production *on the road* to stir up interest prior to its arrival in town. Often arranging for *advertising* and working out promotional gimmicks, effectively a *press agent*.

advertising. Buying media attention in a guaranteed, precise, and targeted way. This includes print, broadcast, outdoor, and direct response.

ancillary rights. Not the *rights* that are actually *licensed*, but other, closely related *rights* to also *license*, so as to make the *license* of stage *rights* worthwhile (i.e., along with stage *rights* from the writer of the *book*, as well as the *composer* and *lyricist* if you planning to produce a musical, there are also *ancillary rights*— the *rights* to make and sell merchandise; the *rights* to produce and distribute a cast album; the *right* to use the authors' bio and picture. *Ancillary rights* are the other *rights* a producer traditionally requires (other than the actual *right* to produce the musical) when they acquire the live stage *rights* to a *property*. See also *rights*.

approval right. Veto power over an aspect or person associated with a production. See also *rights*.

associate producer. An individual who provides or solicits funding of a determined amount of a production's *capitalization*.

at risk. Investment which is available prior to full *capitalization*. See also *pre-formation capital*.

attach. The act of a performer or production team being connected to a production prior to the negotiation and incorporating into the terms of a contract for that production, or before a production *transfers* from one *venue* to another.

back into the budget. The adjustment of the amount of line items in the formulation of a production budget prior to total *capitalization* so that they match those in an *investor's offering papers*.

backer's audition. The presentation of all or selected parts of a play or musical for potential *investors*.

bill (or billing). The ranking of *names* in and *advertising* for a production. The ranking is accomplished not only by the order in which they are listed, but also the size and style of type used and by photographic likenesses and the artwork that are part of the *advertising*.

blind pool. A large sum of money potentially raised for the purpose of investment into a number of production to be selected by the *general partner* of a *limited partnership (LP)*, or *managing member* of a *limited liability company (LLC)*.

Blue Sky Laws. Individual state rules and regulations pertaining to the solicitation of *investors*.

book. (1) The script (story) portion of a musical. (2) selling and routing of a production (i.e., determining which cities the production will play in and when), including negotiating all the terms with the *presenter*, and issuing the contract. Also *booking; booking* agent.

brand. (1) The label which most identifies a product. (2) An *umbrella marketing* term which incorporates strategies including research and positioning, to name generation and tag line creation and design, in order for the *brand* to embody all elements of the *marketing* strategy.

break even. The amount of *gross weekly box office receipts* required to meet the *weekly operating expenses* of a production.

Broadway. A theatre of 700 seats or more located in Manhattan and most probably in midtown.

Broadway Box. The area of midtown New York City from 34th Street to 66th Street and between 6th Avenue and 9th Avenue.

broker. A person who works with a producer as a middle person between the producer and other individuals or organizations to achieve specified end results. This could be in regard to tickets, insurance, or a particular set of trying circumstances.

button. The final chord, musical figure, percussive effect, or what otherwise (possibly including on stage) comes at the very end of a musical number, indicating to the audience that it is completed.

buyout. Compensation paid to a performer prescribed by an Actors' Equity Association Code, Contract, or Agreement, or otherwise, to a member of a production team in order to fulfill a verbal or contractual promise of participation in a production.

call. (1) Notice given of rehearsal or other work session. (2) How much time remains before the curtain goes up (i.e., half hour *call*).

call-board. The bulletin board in the theatre where the *calls* are posted. Sign-in sheets are posted here, and it is where the *closing notice* is posted.

capacity. The amount of money a production can gross at the box office, if every seat in the theatre is sold at the full box office price.

capital. Money or other assets owned by a person or organization, available or contributed, for investing.

capitalize (-ation). The point at which the budgeted amount needed from *investors* in order to begin production is realized, triggering the release of the totality of those funds.

casting. Hiring performers for roles within a production.

close booking. Another production ready to move into a theatre in case the production moving in ahead of it fails early in its run.

closing notice. A piece of paper posted on a theatre's *call-board* that announces to the cast and crew that a production will close in a week's time.

cold reading. A very relaxed hearing of a work read aloud, possibly in a home or other casual setting. See also *informal reading.* Contrast *formal reading; staged reading.*

come down. The time at which a performance is completed, referring to the final curtain coming down.

commercial. An entity created to make a profit. See also *for-profit.* Contrast *non-profit.*

commissioning document. An *option agreement* or other document outlining the terms of such an agreement between the author and producer.

composer. The writer of the music component a musical.

contingent rights. A *buyout* paid to an actor if they are not offered the same role or function in a subsequent contract production of a *property* or if the *property* is produced in another medium. Contrast *conversion rights.*

conversion rights. In an Actors' Equity Association Code, Contract, or Agreement, the *right* of a performer to advance in the same role or function in a subsequent contract production of a *property* or if the *property* is produced in another medium. Contrast *contingent rights.* See also *rights.*

co-production deal. A production arrangement by which a group of *presenters* puts up the financing for a *tour* in the form of: an investment, *advances* against the *guarantee,* or both. See also *guarantee deal; four-wall deal.*

creatives. Any concept, idea, or execution developed by the creative department for presentation to a client. This usually consists of produced work, such as show art presented in window card size (14 x 22) and mounted on illustration board, or tag lines presented in a similar fashion.

dark. A theatre which does not have a current production, or a day on which a theatre with a current production does not have a performance.

deadwood. Unsold tickets to a completed performance.

dedicated message. The impression created by direct response advertising about your *property* or product that is tailored to the consumer. By addressing the consumer at home or on the computer, an opportunity exists to create an impression with little or no competition, and therefore, it has the potential to make a more significant and longer-lasting impact.

develop; development; developmental. The process of readying a *property* for production.

disposition rights. The *right* by legal ownership, to do with a *property* as one pleases, conveying, conferring, or is as otherwise desired. See also *rights*.

enhance; enhancement. The initial financing provided by a **commercial** producer to augment the budget (usually of a *resident* or *nonprofit*) theatre production.

exploitation of rights. Exercising of one's legally designated prerogative to move forward with a respective *right* of ownership of an aspect of a *property*, particularly for the purpose of moving toward production.

fat. Budgeting a line item with more than the projected amount of money believed necessary to achieve the desired result. See also *padding*.

feeders. *Regional* theatres with excellent reputations of *presenting* plays that have gone on to *commercial* success, usually on Broadway.

fence. In a *marketing* campaign, a point such as a date at which it is understood by a consumer that if a ticket has not been purchased, that the price of the ticket will increase.

first-class production. As defined by The Dramatists Guild Approved Production Contract, "a live stage production of the Play on a speaking stage, within the Territory, under Producer's own management, in a regular evening *bill* in a *first class* theatre in a *first class* manner, with a *first class* cast, and a *first class* director." Essentially, productions mounted by Broadway theatres and the other larger theatres in larger cities that utilize a certain Actors' Equity contract.

first-look deal. An arrangement between two entities (usually a *commercial* and a *nonprofit*), where the *commercial* producer has the first *right* to effectuate a *commercial transfer* of a production originating in the *nonprofit* theatre.

(first right of) good faith negotiation. (1) In regard to a *property*, the meaning is that the owner of a *property* cannot sell or *license* any specified *right* without first giving the party having the first *right* the opportunity of entering into negotiations for the specified *right*. (2) In regard to an individual rendering services, the producer may not hire someone else to render those service before offering that individual the position on terms to be negotiated in good faith (i.e., not usury and taking into consideration the prior contributions of that individual). See also *rights*.

formal reading. A rehearsed or generally more prepared hearing of a work read aloud. See also *staged reading*. Contrast *informal reading; cold reading*.

for-profit. An organization that exists for the purpose of making a profit. See also *commercial*. Contrast *nonprofit*.

four-wall deal; four-walling or 4-walling. The complete leasing of a *venue* outside of New York for an *out-of-town tryout* by a producer who then pays 100 percent of all expenses, including *advertising*, stagehand, and musician costs. See also *co-production deal; guarantee deal*.

front money. Money used for a production prior to *offering papers* being drawn up or receipt of total *capitalization*. It is generally used for acquiring the *property*, hiring a *lawyer* and a *general manager*, and printing scripts or other pre-production expenses. See also *up front*.

front of (the) house. Any and all areas apart from the backstage area.

general manager. An individual or company engaged by a producer for the administration of a production, to whom may be delegated all of those producer's responsibilities and prerogatives, beyond *optioning* the play and raising the *capitalization*, that the producer does not wish to assume themselves, including the preparation of the initial production and weekly operating budgets; assisting producer in negotiating contracts for the artistic team according to respective union rules and regulations governing them; *licensing* of the theatre and any and all other contracts and other agreements that may be required (excluding those related to funding); supervise the staffing and hiring of all non-artistic personnel; supervising of all activities relating to the physical aspects of the production and to be responsible for the letting of such contracts, subject to competitive bidding when appropriate; administration of all customary and routine business matters with respect to a production; securing all necessary insurance; working with the company *attorney* in the development of the *offering materials*, furnishing the *attorney* with a copy of all draft agreements for review and comment prior to finalizing any negotiation, engagement, or other commitment on behalf of producer; assisting with the company accountant in the preparation of all required financial statements and the timely preparation and filing of tax and statutory insurance forms and related documentation; supervising the *advertising* for the production and administering all *advertising, marketing,* and promotional expenses; supervise the activities of the *press agent*, as well as any and all *marketing* director(s). All such acts are subject to prior consultation with, and approval by, the producer unless otherwise directed; and does not generally participate in fundraising or *investor relations*.

general partner. In either a *limited liability company* or a *limited partnership,* the producers of the play, who are entitled to make all creative and financial decisions affecting its production.

general reserve; reserve. The portion of the *capitalization* set aside to underwrite *operating losses* between the official press opening, performance, and attaining *break even.*

green room. A convenient retiring room for actors offstage. (It is not usually green.)

gross weekly box office receipts. Every dollar taken in on a weekly basis.

guarantee. (1) An arrangement where a return on an *investor's* income is virtually assured (e.g., a musical about Elvis Presley touring large, pre-Sold Out theatres throughout the South with high *advance* ticket sales). (2) Provide financial security for. (3) In an arrangement between a producer and an *out-of-town presenter,* an amount put up by the producer which is usually fixed, plus a percentage of the *net gross.*

guarantee deal. The most common of *deals* between an *out-of-town* producer and a local *presenter,* developed to diminish the risk for the producer when mounting a *tour* or *sit-down* production. The *presenter* must put up a *guaranteed* amount of money for a performance week, thereby reducing the producer's risk and ensuring the production will arrive. The *presenter* must pay the *guarantee* even if the box office receipts don't meet the required amount. What the *guarantee* buys, however, is only the production at the loading dock. After the *guarantee,* the *presenter* pays for three other categories of expenses for which the *presenter* is also *at risk:* (1) *advertising;* (2) local stagehands, wardrobe, and hair staff; and (3) in the case of a musical, local musicians. After those bills are paid, the *presenter* receives income to pay for theatre rent and administrative costs. Finally, should there be monies after all these bills are paid, the remaining amount splits between the producer and *presenter.* See also *co-production deal; four-wall deal.*

house manager. Person in charge of all of the public areas of the theatre–the lobby, box office, ushers, aisles, lounges, and the auditorium. Not customarily involved with back stage.

house seats. Prime Orchestra section seats controlled by the producer, the release and coordination of which is usually conducted by the *press agent* or *publicist.* Multiple purposes include distribution to *investors, public relations,* and ultimately may be sold at full price to industry insiders or others, but not offered to the general public. Traditionally, these seats may be more available (only just, if at all) to insiders than any other seats to a successful production.

ice. The difference between the listed price of a ticket price and the price paid for the ticket.

Independent Presenters Network (IPN). An association of *presenters*, theatres, and performing arts centers whose members bring Broadway productions to more than 110 cities throughout North America and Japan.

independent. A producer functioning separately from others.

informal reading. A very relaxed hearing of a work read aloud, possibly in one's home or other casual setting. See also *cold reading*. Contrast *formal reading; staged reading*.

internal. A meeting in an *advertising* agency between the creative director and the art directors and copywriters where ideas for an upcoming creative presentation are reviewed and discussed. At this stage, ideas are presented in concrete form and include artistic designs, photographs, or sketches, as well copy taglines or descriptions. Further development or revisions may occur after this meeting.

investor. Someone who provides *capital* to a production who expects to share in the profits but whose money is *at risk*.

investor relations. Establishing credibility, trust, and an otherwise generally meaningful relationship with *investors*. May include strategies such as distributing reviews of a production (including negative ones), opening night tickets, party passes, and the making available of *house seats*.

jump. Moving a production from one town to the next in the course of a *tour*.

key art. The major elements of an *advertising* campaign (e.g., posters, programs, etc.).

lawyer. In theatre, an attorney-at-law proficient at the entertainment industry. See also *theatrical attorney*.

license. Allow, give permission, or otherwise authorize a performance or production of a work, and/or the sale of mementos related to that work.

license agreement. A contract between a theatre owner or operator and a producer setting forth the terms and condition applicable to the use of the theatre in connection with a specified attraction and the responsibilities and obligations of each of the parties.

limited engagement. A run of a length of time specified prior to the opening.

limited liability company (LLC). One of the two forms of *private offerings* used by a producer to raise money (*limited partnership* being the other), in which *managing members* (the counterpart to a *limited partner* or *general partner* of a *limited partnership*), assume limited liability should the project go over budget or lawsuit be instituted for whatever reason. In either a *limited partnership (LP) or limited liability company (LLC)* the *investor* is only exposed up to the limit of his or her investment. Filing fees for this kind of *private offering* are often higher than those of a *limited partnership*. Contrast *limited partnership*.

limited partner. *Investors* who receive a portion of the *net profits* of the play. The *limited partners* have no voice in the creative and financial decisions. The sole obligation of the *limited partners* is to invest the money, and their liability is limited to the amount of their investment. They are isolated from any financial liability beyond their initial investment unless there is an *overcall*. If the play is successful, each *limited partner* will, following the return of his investment, continue to receive his/her proportionate share of the *net profits*. Contrast *general partner*.

limited partnership. One of the two forms of *private offerings* used by a producer to raise money (*limited liability company [LLC]* being the other). A *limited partnership* is a hybrid of the *general partnership* and the corporation. It consists of *general* and *limited partners* (counterpart to a *managing member* of a *limited liability company*), who assume unlimited financial exposure should the project go over budget or a lawsuit be instituted for whatever reason. In either a *limited partnership (LP) or limited liability company (LLC)* the *investor* is only exposed up to the limit of his or her investment. Filing fees for this kind of *private offering* are often higher than those of a *limited liability company*. Contrast *limited liability company*.

limited partnership agreement. A legally binding document that effectuates a *limited partnership*. See also *private placement memorandum; subscription documents*.

Live Nation. One of the world's largest diversified promoters and producers of, *venue* operators and sponsorship/advertising for, live entertainment events including music concerts, theatrical performances, and specialized motor sports events. *Live Nation* owns, operates, or has booking *rights* for 150 *venues* worldwide including 107 domestic and forty-three international *venue* sites. *Live Nation* presents Broadway production in more than forty-four cities in the U.S. and Canada in their Broadway Across America and their Broadway Across Canada series.

load in/load out. The physical act of moving all of a production's equipment into or out of a theatre.

lyricist. The writer of the words to the songs of a musical.

marketing (also marketing director/team). The action or business of promoting and selling products.

(most) favored nations. All similarly associated parties involved with a production being paid and otherwise treated equally (i.e., the cast members being hired on a *most favored nations* basis).

names. Stars of stage, film, television, or other celebrities who have the perceived ability to draw an audience.

net gross. The *gross weekly box office receipts*, less taxes, restoration, and deductions.

net profits. Under a *limited partnership, limited partners*, in return for their investment, customarily receive 50 percent of the *net profit* with the balance going to the *general partners*. The *net profits* are the amounts paid to the *investors* after their investments have been returned. *Net profits* consist of weekly *operating profits* from performances of a play and represent the difference between the *gross weekly box office receipts* and the *weekly operating expenses*.

non-accredited investor. A private individual whose net worth or joint net worth with spouse (including real estate) at the time of investment, is less than $1 million. Contrast *accredited investor*.

nonprofit; not-for-profit. An agency, institution, or organization formed under Internal Revenue Service guidelines which designates that it exist not for private gain, but for public or benefit purposes, and is tax-exempt.

off the top. (1) Any amount deducted from any other amount before any other amounts are deducted. (2) Any amount deducted after reaching *capitalization* from the *net profits* of a production, such as that negotiated for distribution to a *general manager* or *name*. The remaining after amount deducted *off the top*, if any, is the *adjusted net profits*.

Off-Broadway. A theatre with a seating capacity of 100-499 seats located in New York, NY.

Off-Off-Broadway. A theatre with a seating capacity of 99 seats or under located in New York, NY.

offering materials. The legal papers required to raise money, typically a *limited liability company* operating agreement or *limited partnership agreement* and any other accompanying documentation required by reason on the amount being raised and in what states funds will be solicited. See also *offering papers*.

offering papers. The legal papers required to raise money, typically a *limited liability company* operating agreement or *limited partnership agreement* and any other accompanying documentation required by reason on the amount being raised and in what states funds will be solicited. See also *offering materials*.

(on the) road. A production which *tours* regionally, nationally, or in other countries for any length of time, usually with stops in many cities and usually, but not always, following a production in New York. In certain circumstances, such as with a financially successful production, one production (or more) may go *on the road* while one remains in New York.

one-for-two. A situation in which an *investor* who has invested $100,000 in a $1 million production for use *up front*, for example, will receive 5 percent of the *net profits* from the *limited partners'* side (i.e., 10 percent of the 50 percent to which all *investors* are entitled, for having provided 10 percent of the aggregate amount provided by all *investors*) and 2 ½ percent (1 percent of the producer's *net profits* for every 2 percent in which the *investor* is entitled from the *investors'* *net profits*) from the *general partners'* share of *net profits*.

open cold. To open a production in New York City without previous *out-of-town tryouts*.

operating loss. A deficit of cash flow needed to operate a show from *gross weekly box office receipts*.

operating profit. A surplus of cash flow needed to operate a show from *gross weekly box office receipts*.

option. Obtaining the legal *right* to produce a *property*. See also *option agreement*.

option agreement. The document by which the legal *right* to produce a *property* is obtained. See also *option*.

out-of-town. A production outside of New York usually indicating the intent to bring it to New York.

overcall. An additional investment required of the original *investors* when there is a need for more funding.

padding. Budgeting a line item with more than the projected amount of money believed necessary to achieve the desired result. See also *fat*.

paper (the house). The act of giving away tickets to fill the house that gives the appearance of a production in demand.

passive gain. A passive investment is one in which you have no control over the management of the enterprise (stocks, bonds, etc.). Under the current tax code, *passive loss* from a theatrical investment can only be deducted from a *passive gain*. Contrast *passive loss*.

passive loss. A passive investment is one in which you have no control over the management of the enterprise (stocks, bonds, etc.). Under the current tax code, *passive loss* from a theatrical investment can only be deducted from a *passive gain*. Contrast *passive gain*.

pitch. (1) An informal or formalized attempt to sell a *property* to a potential participant or *investor(s)*. (2) A presentation of creative and strategic ideas to the client at the *advertising* agency's expense in order to win the account.

playwright. The author of a play.

preformation capital. Under regulations that guide the *capitalization* process of theatrical ventures, every *investor* has the *right* to require a producer to raise every last penny of the needed *capitalization* before that *investor's* money can be used. The need to start spending substantial amounts on such things as sets and costumes early in the process means that unless he or she is independently wealthy, a producer simply must use *investors'* money long before the last dollar of capital arrives at the bank. Some *investors* can choose to be willing to let the producer use their money prior to full *capitalization*, thereby taking the risk that full amount might never be raised and the production never actually mounted. This is a risk for which there is no reward offered, so what's needed is a significant level of confidence in the producer (presumably based on a track record in which he has never failed to fully *capitalize* in the past), and an amount which, if lost for this reason, wouldn't be crippling to the *investor*. So here again, smaller investments are helpful to the producer. See also *at risk*.

private offering. One of the two types of offerings for raising money (the other being a *public offering*), the guidelines of which provide for the establishment of either a *limited liability company (LLC)*, or a *limited partnership (LP)*. Under this offering, *advertisement* for *investors* is not allowed, and registration with the Securities and Exchange Commission is not required. Contrast *public offering*.

public offering. One of the two types of offerings for raising money (the other being a *private offering*), the guidelines of which provide for the establishment of either a *limited liability company (LLC)*, or a *limited partnership (LP)*. Under this offering, the *advertisement* for *investors* is allowed, and registration with the Securities and Exchange Commission required.

premium market. A condition existing in any given market whereby demand is so great that you can raise your tickets beyond what you deemed your full price initially.

presenter. In *a producer/presenter* relationship, responsible for promoting and selling the production to its local audience, providing a theatre and its administrative staff, hiring local stagehands, musicians, wardrobe, and hair personnel to support the production, and operating the theatre during the period the production is booked. Also handling all functions such as *house management,* ushers, security, box office, and programs. See also *co-production deal; guarantee deal; four-wall deal.*

press agent; press office. A person engaged by a producer to publicize a production, or by an actor, author, director, producer, etc. to publicize him. The job is to incite interest so that the client/production is mentioned in the press, on television and radio, and the public will with to see the production or the person.

priority loan. Non-recourse loan which is returned to the lenders prior to the return of any capital to the *investors.*

private placement memorandum. Document given to potential *investors* that sets forth all the information about a project including among others, the risk factors, the units being offered, descriptions of the *general partners*, agreements relating to the play, use of proceeds, estimated weekly budget, tax matters, *rights* of *general* and *limited partners,* share of losses between *general* and *limited partners,* termination of the partnership, financial reports, other financing, who may invest, the budget, bios of the creative people involved, a description of the production, the areas in which the *investors* participate and the risks involved, among others. A *private placement memorandum* can be avoided if a production's budget is under $1 million, or if all *investors* are *accredited*. See also *subscription documents; limited partnership agreement.*

property. The particular work being produced.

public relations. An encompassing term including an educational aspect directed at both the ticket buyer and the press (editors, reporters, critics, etc.), leading to tangible *publicity* and hopefully increased sales.

publicity (publicist, publicity office or **publicity team).** Implies a campaign involving a measurable amount of exposure for a project such as a newspaper or magazine article, or a segment on a television program. See also *public relations.*

reading. A work read aloud, in public or otherwise. See also *informal reading, formal reading, staged reading, cold reading.*

recoup(-ment). The reach the point at which the total capital invested in a production has been repaid to *investors.*

regional. See also *resident theatre.* Usually refers to theatre that is a member of the League of Resident Theaters and Producers. See also *resident.*

reserve; general reserve. A portion of the *capitalization* set aside to underwrite *operating losses* between the official press opening, performance, and attaining *break even.*

resident. A *nonprofit* theatre that operates outside or within the New York metropolitan area. Usually refers to theatre that is a member of the League of Resident Theaters and Producers. See also *regional.*

rights. The legally valid acquisition of control of stated aspects of intellectual *property.* See also *ancillary rights, approval rights, contingent rights, conversion rights, disposition rights, first right of good faith negotiation, subsidiary rights, underlying rights.*

risk/reward relationship. In *commercial* endeavors, how much one is willing to risk (spend) in order to make a potential profit.

routing. Determining which cities a production *on the road* will play in and when, usually determined by the *booking* agent.

royalty. A share of the proceeds, usually a specified percentage, paid to members of the creative staff in exchange for performing their work.

run-thru. A rehearsal at which all of the elements of a production are performed in the order they will appear.

running expenses. The total of all expenses associated with sustaining a production reduced to their impact on a weekly basis (including accruals and amortizations). Also referred to as and see also *weekly nut.*

second class productions. As defined by The Dramatists Guild, "all performances of the Play other than Stock, Amateur and Ancillary Performances (as those terms are defined in SECTION 11.01 of the Approved Production Contract), Off-Broadway Performances (as defined in SECTION 9.02 of the Approved Production Contract), and First Class Performances and Developmental (i.e. "workshop") Productions."

service package charge. The amount charged by a theatre for specified personnel and services provided by the theatre to the production, usually on a weekly basis.

sit down. Referring to a production

stage foot print. The height and width of the proscenium arch, the width, depth of the stage floor (including offstage), height to the grid, and all impediments.

staged reading. A rehearsed or generally more prepared hearing of a work read aloud. See also *formal reading.* Contrast *informal reading; cold reading.*

stop clause. Found in the theatre *licensing agreement,* the *stop clause* allows the theatre owners to terminate the agreement with a production if the show's *gross weekly box office receipts* fall below a specified amount for a specified period of time.

subscribe(r). Season ticket holder

subscription documents. See *also limited partnership agreement; private placement memorandum.*

subsidiary rights. *Rights licensed* when entering into a legally binding agreement with an author (e.g., stock and amateur *rights*; the *right* to produce in Korea; film and television *rights*). This is not to say that these *rights* are not capable of being acquired, however to the extent that they may not have been as of yet, they are *subsidiary rights.* Participation in the income that the author derives from the exploitation of the play's *subsidiary rights,* as a reward for the investment you have made for premiering the play, is standard (e.g., there may not have been a film sale had the production not occurred and put the play on the map). Standard producer *subsidiary rights* participation may go as high as 40 or 50 percent depending on how many performances and where they were, presented. Participation in the author's *"subsids"* would be from net income (gross to author minus only *off the top* deductions for author's agent). Note: *Subsidiary Rights* in connection with an *option agreement* are different from *subsidiary rights* in the contractual context of the Actors' Equity Association. See also *rights.*

sui generis. Latin term meaning "unique unto itself".

sunsets. The *right* of a *nonprofit* to share in future income lapsing if the author does not enter into a production contract with a *commercial* producer within a certain period of time, such as three years after the close of the *nonprofit's* production.

takedown. Small, black-and-white renditions of full-color and full-size art concepts shown in the creative presentation at an *advertising* agency, intended to give clients an idea of how the art will translate to small units in newsprint.

take-in(date). (1) The loading in to the theatre of the physical production elements (set, lights, sound, costumes, musical instruments, etc.) and the date that it is scheduled to occur. (2) Money collected during any given period (i.e., weekly *take-in*).

theatre restoration charge. A charge paid to a theatre owner for the upkeep a theatre building.

theatrical attorney. A lawyer specializing in entertainment law, specifically theatre. See also *lawyer*.

Tony eligible. To be allowed to compete for Antoinette Perry (Tony) Awards given annually and jointly by The League of American Theatres and Producers and the American Theatre Wing. This award is clearly the most recognizable award in the industry and much is made of its purported ability to affect box office receipts.

tour. When used in conjunction with *for the road* or as in *national tour.*

touring Broadway. Productions originating on *Broadway* that are *touring* or *on the road* in this country or otherwise throughout the world.

transfer. To move from one *venue* to another.

tryout. A production in a *venue* outside of the New York metropolitan area in anticipation of subsequent (usually Broadway) New York production.

umbrella. A *marketing* strategy or campaign incorporating many elements, including advertising on television, radio, outdoor, print, press, promotion, direct mail response marketing, and more recently, e-mail response *marketing*, Internet, and web *marketing*.

underlying rights. The *property* on which another *property* is based (i.e., plays, novels, or movies). It is rare to find a Broadway musical that does not have *underlying rights.*

up front. Use of an investment prior to *capitalization*. See also *front money*.

vehicle. A production in which it is considered desirable by a performer to appear.

venue. Theatre or other space where a production takes place.

weekly nut (nut). The total of all expenses associated with sustaining a production reduced to their impact on a weekly basis (including accruals and amortizations). Also referred to as and see also *weekly operating expenses* or *running expenses.*

weekly license fee. Base weekly rent for a theatre.

weekly operating expenses. The total of all expenses associated with sustaining a production reduced to their impact on a weekly basis (including accruals and amortizations). See also *weekly nut* or *running expenses.*

work for hire. To work for a fixed rate or fee rather than a percentage of future profits.

wraps. The amount of money the box office has taken in for a specified amount of time (e.g., "$200,000 was *wrapped* on Tuesday, $350,000 on Wednesday"); originating from an era when the cash was "wrapped" in pieces of paper.

yield. Generated return.

yield management. Sometimes known as revenue management, the process of understanding, anticipating, and reacting to consumer behavior in order to maximize revenue. It can be used to smooth the demand pattern. In peak season, the productions can increase revenues by increasing the fare on its tickets and in low season, it can increase capacity by offering low prices. Industries that use *yield management* typically have computer systems to measure supply and demand and generate variable price points.

Index

COMMERCIAL THEATER INSTITUTE

The Commercial Theater Institute consists of two separate components, the Three-Day Program, held annually on the last weekend in April, and the Fourteen-Week Program, held on consecutive Monday evenings from early February through the beginning of May.

The Three-Day Program is scheduled for two and a half days and is open to anyone who is interested. All of the resource speakers are working professionals—producers On and Off-Broadway, marketing, press and advertising personnel, theatrical attorneys, and general managers.

The Fourteen-Week Program is limited to twenty-five participants selected from nominations made by producers, general managers, theatrical attorneys, and other professionals. Again, the weekly speakers are working professionals from the industry.

Some present for a full three-hour evening and some share the time. The CTI selection committee chooses members for the program whom they believe will actually be involved in producing in the commercial theatre in the foreseeable future.

For more information on the Commercial Theater Institute, please visit: http://www.commercialtheaterinstitute.com